THE LOEB CLASSICAL LIBRARY

FOUNDED BY JAMES LOEB, LL.D.

EDITED BY

† T. E. PAGE, c.h., litt.d.

† E. CAPPS, ph.d., ll.d.   † W. H. D. ROUSE, litt.d.

L. A. POST, l.h.d.   E. H. WARMINGTON, m.a., f.r.hist.soc.

ST. AUGUSTINE

ST. AUGUSTINE

SELECT LETTERS

WITH AN ENGLISH TRANSLATION BY

JAMES HOUSTON BAXTER, B.D., D.Litt

REGIUS PROFESSOR OF ECCLESIASTICAL HISTORY IN THE
UNIVERSITY OF ST. ANDREWS

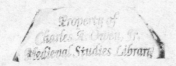

LONDON
WILLIAM HEINEMANN LTD
CAMBRIDGE, MASSACHUSETTS
HARVARD UNIVERSITY PRESS
MCMLXV

ST. AUGUSTINE

SELECT LETTERS

WITH AN ENGLISH TRANSLATION BY

JAMES HOUSTON BAXTER, B.D., D.Litt.

First printed 1930
Reprinted 1953, 1965

Printed in Great Britain

CONTENTS

CONTENTS

CONTENTS

CONTENTS

PREFACE

COMPARED with his *Confessions*, St. Augustine's *Letters* have received but slight attention, even from many of his professed biographers, and for each edition of the one there have appeared, at a moderate estimate, several hundred editions, translations or studies of the other. Yet a man's autobiography gives only his own account and interpretation of himself and his deeds ; his letters, if they are genuine and spontaneous, show him directly, without the distortion of his own explanations and self-justifications. The present selection, barely a quarter of Augustine's extant correspondence, contains, it is hoped, enough to exhibit the human interest of the man and his environment ; excluding almost all the lengthier letters, often of the bulk of minor treatises, and those solely or chiefly concerned with questions of doctrine, I have sought to present those which best reveal him in contact with the varied and busy life of his time.

The Latin text is, for the most part, that of the Vienna *Corpus Scriptorum Ecclesiasticorum Latinorum*, edited in four volumes by Alois Goldbacher. Permission to reprint this was generously granted some ten years ago by the late August Engelbrecht, then Secretary of the Vienna Academy, and this courtesy is here gratefully acknowledged. The large number

and variety of the manuscripts, which would have rendered necessary a fresh and lengthy series of *sigla* for each letter, has made it practically impossible to provide critical notes for all the changes introduced into the text, and many of these have been adopted without remark. Goldbacher's reviewers repeatedly pointed out the difficulties made for the reader by his method of quoting his manuscript authorities, but in an edition of this size no improvement has been attempted, and, as his *apparatus criticus* has supplied the material for improving his text, to it the textual critic is referred.

I have had before me the translations by Poujoulat, Cunningham and Miss Allies. Of these Poujoulat is fluent, but given to avoiding difficulties; Cunningham is, on the whole, accurate, but his dull and over-literal style makes his translation heavy reading, though here and there he finds a phrase which it would have been hard to better; in difficulties I have occasionally adopted or adapted his rendering. Miss Allies gives a paraphrase which is not of much help alongside the Latin.

To Mr. C. J. Fordyce, of Jesus College, Oxford, I am indebted for a careful reading of the greater part of my translation and his high scholarship and accuracy have removed many weaknesses and roughnesses. Messrs. R. and R. Clark's readers and printers have been models of exactness and speed. Finally, I owe a great debt, which I can merely acknowledge, to three men who in this particular field have given me guidance and inspiration: the late John Swinnerton Phillimore, of Glasgow University, to whose scholarship, kindliness and influence no words could be adequate tribute; the late Alois

PREFACE

Goldbacher, the veteran editor, whom I knew only in the last, difficult years of his long and devoted life, but who was even then unwearied in labour and in helpfulness; and, last but not least, Professor Alexander Souter, of Aberdeen University, with whom my friendship during the last twelve years has been an interrupted, but happy, record of "patristic hours," fruitful and stimulating to a degree which those who know him as a scholar and a friend will readily understand.

J. H. B.

St. Andrews, *August* 1930.

INTRODUCTION

I

As befitted the religion of a new and deep and universal brotherhood, Christianity from its first diffusion wove new ties between sundered classes and distant nations and created a fresh and urgent need for intercourse and for communication. Its earliest literature was epistolary and its chief missionary the prince of letter-writers, whose correspondence, early deemed canonical, set an example and provided a model for the following Christian generations. The centuries of persecution may have diminished, though they did not stem, the stream of letters that flowed across the Mediterranean from Church to Church, and in the Christian literature of that time no names are better known than those of Ignatius, Barnabas, Clement, Polycarp, Irenaeus, Dionysius of Corinth, Origen, Dionysius of Alexandria, and Cyprian—letter-writers all. When peace was won and the Church recognized, Christian development on all sides was rapid, until, in the half-century following Julian's failure to revive and restore the glories of ancient paganism, Christian literature in both East and West, and with it Christian " epistolary converse," as its devotees loved to call it, reached its patristic Golden Age.

There was, indeed, much to challenge and to stimulate the eager and observant Christian mind, and to

encourage the exchange of ideas between communities and between individuals. Paganism, by a succession of increasingly severe edicts, was being publicly dismissed from the Empire ; its temples were seized and closed or torn down, or else, when a less puritanical outlook prevailed, turned to Christian uses ; its Altar of Victory, set up in the Senate-house after the Battle of Actium in 31 B.C. and since then, with negligible interruptions, the standing symbol of the Empire's old religion, was finally and irrevocably removed under Theodosius, and paganism, publicly proscribed, was driven to seek shelter and continuance in quiet districts and under new and orthodox disguises. The Church was learning to accommodate itself, not merely to freedom, but to dominance ; like a little water in a large vessel, it spread thinly to take the shape and perform the functions of that which it had displaced ; it had to learn new duties, and in the process it was acquiring that organization which has marked it ever since. At the same time, the internal changes were important and enduring : modes of worship were being evolved which became by slow growth and development the stately and impressive liturgy of the Middle Ages ; in the need for formulation of the standard faith, the boundaries were drawn more and more rigidly between right religion and dangerous error, and Christianity steadily grew more metaphysical as it attempted to express the inexpressible. A new ascetic movement, the parent of ordered community monasticism, had inevitably followed the invasion of the Church by masses to whom Christianity was more a fashion than a faith, and, partly as the result of the conviction that this elect and inner circle

had a better and a surer way to salvation in the renunciation of the world and all its pomp and power, the rich surrendered their property for pious uses and their prospects for a lowlier, chastened life that was to win them higher blessings in the world to come. Partly too, no doubt, it was the conscious or unconscious answer of the harassed and perplexed to the increasing difficulties of the time, the progressive impoverishment of the Empire and the progressive burden of taxation, for, since Constantine had first imposed his super-tribute, material embarrassments had vastly grown, and the only ways of escape were into the senatorial class, which was hard, or into the ranks of the clergy, which was easy. The same economic pressure led to the consolidation and the isolation of those great domains of which the following letters speak more than once ; on them the proprietors became practically independent rulers, and to them, as life grew more and more unsure, the poorer classes gravitated in search of protection against pirates and brigands and the tax-collector. In the arrangements gradually evolved between the owners and the tenants for the cultivation of the land are to be found the beginnings of a system which was to play an important part in the peasant-life of the Middle Ages ; but for the moment its disadvantageous features are more evident. City-life, prosperous and active in the first and second centuries of our era, was suffering a marked decline, and, as patriotic feeling had always found expression in devotion to one's city and a civic pride much narrower and more intense than in our own day, the Empire became more and more an abstraction and society more definitely turned in the

direction of local pre-occupations and aristocratic administration. With the isolation of each territorial unit and its economic and administrative self-sufficiency, centralized sovereignty disappeared before a divided and dissipated control which owed little allegiance and provided little support to the needs or to the idea of an empire. Each *fundus*, Augustine tells us, is a practical independent unit ; it has its own machinery, its own church or churches, and its own bishop. In these *Letters* the reader will often be struck by the existence of such bishops in charge of what are apparently very small churches and very limited territories, and in this fact of decentralization he will find the explanation. The same fact very largely accounts for the persistence of Donatism and the violence of its antagonism to the Catholic Church. The ancient stock, even after nearly six hundred years of Roman civilization, remained largely unchanged ; the Punic language was spoken even in Hippo, and in the country districts it was often the only speech. The enormous extension of landed properties in Africa laid upon the native population a heavy burden of serfdom which provoked acute social and racial hatred, and when, through the generosity of the emperors, the Church itself, in addition to being officially recognized, became a landed proprietor, that opposition which had begun as a simple question of ecclesiastical rivalry was soon augmented by the accession of discontented slaves who were prompted to rebellion by economic oppression and social grievances. Their armed bands of *circumcelliones* wandered round the country, attacking and burning property and wreaking the most violent vengeance upon landowners and Catholic priests,

pouring vinegar and salt water down their throats, putting lime into their eyes, and cudgelling them to death. The African provinces were completely at their mercy : debtors' tablets were seized and destroyed ; the roads were infested with brigands, and life was safe neither on the country domains nor outside them. At Hippo Augustine found his Catholic Christians denied bread by the Donatist baker and his people often driven by force to join the Donatist party. On one occasion he himself only escaped with his life by losing his way and so avoiding an ambush they had laid for him. During the short rebellion under Gildo, a count of Africa who had turned the social and religious ferment to his own ends, the threat not only to Africa, but to Rome, reached its most dangerous point. The rebel had chosen his moment well, for the Rhine frontier was crumbling. Alaric was threatening Italy, and the arrest of the corn supply from Numidia added actual famine to potential fear. Stilicho was campaigning in the East, and only in 398 was he able to deal with Gildo the Moor. The rebellion was soon put down, but already a few of the Donatists had begun to look to the Catholic Church as the only agent which could reestablish peace and order. The outrageous violence of their supporters recoiled upon their own head, for a period of drastic repression was now adopted by both Church and State. Donatist churches were destroyed ; Donatist property was confiscated, and the right of buying, selling, or bequeathing property was taken away. In February 405 the Emperor Honorius promulgated the law known as the " Edict of Union," which made schism penal, and, though its immediate effect was to drive the Circumcellions to

greater exasperation and outrage, it did in time produce some degree of peace. Yet in 410 the council of African bishops assembled at Carthage sought from the Emperor powers to convene Catholics and Donatists in a Conference, at which the points at variance should be discussed. In June 411 the two parties met at Carthage under the presidency of the tribune Marcellinus, who after hearing both sides gave judgement for the Catholics. All rescripts giving toleration or favour to the Donatists were repealed and previous condemnations of their sect and error were confirmed. Heavy penalties were to be inflicted upon their adherents; their clergy were to be deported, and their churches handed over to the Catholics. Fresh outbreaks of fury resulted; Restitutus, a priest of Hippo, was murdered and another cleric suffered mutilation, but the work of restoration and incorporation went on. Yet there can be no doubt that the success of the Vandals in Africa was in a considerable measure facilitated by the presence of large bodies of malcontents among the native population. The ten years of warfare that preceded the fall of Carthage in 439 were rendered appalling by the wanton ferocity of the fanatical native peasantry, who under protection of the invaders burned the villas of their masters and gave the whole countryside over to pillage and destruction. During the Vandal occupation of Africa (A.D. 430–533), the Donatists seem to have escaped the persecution meted out by the Arian conquerors to the Catholic party, and from the reconquest by the Byzantine emperors until in 637 the Saracen invaders swept across Africa destroying Church and State alike, occasional glimpses of

Donatist activity reappear, to show that they had by no means abandoned their opposition to orthodoxy or yielded to the pressure of the long series of edicts designed to crush them.

In its chronological details their history possesses only a restricted interest ; its importance lies rather in the system of Catholic doctrines which were formulated in the refutation of their errors. The real origins of the schism are to be found in the era of the persecutions, when many of the terrorized Christians of North Africa surrendered to the imperial agents the Sacred Books of the Faith. When peace came, the question of discipline arose : were those who had thus handed over the Scriptures to be received back to full communion, or was their character as Christians and as officers of the Church not entirely impaired by that act of faint-heartedness and treason ? If a minister was thus unworthy, did his personal unworthiness destroy the efficacy of the Sacraments which he dispensed ? The party of zealots, many of whom declared that they had refused to surrender the Holy Books or had sought the honours of martyrdom by proclaiming their possession of them and their defiance of the persecuting edict, maintained the position that as the Bishop of Carthage had been ordained by a *traditor*, his consecration was invalid and the Catholics, who persisted in communion with him, were in consequence cut off from the true Church. This rigorism was not new in Africa : Tertullian had argued, a century before, that the Christian had no right to avoid persecution, since in so doing he is thwarting the will of God by whom the persecution has been allowed to come about ; Cyprian and the majority of his fellow-

bishops held that baptism could not be validly administered by heretics, since they could not give what they did not possess. The Donatists, in turn, made the validity of a Sacrament depend upon the character of the minister ; holiness is the keynote of the Church, and when that has been impaired, apostolicity and catholicity are of no avail. The Church is a society of saints, not a school for sinners. So, since to their mind the whole Catholic body was composed of traditors and the sons of traditors, all who came over from its ranks to theirs must be re-baptized. On the point of fact, the betrayal of the Scriptures by representatives of the Catholic Church, they were proved by ample evidence to be in the wrong. On the point of doctrine, it was left for Augustine to emphasize the distinction between sacramental validity and efficacy and to give authoritative expression to the Cyprianic and ecclesiastical conceptions of the nature and the unity of the Church, the necessity of inclusion in it for salvation, and the apostolicity of its episcopate. Further, in his polemic against Donatism, he was led to forgo his earlier opinion in favour of freedom of thought, and to enunciate the theory of religious intolerance. To this momentous step his progress was gradual, and he was never, indeed, very happy about the employment of civil power in the coercion of the heretics. In the first period of the controversy, from 391 to about 404, he sought to win the Donatists to unity through argument and persuasion ; then, for a year or two, in face of the fruitlessness of that policy, he hesitated and held back, before finally accepting the edict of 405 with its penal laws against the heretics and supporting with his authority the theory that it is the duty

of the Catholic prince to establish Catholic unity. The action of the emperors in using force to destroy heresy he thereafter vigorously defended, although in actual practice he sought as far as lay in his power to prevent the infliction of the extreme penalties of torture and death. Yet his theory of the coercion of heretics contains in germ the whole system of spiritual tyranny which came to a full development in the Inquisition, and his authority was invoked for the perpetration of cruelties from which he certainly would have shrunk with horror. His doctrine of the Church provided the basis for the mediaeval conception of an omnipotent institution, capable of using the secular State as the executive of its declared will, possessed of an essential and inalienable prerogative as the Body and Kingdom of Christ, and exercising a divine right in its organization and in the suppression of all free inquiry and free speech. But he never completely resolved the inconsistency between his theory of the Church Catholic and his theological doctrine of Grace ; on the one hand, the Church is the visible Society bound together by the Sacraments and the hierarchy ; on the other, it is the sum total of all those who, whether within the visible Church or without, are predestined by God to eternal life. Between these two his thought wavered, and he transfers to the visible Society much of the ideal character of the final Kingdom of God. In this identification of the Kingdom of God with an organized ecclesiastical government he supplied the framework for the mediaeval Church, but the real disparity between the hierarchical idea and his doctrine of Grace was not realized and faced until the days of Wyclif and Hus and the Reformation.

INTRODUCTION

II

The controversy between Augustine and Pelagius, in the course of which were evolved those theories of Grace, Predestination, and Freewill specifically designated Augustinianism, occupies a relatively small space in the present collection of letters, for the majority of those in which Augustine sets forth his own views or discusses the theories of his opponents are either too lengthy or too technical for our purpose here. Yet in many ways it was the most important of the ecclesiastical questions with which Augustine was engaged, and the one into which he threw himself with the most fervour and conviction. His controversy with the Manichaeans concerning the nature of evil had already turned his attention to the problem of sin, its sway over the human heart, and its punishment, and the writings he had circulated on the subject had marked him out as a leader of Christian thought. Moreover, it was a phrase from his own *Confessions*: *Da quod iubes et iube quod vis* (Bk. x. 40, 44, 60) to which Pelagius originally took exception, and it was in Africa that the new doctrines first took hold and were first condemned. When Pelagianism spread to the various countries around the Mediterranean, it was to Augustine that all men turned in hope of definition in a problem which affected every Christian in his attitude towards evil and towards the salvation offered by the Church in Christ as a deliverance from evil. The dispute here concerned man as a more immediate and inward aspect of the problem which had earlier engaged Augustine's mind ; with the Manichaeans the discussion had centred round the metaphysical and cosmological problem, evil as it existed

in the universe, its origin and its relation to the Creator. Against Pelagianism Augustine was chiefly engaged in discussing the nature of evil as it is manifested in the heart of man, the corruption of the human will, man's responsibility for all the sin that exists in the world, and the place of human freedom in God's scheme of salvation. Partly deriving from those Christological heresies which regarded Jesus as a sinless man inhabited by the divine Logos and so promoted to the dignity of being God, and partly drawing upon the Stoic doctrine of human perfectibility and of virtue as the life according to nature, Pelagianism was an outbreak of paganism within the Church which threatened not only to blot out that condescension of God to man that makes all religion something more than mere ethics, but also to deny that fundamental doctrine of Christianity, the necessity and the power of the Atonement. Of the stages in this controversy, a few indications will be found in the Letters here selected: the first, at Carthage, when Celestius was condemned; the second, in Palestine, where Pelagius's specious arguments misled two Eastern synods into approval of his case; and the third, at Rome, where at first the Roman bishop, Zosimus, pronounced Pelagius orthodox and afterwards, under pressure from the Church at Carthage, declared his theories anathema. But the problem, once ventilated, continued to trouble the Western Church, and even in his own day Augustine found many critics of his system as he has continuously found both critics and supporters since. If his views have not found universal acceptance in detail, those which he attacked have been with one accord rejected, though they are ever ready to return to

favour as often as men lose their sense of the reality of sin and the Church fails to insist upon the cardinal need of redemption. If Augustine based his general argument upon theories which were inconsistent with his other teaching, if the sharp-witted Julian of Eclanum made short work of much of his doctrine, at least in the age-long controversy between "morals as against religion, free-will as against grace, reason as against revelation, and culture as against conversion," Augustine undoubtedly saved the cause of Christianity. He re-discovered and re-interpreted St. Paul; it might even be said that he re-lived the Pauline experience and re-expressed the Pauline contribution to Christian doctrine, and for that it is a becoming recognition that the only two conversion anniversaries in the Church's calendar should be those of the two men who were so closely akin. It was by this side of his teaching, so irreconcilable with his catholicism, that he became the teacher and the inspiration of Gottschalk and the Jansenists, of Luther and of Calvin.

III

Before the Roman conquest of 146 B.C. Carthage had been a Phoenician colony since the ninth century and Utica for three centuries more, and in the commercial centres along the coast and in the valleys cultivated for their support Punic civilization had left deep and abiding traces. At best, the Romanization of North Africa was but partial and external. Primarily an agricultural province, Africa had to be systematically organized, preserved in orderliness and defended along the desert frontier, so that the rich harvests of wheat, wine, olives, and grapes, so necessary for the

markets and the mouths of Rome, might be fully
developed, safely gathered, and speedily transported.
The coastal towns, Hadrumetum, Carthage, Hippo,
and others, were active ports and shipbuilding
centres, with a considerable population of Roman
agents and officials, yet even there the basic elements
were Punic and so remained. In spite of the influence exerted by the many municipalities scattered
throughout the country, the existence of those extensive estates which have been already mentioned,
and on them of a small, exclusive, and enormously
wealthy class of proprietors alongside a vast population
of serfs, made it possible to have considerable material
progress without a corresponding extension of culture.
Since the reign of Trajan, the soldiers of the Third
Legion who on discharge from service settled in the
veteran-colonies were almost all of African birth, and
their influence in Romanizing the country was small.
Through long contact and acquiescence the native
inhabitants had adapted themselves to Roman forms
and institutions, but the economic and social life
developed by the conquerors, the laws and language
they imposed and the religion they practised, made
no deep impression upon a race that in speech, culture,
and tradition was oriental. Although Africa, like the
other provinces, shows abundant evidence of the cult
of the Hellenic deities and the adoption of the old
mythology, and although the official cult of Rome
and the Emperor was naturally observed as an expression of subjection, devotion, and loyalty, these
forms of religion were only engrafted upon an older
and deeper set of beliefs and superstitions, which they
could neither displace nor destroy. As might be expected, the imported religion found its chief devotees

among the higher urban classes. The numerous monuments raised to the honour of the sovereign City or the Emperor were promoted either by the municipalities themselves or by those who had held office in them as magistrates. But among the humbler classes it was otherwise, and if they shared in the ceremonies and the games celebrated in the name of the imperial religion, their intimate and personal devotions were paid to other deities thinly disguised under Roman appellations. The inscriptions bear witness to the great popularity of Saturn throughout all North Africa, and Tertullian several times records the widespread nature of that cult, but at bottom it was, and remained, the cult of a Phoenician deity, Baal-Hammon. Similarly, the cult of Juno Caelestis or the Dea Caelestis or Diana concealed that of the old Punic goddess, Tanit, goddess of the crescent moon, parent of all things, mistress of all elements. In the old Carthaginian religion Baal and Tanit were the two supreme divinities, or rather the original divine being, conceived under male and female forms. Of their offspring, Eschmoun and Melqart were the most notable, and they continued to be worshipped after the Roman conquest under the names of Esculapius and of Hercules. In the course of time certain changes were produced by this identification of the older religion with the new. The Phoenicians of Tyre and Sidon had refrained, like the Jews, from the representation of their divinities in human form, and in North Africa, too, the stones raised in honour of Baal or Tanit originally bore only symbols, the disk, the crescent, or the caduceus. Under Roman influence, the employment of more or less artistic human figures and features gradually became the custom, and the

xxvi

syncretistic paganism of the North African passed from being symbolical to being anthropomorphic. Further, the Punic religion in its native state had been more closely akin to the strict monotheism of the Hebrews than to the picturesque polytheism of the Hellenes. Its twofold divinity, Baal-Tanit, was more a cosmological conception than a religious or poetical; though two in name, they symbolized the two correlative aspects of the ultimate being, the male and generative, and the female and reproductive. But around them had grown up no art and no mythology; their functions remained vague and indeterminate, and their personality ill-defined. That was why their identification with any single one of the figures of the Roman pantheon was uncertain; Tanit appears under the varying appellations of Diana, Ceres, or Venus, and Baal masquerades under the designations of Saturn, Jupiter, Liber Pater, Mercury, Pluto, or Apollo. Here already was a suggestion of that monotheistic tendency which later African paganism displays so markedly. Since none of the characters of Roman mythology exactly fitted or completely expressed the nature of that almost impersonal deity which the Phoenicians had introduced, it was the easier to claim, as does Maximus of Madaura, that behind the multiple names of divinities worshipped by mankind there was a common God, the Father of them all. And again, in the centuries of Roman domination, the worship even of Baal had gradually receded into the background, and that of Tanit, in the character of Caelestis, had become more and more widespread, until she was an object of veneration, not only in her well-known and beautiful temple at Carthage, but also in Numidia, Spain, Mauretania, and in Rome

INTRODUCTION

itself. Thus, though transformed by the acceptance
of a mythology which was at best an inadequate and
ill-fitting cloak for its original bareness and simplicity,
though adopting Roman nomenclature and con-
structing its sanctuaries upon the model of those in
Roman use, this Punic paganism persisted behind and
below all that the conquerors imposed. In reality,
they had not attempted a religious revolution. It was
enough that political and industrial ends were served
by external conformity to the State religion as a
symbol of authority and by participation in its games,
its ceremonies, and its festivals.

What the Christian Church from the time of Constantine had been steadily attempting to repress and
eradicate was this official Roman paganism, the ally and
the expression of Roman imperialism. The distinction drawn above between the Punic basis of religion
and the veneer of terminology, mythology, and rite
which accompanied the conquest and settlement,
must be borne in mind for the understanding of
the Church's attitudes and policies towards paganism during the lifetime of Augustine. The reign of
Julian (361–363) had been followed by nearly twenty
years of vacillation and partial tolerance of paganism
which Augustine himself must have clearly remembered, but from the time of the emperor Gratian on-
wards a succession of imperial edicts forbade with
increasing severity the observance of pagan practices ;
sacrifices were proscribed, the immunities enjoyed by
priests and vestals were withdrawn, the revenues and
property of pagan temples were confiscated, and the
statues of heathen deities were overthrown and their
temples closed. Those most affected by this legislation were naturally of the official class, the magistrates

and the wealthier and Romanized families of the municipalities. For them the State religion had been indissolubly bound up with politics ; the dignity of perpetual flamen was the climax of the municipal *cursus honorum*, while the priests of Rome and Augustus had not infrequently discharged the various public offices in their city before achieving the crowning honour of their career. In Timgad, for example, about two-thirds of the curia had fulfilled religious functions as flamines, pontiffs, augurs, or provincial high-priests ;[a] at Madaura the public character of the pagan sacrifices is emphasized by Augustine's correspondent Maximus, and the municipal senate was apparently composed entirely of adherents of the older cult.[b] The town of Sufes might be alleged as an example of popular resentment against the closing of the temples, yet it is not unlikely that the massacre of some sixty Christians there as a result of the legislation of 399 [c] was instigated by the magistrates and that, in any case, the level of Romanization was more than usually high, for that town owed its origin to the strategic position it occupied on the edge of the area of Punic infiltration around Mactar, and its population, as that of a frontier fort, may have been largely Roman. But in general the suppression of official paganism concerned the wealthier and the more cultured classes

[a] This was between A.D. 364 and 367, certainly, but there is evidence of a correspondingly high proportion of pagans among municipal officers elsewhere in Augustine's own day. The vicar of Africa in 395 and the pro-consul in 394 were apostates ; the pro-consul in 400 was fanatically pagan. It was this condition of things which provoked Augustine's regretful remark (*In Ps.* 54, 13): *ille nobilis si Christianus esset, nemo remaneret paganus.*

[b] See Nos. 5, 6, and 55 *infra*.   [c] See No. 16 *infra*.

from whom were drawn the administrators and the civil servants, the educated and the literary. The inevitable result was the loss to Christianity of those who represented the finer sides, not only of paganism, but of the antique culture, and the alienation of ecclesiastics from the art and literature of the ancient world. In the absence of a laity accustomed to the management of affairs, the whole working of the Church fell more and more upon the clergy, and the development of Christianity was accompanied by the development of ecclesiasticism. Being out of touch with the personnel of the government, the Church was hardly in a position to act as an intermediary between the State and the indigenous population, and probably the hostility of the governing class counted for something against Christianity when the barbarians began to arrive.

In this direction, indeed, the Church had since the time of Constantine been steadily assuming the functions and the duties earlier the prerogative of the State religion, paganism, and the final rejection of that religion left the ground clear for Christianity and gave sanction to those activities in which it had already discredited and displaced its competitor. In many respects the gradual association with political departments and secular concerns was a valuable preparation for the coming days of administrative dislocation and paralysis, when the machinery of the Roman Empire was reduced almost to impotence through the barbarian invasions. The tasks and the attributes of civil officialdom increasingly devolved upon the clergy, and, in Africa during the century before the irruption of the Vandals, it meant the developing alliance of Church and State and the identification,

INTRODUCTION

in the eyes of the native inhabitants, of Christianity
with the Roman conqueror. It was among these
peoples that the earliest successes of the Church had
been achieved; missionary enterprise had begun in
the coastal towns and followed the Roman roads inland, but the first Christians were recruited from the
lower classes, as were later the majority of the converts
to monasticism. Now the victorious Church, through
the generosity of the emperors and the devotion of
its members, acquired or inherited vast tracts of land
and became itself a proprietor and employer, bound
to the same system of exploitation as had character-
ized the civil régime. The owners of large estates
who were Christians compelled their dependents to
accept the faith, on the principle *cujus regio, ejus
religio*, and built Christian churches or chapels upon
their land for the use of their workers. The bishops
obtained judicial privileges which, if they added
enormously to their labour, added no less to their
prestige. Following more or less closely the civil
boundaries, the Church had organized its dioceses
into the six provinces into which Diocletian had
divided North Africa: Pro-consular Africa had its
metropolis at Carthage, Numidia at Cirta, Byzacenum
at Hadrumetum, Tripolitana at Tripoli, the two
Mauretanias at Sitifis and Caesarea. A clue to the
nature of the Christian population is supplied by the
interesting phenomenon of an unusually numerous
episcopate: practically every important town had its
own bishop, and not a few of the manorial churches
besides. In the course of the fourth century there
are no fewer than seven hundred bishoprics, and even
admitting that roughly one half of these were due to
Donatist rivalry, the remainder is still disproportion-

ately large for a province even so extensive as North Africa. It is clear that the normal Christian congregation was recruited from the more civilized inhabitants and from the serfs on estates of Christian masters. There still remained a great number of natives outside the towns, to whom the increasing strength and organization of the Church suggested that it was only another instrument for native oppression. It has been often suggested that the most formidable heresies that confronted the Church arose in those provinces where Hellenistic or Roman culture was least assimilated, in Arian Egypt, Monophysite Syria, and Donatist Africa, and here, at least, the union of orthodoxy with the State brought to a head that national feeling which was already partially aroused by the heavy burden of taxation, the compact and depressing system of land-holding, and the undoubted increase of economic difficulties. Donatism began within the Church ; it ended as a social revolution.

Though Christianity had successfully overcome paganism in this public sphere and acquired its official status and privileges, that deeper and more indigenous religion upon which paganism had been a loyal veneer presented a problem less easily solved. Public ceremonies and rites could be forcibly suppressed, but superstitions persisted alongside and within Christianity, and here the Church was unable to secure more than an unequal compromise. Augustine repeatedly speaks of the extent of Christianity and the growing extinction of paganism, but while the composition of his *De Civitate Dei* shows the survival of paganism among the lettered classes, his *Sermons*, and casual remarks elsewhere, show how deeply it still in-

fluenced the conduct of the people. One of the most important of his *Letters* [a] contains a graphic picture of the celebration of Agapae in cemeteries and in the chapels of the martyrs, and Augustine himself recognizes in this the persistence of the ancient Parentalia. To combat the evil of drunkenness at the martyrs' tombs, the Church turned the offering of bread and wine into an offering of the Eucharist; roofed over the tomb, now become an altar, and called the new building a chapel, where the saint's career might be depicted in picture and in play and where the burial of the faithful might show their veneration for the saint and their belief in the virtue of his near presence. But other practices yielded less speedily and less completely. The consulting of astrologers was widespread, and Augustine himself, as he tells in the *Confessions*,[b] had the habit as a young man. Even members of the Church observed pagan customs and required admonition to refrain from such habits as the celebration of New Year's Day by the giving of presents, the singing of ribald songs, attendance at the theatre and at banquets. From these and other references in Augustine's works, it is clear that the Christianity of the time bore the strong imprint of the character of those by whom it was received. The problem of dealing with survivals from earlier cults remained a difficulty for long thereafter. It troubled St. Augustine of Canterbury and evoked two differing replies from Pope Gregory the Great; it received solution by way of compromise from Gregory Thaumaturgus and by way of stern de-

[a] No. 10 *infra*.
[b] *Conf.* iv. 3, 4; see the interesting account of the Carthaginian astrologer Albicerius in *C. Acad.* i. 6. 17 ff.

nunciation of any association with paganism from the Popes consulted by the Franciscan missionaries to China in the seventeenth and eighteenth centuries. Yet if these pagan characteristics were conspicuous in the African converts, it could hardly have been otherwise. By the aid of the imperial laws the Church had eventually succeeded in effacing paganism as an official cult ; through the Councils it preserved its doctrine free from subtle semi-paganized interpretation and misconstruction, and in such writings as Augustine's *City of God* it created a historical background against which its development could be seen as a vast providential purpose and its organization as a reflection and anticipation of the Eternal Kingdom of God. But in the lower levels of everyday practice among its ordinary believers Christianity was forced to accept and to sanction much that was undoubtedly of pagan origin and with which, strictly speaking, it had nothing whatever to do. In the pagan festivals are to be found the beginnings of the Christian year ; the worship of Tanit or Astarte or Caelestis may have encouraged the veneration of the Virgin Mother ; the lesser deities of popular superstition were certainly the prototypes of the Christian saints or demons ; the belief in magic and divination, probably the most energetic pagan sentiment of the time, continued both in and below Christianity and would not be cast out. It is possible to condemn the compromising spirit and to see in that century of Christian interpenetration with alien and indefensible customs the ironical vengeance of the paganism which, publicly ejected and condemned, returned to cloak itself under various licit and respectable guises, but it is perhaps kinder to find in that slow achievement the evidence

of a divine capacity to absorb theories and customs that could be eradicated only by a toilsome process of education and enlightenment, to consecrate them by their admission among holier habits and to utilize them as steps towards a purer and a higher life.

IV

To the Christians of the fourth and fifth centuries the writing of letters was more than a personal and occasional pleasure. A bishop was tied to his see and not infrequently, as with Augustine, his people were unwilling to allow him to be absent from them, so for such as he correspondence was a necessity. There were official letters communicating the decision of local synods, and others demanded in the exercise of episcopal duties and discipline. These *litterae formatae* might be certificates of church communion to Christians who were compelled to travel and were in this way commended to bishops elsewhere (*litterae communicatoriae*); they might be letters granting authority to local clergy to remove to another diocese with credentials from their own bishop (*litterae dimissoriae*); they might be simple letters of introduction (*commendatoriae*). But in addition correspondence was a means, often the only one, of publicity: it supplied news, discharged the function of exhortation and encouragement, served as a bond between churches and between individuals, and not seldom did duty as an open pamphlet or treatise. A good many of Augustine's letters have this official or semi-official character, and, covering as they do a period of forty-five years, they are invaluable documents for the history of his age. The majority of them treat of the heresies, principally

Donatism ; a smaller number treat of paganism, and several others discuss such matters as church discipline, the right of sanctuary, and monasticism. Most of the purely personal letters have been relegated by the editors, because of the difficulty of dating them, into the fourth section (Epp. ccxxxii.–cclxx.), and among these will be found some of the most interesting of the whole collection : his reply to the magistrates of Madaura discussing paganism (No. 55), his letter to Possidius concerning the painting of the face and the wearing of ornaments and amulets (No. 56), his brief account and examination of astrology (No. 57) and his discussion of the matrimonial shortcomings of Ecdicia and the duties of a Christian wife (No. 60). In these more particularly he manifests his friendly and helpful pastoral care for his people, his understanding of human nature and his sound common sense. Here, with a regrettable infrequency, he becomes intimate and human, and the official, the bishop, the philosopher, the theologian, sink into the background as the man appears.

In general, the letters of the time were written upon papyrus (*charta*). On one occasion [a] Augustine excuses himself for writing on parchment, because at the moment neither papyrus nor tablets were available : his ivory tablets he had sent to the uncle of his correspondent and he asks for their speedy return. His habit was to dictate to scribes ; [b] not seldom at the end of a letter he has added a sentence of greeting or exhortation in his own hand, though the carelessness of copyists has considerably reduced the

number of the marginal annotations *Et alia manu.*[a]
The letter finished, it was folded and sealed, and
Augustine tells a correspondent on one occasion the
emblem on his seal : it depicts a human face in profile,
perhaps that of the writer himself. The bearers of
the missives were almost always private individuals,
and only rarely was it possible to secure the services
of the public *tabellarii.* Sometimes the writer was
fortunate enough to find someone travelling at least
near to the person he desired to address, as when
Augustine transmits a letter to Paulinus of Nola by
Fortunatianus, who is journeying to Rome.[b] More
usually one of his own clergy, a presbyter or a deacon,
was entrusted with the letter and made a special
journey in order to deliver it ;[c] once or twice an
acolyte is sent with letters,[d] and once the agent of a
Roman lady carries letters to the African shore and
employed someone to bear them thence to Augustine
at Hippo.[e] Naturally, a special bearer was always
insistent upon receiving an answer and no less insistent upon the need for an early departure. Of all
letters, received or transmitted, Augustine appears
to have kept copies ; in writing to Jerome,[f] for
example, he speaks of his own earlier communications ;
sometimes he quotes verbally from them, and one letter
at least owes its preservation only to his inclusion of
it in a later treatise.[g] In the list of his works com-
piled by Possidius, many of his letters are mentioned
as existing in the library of the church of Hippo, and
Augustine in his *Retractations* amends or qualifies

---

[a] *e.g.* No. 36 *infra.* [b] Ep. lxxx.
[c] Epp. xciv., xcv., xcvii., etc.
[d] No. 43. 1. [e] No. 26.
[f] Epp. clxvi., ccii. A. [g] No. 36.

some of the statements he had made throughout the years in his correspondence. In preserving the letters he had received, Augustine must have dated them and at times supplied a name where the writer's identity was not conspicuous ; thus, the superscription to the letter from Maximus of Madaura would in all probability come from the hand of Augustine alone. Again, the rich manuscript tradition for the correspondence exchanged between Augustine and Jerome suggests that each recipient edited it separately. There is a double tradition, as there is for the letters exchanged between Augustine and Paulinus of Nola, so it appears practically certain that there was also a double edition.

To a reader unaccustomed to Christian Latin letters the use of honorific titles will appear at first strange and cumbersome. These occur in endless variety, and the translator is confronted with the difficulty of either rendering the phrase by a periphrasis or of adopting and capitalizing a word which in English is not ordinarily so employed. Such terms as *Beatitudo tua, Amplitudo tua, Magnanimitas tua, Venerabilitas tua, Benivolentia tua, Dilectio tua,* can hardly be literally rendered, and even where an English phrase like " Your Grace " can be used, it has associations not always appropriate to the context. The employment of these honorific titles begins in the epistolary literature of the third century and becomes increasingly frequent until the time of Justinian, when certain changes were made in terminology and descriptive titles assigned to certain ranks of imperial officials. Within the Church, the development of such a nomenclature was no doubt the inevitable accompaniment of the development of a hierarchy, and as the dignity of

the clergy was augmented and encouraged by the State, their titles became more and more pompous and ornate. Meantime, in Augustine's age, they are upon the whole elastic and variable. A few titles are the prerogative of the Emperor or of bishops in general ; some others are confined in use to the laity, but as yet there is hardly visible any such definite gradation as marks the civil officials into the three classes of *illustres*, *spectabiles*, and *clarissimi*, corresponding to the *magistratus maximi*, *medii* and *minores*. The title bestowed by a writer upon his correspondent depends upon the circumstances of their respective relations, the purpose of the letter, and the degree of veneration and respect which the writer thought proper to assume. Epistolary language of the period is exaggeratedly deferential, and the employment of the infinite varieties of honorific terms of address is only symptomatic of the rhetorical and pompous style in vogue among pagans and Christians alike.

V

As a letter-writer Augustine certainly lacks the point and the passion of his contemporary, Jerome ; his style has little of the movement and the *color poeticus* of Ambrose, and nothing of the tedious loquacity and rotundity of Paulinus. To a modern reader it seems strange that one of his friends could compare his prose to that of Cicero, for as a rule it is comparatively undistinguished and unobtrusive. Critics and biographers have emphasized his early training in rhetoric and his adoption of public speaking as a career, yet their insistence upon the rhetorical nature of his prose is over-done. He does like, at

times, to seize hold of a word or phrase in an opponent's letter, and to play upon the word or the idea for the duration of his reply ; [a] he has a fondness for jingle and assonance, and many of his most quoted phrases owe their popularity as much to their balance, point, and rhyme, as to their meaning. But even granting all this, we fall short of accuracy in describing his language as " rhetorical " and in crediting his early and pre-Christian studies with a permanent and unmistakable moulding of his style. In reality, if he be compared with his contemporaries, none has emerged so far from enslavement to rhetoric ; no one of them shows less solicitude than he for the frills and flourishes of mere ornament. Of a sober and introspective nature, he is too much in earnest about the truth to be anything but direct, weighty, and unadorned. He made Christian Latin a more pliant and forceful speech than any of his predecessors except that other African, Tertullian. Under stress of his ideas or his emotions it becomes a grave and sonorous vehicle for great and moving thoughts, and only at occasional moments does he condescend to think as much of his method and manner of utterance as of his message. Rhetoric formed indeed the chief staple of contemporary education and Augustine did not escape from the heritage of his age, yet in many respects he is one of the greatest, as well as the last, of the masters of Latin eloquence.

It was Augustine's merit that, in an age of definite transition, he stood at the boundary-line of old and new and linked hands with both. In him the contribution of the passing ancient civilization was concentrated and epitomized : he had learned through his accept-

[a] See, for example, No. 24, and others *passim.*

INTRODUCTION

ance of Manicheism much of the thought and the perplexities of the Orient, and as an African, sharing the blood of the Roman and the Phoenician, he could understand and participate in the Eastern and the Western both ; he had come through his Neoplatonic sympathies to know something of the legacy of Hellenic philosophy, and from it, too, he gathered much that influenced and enriched his interpretation of Christian problems. With him, the centre of theological discussion changes finally from East to West. The preceding century had witnessed an Eastern heresy combating Eastern Councils, but the results of that long struggle he summed up, perhaps not altogether understanding it, and passed on with his imprint to the Western Church of later times. For all succeeding centuries he remains a source, an inspiration, and an originator. Rich and complex and powerful, his mind had gathered up all that was best in the past, and the story of his influence is the story of Christian thought from his own day till now. He inspired both the scholastic philosopher and the mystic ; to the religious orders he was a veritable father and founder ; to the Christian constitutionalist his Donatist synthesis and his vision and interpretation of the two Cities was fundamental and authoritative ; to the Christian individualist his Pauline theory of Grace came as a challenge and a revelation. Yet no less he was unmistakably the child of his own age —or perhaps it is because of this that he became the heritage of all time, for, if he survived the capture of Rome, Roman civilization survived him but a few months in North Africa. Confronted with what, to blinder eyes, appeared to be the end of all things, he has all the unhappiness and questioning of a time of

collapse and desperate gloom, but to the ultimate and permanent problems of humanity he gave an answer, or a series of answers, not without a very sober realization of the sorrow of the times and the gravity of the inescapable issues, which by its insight, wisdom, and indomitable faith gave assurance to mankind in centuries of trial and darkness and provided a starting-point, when opportunity was ripe, for new inquiry and new achievements.

CHRONOLOGY

354. Augustine born at Tagaste, November 13.

361–363. Julian Emperor.

370. Studies at Carthage.

374. Ambrose becomes bishop of Milan.

376. Teaches rhetoric at Carthage. The Goths cross the Danube.

379–395. Reign of Theodosius.

383. Goes to Rome.

384. Appointed public teacher of rhetoric at Milan.

386. His conversion (July or August).

387. Returns to Milan after a period of retirement at Cassiciacum. Is baptized by St. Ambrose. Sets out for Africa with Monnica, his mother, who dies at Ostia. Returns to Rome.

388. Returns to Africa (July or August).

388–391. Selling his patrimony at Tagaste, Augustine adopts a monastic mode of life with some friends.

391. Ordained presbyter at Hippo Regius.

394. Ordained bishop-coadjutor.

396. On Valerius's death, he becomes sole bishop.

397. Death of St. Ambrose.

c. 400. Writes the *Confessions*.

402–403. Prudentius in Rome.

406. The Germans cross the Rhine.

407. The Roman legions withdrawn from Britain.

408. Death of Claudian. Execution of Stilicho.

410. Sack of Rome by Alaric, August 23.

411. Conference at Carthage with the Donatists (June).

412. First writings against the Pelagians.

420. Death of Jerome.

425–455. Valentian III. Emperor in the West.

426. Augustine nominates his coadjutor as successor.

427. Revolt of Count Boniface.

429. The Vandals enter Africa and besiege Hippo.

430. Death of Augustine, August 28.

431. Death of Paulinus of Nola.

439. The Vandals capture Carthage.

BIBLIOGRAPHY

SEE, in general, the bibliographies in M. Schanz, *Geschichte der römischen Litteratur*, iv. 2 (Munich, 1920), pp. 454-457 ; Otto Bardenhewer, *Geschichte der altkirchlichen Literatur*, iv. (Freiburg-im-Breisgau, 1924), pp. 497-500 ; *Bibliothèque Nationale : Catalogue des ouvrages de s. Augustin conservés au département des imprimés* (Extrait du tome v du Catalogue général) (Paris, 1901) ; Paul Monceaux, *Histoire littéraire de l'Afrique chrétienne*, tome vii : " Saint Augustin et le Donatisme " (Paris, 1923), pp. 129-146 (" Lettres d'Augustin relatives au Donatisme ") and pp. 279-286 ("Tableau chronologique des lettres d'Augustin relatives au Donatisme "). The longer studies of St. Augustine may often be consulted with advantage, especially that by Portalié in the *Dictionnaire de Théologie Catholique*, vol. i., cols. 2268-2472, but on the whole they pay little attention to the letters. The best recent general bibliography of studies on Augustine is that of Étienne Gilson, " Bibliographie des principaux travaux relatifs à la philosophie de saint Augustin jusqu'en 1927," which forms pp. 309-331 of his *Introduction à l'étude de Saint Augustin* (Paris, 1929).

I. MANUSCRIPTS

Owing to the great number and variety of the manuscripts, no account of them can be attempted here. For full information see Goldbacher's fifth volume (*Corpus Scriptorum Eccl. Lat.*, vol. lviii. : *S. Augustini Epistulae*, pars v. Vienna-Leipzig, 1923), pp. xi-lxxx, which supersedes his early study, " Ueber d. Handschriften der Briefe

BIBLIOGRAPHY

des hl. Augustinus " (*Sitzungsberichte der kl. Akad. Wien*, Hist.-Phil. Klasse. Bd. lxxiv. (1873) pp. 275-284). For manuscripts of recently discovered letters see Morin, under " Editions," below, and for an English manuscript see Cowper, H. S., " A thirteenth-century manuscript of the Epistolae of St. Augustine, formerly belonging to Conishead Priory " (*Transactions of the Cumberland and Westmorland Antiquarian Society*, N.S. vol. 27, 1926-7, pp. 48-53).

There is an interesting paper by Henri Bordier, " Restitution d'un manuscrit du VIe siècle mi-parti entre Paris et Genève, contenant des lettres et des sermons de S. Augustin " (*Mémoires et documents de la Société d'histoire de Genève*, tome xvi., 1869, pp. 82-126 ; also in *Études paléographiques et historiques*, by L. Delisle, A. Rillier, H. Bordier, Genève et Bâle, 1866).

II. EDITIONS

The earliest editions (Johannes de Amerbach, 1493 ; Erasmus, 1528, 1569) possess only a bibliographical interest. The editors of the Louvain edition of the complete works of Augustine (1576) added 29 new letters, some of which are found also as *anecdota* in the *Supplementum* to Augustine by Hieronymus Vignier (Paris, 1654-1655). A separate edition of the Letters was given in 1668 by L. F. Reinhart, who added seven more to the *corpus*. But an epoch-making recension and re-arranging appeared just a hundred years later, in the edition of the complete works prepared by the Benedictines of St. Maur. They added 16 letters, making a total of 270, of which number 53 were addressed to Augustine, the remainder being written by him, sometimes in conjunction with others. These 270 the Maurist editors arranged in four groups, as nearly chronological as they could place them. The first (Epp. i.-xxx.) belongs to the years before his elevation to episcopal rank (A.D. 386-395) ; the second (Epp. xxxi.-cxxiii.) to the years 396-410 ; the third (Epp. cxxiv.-ccxxxi.)

xlv

from 411–430 ; and the last group (Epp. ccxxxii.-cclxx.) contains the letters that cannot be dated.

The Maurist edition was several times reprinted, the best-known reprint being that of Gaume (Paris, 1836). Goldbacher's edition began to appear in 1895, after twenty-two years of preparation ; in the Vienna *Corpus Scriptorum Eccl. Latinorum* it forms vols. 34 (parts 1 and 2, containing Epp. i.-xxx. and xxxi.-cxxiii., 1895, 1898), 44 (part 3, Epp. cxxiv.-clxxxiv., 1904) and 57 (Epp. clxxv.-cclxx., 1911). The final volume, containing prefaces and indices, was not issued until 1923, fifty years after the editor had begun his long task.

Meanwhile, the original *corpus* of 270 letters had been increased by several fortunate, if meagre, discoveries. Goldbacher inserted between Epp. clxx. and clxxi. a portion of a letter preserved in the Commentary of Primasius on the Apocalypse ; this fragment was re-edited after Goldbacher by Haussleiter in Zahn's *Forschungen zur Geschichte d. neutest. Kanons*, fasc. iv. (Erlangen, 1891) ; and also two letters (Epp. clxxxiv. and ccii.A) published by G. Bessel in 1732 and 1733. Further, Goldbacher found two letters (Epp. xcii.A and clxxiii.A) which he first published in *Wiener Studien*, Bd. xvi. (1894) pp. 72-77. In the *Revue Bénédictine*, vol. xiii. (1896) pp. 481-486, Dom Germain Morin published the text of an unprinted letter addressed to Valentinus, abbot of Hadrumetum (see No. 50 *infra*), of which, by the discovery of another manuscript, he was able to give a better text in the same review, vol. xviii. (1901) pp. 241-244. This letter has unfortunately found no place in Goldbacher's edition.

In the present year two small volumes have been announced (*S. Eusebii Hieronymi et Aurelii Augustini epistulae mutuae*, ed. Jos. Schmid, and *S. Aurelii Augustini liber de videndo Deo, seu Epistula 147*, ed. Michael Schmaus = *Florilegium Patristicum*, Nos. xxii. and xxiii.). Of these only the second has appeared at the time of going to press ; it is a faithful reproduction of Goldbacher's text, with a slight introduction and the minimum of textual notes.

BIBLIOGRAPHY

III. Translations

(a) English

Letters of Saint Augustine. Translated by the Rev. J. G. Cunningham. Edinburgh, 1872–1875. 2 vols. Pp. 440, 480.

[Contains 160 letters. An American edition was published by Scribners.]

Letters of St. Augustine. Selected and translated by Mary H. Allies. London, 1890. Pp. 342.

[Contains 33 letters.]

(b) French

Épistres choisies de S. Augustin, traduites en françois par Monsieur Giry. Paris, 1653.

Les Épistres choisies de S. Augustin, mises en françois par le sieur Picard de La Cande. Paris, 1653. 8vo.

Les Lettres de saint Augustin, traduites en françois sur l'édition nouvelle des Pères Bénédictins . . . (par Ph. Goibaud Du Bois). Paris, 1684. 2 vols., folio.

[There was an edition of 1684 in 6 vols. 8vo, and later editions in 1701, 1707, 1718, 1737.]

Lettres nouvelles de saint Augustin, traduites en françois [par dom J. Martin], accompagnées de notes critiques, historiques et chronologiques. Paris, 1734. 8vo.

Lettres de saint Augustin, traduites en français et précédées d'une introduction, par M. Poujoulat. Paris, 1858. 4 vols., 8vo.

La Vie heureuse. Lettres choisies de S. Augustin. Orléans, 1873. 16mo.

(c) German

Kranzfelder, Th. *Augustinus. Ausgewählte Briefe.* Kempten, 1878–1879. 2 vols. (Bibliothek der Kirchenväter.)

Hoffmann, Alfred. *Des hl. Augustinus ausgewählte Briefe.* Kempten and Munich, 1917. 2 vols. Pp. 484, 440. (Bibliothek der Kirchenväter, 29, 30.)

[A revision of Kranzfelder.]

BIBLIOGRAPHY

(d) Italian

S. Agostino. *Lettere scelte e di altri a lui scritte fra cui di S. Gerolamo.* Torino, 1871–1873. 2 vols.

S. *Agostino. Lettere xxxiii.* Traduzione di Giov. Neapoli. Torino, 1887. Pp. xxxii. + 272.

IV. STUDIES

(a) GENERAL

Banks, J. S. " Augustine as seen in his letters " (*London Quarterly Review*, vol. ccxi., 1914, pp. 86-97).

de Bruyne, Donatien. "Notes sur les lettres de s. Augustin" (*Revue Bénédictine*, t. xxiii, 1927, pp. 523-530).

Dubelman, J. F. P. *Das Heidenthum in Nordafrika nach den Briefen des hl. Augustinus.* Bonn, 1859. 4to. Pp. 26.

Ginzel, J. A. " Der Geist des hl. Augustinus in seinen Briefen," in his *Kirchenhistorische Schriften*, Bd. i. (Wien, 1872) pp. 123-245.

Karsten, H. T. " De brieven van den kerkvader Augustinus " (*Verslagen en mededeelingen d. k. Akad. van Wetenschappen*, Vierde Reeks, Tiende Deel, 1911, pp. 226-258).
[On Neoplatonic influences in the Letters.]

Montgomery, W. " Augustine's correspondence," in his *St. Augustine : Aspects of his life and thought.* London, 1914, pp. 66-98.

Moorrees, F. D. *De Organisatie van de christelike Kerk van Noord-Afrika in het licht van de brieven van Augustinus.* Groningen-Hague, 1926. Pp. 122.

Parsons, Wilfrid. *A Study of the Vocabulary and Rhetoric of the Letters of St. Augustine.* Washington, 1923. Pp. 281.
[See my review in *Bulletin Du Cange*, t. i., 1924-5. Pp. 251-254.]

xlviii

BIBLIOGRAPHY

Sparrow-Simpson, W. J. *The Letters of St. Augustine.* London, 1919. Pp. 336.

Thimme, W. *Augustin : Ein Lebens- und Characterbild, auf Grund seiner Briefe.* Göttingen, 1910. Pp. 206.

(b) SPECIAL

(1) On Augustine's Correspondence with Jerome

Barberiis, Philippe de. *Discordantiae SS. Hieronymi et Augustini.* Rome, 1481.

Bindesboll, Severin. *Augustinus et Hieronymus de s. Scriptura ex Hebraeo interpretanda disputantes.* Copenhagen, 1825.

Dufey, A. "Controverse entre s. Jerome et s. Augustin d'après leurs lettres " (*Revue du Clergé français*, tome xxv., 1901, pp. 141-149).

Dorsch, Aem. "St. Augustinus und Hieronymus über die Wahrheit der biblischen Geschichte " (*Zeitschrift für Katholische Theologie*, 1911, pp. 421-448, 601-664).

Haitjema, Th. " De Briefwisseling tuischen Augustinus en Hieronymus " (*Tijdschrift voor Geschiedenis*, vol. xxxvi., 1921, pp. 159-198).

Malfatti, E. "Una controversia tra S. Agostino e S. Girolamo " (*La Scuola Cattolica*, 1921, pp. 321-338, 402-426).

Möhler, J. A. "Hieronymus und Augustinus im Streit über Gal. 2. 14 " in his *Gesammelte Schriften und Aufsätze*, Bd. i., Regensburg, 1839, pp. 1-18.

Overbeck, F. *Ueber die Auffassung des Streites des Paulus mit Petrus in Antiochen bei den Kirchenvätern.* Basel, 1877.

—— " Aus dem Briefwechsel des Augustinus mit Hieronymus " (*Historische Zeitschrift*, Bd. vi., 1879, pp. 222-259).

Tourscher, F. E. "The Correspondence of St. Augustine and St. Jerome " (*American Ecclesiastical Review*, 1917, vol. lvii. pp. 476-492, 1918, vol. lviii. pp. 45-56).

BIBLIOGRAPHY

(2) On Particular Letters

Epp. xvi.-xvii. :

Baxter, J. H. "The Martyrs of Madaura, A.D. 180" (*Journal of Theological Studies*, vol. xxvi., 1924, pp. 21-37).

Beyerhaus, Gisbert. "Philosophische Aussetzungen in Augustins Briefen" (*Rheinisches Museum*, N.F. vol. lxxv., 1926, pp. 6-45).

Usener, H. "Vergessenes" (*Rheinisches Museum*, N.F. vol. xxviii., 1873, pp. 407-409).

Ep. xxvi. :

Zelzner, M. *De carmine Licentii ad Augustinum.* (Dissertation.) Arnsberg, Westphalia, 1915.

Ep. xxviii. 6 :

Weyman, Carl, "Infinitiv auf -uiri bei Augustin" (*Archiv für lat. Lexikographie u. Grammatik*, vol. ix., 1896, p. 492).

Ep. xli. :

Georges, Karl Ernst. "Miscellen" (*Jahrbücher für class. Philologie*, vol. 123, 1881, p. 807).

Ep. xlviii. :

The Judgement of the learned and pious St. Augustine concerning penal laws against conventicles and for Unity in Religion. Deliver'd in his 48th Epistle to Vincentius. London, 1670.

Ep. lxviii. 2 :

Schenkl, R. "Zu Hieronymus s. Augustinus Epist. lxviii., § 2" (*Wiener Studien*, Bd. xix, 1897, p. 317).

Ep. xciii. :

Herzog, E. "Ein Schreiben Augustins über kirchen-politischen Zwang" (*Internat. kirchliche Zeitschrift*, vol. 6, 1916, pp. 1-26).

Ep. cii. 6 :

Rottmanner, Odilo. "S. Augustin, Epist. 102, 6" (*Revue Bénédictine*, tome xvii., 1900, p. 315).

1

BIBLIOGRAPHY

Epp. ciii.-cvi. (also Epp. cli., cliii. 20, cclxviii.) :

Martroye, F. " S. Augustin et la législation " (*Bulletin de la Société nationale des Antiquaires de France*, 1915, pp. 166-168, 223-229 ; 1917, p. 101 ; 1918, pp. 108-118, 165-166).

Ep. cxxv. :

Daux, C. " Un Incident à la Basilique d'Hippone en 411 " (*Revue des Questions Historiques*, tome lxxx., 1906, pp. 31-73).

Ep. clix. :

Tourscher, F. E. " Some letters of St. Augustine. A Study " (*American Ecclesiastical Review*, 1919, vol. lxix. pp. 609-625).

Ep. clxiv. :

Hundhausen, L. J. *Die beiden Pontificalschreiben des Apostelfürstens Petrus.* Mainz, 1873, pp. 343 ff.

Ep. clxxxix. :

Moffatt, J. " St. Augustine's Advice to an Army Officer " (*Expositor*, vol. xi. series 8, 1916, pp. 409-420).

Ep. ccxi. (The " Rule ") :

The literature on the *Rule* is too lengthy to be given here, but reference may be made to the article " Règle de S. Augustin " in *Dictionnaire de Théologie Catholique*, vol. 1, cols. 2472-2483, and to an interesting paper by Eliz. Speakman, "The Rule of St. Augustine" in *Historical Essays . . . Owens College, Manchester* (1907), pp. 57-75.

The following studies are directly concerned with Augustine's letter in itself, not as the foundation-statute of an order.

Baxter, J. H. " St. Augustine's *Rule* " (*Journal of Theological Studies*, vol. xx., 1919, pp. 352-355).
  [A reply to V. M'Nabb, below.]

li

BIBLIOGRAPHY

Baxter, J. H. " On a place in St. Augustine's *Rule* "
(*Journal of Theological Studies*, vol. xxiii., 1922, pp.
188-190).

[On the reading *Deo natis* in § 4.]

Capelle, B. " L'Epître 211ᵉ et la Règle de Saint Augustin " (*Analecta Praemonstratensia*, tome iii., 1927, pp.
369-378).

[A criticism of Goldbacher's text.]

Lambot, C. " La Règle de s. Augustin et s. Césaire "
(*Revue Bénédictine*, t. xli., 1929, pp. 333-341).

McNabb, Vincent. " Was the Rule of St. Augustine
written for St. Melania the Younger ? " (*Journal of
Theological Studies*, vol. xx., 1919, pp. 242-249).

Schroeder, P. " Die Augustinerchorherrenregel : Ent-
stehung, kritischer Text und Einführung der Regel "
(*Archiv für Urkundenforschung*, 1926, pp. 271-306).

Ep. cclxii. :

Lettre de saint Augustin (262ᵐᵉ). *Saint Augustin
adresse des reproches et des conseils à une femme mariée.*
Lyon, 1861. 8vo.

SELECT LETTERS OF
ST. AUGUSTINE

S. AURELI AUGUSTINI EPISTULAE

No. 1 (Ep. II)

ZENOBIO AUGUSTINUS

Bene inter nos convenit, ut opinor, omnia, quae
corporeus sensus adtingit, ne puncto quidem temporis eodem modo manere posse, sed labi, effluere et
praesens nihil obtinere, id est, ut latine loquar, non
esse. Horum itaque amorem perniciosissimum poe-
narumque plenissimum vera et divina philosophia
monet frenare atque sopire, ut se toto animus, etiam
dum hoc corpus agit, in ea, quae semper eiusdem
modi sunt neque peregrino pulchro placent, feratur
atque aestuet. Quae cum ita sint et cum te verum
ac simplicem, qualis sine ulla sollicitudine amari
potes, in semet ipsa mens videat, fatemur tamen
congressum istum atque conspectum tuum, cum a
nobis corpore discedis locisque seiungeris, quaerere nos eoque, dum licet, cupere fratribus. Quod
profecto vitium, si te bene novi, amas in nobis et,
cum omnia bona optes carissimis et familiarissimis

---

[a] Written at Cassiciacum towards the end of 386, while
Augustine was still in retirement and immersed in philosophical studies. In these Zenobius was keenly interested,
and to him Augustine dedicated the treatise *De Ordine*
(A.D. 386). He afterwards became a keeper of public records
(*magister memoriae*, Ep. cxvii.).

2

LETTERS OF ST. AUGUSTINE

No. 1 (Ep. II)

(A.D. 386)

AUGUSTINE TO ZENOBIUS [a]

We are quite agreed, I think, that everything that
is the object of our bodily senses is incapable of
remaining a single moment in the same state, but is in
motion and transition and possesses no actuality, that
is, in plain language, has no real existence. In consequence, true, divine philosophy admonishes us to
check and mitigate our affection for such things, as
being very baneful and productive of detriment, so
that even while in control of this mortal body, the
soul may with intensity and fervour pursue those
things that are ever the same and satisfy with no
transient charm. Although this is true and although
my mind envisages you in your simple and unalloyed
character, as an individual who may be loved without
disquietude, still I must confess that when you are
absent in body and distant in space, I miss the pleasure
of meeting and seeing you, and desire it, when it can
be had, for the brethren. This fault, if I know you
aright, you are glad to find in me, and, although you
pray for every good thing for your dearest and closest

3

tuis, ab hoc eos sanare metuis. Si autem tam potenti
animo es, ut et agnoscere hunc laqueum et eo captos
inridere valeas, ne tu magnus atque alius. Ego quidem
quamdiu desidero absentem, desiderari me volo.
Invigilo tamen, quantum queo, et nitor, ut nihil
amem, quod abesse a me invito potest. Quod dum
officio, commoneo te interim, qualiscumque sis, in-
choatam tecum disputationem perficiendam, si curae
nobismet ipsis sumus. Nam eam cum Alypio perfici
nequaquam sinerem, etiam si vellet. Non vult
autem ; non enim est humanitatis eius non mecum
operam dare, ut in quam multis possemus litteris te
nobiscum teneamus nescio qua necessitate fugientem.

No. 2 (Ep. IV)

NEBRIDIO AUGUSTINUS

1 Mirum admodum est, quam mihi praeter spem
evenerit, quod, cum requiro, quibus epistulis tuis
mihi respondendum remanserit, unam tantum inveni,
quae me adhuc debitorem teneret, qua petis, ut tanto
nostro otio, quantum esse arbitraris tecum aut nobis-

---

 [a] Alypius was born, like Augustine, at Tagaste, but
was slightly younger. He attended Augustine's lectures in
Carthage, became a Manichee when he did, followed him
to Italy and was present during the struggle that preceded
Augustine's conversion. They were baptized together, then
shared the monastic life at Tagaste from 391 to 394, when
Alypius visited Jerome at Bethlehem. Alypius became
bishop of Tagaste some months before Augustine's elevation
to Hippo, and held that post till his death about 430.

 [b] Nebridius, born near Carthage, had accompanied
Augustine to Rome and Milan, " for no other reason than

friends, you are reluctant to see them cured of it. But if you have attained such strength of mind that you can both discern this pitfall and make mockery of those who have fallen into it, then you are indeed great and different from me, for I want my absent friend to miss me as long as I miss him. Yet, as far as I can, I watchfully strive to set my affections upon nothing that can cause me regret by its absence. Though engaged in this preventive course, I remind you in the meantime, whatever be your state of mind, that we must, if we care for each other, finish the discussion I had begun with you, for I should certainly not allow Alypius *a* to help in finishing it, even if he wanted to, which he doesn't. His kindly nature would make him second my efforts to keep contact with you by as many letters as I can send, even when your duties drive you farther away from us.

No. 2 (Ep. IV)

(A.D. 387)

AUGUSTINE TO NEBRIDIUS *b*

It is quite curious how surprised I am to dis- 1 cover, on inquiring what letters of yours I have still to answer, that I am in your debt for only one. In it you ask me to tell you what progress I have made, with the abundant leisure you think I have or wish, as

that he might live with me in the most ardent pursuit of truth and wisdom " (*Confessions*, vi. 17). He had not joined the party at Cassiciacum, and this and the following letter show his anxiety to be beside Augustine, sharing his life and studies. He died soon after Augustine's conversion.

cum cupis, indicemus tibi, quid in sensibilis atque intellegibilis naturae discernentia profecerimus. Sed non arbitror occultum tibi esse, si falsis opinionibus tanto quisque inseritur magis, quanto magis in eis familiariusque volutatur, multo id facilius in rebus veris animo accidere. Ita tamen paulatim ut per aetatem proficimus. Quippe cum plurimum inter puerum et iuvenem distet, nemo a pueritia cotidie interrogatus se aliquando iuvenem dicet.

2 Quod nolo in eam partem accipias, ut nos in his rebus quasi ad quandam mentis iuventutem firmioris intellegentiae robore pervenisse existimes. Pueri enim sumus, sed, ut dici adsolet, forsitan belli ; et non male. Nam plerumque perturbatos et sensibilium plagarum curis refertos illa tibi notissima ratiuncula in respirationem levat, mentem atque intellegentiam oculis et hoc vulgari aspectu esse meliorem. Quod ita non esset, nisi magis essent illa, quae intellegimus, quam ista, quae cernimus. Cui ratiocinationi utrum nihil valide inimicum sit, peto mecum consideres. Hac ego interim recreatus, cum deo in auxilium deprecato et in ipsum et in ea, quae verissime vera sunt, adtolli coepero, tanta non numquam rerum manentium praesumptione compleor, ut mirer interdum illa mihi opus esse ratiocinatione, ut haec esse credam quae tanta insunt praesentia, quanta sibi quisque ipse fit praesens. Recole tu

---

[a] This phrase is difficult: I take *arbitraris tecum* to mean "think within yourself," on the analogy of *cogitare tecum* (for which see, *e.g.*, Vulgate, Gen. xx. 11, Mark xi. 31, etc.), and *nobiscum cupis* as "join me in wishing." But Nebridius's desire to share Augustine's monastic life (see *infra*) makes it possible that *nobiscum cupis* means "desire to enjoy in my company."

[b] Or, perhaps, "and the phrase is not inappropriate."

I do, that I had,[a] in discriminating between nature as perceived by the senses and as known to the intellect. I think, however, you are not unaware that, if one becomes more thoroughly enmeshed in false opinions the more deeply and familiarly one wallows in them, the same happens much more readily to the mind in things that are real. My progress is gradual, like the advance of age. There is a very great difference between a boy and a mature man, yet no one, if asked each day from boyhood on, will at any given time declare that he has reached maturity.

I don't want you to take this to mean you are 2 to assume that, through the vigour of a more robust understanding, I have attained in such matters a kind of mental maturity. I am still mentally a boy ; let us hope a fine, strapping one, as the phrase goes, but I am not badly off either.[b] For generally, when I am unsettled and oppressed with the anxieties arising from the impingement of sensations, I am raised to a fresher atmosphere by this brief reasoning, which you know so well : "The mind and understanding are superior to the eyes and the common faculty of sight. That would not be so, unless the things we conceive were more real than those we perceive." Please examine with me whether there be anything that strongly conflicts with this line of reasoning. For the present I find it stimulating ; yet, when I have asked God's help and have begun to rise towards Him and towards those things that are most really real, I am sometimes filled with such a foretaste of the things that abide, that I occasionally wonder at my needing the help of this reasoning to believe in the existence of those things that are as real within me as any man can be to himself.

quoque ; nam te fateor huius rei esse diligentiorem,
ne quid forte nesciens rescriptis adhuc debeam.
Nam mihi non facit fidem tam multorum onerum,
quae aliquando numeraveram, tam repentina de-
positio, quamvis te accepisse litteras meas non
dubitem, quarum rescripta non habeo.

No. 3 (Ep. X)

NEBRIDIO AUGUSTINUS

1   Numquam aeque quicquam tuarum inquisitionum
me in cogitando tenuit aestuantem atque illud, quod
recentissimis tuis litteris legi, ubi nos arguis quod
consulere neglegamus, ut una nobis vivere liceat.
Magnum crimen et, nisi falsum esset, periculosissimum. Sed cum perprobabilis ratio demonstrare
videatur hic nos potius quam Carthagini vel etiam in
rure ex sententia posse degere, quid tecum agam, mi
Nebridi, prorsus incertus sum. Mittaturne ad te
accommodissimum tibi vehiculum ? Nam basterna
innoxie te vehi posse noster Lucinianus auctor est.
At matrem cogito, ut quae absentiam sani non
ferebat, inbecilli multo minus esse laturam. Veniam-
ne ipse ad vos ? At hic sunt, qui neque venire mecum queant et quos deserere nefas putem. Tu enim
potes et apud tuam mentem suaviter habitare ;
hi vero ut idem possint, satagitur. Eamne crebro
et redeam et nunc tecum, nunc cum ipsis sim ? At
hoc neque simul neque ex sententia vivere est. Non

---

[a] By the autumn of 388 Augustine had retired to his
native town, Tagaste, where he was practising the monastic
life with a few friends. Nebridius was now at Carthage,
but was still anxious to join the company.

Try you to remember, for I admit that you are more attentive to such details, in case I still owe you replies without knowing it. I can hardly believe I have so speedily discharged tasks I had once reckoned so numerous. Yet I am sure you must have had letters from me, to which I have received no answers.

No. 3 (Ep. X)

(A.D. 389)

AUGUSTINE TO NEBRIDIUS [a]

Never has any of your problems kept me so 1 troubled in mind as the remark you made in your last letter, reproaching me for failing to plan how we may live together. A serious charge, and were it not untrue, very threatening to our friendship. But since quite satisfactory reasons seem to show that we can lead our ideal life here better than at Carthage or in the country, I am altogether in doubt how I should deal with you, Nebridius. Am I to send you our most suitable conveyance ? Our friend Lucinianus tells me that you can now ride in a sedan chair without any harm. But then your mother comes to my mind : if she cannot endure your absence when you are well, she will endure it much less when you are ill. Am I to come to you myself ? But there are people here who cannot come with me and whom I think it criminal to leave behind. For you can be happily at home with your own mind, while these others are only striving towards that attainment. Am I to make frequent journeys back and forward, living with you part of the time and the other part with them ? But that is neither living together nor living the ideal life. The

enim brevis est via, sed tanta omnino, cuius per-
agendae negotium saepe suscipere non sit ad optatum
otium pervenisse. Huc accedit infirmitas corporis,
qua ego quoque, ut nosti, non valeo, quod volo, nisi
omnino desinam quicquam plus velle, quam non
valeo.

2 Professiones ergo, quas quietas et faciles habere
nequeas, per totam cogitare vitam non est hominis
de illa una ultima, quae mors vocatur, cogitantis, de
qua vel sola intellegis vere esse cogitandum. Dedit
quidem deus paucis quibusdam, quos ecclesiarum
gubernatores esse voluit, ut et illam non solum ex-
pectarent fortiter, sed alacriter etiam desiderarent
et harum obeundarum labores sine ullo angore sus-
ciperent; sed neque his, qui ad huius modi admini-
strationes temporalis honoris amore raptantur, neque
rursum his, qui cum sunt privati, negotiosam vitam
appetunt, hoc tantum bonum concedi arbitror, ut
inter strepitus inquietosque conventus atque dis-
cursus cum morte familiaritatem, quam quaerimus,
faciant; deificari enim utrisque in otio licebat. Aut
si hoc falsum est, ego sum omnium ne dicam stultis-
simus, certe ignavissimus, cui nisi proveniat quaedam
secura cessatio, sincerum illud bonum gustare atque
amare non possum. Magna secessione a tumultu
rerum labentium, mihi crede, opus est, ut non duritia,
non audacia, non cupiditate inanis gloriae, non super-
stitiosa credulitate fiat in homine nihil timere. Hinc
enim fit illud etiam solidum gaudium nullis omnino
laetitiis ulla ex particula conferendum.

journey is not short, sufficiently long, in fact, that the
effort to perform it often would prevent our having the
leisure we long for.   In addition, there is my physical
weakness ; because of it, as you know, I am not able
to do what I wish, unless I altogether give up wishing
to do anything that I am not strong enough for.

To go through life planning journeys that cannot **2**
be undertaken without disturbance and trouble does
not become one who is planning for that last journey
we call death ; with it alone, as you are aware, should
our real plans be concerned.   It is God's gift to
some few men, whom He has appointed to rule over
churches, not only to await death manfully but even to
desire it eagerly, and to undertake the toil of those
other journeys without any vexation.   But in my
opinion neither those who are impelled to such administrative tasks by love of worldly position, nor those
who, though occupying no public post, hunger for
a life of affairs, have been granted the great boon of
acquiring amid their clamour and their restless run-
ning hither and thither that familiarity with death that
we are seeking ; both classes might have become godly
in retirement. If this be untrue, then I am of all men,
I won't say the most foolish, but certainly the most
slothful, for I cannot relish and enjoy that real boon,
unless I obtain release from work and worry.   Complete withdrawal from the turmoil of transitory things
is, believe me, essential before a man can develop that
fearlessness in the face of death which is based neither
on insensibility nor on foolhardy presumption, neither
on the desire for empty glory nor on superstitious
credulity.   It is that which is the origin of that solid
joy with which no pleasure from any transitory source
is in any way to be compared.

11

§ Quod si in natura humana talis vita non cadit, cur
aliquando evenit ista securitas? Cur tanto evenit
crebrius, quanto quisque in mentis penetralibus
adorat deum? Cur in actu etiam humano plerumque ista tranquillitas manet, si ex illo adyto ad
agendum quisque procedat? Cur interdum et cum
loquimur, mortem non formidamus, cum autem non
loquimur, etiam cupimus? Tibi dico, non enim hoc
cuilibet dicerem, tibi, inquam, dico, cuius itinera in
superna bene novi, tune, cum expertus saepe sis,
quam dulce vivat, cum amori corporeo animus moritur, negabis tandem totam hominis vitam posse in-
trepidam fieri, ut rite sapiens nominetur? Aut hanc
affectionem, ad quam [1] ratio nititur, tibi accidisse
umquam, nisi cum in intimis tuis ageres, asserere
audebis? Quae cum ita sint, restare unum vides, ut
tu quoque in commune consulas, quo vivamus simul.
Quid enim cum matre agendum sit, quam certe frater
Victor non deserit, tu multo melius calles quam ego.
Alia scribere, ne te ab ista cogitatione averterem,
nolui.

No. 4 (Ep. XV)

ROMANIANO AUGUSTINUS

1 Non haec epistula sic inopiam chartae indicat, ut
membranas saltem abundare testetur? Tabellas
eburneas, quas habeo, avunculo tuo cum litteris misi.
Tu enim huic pelliculae facilius ignosces, quia differri

---

[1] quam *Goldbacher*: ad quam *A. Souter*.

[a] A wealthy citizen of Tagaste, who had shown great
generosity to Augustine when studying in Carthage, and also
later. To him Augustine dedicated his *Contra Academicos*
(A.D. 386) and the *De Vera Religione*, mentioned below.

But if human nature does not admit of such a 3 life, why does that calmness of spirit ever befall us ? Why does it befall us more frequently in proportion as each man worships God in the secret places of his mind ? Why even amid ordinary mortal concerns does that peace, as a rule, linger on, when one goes forth from that inner shrine to do his part ? Why is it that sometimes, even in conversation, death has no terrors for us, and, when conversation is stilled, it even allures us ? I say to you (and I would not say it to everyone)—I say to you, knowing well, as I do, your journeyings to the upper world, will you, after frequent experience of the sweet life the soul lives when it dies to bodily affections, deny that a man's whole life can at length become so exempt from fear that he may rightly be called wise ? Or will you venture to maintain that that state of mind, towards which reason strives, has ever befallen you, save when you were communing with your own heart ? This being so, you see this one thing only remains for you—to consider for our mutual advantage how we may live together. You know much better than I do what is to be done with your mother ; in any case your brother Victor is not leaving her. I write no more, for fear of diverting you from consideration of that problem.

No. 4 (Ep. XV)
(A.D. 390)

AUGUSTINE TO ROMANIANUS[a]

Does this letter not show that, if we are short of 1 papyrus, we have at least abundance of parchment ? The ivory tablets I possess I have sent to your uncle with a letter ; you will the more easily forgive this

non potuit, quod ei scripsi, et tibi non scribere etiam
ineptissimum existimavi. Sed tabellas, si quae ibi
nostrae sunt, propter huius modi necessitates mittas
peto. Scripsi quiddam de catholica religione, quantum dominus dare dignatus est, quod tibi volo ante
adventum meum mittere, si charta interim non desit.
Tolerabis enim qualemcumque scripturam ex officina
Maiorini. De codicibus praeter libros de Oratore
totum mihi excidit. Sed nihil amplius rescribere
potui, quam ut ipse sumeres, quos liberet, et nunc
in eadem maneo sententia. Absens enim quid plus
faciam, non invenio.

2   Gratissimum mihi est, quod in ultima epistula me
participem domestici tui gaudii facere voluisti. Sed

> mene salis placidi vultum fluctusque quietos
> ignorare iubes?

quamquam nec me iubeas nec ipse ignores. Quare
si ad melius cogitandum quies aliqua data est, utere
divino beneficio. Nec enim nobis debemus, cum
ista proveniunt, sed illis, per quos proveniunt, gratu-
lari, quoniam iusta et officiosa et pro suo genere
pacatior atque tranquillior rerum temporalium ad-
ministratio recipiendorum aeternorum meritum gignit, si non teneat, cum tenetur, non implicet, cum
multiplicatur, si non, cum . . . putatur, involvat.

---

^a His treatise *De Vera Religione*, written at Tagaste,
389-390.   ^b The allusion is unknown.

^c Cicero's, no doubt; the fact that it had survived
Augustine's many journeys may be explained by the
supposition that he used it as a text-book during his career
as a public teacher of rhetoric.

^d Virg. *Aen.* v. 848-849.

^e The text here is doubtful: Goldbacher marks the lacuna,
but perhaps *amputatur* would satisfy the palaeography and
the sense.

bit of skin, since my message to him could not be postponed, and I considered it very impolite not to write to you. If you have any tablets of mine beside you, please send them back for such emergencies as this. I have written something, as far as the Lord has deigned to grant me, on the Catholic Religion [a]; I want to send it to you before I come, if meanwhile paper does not fail me, for you will tolerate any kind of writing from the workshop of Majorinus.[b] Of the manuscripts everything has disappeared except the books *On the Orator*,[c] but I could not do any more in my reply than tell you to take those you wanted, and I am still of the same mind. I don't know what more I can do in my absence.

It gave me very great pleasure that in your last 2 letter you wanted to give me a share in your personal happiness, but

> bid'st thou me
> Ignore the portent of the sea's still face
> And slumbering waves?[d]

Yet you don't bid me, nor do you ignore it. So, if you do obtain some quietness for deeper reflection, avail yourself of what is a heavenly boon. For when such good fortune befalls us, we should not congratulate ourselves, but those through whom it has befallen us. If men discharge their temporal duties in a manner that is just and scrupulous and, considering their nature, more than ordinarily serene and composed, they grow more worthy of having eternal things committed to them, provided always that such temporal duties, when laid hold of, do not lay hold of them, do not enfold as they grow manifold, do not enmesh when they are pruned.[e] It has been

15

Ipsius enim veritatis ore dictum est : *Si in alieno fideles non fuistis, vestrum quis dabit vobis?* Laxatis ergo curis mutabilium rerum bona stabilia et certa quaeramus, supervolemus terrenis opibus nostris. Nam et in mellis copia non frustra pennas habet apicula ; necat enim haerentem.

No. 5 (Ep. XVI)

[AUGUSTINO MAXIMUS]

1 Avens crebro tuis affatibus laetificari et instinctu tui sermonis, quod me paulo ante iucundissime salva caritate pulsasti, paria redhibere non destiti, ne silentium meum paenitudinem appellasses. Sed quaeso, ut, si haec quasi seniles artus esse duxeris, benignarum aurium indulgentia prosequaris. Olympum montem deorum esse habitaculum sub incerta fide Graecia fabulatur. At vero nostrae urbis forum salutarium numinum frequentia possessum nos cernimus et probamus. Et quidem unum esse deum summum sine initio, sine prole naturae ceu patrem magnum atque magnificum quis tam demens, tam mente captus neget esse certissimum ? Huius nos virtutes per mundanum opus diffusas multis vocabulis invocamus, quoniam nomen eius cuncti proprium videlicet ignoramus. Nam deus omnibus religionibus

---

a Luke xvi. 12.

b Maximus is otherwise unknown, but probably he had been one of Augustine's teachers at Madaura, the town to which his letter refers. Most notable as the birthplace of Apuleius, Madaura was a noted centre of pagan life and culture, and paganism seems to have lingered there long and tenaciously (see Ep. ccxxxii. *infra*).

16

said by the mouth of Truth Himself : *If ye have not been faithful in that which is another's, who shall give you that which is your own ?* [a] Let us then relax our anxiety for transitory things and seek goods that are abiding and sure. Let us soar above our earthly possessions, for even when honey is abundant, the bee has not its wings for nothing : for if it stick in the honey, it dies.

No. 5 (Ep. XVI)

(A.D. 390)

MAXIMUS [b] THE GRAMMARIAN TO AUGUSTINE

I find interest and pleasure in frequent talk 1 with you and in your provocative conversation, so, since you recently attacked me without unpleasantness and without disturbing our friendly relations, I make haste to give you back as good as you gave : otherwise you might have thought my silence implied a change of mind. But I beg you, if you consider my reply shows the stiffness of old age, to attend to it with a kindly ear. There is no sure evidence for the Greek fable that Mount Olympus is the dwelling-place of the gods, but we see and feel sure that the market-place of our own town is occupied by a crowd of beneficent deities. And indeed, who is so foolish, so mentally astray, as to deny the very certain truth that there is one supreme god, without beginning, without natural offspring, like a great and splendid father ? His powers that permeate the universe he has made we call upon by many names, since to all of us his right name is of course unknown. For god is a name

17

commune nomen est. Ita fit, ut, dum eius quasi
quaedam membra carptim variis supplicationibus
prosequimur, totum colere profecto videamur.

2 Sed inpatientem me esse tanti erroris dissimulare
non possum. Quis enim ferat Iovi fulmina vibranti
praeferri Migginem, Iunoni, Minervae, Veneri Ves-
taeque Sanamem et cunctis, pro nefas ! diis inmortalibus archimartyrem Namphamonem ? Inter
quos Lucitas etiam haud minore cultu suspicitur
atque alii interminato numero, diis hominibusque
odiosa nomina, qui conscientia nefandorum facinorum specie gloriosae mortis scelera sua sceleribus
cumulantes dignum moribus factisque suis exitum
maculati reppererunt. Horum busta, si memoratu
dignum est, relictis templis, neglectis maiorum
suorum manibus stulti frequentant, ita ut praesagium
vatis illius indigne ferentis emineat :

> inque deum templis iurabit Roma per umbras.

Sed mihi hac tempestate propemodum videtur bellum
Actiacum rursus exortum, quo Aegyptia monstra in
Romanorum deos audeant tela vibrare minime dura-
tura.

3 Sed illud quaeso, vir sapientissime, uti remoto
facundiae robore atque exploso, qua cunctis clarus
es, omissis etiam, quibus pugnare solebas, Chrysip-
peis argumentis postposita paululum dialectica, quae

---

[a] Namphamo is commonly described by the text-books of
Church history as one of the earliest Christian martyrs in
Africa, and his date is given as *circa* A.D. 180. I have shown,
in the *Journal of Theological Studies*, vol. xxvi. (1924),
pp. 21-37, that this view is untenable, that his correct date is
probably about the middle of the fourth century, and that

common to all cults, and so it is that while with differing prayers we pursue, as it were, his members piecemeal, we seem, in truth, to worship him entire.

But I cannot disguise my impatience with such a 2 misconception as yours. For who could bear to see Miggo esteemed above Jove, wielder of thunderbolts, Saname above Juno, Minerva, Venus, and Vesta, and your head-martyr, Namphamo [a] (save the mark!), above all the immortal gods ? Among these Lucitas is honoured with a cult hardly inferior ; and others endless in number, names hateful to gods and men, who, villains that they were, and heaping crime on crime, met an end befitting their character and deeds, vaunting of their death as glorious though inwardly well aware of their unspeakable offences. Fools flock to their tombs, I'm ashamed to say, forsaking the temples and abandoning the worship of their ancestors, so that the prediction of the scornful bard is clearly fulfilled :

And in God's temples Rome shall swear by shades.[b]

This time seems to me to be almost another battle of Actium, in which the monsters of Egypt are daring to brandish against the Roman gods weapons doomed to speedy destruction.

But I beg you, my learned friend, to reject, as 3 unworthy of you, that vigorous eloquence which has brought you to universal fame, to abstain from those Stoic arguments that are your usual weapons, and to renounce for a while the logic which devotes all

he was a Donatist or Circumcellion. The others mentioned here with him are not known, but were probably of the same party. On the arguments advanced by Maximus see p. 30, note.

  [b] Lucan, *B.C.* vii. 459.

nervorum suorum luctamine nihil certi cuiquam re
linquere nititur, ipsa re adprobes, qui sit iste deus,
quem vobis Christiani quasi proprium vindicatis et
in locis abditis praesentem vos videre componitis.
Nos etenim deos nostros luce palam ante oculos atque
aures omnium mortalium piis precibus adoramus et
per suaves hostias propitios nobis efficimus et a
cunctis haec cerni et probari contendimus.

4   Sed ulterius huic certamini me senex invalidus
subtraho et in sententiam Mantuani rhetoris libenter
pergo :

> trahat sua quemque voluptas.

Post haec non dubito, vir eximie, qui a mea secta
deviasti, hanc epistulam aliquorum furto detractam
flammis vel quolibet pacto perituram. Quod si acciderit, erit damnum chartulae, non nostri sermonis,
cuius exemplar penes omnes religiosos perpetuo
retinebo. Dii te servent, per quos et eorum atque
cunctorum mortalium communem patrem universi
mortales, quos terra sustinet, mille modis concordi
discordia veneramur et colimus.

No. 6 (Ep. XVII)

[MAXIMO AUGUSTINUS]

1   Seriumne aliquid inter nos agimus, an iocari libet ?
Nam sicut tua epistula loquitur, utrum causae ipsius
infirmitate, an morum tuorum comitate sit factum, ut

---

[a] A very common charge against the Christians, arising
no doubt from a misunderstanding of their private celebration of the Eucharist. It is made by Pliny and Fronto,
among others, and is discussed and repudiated by all the
Apologists, until in the third century it gradually disappears.

[b] Virg. *Buc.* ii. 65.

the strength of its sinews to robbing every man of certainty. Prove by the facts themselves who is that god whom you Christians claim as your peculiar property and whose presence you feign to see in secret places.[a] We indeed with reverent prayers worship our gods in daylight, openly before the eyes and ears of all mortals, and we earn their favour by acceptable sacrifices, taking pains to let our actions be seen and approved by everyone.

But I am a feeble old man, so I withdraw from 4 any further contest and gladly give my adherence to that sentiment of the eloquent Mantuan :

Let each man be drawn by his own pleasure.[b]

After this, my distinguished friend, seceder that you are from my own faith, I fully expect that some thieves will steal this letter and that it will be burned or otherwise destroyed. In that event, it will only be the papyrus that will be lost, not what I have said, for I shall for ever keep a copy of it accessible to all the devout. May the gods keep you ! Through them all we mortals whom earth bears worship and adore in a thousand ways and with harmonious variance one who is the common father both of the gods and of all mortal men.

No. 6 (Ep. XVII)

(A.D. 390)

AUGUSTINE TO MAXIMUS THE GRAMMARIAN

Is it a serious discussion we are engaged in, or 1 do you want only to be amused ? The tone of your letter leaves me wondering whether your preference for humorous remarks to studied arguments is the

malles esse facetior quam paratior, incertum habeo.
Primo enim Olympi montis et fori vestri comparatio
facta est, quae nescio quo pertinuerit, nisi ut me
commonefaceret et in illo monte Iovem castra po-
suisse, cum adversus patrem bellum gereret, ut ea
docet historia, quam vestri etiam sacram vocant, et
in isto foro recordarer esse in duobus simulacris unum
Martem nudum, alterum armatum, quorum dae-
monium infestissimum civibus porrectis tribus digitis
contra conlocata statua humana comprimeret. Ergone umquam ego crediderim mentione illius fori
facta numinum talium memoriam mihi te renovare
voluisse, nisi iocari potius quam serie agere maluisses ?
Sed illud plane, quod tales deos quaedam dei unius
magni membra esse dixisti, admoneo, quia dignaris,
ut ab huius modi sacrilegis facetiis te magnopere
abstineas. Si quidem illum deum dicis unum, de
quo, ut dictum est a veteribus, docti indoctique con-
sentiunt, huiusne tu membra dicis esse, quorum iam
immanitatem vel, si hoc mavis, potentiam mortui
hominis imago compescit ? Plura hinc possim dicere ; vides enim pro tua prudentia, quam late locus
iste pateat reprehensioni. Sed me ipse cohibeo, ne a
te rhetorice potius quam veridice agere existimer.

2   Nam quod nomina quaedam mortuorum Punica
collegisti, quibus in nostram religionem festivas, ut
tibi visum est, contumelias iaciendas putares, nescio,

result of your having a feeble case, or simply of your affability. First you make a comparison between Mount Olympus and your own market-place, the point of which I fail to see ; unless it was your intention to remind me that it was in that mountain Jove pitched his camp when fighting against his father, according to the tale your co-religionists call sacred, and to remind me of the two images of Mars in that same market-place, one of them armed, the other in his tunic, while a human statue, standing over against them, uses three outstretched fingers to curb their evil influence that threatens your townsmen so direfully. So should I ever have believed that in mentioning your market-place you wanted to revive my recollection of such deities, if it had not been your intention to be facetious rather than to have a serious discussion ? But as to your statement that such gods are portions of one great god, I give you plain warning : please refrain altogether from such irreverent jocularity. If you are really referring to the unity of that god about whom, as the ancients have it, learned and unlearned are in agreement, do you describe as portions of him those whose frightfulness, or, if you prefer the word, power, is kept in check by the statue of a single dead man ? I could say a good deal more about this point : you are intelligent enough to see how far that remark of yours lays you open to censure. But I refrain, in case you imagine that I am quarrelling about words rather than seeking truth.

You have gathered together some Punic names 2 of dead people, with the intention of making use of them to cast on our religion what you supposed to be witty abuse : I am not sure if I should refute your

utrum refellere debeam, an silentio praeterire. Si enim res istae tam videntur leves tuae gravitati, quam sunt, iocari mihi non multum vacat ; si autem graves tibi videntur, miror, quod nominum absurditate commoto in mentem non venerit habere vos et in sacerdotibus Eucaddires et in numinibus Abaddires. Non puto ego ista tibi, cum scriberes, in animo non fuisse, sed more humanitatis et leporis tui commonefacere nos voluisti ad relaxandum animum, quanta in vestra superstitione ridenda sint. Neque enim usque adeo te ipsum oblivisci potuisses, ut homo Afer scribens Afris, cum simus utrique in Africa constituti, Punica nomina exagitanda existimares. Nam si ea vocabula interpretemur, Namphamo quid aliud significat quam boni pedis hominem ? Id est, cuius adventus adferat aliquid felicitatis, sicut solemus dicere secundo pede introisse, cuius introitum prosperitas aliqua consecuta sit. Quae lingua si inprobatur abs te, nega Punicis libris, ut a viris doctissimis proditur, multa sapienter esse mandata memoriae ; paeniteat te certe ibi natum, ubi huius linguae cunabula recalent. Si vero et sonus nobis noster non rationabiliter displicet et me bene interpretatum illud vocabulum recognoscis, habes quod suscenseas Vergilio tuo, qui Herculem vestrum ad

---

^a Abaddir is a Phoenician deity, probably to be identified with Baal Addir or Baal Hammon; the word itself is Punic for " Mighty Father." The Eucaddires were perhaps the priests of that cult, but the word is not found elsewhere.

^b Punic was still widely spoken, and Augustine several times speaks of the need for priests speaking that tongue. Arnobius Junior, writing in the fifth century, says Punic was still the language of the people of the little Syrtes, and a bilingual inscription has been found as late as 539 (*Corpus*

taunts or pass them over in silence. If such matters appear to a man of your sense to be as unimportant as they really are, I have not much time to spare for such pleasantry ; if they appear to you important, I am surprised that if absurd names appeal to you, you did not remember that among your priests you have the Eucaddires, and among your deities the Abaddires.[a] I do not suppose that these did not occur to you when you were writing, but in your usual genial and witty way you wanted to amuse me by reminding me how many laughable things are to be found in your superstitions. Nor could you have forgotten yourself so far as to imagine that Punic names were to be railed at, when you, an African, were writing to Africans and seeing that we are both living in Africa. If we interpret those words, what does Namphamo mean but "the man with the lucky foot"? That is, the man whose coming brings some good fortune, just as we say that one whose arrival has been attended by some stroke of luck has entered with a prosperous foot. If you disapprove of Punic as a language, then you must refuse to admit that many wise things have been recorded in Punic books, as is declared by learned men; you must even feel shame that you were born in a district in which the cradle of that language is still warm.[b] If it is unreasonable that the sound of our own tongue should give us offence and if you grant that I have rightly interpreted that name, you have just cause to feel annoyed with your friend Virgil,

Inscr. Lat. viii. 4677). Of Punic literature only a few specimens are mentioned: Varro and Columella refer with praise to a treatise on Agriculture by Mago; Sallust had Punic chronicles translated to him, and Suidas cites one Charon of Carthage who wrote biographies.

sacra, quae illi ab Evandro celebrantur, invitat hoc modo :

> et nos et tua dexter adi pede sacra secundo.

Secundo pede optat ut veniat. Ergo venire optat Herculem Namphamonem, de quo tu multum nobis insultare dignaris. Verum tamen si ridere delectat, habes apud vos magnam materiam facetiarum : deum Stercutium, deam Cluacinam, Venerem Calvam, deum Timorem, deum Pallorem, deam Febrem et cetera innumerabilia huiusce modi, quibus Romani antiqui simulacrorum cultores templa fecerunt et colenda censuerunt. Quae si neglegis, Romanos deos neglegis, ex quo intellegeris non Romanis initiatus sacris, et tamen Punica nomina tamquam nimium Romanorum altaribus deditus contemnis ac despicis.

3   Sed mihi videris omnino plus quam nos fortasse illa sacra nihili pendere, sed ex eis nescio quam captare ad huius vitae transitum voluptatem, quippe qui etiam non dubitaveris ad Maronem confugere, ut scribis, et eius versu te tueri, quo ait :

> trahit sua quemque voluptas.

Nam si tibi auctoritas Maronis placet, sicut placere significas, profecto etiam illud placet :

> primus ab aetherio venit Saturnus Olympo
> arma Iovis fugiens et regnis exul ademptis

et cetera, quibus eum atque huius modi deos vestros

ᵃ Virg. *Aen.* viii. 302.   ᵇ Virg. *Buc.* ii. 65.
ᶜ Virg. *Aen.* viii. 319-320.

who in these words invites your Hercules to the rites celebrated in his honour by Evander :

> Us and thy rites with prosperous foot approach,
> In favouring mood.[a]

He prays him to come " with prosperous foot "; that is, he wants Hercules to come as Namphamo, in whom it pleases you to find much to taunt us with. But if you do take delight in jests, you have in your own religion ample material for ridicule : Stercutius, your god of manure, Cluacina, your goddess of purification, Bald Venus, your god Fear, your god Pallor, your goddess Fever, and countless others of the same kind, to whom the ancient Romans, worshippers of idols, built temples and thought worship should be offered. If you neglect them, you are neglecting Roman gods, thereby making it understood that you were not initiated into Roman rites, and yet you scorn and despise Punic names like one excessively devoted to the altars of Rome.

But altogether your depreciation of those rites 3 seems perhaps greater than ours, though you gain from them some vague pleasure for life's journey. You had no hesitation even in invoking the authority of Virgil, as you say, and in shielding yourself by that line in which he says :

> Each man is drawn by his own pleasure.[b]

If you are satisfied with Virgil's authority, as you indicate that you are, then you will certainly be satisfied with these lines too :

> From high Olympus first came Saturn down,
> Fleeing Jove's arms, an exile from his realm,[c]

and so on. By these lines the poet wants to show that

vult intellegi homines fuisse. Legerat enim ille mythicam[1] historiam vetusta auctoritate roboratam, quam etiam Tullius legerat, qui hoc idem in dialogis plus, quam postulare auderemus, commemorat et perducere in hominum notitiam, quantum illa tempora patiebantur, molitur.

4 Quod autem dicis eo nostris vestra sacra praeponi, quod vos publice colitis deos, nos autem secretioribus conventiculis utimur, primo illud abs te quaero, quo modo oblitus sis Liberum illum, quem paucorum sacratorum oculis committendum putatis. Deinde tu ipse iudicas nihil aliud te agere voluisse, cum publicam sacrorum vestrorum celebrationem commemorares, nisi ut nobis decuriones et primates civitatis per plateas vestrae urbis bacchantes ac furentes ante oculos quasi specula poneremus. In qua celebritate si numine inhabitamini, certe videtis quale illud sit, quod adimit mentem ; si autem fingitis, quae sunt ista etiam in publico vestra secreta ? Vel quo pertinet tam turpe mendacium ? Deinde cur nulla futura canitis, si vates estis ? Aut cur spoliatis circumstantes, si sani estis ?

5 Cum igitur haec nos et alia, quae nunc praeter-

---

[1] MSS. multam, *Goldbacher* mysticam.

^a Cf. *De nat. deorum*, i. 42, 119.

^b Though forbidden by the Senate in 186 B.C. (Livy xxxix. 8-19), the Bacchanalia were later revived, and are often attacked by Christian writers. The celebration was confined to the initiate, who, feigning frenzy, claimed the indwelling presence of their god and practised many cruel and orgiastic rites. The language of Arnobius (*Adv. Nat.* v. 19) closely resembles Augustine's, and adds several other details: "Bacchanalia etiam praetermittemus inmania quibus nomen Omophagiis graecum est, in quibus furore mentito et sequestrata pectoris sanitate circumplicatis vos anguibus atque ut vos plenos dei numine ac maiestate doceatis, caprorum

28

Saturn and such-like gods of yours were once men ; he had read that mythical tale confirmed by ancient authority and known to Tully as well, for in his Dialogues [a] he draws attention to the same fact more explicitly than we should venture to ask, and tries, as far as those days allowed, to put it before men's notice.

Then again, you state that your rites are to be 4 preferred to ours, on the ground that your worship is public, while we use more secret places of meeting. First, I ask you how it comes that you have forgotten your god Bacchus ; you think he should be entrusted only to the eyes of the few who are initiated. Then you convict yourself of having had no other intention, in mentioning the public celebration of your rites, than that of making us envisage, as in a mirror, your senators and notable townsmen raging and revelling through your city streets. If in that celebration you have the presence of a deity within you, you surely see what kind of being he is, when he destroys your reason. But if this is only an assumed madness, what are those secret rites that you actually practise in public ? Or what is the object of so vile a piece of deceit ? Or again, if you are inspired seers, why do you foretell no future events ? Or why do you rend the clothes of the bystanders, if you are in your right mind ? [b]

Since your letter has recalled to me these facts 5

reclamantium viscera cruentatis oribus dissipatis " (and also *infra*). See, too, Aug. *C.D.* vi. 9 and xviii. 13. There seems little evidence for this rending of bystanders' clothes, but probably this is what is implied in Plautus, *Bacch.* 974 *sqq.* and *Aulul.* 408 " neque ego umquam nisi hodie ad Bacchas veni in bacchanal coquinatum, | ita me miserum et meos discipulos fustibus male contuderunt."

mittenda existimo, per epistulam tuam feceris re-
cordari, quid nos derideamus deos vestros, quos abs
te ipso subtiliter derideri nemo non intellegit, qui et
ingenium tuum novit et legit litteras tuas ? Itaque
si aliquid inter nos de his rebus vis agamus, quod
aetati prudentiaeque tuae congruit, quod denique de
nostro proposito iure a carissimis nostris flagitari
potest, quaere aliquid nostra discussione dignum et
ea pro vestris numinibus cura dicere, in quibus non
te causae praevaricatorem putemus, quod nos magis
commoneas, quae contra illos dici possint, quam pro
eis aliquid dicas. Ad summam tamen ne te hoc
lateat et in sacrilega convicia inprudentem trahat,
scias a Christianis catholicis, quorum in vestro oppido
etiam ecclesia constituta est, nullum coli mortuorum,
nihil denique ut numen adorari, quod sit factum et
conditum a deo, sed unum ipsum deum, qui fecit et
condidit omnia. Disserentur ista latius ipso vero et
uno deo adiuvante, cum te graviter agere velle
cognovero.

---

a In addition to the Donatists.

Note.—The two preceding letters are among the best
known and most frequently cited of Augustine's correspondence. Voltaire, for example, several times (*Dict. Philoso-
phique, s.vv.* " Dieu," " Idole "; *Traité sur la Tolérance,* ch.
9; " Notice sur Maxime de Madaure " at the head of his
Sophronime et Adelos) quotes Maximus as evidence that the
polytheism of his time was tolerant, philosophical, and deistic.
The monotheistic explanation was by now current among the
better educated pagans (*cf. P.L.* iii. 1107 " gentiles quamvis
idola colant, tamen summum Deum Patrem creatorem cog-
noscunt et confitentur "; Maximus's own words are almost a
literal translation of the verse quoted by Lactantius, *Inst.* i. 6.
15 εἶς θεός, ὃς μόνος ἄρχει, ὑπερμεγέθης, ἀγένητος); but it was
largely inspired by the struggle against Christianity and it was
30

and others which I think it better to pass over for the
present, why should I make fun of your gods, when
anyone who knows your type of mind and reads your
letter can see that you yourself poke stealthy fun at
them ? So, if you want us to discuss this topic in a
manner befitting your age and good sense and answer-
ing the just demands of my close friends from one of
my profession, look for some theme worthy of debate
between us, and do your best to put forward on your
gods' behalf arguments that will not make me think
you are betraying your own case; for you certainly did
suggest to me what can be said against them, rather
than advance any statement on their behalf. Finally, I
want to tell you something you should know, to keep
you from being inadvertently drawn into irreverent
gibes : Catholic Christians, who have a church established in your town too,[a] worship no dead man and
adore nothing as a deity that was made and created
by God; they worship only God himself, who made
and created everything.

I shall enlarge on these facts by the help of our one
true God, when I am assured that you want to treat
them seriously.

never more than a controversial argument, forgotten in polytheistic practice. His case for paganism is largely aesthetic and
sentimental; in attacking Christianity he undoubtedly strikes
at the weakest point of its popular observance, the cult of
saints and martyrs, the concession made by Christianity to
local, polytheistic hero-worship. But he confuses Donatism,
strong in the region round Madaura, with orthodox Christianity, and his remarks about the villainous character of those
popular objects of veneration are beside the mark. Augustine in reply attacks the disreputable cults and practices
of paganism and treats Maximus's arguments, both for
paganism and against Christianity, with contempt.

No. 7 (Ep. XXI)

DOMINO BEATISSIMO ET VENERABILI ET IN
CONSPECTU DOMINI SINCERA CARITATE
CARISSIMO PATRI VALERIO EPISCOPO
AUGUSTINUS PRESBYTER IN DOMINO
SALUTEM

1 Ante omnia peto, ut cogitet religiosa prudentia
tua nihil esse in hac vita et maxime hoc tempore
facilius et laetius et hominibus acceptabilius episcopi aut presbyteri aut diaconi officio, si perfunctorie
atque adulatorie res agatur, sed nihil apud deum
miserius et tristius et damnabilius ; item nihil esse in
hac vita et maxime hoc tempore difficilius, laborio-
sius, periculosius episcopi aut presbyteri aut diaconi
officio, sed apud deum nihil beatius, si eo modo militetur, quo noster imperator iubet. Quis autem iste sit
modus, nec a pueritia nec ab adulescentia mea didici.
Et eo tempore, quo discere coeperam, vis mihi facta
est merito peccatorum meorum—nam quid aliud
existimem nescio,—ut secundus locus gubernaculo-
rum mihi traderetur, qui remum tenere non noveram.

2 Sed arbitror dominum meum propterea me sic
emendare voluisse, quod multorum peccata nauta-
rum, antequam expertus essem, quid illic agitur,
quasi doctior et melior reprehendere audebam.
Itaque posteaquam missus sum in medium, tunc

---

* Valerius was bishop of Hippo when Augustine returned
to Africa in 388. By birth a Greek, he had difficulty in
preaching in Latin. When Augustine was visiting Hippo
in 391, he was forcibly ordained to assist Valerius, and this
letter was written soon after the ordination, probably from
Tagaste, whither Augustine had no doubt returned to
terminate his affairs there. Augustine always speaks of

No. 7 (Ep. XXI)

(A.D. 391)

TO BISHOP VALERIUS,[a] MY LORD MOST SAINTLY
AND VENERABLE, MY FATHER WARMLY
CHERISHED BEFORE THE LORD WITH
SINCERE AFFECTION, AUGUSTINE, PRIEST,
SENDS GREETING IN THE LORD

First and foremost, I beg your wise Holiness to 1
consider that there is nothing in this life, and especially in our own day, more easy and pleasant and acceptable to men than the office of a bishop or priest or
deacon, if its duties be discharged in a mechanical and
sycophantic way, but nothing more worthless and
deplorable and meet for chastisement in the sight of
God ; and, on the other hand, that there is nothing in
this life, and especially in our own day, more difficult,
toilsome and hazardous than the office of a bishop or
priest or deacon, but nothing more blessed in the sight
of God, if our service be in accordance with our Captain's orders.[b] But how that is to be done I learned
neither in my boyhood nor in my youth, and just as
I had begun to learn, I was compelled by reason
of my sins to assume the second place at the helm,
although I did not know how to hold an oar.

But I imagine that it was my Lord's intention 2
to chastise me because I was bold enough to rebuke
many sailors for their faults, as though I were a wiser
and a better man, before experience had taught me
the nature of their work. So, on being sent into
their midst, I then began to realize how presump-

Valerius with great respect and affection. Valerius retired
in 396, and Augustine succeeded him.

[b] 1 Tim. i. 18-19 ; 2 Tim. ii. 4.

sentire coepi temeritates reprehensionum mearum,
quamquam et antea periculosissimum iudicarem hoc
ministerium. Et hinc erant illae lacrimae, quas me
fundere in novitate ordinationis meae nonnulli fratres
animadverterunt, et nescientes causas doloris mei
quibus potuerunt sermonibus, qui omnino ad vulnus
meum non pertinerent, tamen bono animo consolati
sunt. Sed multo, valde multo amplius expertus
sum, quam putabam, non quia novos aliquos fluctus
aut tempestates vidi, quas ante non videram vel non
audieram vel non legeram vel non cogitaveram, sed
ad eas evitandas aut perferendas sollertiam et vires
meas omnino non noveram et alicuius momenti
arbitrabar. Dominus autem inrisit me et rebus
ipsis ostendere voluit me ipsum mihi.

3   Quod si non damnando, sed miserando fecit—hoc
enim spero certe vel nunc cognita aegritudine mea,
—debeo scripturarum eius medicamenta omnia per-
scrutari et orando ac legendo agere, ut idonea valitudo animae meae ad tam periculosa negotia tribuatur. Quod ante non feci, quia et tempus non
habui ; tunc enim ordinatus sum, cum de ipso vacationis tempore ad cognoscendas divinas scripturas
cogitaremus et sic nos disponere vellemus, ut nobis
otium ad hoc negotium posset esse. Quod verum
est, nondum sciebam, quid mihi deesset ad tale opus,
quale me nunc torquet et conterit. Quod si propterea in re ipsa didici, quid sit homini necessarium,

---

a This was early in 391 (*cf.* § 4 " until Easter "), when
Augustine was in his thirty-sixth year. Among his earliest
actions at Hippo was the founding of a monastery—his
second, that at Tagaste remaining in the charge of Alypius.
For other accounts of this forcible ordination see *Serm.*

tuous were my rebukes, although even before that time I had concluded that this occupation was fraught with great hazards. That was the cause of those tears which some of the brethren noticed me shedding when I was newly ordained [a]; they said all they could to console me, but, though their intentions were good, their words had no bearing whatever on my trouble, as they did not know the reasons for my grief. But experience has revealed the hazards far, far more fully than even anticipation; it is not that I have observed some new breakers or storms unknown to me by previous observation or report or reading or meditation, but that I completely miscalculated my ability and strength to avoid them or endure them and reckoned it to be of some worth. But the Lord mocked me and by actual experience sought to show me just what I am.

If He did this in mercy and not in judgement, as I 3 confidently hope now that I at last recognize my weak points, it is my duty to investigate all the remedies to be found in His Scriptures and to see that prayer and study procure for my soul adequate strength for such dangerous tasks. I had no time before the ceremony, so I failed to do it then : I was ordained just when I was planning for a period of leisure in order to make myself acquainted with the Holy Scriptures, and when I was arranging to obtain some spare time for that task. The truth is, I did not realize my lack of qualifications for the duties that now vex and harass me. If experience has taught me what is requisite for one

ccclv. 2 and Possid. *Vit. Aug.* iv. Ordination by compulsion was at this time not uncommon : Ambrose, Martin of Tours, Chrysostom and Paulinus were ordained by force, as was also Jerome's brother, Paulinianus.

qui populo ministrat sacramentum et verbum dei, ut
iam mihi non liceat adsequi, quod me non habere
cognovi, iubes ergo, ut peream, pater Valeri ? Ubi
est caritas tua ? Certe diligis me ? Certe diligis
ipsam ecclesiam, cui me sic ministrare voluisti ? Et
tamen certus sum, quod et me et ipsam diligis. Sed
putas me idoneum, cum ego melius me noverim, qui
tamen nec ipse me nossem, nisi experiendo didicissem.

4   Sed dicit fortasse sanctitas tua : vellem scire, quid
desit instructioni tuae. Tam multa autem sunt, ut
facilius possim enumerare quae habeam, quam quae
habere desidero. Auderem enim dicere scire me et
plena fide retinere, quid pertineat ad salutem nostram. Sed hoc ipsum quo modo ministrem ad salutem aliorum *non quaerens, quod mihi utile est, sed quod
multis, ut salvi fiant* ? Et sunt fortasse aliqua, immo
non est dubitandum esse in sanctis libris conscripta
consilia, quibus cognitis et adprehensis possit homo
dei rebus ecclesiasticis ordinatioribus ministrare aut
certe inter manus iniquorum vel vivere conscientia
saniore vel mori, ut illa vita non amittatur, cui uni
christiana corda humilia et mansueta suspirant. Quo
modo autem hoc fieri potest, nisi, quem ad modum
ipse dominus dicit, petendo quaerendo pulsando, id
est orando legendo plangendo ? Ad quod negotium
mihi parvum tempus velut usque ad pascha impetrare volui per fratres a tua sincerissima et venerabili
caritate et nunc per has preces volo.

5   Quid enim responsurus sum domino iudici ? Non

---

^a 1 Cor. x. 33.
^b Matt. vii. 7-8 ; Luke xi 9-10.

who dispenses God's word and sacrament to the people, only now to be debarred from acquiring what I know I do not possess, are you, Father Valerius, simply decreeing my ruin? Where is your affection for me? Do you really love me? Do you really love the Church which you want me to serve with this poor equipment? Yet I am sure that you love us both, but you think me quite well equipped, though I know myself better; but I should not have acquired this knowledge, had it not been taught me by experience.

But perhaps your Holiness replies: " I should like **4** to know wherein your training is deficient." It has so many deficiencies that it would be easier for me to enumerate the things I have acquired than those I want to acquire. I might venture to say that I know and hold with complete trust what belongs to our salvation. But how am I to minister even that for the salvation of others, not seeking mine own profit, but the profit of many, that they may be saved [a]? Perhaps there are some admonitions written in the holy books—nay, it is certain that there are—which, if a man of God grasp and apply them to himself, will enable him to discharge his more ordinary clerical duties, or at least amidst the wicked to keep so sound a conscience that, whether living or dying, he lose not that life for which alone humble and gentle Christian hearts long. But how can this be done, except, as the Lord Himself says, by asking, seeking and knocking,[b] that is, by prayer, study and beating of the breast? It was for this task that I sought through my brethren to obtain from your dear Reverence a short space of time, say until Easter, and to that I now add this present supplication.

For what answer am I to make to the Lord, when **5**

37

poteram ista iam quaerere, cum ecclesiasticis negotiis impedirer ? Si ergo mihi dicat : *serve nequam*, si villa ecclesiae calumniosum aliquem pateretur, cuius fructibus colligendis magna opera inpenditur neglecto agro, quem rigavi sanguine meo, si quid agere pro ea posses apud iudicem terrae, nonne omnibus consentientibus, nonnullis etiam iubentibus et cogentibus pergeres et, si contra te iudicaretur, etiam trans mare proficiscereris ? Atque hoc modo vel annuam vel amplius absentiam tuam nulla querella revocaret, ne alius possideret terram non animae sed corpori pauperum necessariam, quorum tamen famem vivae arbores meae multo facilius mihique gratius, si diligenter colerentur, explerent. Cur ergo ad discendam agriculturam meam vacationem temporis tibi defuisse causaris ? Dic mihi, quid respondeam ; rogo te an forte vis dicam : senex Valerius dum me omnibus rebus instructum esse credidisset, quanto amplius me dilexit, tanto minus discere ista permisit ?

6   Adtende omnia ista, senex Valeri ; obsecro te per bonitatem et severitatem Christi, per misericordiam et iudicium eius, per eum, tantam qui tibi inspiravit erga nos caritatem, ut ne te nec pro lucro animae nostrae audeamus offendere. Sic autem mihi dominum et Christum testem facis innocentiae et caritatis et sinceri affectus quem circa nos habes, quasi ego non de his iurare omnibus possum. Ipsam ergo

<hr/>

[a] Matt. xviii. 32 ; Luke xix. 22.

[b] In Africa and Spain the title *Senex* was given to the Metropolitan, since the senior Bishop in those two countries usually held that dignity. The Bishop of Carthage was Primate from his possession of that see, but from 305 there was a Primate of Numidia as well, and later of Tripolitana, the Mauretanias, and Byzacenum. *Cf.* Leo Magn. *Ep.* iv. " in singulis Africae provinciis antiquitus primates institue-

He judges me? That I had no opportunity for self
improvement in the embarrassment of clerical duties?
If He were to say to me: "Thou wicked servant,[a] if
some rogue were preying upon the Church's property,
the fruits of which are gathered with great expenditure of effort, and your intervention before an earthly
bar could be of some avail, would not everyone agree
and some even command and compel you to abandon
the field that I watered with My own Blood and proceed to court, and if the verdict were unfavourable,
even to make the journey across the sea? You
might spend a year or more without being recalled by
grumbling, in preventing the land needful for the
bodily, not the spiritual, welfare of the poor from
falling into other hands; yet their hunger would be
appeased much more easily and more satisfactorily to
Me, by My living trees, if they were carefully tended.
Why then do you complain that you had no leisure
to learn My husbandry?" Tell me, what answer
could I make? I wonder if you would like me to say:
"But the Senior [b] Valerius thought my training was
complete and, out of his great love for me, gave me
all the less opportunity to acquire what I lacked"?

Consider all these points, Senior Valerius; I en- **6**
treat you by the goodness and severity of Christ,
by His mercy and judgement, by Him who inspired
you with such affection for me that even to gain my
own soul I would not venture to displease you. You
call upon the Lord and Christ to bear witness to me
of the single-mindedness and liking and warm affection you have towards me, as if I could not take an
oath myself on them all. To that liking and affection

bantur non secundum potentiam alicuius civitatis, sed
secundum tempus suae ordinationis."

caritatem et affectum inploro, ut miserearis mei et
concedas mihi ad hoc quod rogavi, tempus quantum
rogavi, atque adiuves me orationibus tuis, ut non sit
inane desiderium meum nec infructuosa ecclesiae
Christi atque utilitati fratrum et conservorum meorum absentia mea. Scio quod illam caritatem pro
me orantem maxime in tali causa non despicit dominus et eam sicut sacrificium suavitatis accipiens
fortassis breviore tempore, quam postulavi, me salu-
berrimis consiliis de scripturis suis reddet instructum.

No. 8 (Ep. XXII)

AURELIO EPISCOPO AUGUSTINUS PRESBYTER

1 I. Qua gratia responderem litteris sanctitatis tuae,
cum diu haesitans non reperirem—omnia enim vicit
affectus animi mei, quem iam sponte surgentem lectio
epistulae tuae multo ardentius excitavit,—commisi
me tamen deo, qui pro viribus meis operaretur in me,
ut ea rescriberem, quae utrique nostrum studio in
domino et cura ecclesiastica pro tua praestantia et
mea obsecundatione congruerent. Atque illud primum, quod orationibus meis te adiuvari credis, non
solum non defugio, verum etiam libenter amplector.
Ita enim etsi non meis, at certe tuis me dominus
noster exaudiet. Quod fratrem Alypium in nostra
coniunctione mansisse, ut exemplo sit fratribus curas
mundi huius vitare cupientibus, benivolentissime

---

^a Augustine first met Aurelius at Carthage in 388, when
Aurelius was a deacon (*Civ. Dei*, xxii. 8. 3), and there were
laid the beginnings of a long and close friendship. Aurelius
succeeded to the see of Carthage in 391 or 392, and was
still in office in 426. To him Augustine dedicated his *De
Trinitate*, *De Gestis Pelagii*, and *De Opere Monachorum*.

I appeal : pity me and give me the time I want for the
thing I want ; give me the aid of your prayers, that
my desire be not in vain and my absence not without
fruit to the Church of Christ and the welfare of my
brethren and fellow-servants. I am sure that the
Lord does not despise such affection when it expresses itself in prayer for me, especially in a
matter of this kind. He will accept it as a sweet
sacrifice, and perhaps in a shorter time than I have
asked for will provide from the health-giving counsels
of His Scriptures the instruction I need.

No. 8 (Ep. XXII)

(A.D. 392)

TO BISHOP AURELIUS^a FROM AUGUSTINE, PRIEST

I. After long hesitation I have not discovered how **1**
most gratefully to reply to your Holiness's letter, for
all my efforts were thwarted by my heartfelt emotion,
which rising of its own accord was much more warmly
stirred by the reading of your letter. But I cast myself upon God that He might work in me according
to my strength, so that I should reply to you as befitted our mutual zeal in the Lord and our care for His
church, you in your exalted station and I in my
subordinate post. And, first, so far from declining
your assurance that you believe my prayers avail for
you, I gladly welcome it, for in this way the Lord will
hear and answer me, if not through my own prayers,
then certainly through yours. I am more grateful to
you than I can well express for your kindly approval
of brother Alypius's action in remaining a member of
our fellowship, as an example to the brethren who

41

accepisti, ago gratias, quas nullis verbis explicare possim; deus hoc rependat in animam tuam. Omnis itaque fratrum coetus, qui apud eos coepit coalescere, tanta tibi praerogativa obstrictus est, ut locis terrarum tantum longe disiunctis ita nobis consulueris tamquam praesentissimus spiritu. Quapropter precibus, quantum valemus, incumbimus, ut gregem tibi commissum tecum dominus sustinere dignetur nec te uspiam deserere, sed adesse *adiutor in opportunitatibus faciens* cum ecclesia sua *misericordiam* per sacerdotium tuum, qualem spiritales viri ut faciat lacrimis eum gemitibusque interpellant.

2 Scias itaque, domine beatissime et plenissima caritate venerabilis, non desperare nos, immo sperare nos vehementer, quod dominus et deus noster per auctoritatem personae, quam geris, quam non carni, sed spiritu tuo inpositam esse confidimus, multas carnales foeditates et aegritudines, quas Africana ecclesia in multis patitur, in paucis gemit . . . conciliorum gravi ense et tua gravitate posse sanari. Cum enim apostolus tria breviter genera vitiorum detestanda et vitanda uno in loco posuerit, de quibus innumerabilium peccatorum exsurrexit seges, unum horum, quod quidem secundo loco posuit, acerrime in ecclesia vindicatur; duo autem reliqua, id est primum et ultimum, tolerabilia videntur hominibus atque ita paulatim fieri potest, ut nec vitia iam putentur. Ait enim vas electionis: *Non in comissationibus et ebrietatibus, non in cubilibus et inpudicitiis, non*

---

[a] Ps. ix. 10; xvii. 51.

[b] There is an anacoluthon here, and Goldbacher has marked a lacuna. The last clause (*conciliorum . . . sanari*) is a *locus vexatissimus*, and the variants so numerous that the textual critic must be referred to Goldbacher's apparatus.

wish to withdraw from the cares of this world. May God recompense your soul for this! The whole company of brethren that has begun to form around them is therefore bound to you with great gratitude, for you looked after our interests as if very present in spirit, although our abode is so far removed from yours in space. So we devote our best strength to praying that the Lord will deign to uphold with you the flock committed to your care and that He will never leave you but be a present help in time of trouble,[a] showing with His Church such mercy through your ministry as spiritual men implore Him with tears and groanings to show.

Let me assure you, therefore, my Lord most **2** revered, worthy of all devotion and of overflowing affection, that we are not without hope—nay, are rather strongly hopeful—that through the authority you bear, laid, as we trust, not on your flesh, but on your spirit, our Lord and God may use the weighty sword of councils and your own weight for the healing of the many carnal sores and disorders which the African Church is suffering in so many quarters and lamenting in so few.[b] In one passage the Apostle has set down to be hated and shunned three classes of vice from which has sprung an incalculable crop of sins. One of them, which he places only in the second rank, the Church punishes most severely; the other two, the first and the last-mentioned, appear to men to be quite tolerable, and so they may gradually come to be looked upon as not sins at all. The words of the Chosen Vessel[c] are these: "Not in rioting and drunkenness, not in chambering and

---

[c] St. Paul, so called from the words of Acts ix. 15.

in contentione et zelo ; sed induite vos dominum Iesum Christum et carnis curam ne feceritis in concupiscentiis.

3 Horum ergo trium cubilia et inpudicitiae ita magnum crimen putatur, ut nemo dignus non modo ecclesiastico ministerio, sed ipsa etiam sacramentorum communione videatur, qui se isto peccato maculaverit. Et recte omnino. Sed quare solum ? Comissationes enim et ebrietates ita concessae et licitae putantur, ut in honore etiam beatissimorum martyrum non solum per dies sollemnes, quod ipsum quis non lugendum videat, qui haec non carneis oculis inspicit, sed etiam cotidie celebrentur. Quam foeditatem, si tantum flagitiosa et non etiam sacrilega esset, quibuscumque tolerantiae viribus sustentandam putaremus. Quamquam ubi est illud, quod cum multa vitia enumerasset idem apostolus, inter quae posuit ebriosos, ita conclusit, ut diceret : *cum talibus nec panem edere* ? Sed feramus haec in luxu et labe domestica et eorum conviviorum quae privatis parietibus continentur, accipiamusque cum eis corpus Christi, cum quibus panem edere prohibemur : saltem de sanctorum corporum sepulcris, saltem de

---

[a] Rom. xiii. 13-14.   [b] 1 Cor. v. 11.

[c] This practice of drunkenness at the martyrs' tombs was widespread (Ps.-Cypr. *Dupl. Martyr.* 25 "annon videmus ad martyrum memorias Christianum a Christiano cogi ad ebrietatem?" Ambr. *Helia* xvii. 62 "calices ad sepulchra martyrum deferunt atque illic in vesperam bibunt," etc.). It was a survival of the old pagan custom of celebrating Parentalia or Feralia on the tombs of the dead, but, as Augustine says, the Church attempted to arrest this licence, not by complete suppression, but by converting the offering of bread and wine laid on the tombs (see *Conf.* vi. 2) to a nobler use. The martyr's tomb was made an altar, round which was built the chapel dedicated to him and called by his name; this explains why, in the fourth century, churches

wantonness, not in strife and envying; but put ye
on the Lord Jesus Christ, and make not provision
for the flesh, to fulfil the lusts thereof." [a]

Of these three classes, chambering and wantonness **3**
are considered so great an offence that no one who
has defiled himself with that sin is considered worthy
not merely of holding office in the Church, but even of
participation in the sacraments. And quite rightly
so, but why single out these ? Rioting and drunkenness are considered so permissible and tolerable that
they are practised not only on holy days, when the
blessed martyrs are honoured,—a lamentable sight
to anyone who looks on such festivities with more
than a carnal eye,—but even on any and every day.
Were this depravity only immoral and not sacrilegious
as well, we might think of putting up with it with
what power of endurance we could. And yet, what
about the same Apostle's statement, when he ends his
lengthy list of vices, among which drunkenness finds
a place, by saying: "With such an one not even to eat
bread" [b]? Are we to put up with it in the disgraceful
debauchery of private life and of those festivities that
are confined to private houses, and receive the Body
of Christ in the company of those with whom we are
forbidden to eat bread ? At least let such a disgraceful practice be removed from the cemeteries [c] where

were built outside the towns, for the cemeteries were there;
only in the tenth century did the church reach the middle of
the town. Further, the martyr's fame and sanctity encouraged burial near him; hence the habit of burial within the
church, and later around it. So throughout the Middle
Ages the church and the cemetery were the sacred place of
the people : there they held their plays, their dances (Giraldus
Cambrensis describes one in Wales in 1188, *Itin. Kambr.*
i. 2), their revels and even their drinking-bouts, in spite of
repeated prohibitions by Church Councils.

locis sacramentorum, de domibus orationum tantum
dedecus arceatur. Quis enim audet vetare privatim,
quod cum frequentatur in sanctis locis, honor martyrum nominatur ?

4   Haec si prima Africa temptaret auferre, a ceteris
terris imitatione digna esse deberet ; cum vero et
per Italiae maximam partem et in aliis omnibus aut
prope omnibus transmarinis ecclesiis, partim quia
numquam facta sunt, partim quia vel orta vel in-
veterata sanctorum et vere de vita futura cogitantium
episcoporum diligentia et animadversione extincta
atque deleta sunt, . . . dubitare quo modo possumus tantam morum labem vel proposito tam
lato exemplo emendare ? Et nos quidem illarum
partium hominem habemus episcopum, unde magnas
deo agimus gratias. Quamquam eius modestiae
atque lenitatis est, eius denique prudentiae et
sollicitudinis in domino, ut, etiam si Afer esset,
cito illi de scripturis persuaderetur curandum, quod
licentiosa et male libera consuetudo vulnus inflixit,
sed tanta pestilentia est huius mali, ut sanari prorsus,
quantum mihi videtur, nisi concilii auctoritate non
possit, aut, si ab una ecclesia inchoanda est medicina,
sicut videtur audaciae mutare conari quod Carthaginiensis ecclesia tenet, sic magnae inpudentiae est
velle servare quod Carthaginiensis ecclesia correxit.
Ad hanc autem rem quis alius episcopus esset op-
tandus, nisi qui ea diaconus execrabatur ?

5   Sed quod erat tunc dolendum, nunc auferendum

the bodies of the saints are laid, and from the place where the sacraments are celebrated, and from the house of prayer. For who dare forbid the use in private of that which, when practised in holy places, is called a tribute to the martyrs ?

If Africa were the first to attempt the removal of **4** these abuses, she would be worthy of imitation by all other countries. But since they have been repressed and done away with through the greater part of Italy and in all, or nearly all, the other churches across the sea, partly because they were never in use, partly because, when they did arise or were of long standing, the scrupulousness and censure of saintly bishops, truly contemplating the life to come . . . how can we hesitate to correct this grave moral corruption, especially after the precedent set by so many others ? We have, too, as bishop a man belonging to those regions, for which fact we heartily thank God. Yet he is of such moderation and gentleness, such wisdom and zeal in the Lord, that, even if he were an African, he would readily have been persuaded from the Scriptures to undertake the cure of the wound that this dissolute and disorderly custom has inflicted. But the disease wrought by this evil habit has become so chronic that complete recovery seems to me to be impossible, unless by the authority of a council ; or if any one church has to begin the treatment, it appears foolish to try to change anything the Church of Carthage retains, and very presumptuous to desire to keep anything the Church of Carthage has rectified. And to carry through that reform here, what bishop could be more desirable than the one who, as a deacon, denounced such abuses ?

But what at that time you could only deplore must **5**

47

est, non aspere sed, sicut scriptum est, *in spiritu lenitatis et mansuetudinis*. Dant enim mihi fiduciam litterae tuae, indices germanissimae caritatis, ut tecum tamquam mecum audeam conloqui. Non ergo aspere, quantum existimo, non duriter, non modo imperioso ista tolluntur, magis docendo quam iubendo, magis monendo quam minando. Sic enim agendum est cum multitudine, severitas autem exercenda est in peccata paucorum. Et si quid minamur, cum dolore fiat de scripturis comminando vindictam futuram, ne nos ipsi in nostra potestate, sed deus in nostro sermone timeatur. Ita prius movebuntur spiritales vel spiritalibus proximi, quorum auctoritate et lenissimis quidem sed instantissimis admonitionibus cetera multitudo frangatur.

6 Sed quoniam istae in cimiteriis ebrietates et luxuriosa convivia non solum honores martyrum a carnali et inperita plebe credi solent, sed etiam solacia mortuorum, mihi videtur facilius illis dissuaderi posse istam foeditatem ac turpitudinem, si et de scripturis prohibeatur et oblationes pro spiritibus dormientium, quas vere aliquid adiuvare credendum est, super ipsas memorias non sint sumptuosae atque omnibus petentibus sine typho et cum alacritate praebeantur neque vendantur ; sed si quis pro religione aliquid pecuniae offerre voluerit, in praesenti pauperibus eroget. Ita nec deserere videbuntur memorias suorum, quod potest gignere non levem cordis dolo-

---

^a Gal. vi. 1 ; 1 Cor. iv. 21.

48

now be repressed, not harshly, but as Scripture puts it, in the spirit of gentleness and meekness.[a] Your letter, revealing as it does deep brotherly affection, encourages me to talk to you as I would to myself. It is not by harshness, in my opinion, or by severity, or by over-bearing methods, that such evils are removed, but by education rather than by formal commands, by persuasion rather than by intimidation. That is the kind of treatment to use with men in the mass, while severity should be employed against the sins of individuals. If there be any intimidation, let it be done with sorrow by the threats of future punishment from the Scriptures, then the fear we inspire will not be of ourselves or our authority, but of God speaking in us. In this way an impression will first be made on the spiritually minded or on those most nearly so, and by their influence and gentle, but urgent, expostulation the rest of the crowd will be subdued.

But since those drunken revels in cemeteries and **6** those social orgies are usually considered by the carnal and ignorant laity not only to honour the martyrs but also to comfort the dead, they could, I think, be more easily prevailed upon to abandon that scandalous and vicious practice, if, besides forbidding it on Scriptural grounds, we ensure that the offerings made upon tombs for the spirits of those who have fallen asleep (and we must surely believe that they are of some avail) be not extravagant and be tendered without ostentation or reluctance to any who seek them, but be not sold. If any person wishes from religious motives to make an offering in coin, let him distribute it to the poor on the spot. In this way people will not have the appearance of neglecting their own burial-places, which might pro-

rem, et id celebrabitur in ecclesia, quod pie honeste-
que celebratur. Haec interim de comissationibus
et ebrietatibus dicta sint.

7   II. De contentione autem et zelo quid me attinet
dicere, quando ista vitia non in plebe, sed in nostro
numero graviora sunt? Horum autem morborum
mater superbia est et humanae laudis aviditas, quae
etiam hypocrisin saepe generat. Huic non re-
sistitur, nisi crebris divinorum librorum testimoniis
incutiatur timor et caritas dei, si tamen ille, qui hoc
agit, se ipsum praebeat patientiae atque humilitatis
exemplum minus sibi adsumendo, quam offertur, sed
tamen ab eis, qui se honorant, nec totum nec nihil
accipiendo et id, quod accipitur laudis aut honoris,
non propter se, qui totus coram deo esse debet et
humana contemnere, sed propter illos accipiatur,
quibus consulere non potest, si nimia deiectione
vilescat. Ad hoc enim pertinet, quod dictum est:
Nemo iuventutem tuam contemnat, cum ille hoc dixerit,
qui alio loco ait: *Si hominibus placere vellem, Christi
servus non essem.*

8   Magnum est de honoribus et laudibus hominum
non laetari, sed et omnem inanem pompam prae-
cidere et, si quid inde necessarium retinetur, id
totum ad utilitatem honorantium salutemque conferre. Non enim frustra dictum est: *Deus confringet
ossa hominibus placere volentium.* Quid enim lan-
guidius, quid tam sine stabilitate ac fortitudine,
quod ossa significant, quam homo quem male loquen-

---

duce no slight heart-soreness, and the ceremonies in church will be conducted with piety and decorum. So much then, meanwhile, for rioting and drunkenness.

II. Then again, concerning strife and envying, what **7** right have I to speak, since such sins are more serious among ourselves than among the laity ? These evils are the offspring of pride and eagerness for the praise of men, which often begets hypocrisy as well. The only way they can be resisted is by instilling the fear and love of God with repeated arguments from the holy books, provided that one who follows this method shows himself a pattern of patience and humility, arrogating to himself less honour than is offered him and yet accepting from those who pay him honour neither everything nor nothing, but accepting whatever honour and praise is offered him, not on his own behalf, since he ought to be living with a sole eye to God and to despise merely mortal rewards, but for their sakes whose welfare he cannot promote if he depreciate himself so much that he loses men's esteem. That is the point of the saying, " Let no man despise thy youth," *a* although he who said those words remarks in another place, " If I yet pleased men, I should not be the servant of Christ." *b*

It is a great matter not to rejoice in human praise **8** and honours but to discard all empty ostentation, and, if any of it must be kept, to turn it all to the use and the well-being of those who honour us. Not for nothing has it been said, " God will break the bones of those who seek to please men" *c*; for what is more feeble, more lacking in steadfastness and strength (for this is what " bones " symbolize), than an individual who is unnerved by the voice of slander, when he knows that

51

tium lingua debilitat, cum sciat falsa esse quae dicuntur ? Cuius rei dolor nullo modo animae viscera
dilaniaret, si non amor laudis eius ossa confringeret.
Praesumo de robore animi tui ; itaque ista quae
tecum confero, mihi dico ; dignaris tamen, credo,
mecum considerare quam sint gravia, quam difficilia.
Non enim huius hostis vires sentit, nisi qui ei bellum
indixerit, quia, etsi cuiquam facile est laude carere,
dum denegatur, difficile est ea non delectari, cum
offertur.   Et tamen tanta mentis in deum debet esse
suspensio, ut, si non merito laudemur, corrigamus
eos, quos possumus, ne arbitrentur aut in nobis esse,
quod non est, aut nostrum esse, quod dei est, aut ea
laudent, quae quamvis non desint nobis aut etiam
supersint, nequaquam tamen sint laudabilia, velut
sunt bona omnia, quae vel cum pecoribus habemus
communia vel cum impiis hominibus. Si autem
merito laudamur propter deum, gratulemur eis
quibus placet verum bonum, non tamen nobis quia
placemus hominibus, sed si coram deo tales sumus,
quales esse nos credunt, et non tribuitur nobis sed
deo, cuius dona sunt omnia quae vere meritoque
laudantur.   Haec mihi ipse canto cotidie vel potius
ille cuius salutaria praecepta sunt, quaecumque sive
in divinis lectionibus inveniuntur sive quae intrinsecus animo suggeruntur. Et tamen vehementer
cum adversario dimicans saepe ab eo vulnera accipio,
cum delectationem oblatae laudis mihi auferre non
possum.

9 Haec propterea scripsi, ut, si tuae sanctitati iam

what is being said against him is untrue ? The pain
of receiving such treatment would certainly not rend
his inmost soul, unless the love of praise were " breaking his bones." I have every confidence in your
strength of mind, so what I am discussing with you
I am applying to myself ; still, you are good enough,
I think, to consider with me how serious and difficult
a matter this is. Only one who has declared war on
that foe realizes his power, for, although it is easy to
do without praise, when it is denied us, it is hard not
to take pleasure in it, when it is offered. And yet
our minds ought to be so completely uplifted to God
that, if we are undeservedly praised, we may correct
those we can, lest they should think we possess gifts
that are not ours, or that the gifts we have from God
are our own, or praise qualities we do possess and
even possess in a marked degree, but which are in
no way matters for praise, for example all those
advantages we share with animals or with unchristian
men. But if we are deservedly praised for God's sake,
we should congratulate those who find pleasure in
what is truly good, and not ourselves for pleasing
men, and that only if we are in the eyes of God what
they take us to be and offer the praise not to us, but
to God ; for everything that is truly and deservedly
praised is a gift from Him. This is what I keep on
saying to myself each day, or rather He does, from
whom come whatever salutary counsels are found
in Scripture readings or are suggested to the mind
from within. Yet, strenuously as I struggle with the
adversary, I often receive wounds from him, since I
cannot rid myself of delight in the praise that is
offered me.

Your Holiness may have no further need for 9

non sunt necessaria, sive quod plura ipse huius modi
cogites atque utiliora sive quod tuae sanctitati
medicina ista non opus sit, mala tamen mea nota
sint tibi sciasque, unde pro mea infirmitate deum
rogare digneris. Quod ut inpensissime facias, obsecro per humanitatem illius, qui praeceptum dedit,
ut invicem onera nostra portemus. Multa sunt,
quae de nostra vita et conversatione deflerem,
quae nollem per litteras ad te venire, sed inter cor
meum et cor tuum nulla essent ministeria praeter
os meum et aures tuas. Si autem venerabilis nobis
omniumque nostrum tota sinceritate carissimus,
cuius in te vere fraternam, cum praesens essem, benignitatem studiumque perspexi, senex Saturninus
si dignatus fuerit, quando opportunum videbit, ad nos
venire, quicquid cum eius sanctitate et spiritali
affectu conloqui potuerimus, aut nihil aut non multum
distabit, ac si cum tua dignatione id ageremus. Quod
ut nobiscum ab eo petere atque impetrare digneris,
tantis precibus posco, quantis verba nulla sufficiunt.
Absentiam enim meam tantum longe Hipponienses
vehementer nimisque formidant neque ullo modo
mihi sic volunt credere ut et ego vobis.

Agrum fratribus datum provisione et liberalitate
tua didicimus ante epistulam tuam per sanctum
fratrem et conservum nostrum Parthenium, a quo
multa alia, quae audire desiderabamus, audivimus.
Praestabit dominus, ut etiam cetera, quae adhuc
desideramus, impleantur.

---

counsels of this kind, either because your own reflection has suggested a richer store of beneficial
principles, or else because your Holiness has passed
the stage of requiring remedies of this kind. My
purpose in writing as I have done is to make you aware
of my vices and to let you know what, in view of my
weakness, you might ask God for. I beseech you by
the humanity of Him who has laid down the rule that
we should bear each other's burdens,[a] to do this most
earnestly. There is much in my life and conduct
that I deplore, but I should prefer that it should not
reach you by letter ; between my heart and your
heart there should be no intermediary save my
mouth and your ears. If our venerated Senior,
Saturninus, whom we all regard with very genuine
affection, and whose really brotherly kindness and
concern for you I saw when I was with you, will deign
to visit us when he sees it convenient, any conversation I may have with that holy and warm-hearted
and spiritually-minded man will be little, if any,
different from what I might have with your Grace.
With entreaties that surpass all expression I urge you
to be good enough to join me in asking and obtaining
a visit from him. The people of Hippo are much afraid,
indeed excessively so, to let me go so far away from
them, and they are in no wise willing to trust me, as I
trust you.

Before your letter reached me, I learned through
our saintly brother and fellow-servant, Parthenius,
of the ground provided for our brethren by your forethought and generosity. He gave us besides much
news that we were anxious to have. The Lord will
grant the fulfilment of the other things also for which
we are still anxious.

ST. AUGUSTINE

No. 9 (Ep. XXVIII)

DOMINO DILECTISSIMO ET CULTU SINCERIS-SIMO CARITATIS OBSERVANDO ATQUE AMPLECTENDO FRATRI ET CONPRESBYTERO HIERONYMO AUGUSTINUS

1 I. Numquam aeque quisquam facie cuilibet in-notuit quam mihi tuorum in domino studiorum quieta laetitia et vere exercitatio liberalis. Quamquam ergo percupiam omnino te nosse, tamen exiguum quiddam tui minus habeo, praesentiam videlicet corporis. Quam ipsam etiam, posteaquam te beatis-simus nunc episcopus tunc vero iam episcopatu dignus frater Alypius vidit remeansque a me visus est, negare non possum magna ex parte mihi esse relatu eius inpressam et ante reditum, cum te ille ibi vide-bat, ego videbam sed oculis eius. Non enim animo me atque illum sed corpore duos, qui noverit, dixerit, concordia dum taxat et familiaritate fidissima, non meritis, quibus ille antecellit. Quia ergo me primitus communione spiritus, quo in unum nitimur, deinde illius ex ore iam diligis, nequaquam inpudenter quasi aliquis ignotus commendo germanitati tuae fratrem Profuturum, quem nostris conatibus, deinde adiu-

---

ᵃ Written from Hippo. Jerome was at Bethlehem, but through a series of mishaps this letter was not delivered until nine years later.

ᵇ Profuturus was a member of Augustine's monastery at Hippo. He was prevented from setting out with this
56

No. 9 (Ep. XXVIII)

(A.D. 394 or 395)

AUGUSTINE TO JEROME, MY BELOVED LORD,
MY BROTHER AND FELLOW-PRIEST, WORTHY
OF ESTEEM AND HONOUR AND DEVOTED
AFFECTION [a]

I. Never did any man know another's features 1
as well as I have come to know what peaceful joy
you find in your studies in the Lord and what truly
noble application you give to them. My desire for
thorough acquaintance with you is of the strongest,
yet I lack only one small portion of you, namely
your bodily presence. But, I can assure you, even
that has been to a large extent imprinted on my mind
by the account given me by brother Alypius, now
a much revered bishop, but even then, when he saw
you, well worthy of that office. I saw him on his
return, but even before then, while he was seeing
you there, I too saw you, though with his eyes.
For anyone who knows us both would say that he
and I are distinct individuals in body only, not in
mind ; I mean in our harmoniousness and trusty
friendship, not in merit, in which he far outstrips me.
So it is not presumptuous of me, as if I were a
stranger to you, since you already cherish affection
for me from the unity of spirit, first of all, that makes
us strive for one common end and then, from what
Alypius has told you of me, to commend to your
fraternal kindness our brother Profuturus [b] ; it is my
hope that through my efforts on his behalf and then

letter by his appointment to the see of Cirta and died before
403 (Ep. lxxi. 2). To him is addressed No. 13 *infra*.

torio tuo, vere profuturum speramus, nisi forte quod
talis est, ut ipse tibi per eum fiam commendatior
quam ille per me. Hactenus fortasse scribere de-
buerim, si esse vellem epistularum sollemnium more
contentus. Sed scatet animus in loquelas communi-
candas tecum de studiis nostris quae habemus in
Christo Iesu domino nostro, qui nobis multas utilitates
et viatica quaedam demonstrati a se itineris etiam
per tuam caritatem non mediocriter ministrare
dignatur.

2 II. Petimus ergo et nobiscum petit omnis Africanarum ecclesiarum studiosa societas, ut interpretandis
eorum libris qui graece scripturas nostras quam optime tractaverunt, curam atque operam inpendere
non graveris. Potes enim efficere, ut nos quoque
habeamus tales illos viros et unum potissimum, quem
tu libentius in tuis litteris sonas. De vertendis autem
in linguam latinam sanctis litteris canonicis laborare
te nollem, nisi eo modo quo Iob interpretatus es, ut
signis adhibitis, quid inter hanc tuam et LXX, quorum
est gravissima auctoritas, interpretationem distet,
appareat. Satis autem nequeo mirari si aliquid
adhuc in hebraeis exemplaribus invenitur, quod tot
interpretes illius linguae peritissimos fugerit. Omitto
enim LXX, de quorum vel consilii vel spiritus maiore
concordia quam si unus homo esset, non audeo in ali-
quam partem certam ferre sententiam, nisi quod eis
praeminentem auctoritatem in hoc munere sine controversia tribuendam existimo. Illi me plus movent,

---

^a Origen.

through your assistance he really will " profit "—except perhaps that he is the kind of man who will give you a better opinion of me than I have given you of him. At this point I should perhaps have laid down my pen if I were satisfied with the usual formal letter, but so many remarks swarm into my mind that I must exchange with you about the studies with which we are occupied in Jesus Christ, our Lord, who even through your Charity is pleased to provide us, in no stinted manner, with many benefits and, so to speak, resources for the journey He has prescribed.

II. We beg you then (and we are joined in this by 2 all the company of students in the African churches) not to refuse to devote toil and trouble to translating the works of those who have so excellently expounded our Scriptures in Greek. You can put us in possession of those notable commentators and of one in particular, whose name you utter in your writings with more than usual pleasure.[a] But in translating the holy canonical writings into Latin I should not like you to follow any other method than that in which you translated Job, namely by applying signs to show wherein your translation differs from that of the Seventy, whose authority is of the weightiest. But I should be incredibly surprised if anything is found at this time of day in the Hebrew manuscripts that has escaped so many translators possessing expert knowledge of that language. I leave the Seventy out of account ; of their unanimity of mind or of inspiration, greater than if only one man had been concerned, I should not venture to express a definite opinion in any direction, except that I think there can be no question that in this sphere they must be conceded an outstanding authority. I am more

qui, cum posteriores interpretarentur et verborum
locutionumque hebraearum viam atque regulas mor-
dacius, ut fertur, tenerent, non solum inter se non
consenserunt, sed etiam reliquerunt multa, quae
tanto post eruenda et prodenda remanerent. Si
enim obscura sunt, te quoque in eis falli posse creditur ; si manifesta, illos in eis falli potuisse non creditur. Huius igitur rei pro tua caritate expositis
causis certum me facias obsecraverim.

3   III. Legi etiam quaedam scripta, quae tua dicerent-
tur, in epistulas apostoli Pauli, quarum ad Galatas cum
enodare velles, venit in manus locus ille, quo apostolus Petrus a perniciosa simulatione revocatur. Ibi
patrocinium mendacii susceptum esse vel abs te tali
viro vel a quopiam, si alius illa scripsit, fateor, non
mediocriter doleo, donec refellantur, si forte refelli
possunt, ea quae me movent. Mihi enim videtur
exitiosissime credi aliquod in libris sanctis esse mendacium, id est, eos homines per quos nobis illa scriptura
ministrata est atque conscripta, aliquid in libris suis
fuisse mentitos. Alia quippe quaestio est, sitne aliquando mentiri viri boni, et alia quaestio est, utrum

---

^a This controversy between Augustine and Jerome became
famous in the history of the Church. St. Peter's inconsistent
conduct at Antioch, in first eating with the Gentiles and later
withdrawing from them (Gal. ii. 11-14), was found difficult
to explain ; both heretics and pagans used the incident to
discredit either Paul or Peter and the Church as well. One
commentator, Clement of Alexandria, cut the knot by declaring that the Cephas mentioned in Galatians was not St.
Peter, but a disciple of the same name ; Origen invented the
disingenuous and worse theory that the dispute between the
two apostles was simulated in order the more severely to
condemn the Judaizers. This view found wide acceptance :
it was defended and urged by Chrysostom and, in the West,
with characteristic vigour, by Jerome. Augustine here and

concerned about the later translators; they are said to have possessed a more thorough grip of the course and the rules of Hebrew words and phrases, and yet they are not only at variance with each other, but have also left many points that have remained to be unearthed and brought to light after so long. For if these points are obscure, then it is quite credible that you too may go astray in them; if they are clear, it is incredible that they could have gone astray in them. I should like to ask you of your kindness to explain the reasons for this state of things and to give me some assurance about it.

III. I have been reading some books that are said 3 to be by you, on the Epistles of the Apostle Paul; in seeking to expound Galatians, you reached that passage in which the Apostle Peter is withheld from a piece of pernicious deceit.[a] To see there the defence of falsehood undertaken by a man like you or by some other person (if another person was the author) has caused me, I confess, no small grief, which I shall continue to feel until the objections that trouble my mind are disproved, if they really can be disproved. For it seems to me very disastrous to believe that there can be any falsehood in the sacred books—I mean that those men who wrote and transmitted to us the Scripture, in any way lied in what they wrote. They are two quite different questions, whether it ever accords with a good man's character to lie, and whether a writer of the Holy

in other letters denounces this interpretation as subversive of the whole authority of Scripture. Jerome eventually accepted Augustine's view, which became generally accepted. A full account of the controversy is given in Lightfoot's commentary on Galatians, pp. 128-132.

scriptorem sanctarum scripturarum mentiri opor-
tuerit, immo vero non alia, sed nulla quaestio est.
Admisso enim semel in tantum auctoritatis fastigium
officioso aliquo mendacio, nulla illorum librorum particula remanebit, quae non, ut cuique videbitur vel
ad mores difficilis vel ad fidem incredibilis, eadem
perniciosissima regula ad mentientis auctoris consilium officiumque referatur.

4   Si enim mentiebatur apostolus Paulus, cum apostolum Petrum obiurgans diceret : *Si tu, cum sis Iudaeus,
gentiliter et non iudaice vivis, quem ad modum gentes
cogis iudaizare?* et recte illi videbatur Petrus
fecisse, quem non recte fecisse et dixit et scripsit,
ut quasi animos tumultuantium deleniret, quid re-
spondebimus, cum exsurrexerint perversi homines
prohibentes nuptias, quos futuros ipse praenuntiavit,
et dixerint totum illud, quod idem apostolus de
matrimoniorum iure firmando locutus est, propter
homines, qui dilectione coniugum tumultuari poterant,
fuisse mentitum, scilicet non quod hoc senserit, sed
ut illorum placaretur adversitas ? Non opus est
multa commemorare. Possunt enim videri etiam de
laudibus dei esse officiosa mendacia, ut apud homines
pigriores dilectio eius ardescat. Atque ita nusquam
certa erit in sanctis libris castae veritatis auctoritas.
Nonne adtendimus eundem apostolum cum ingenti
cura commendandae veritatis dicere : *Si autem
Christus non resurrexit, inanis est praedicatio nostra,*

---

   a Officiosum mendacium is difficult to translate : it is a lie
told from a sense of duty, from a wish to glorify God.
   b Gal. ii. 11-14.   *c* 1 Tim. iv. 1-3.
   d 1 Cor. vii. 10-16.

Scriptures should have lied—nay, they are not really different questions, there is no question about it. Admit even a single well-meant falsehood [a] into such an exalted authority, and there will not be left a single section of those books which, if appearing to anyone to present difficulties from the point of view of practice or to be hard to believe from the point of view of doctrine, will escape, by the same very baneful principle, from being classified as the deliberate tact of an author who was lying.

If the Apostle Paul was lying when he rebuked [4] the Apostle Peter with the words, " If thou, being a Jew, livest after the manner of the Gentiles and not as do the Jews, why compellest thou the Gentiles to live as do the Jews ? " [b] and he approved of Peter's action while condemning him by word and pen with the ostensible object of soothing the mind of those who were raging against him, what answer shall we make when perverse men arise and forbid marriage (as the Apostle foretold would happen [c]), declaring that all that he said about strengthening the marriage-bond [d] was a lie told for the sake of those men who from love of their wives might have made an uproar, that clearly those were not his real sentiments, but were meant to allay their antagonism ? There is no need to give many illustrations. There might appear to be well-meant falsehoods even about the praise of God, aiming at inflaming love for Him in men comparatively hard of heart, and on those terms nowhere in the holy books would the authority of unadulterated truth stand unchallenged. Do we not observe the great care with which the same apostle commends truth in the words : " And if Christ be not risen, then is our preaching vain and your faith is also

inanis est et fides vestra. Invenimur autem et falsi
testes dei, quia testimonium diximus adversus deum,
quod suscitaverit Christum, quem non suscitavit? Si
quis huic diceret : " Quid in hoc mendacio per-
horrescis, cum id dixeris quod, etiam si falsum sit, ad
laudem dei maxime pertinet," nonne huius detestatus
insaniam quibus posset verbis et significationibus
in lucem penetralia sui cordis aperiret, clamans non
minore aut fortasse etiam maiore scelere in deo
laudari falsitatem quam veritatem vituperari ? Agendum est igitur, ut ad cognitionem divinarum scripturarum talis homo accedat, qui de sanctis libris tam
sancte et veraciter existimet, ut nolit aliqua eorum
parte delectari per officiosa mendacia, potiusque id,
quod non intellegit, transeat, quam cor suum prae-
ferat illi veritati. Profecto enim cum hoc dicit, credi
sibi expetit et id agit, ut divinarum scripturarum
auctoritatibus non credamus.

5   Et ego quidem qualibuscumque viribus quas
dominus suggerit, omnia illa testimonia quae adhibita
sunt adstruendae utilitati mendacii, aliter oportere
intellegi ostenderem, ut ubique eorum firma veritas
doceretur. Quam enim testimonia mendacia esse
non debent, tam non debent favere mendacio. Sed
hoc intellegentiae relinquo tuae. Admota enim
lectioni diligentiore consideratione, multo id fortasse
facilius videbis quam ego. Ad hanc autem considerationem coget te pietas, qua cognoscis fluctuare
auctoritatem divinarum scripturarum, ut in eis quod

------

^a 1 Cor. xv. 14-15.

vain ; yea, and we are found false witnesses of God,
because we have testified of God that He raised up
Christ ; whom He raised not up "ᵃ? If anyone should
say to him : "What is it in this lie that shocks you,
when, even if what you say is untrue, it very greatly
redounds to the glory of God?" would he not denounce
the madness of such a suggestion and with every
available word and sign open to the light the inmost
secrets of his heart, declaring that to praise falsehood
in God was no less a sin, perhaps even a much greater
one, than to cast aspersion upon His truth? An
effort must be made to bring to a knowledge of
the sacred Scriptures a man who will have such
a reverent and truthful opinion of the holy books
that he would refuse to find delight in a well-meant
falsehood anywhere in them, and would rather pass
over what he does not understand than prefer his
own intelligence to their truth. For indeed when
he expresses such a preference, he demands credence
for himself and attempts to destroy our confidence
in the authority of the holy Scriptures.

For my part I would use all the strength the Lord 5
supplies to show that all those texts that are adduced
to prove the expediency of falsehood ought to be
understood in another sense, so that everywhere their
unimpeachable veracity might be made apparent.
For just as texts ought not to be lies in themselves,
so they should lend no support to lies. But I leave
this matter to your own intelligence ; if you apply a
more attentive consideration to the reading of them,
you will perhaps see this more easily than I do. To
that consideration you will be compelled by the
reverent spirit that makes you recognize that the
authority of the holy Scriptures becomes unsettled,

vult quisque credat, quod non vult non **credat**, si
semel fuerit persuasum aliqua illos viros per quos
nobis haec ministrata sunt, in scripturis suis officiose
potuisse mentiri, nisi forte regulas quasdam daturus
es, quibus noverimus ubi oporteat mentiri et ubi non
oporteat. Quod si fieri potest, nullo modo mendaci-
bus dubiisque rationibus id explices quaeso, nec me
onerosum aut inpudentem iudices per humanitatem
veracissimam domini nostri. Nam ut non dicam nulla,
certe non magna culpa meus error veritati favet, si
recte in te potest veritas favere mendacio.

6   IV. Multa alia cum sincerissimo corde tuo loqui
cuperem et de christiano studio conferre, sed huic
desiderio meo nulla epistula sat est. Uberius id
possum per fratrem quem miscendum et alendum
dulcibus atque utilibus sermocinationibus tuis misisse
me gaudeo. Et tamen, quantum vellem, nec ipse,
quod eius pace dixerim, forsitan capit. Quamquam
nihilo me illi praetulerim; ego enim me fateor tui
capaciorem, sed ipsum video fieri pleniorem, quo me
sine dubitatione antecellit. Et posteaquam redierit,
quod domino adiuvante prosperatum iri spero, cum
eius pectoris abs te cumulati particeps fuero, non est
impleturus quod in me adhuc vacuum erit atque
avidum sensorum tuorum. Ita fiet, ut ego etiam
tunc egentior sim, ille copiosior. Sane idem **frater**

so that anyone may believe what he likes in them and disbelieve what he does not like, if it be once admitted that those men through whom they were delivered to us could in their writings have uttered some well-meant lies. But perhaps you mean to provide us with some rules for discerning when lying is expedient and when it is not. If this can be done, I beg you not to couch your explanation in terms that are false or equivocal, nor, by the very true humanity of our Lord, to consider me burdensome or presumptuous. For a mistake on my part that favours truth is, I will not say no fault at all, but certainly no serious fault, if in you the truth can rightly favour lying.

IV. There are many other matters about which 6 I should like to have converse with your friendly spirit and to discuss with reference to Christian studies, but for this desire of mine no letter is sufficient; I can do that more fruitfully through the brother whom I am glad to send to be admitted to the nurture of your pleasant and profitable conversation. And yet even he (I apologize to him for saying this) has perhaps not the capacity to receive all I should like. But still I should not reckon myself his superior in any respect, for I confess that I have more room for receiving from you than he has; but I see him becoming fuller of you, and in that there is no doubt that he surpasses me. When he returns, as I trust he will succeed in doing with God's help, and shares with me his understanding that you have richly stored, he is not likely to satisfy the void and the eagerness that I shall still have for your thoughts and feelings, and so I shall even then be the poorer and he the richer. The same brother, however,

aliqua scripta nostra fert secum.   Quibus legendis si
dignationem adhibueris, etiam sinceram fraternam-
que severitatem adhibeas quaeso.   Non enim aliter
intellego, quod scriptum est : *Emendabit me iustus
in misericordia et arguet me ; oleum autem peccatoris
non inpinguet caput meum,* nisi quia magis amat
obiurgator sanans quam adulator unguens caput.
Ego autem difficillime bonus iudex lego, quod scripserim, sed aut timidior recto aut cupidior.   Video
etiam interdum vitia mea, sed haec malo audire a
melioribus, ne, cum me recte fortasse reprehendero,
rursus mihi blandiar et meticulosam potius mihi
videar in me quam iustam tulisse sententiam.

No. 10 (Ep. XXIX)

EPISTULA PRESBYTERI HIPPONIENSIUM RE-GIORUM AD ALYPIUM EPISCOPUM TA-GASTENSIUM DE DIE NATALIS LEONTII QUONDAM EPISCOPI HIPPONIENSIS

1   De negotio interim quod non curare non possum,
nihil certum scribere potui absente fratre Macario,
qui cito dicitur rediturus, et quod deo adiuvante
peragi potuerit, peragetur.   De nostra autem pro
eis sollicitudine quamquam fratres nostri cives qui
aderant, securos vos facere possent, tamen digna res

---

a Ps. cxl. 5.   Translated from the Septuagint.

b Leontius suffered martyrdom about 303.   A church
built by him, the *basilica Leontiana,* is several times mentioned by Augustine (here and *Serm.* 260, 262).   "That
festival" (§ 2) is the celebration of his martyrdom beside
his tomb, with that licence which Augustine has in general
terms already denounced in No. 8 above.

carries with him some of my writings, to which, if you have the condescension to read them, please apply an unbiased and brotherly severity. For I take the words of Scripture, "The righteous shall correct me with pity and reprove me, but the oil of the sinner shall not anoint my head," [a] to mean this, that he is the greater friend whose censure heals than he whose flattery anoints the head. When I myself read over what I have written, I find the greatest difficulty in judging it rightly, being either over-cautious or over-rash. I catch occasional sight of my faults, but I prefer to hear of them from better men, lest after censuring myself, perchance rightly, I fall again into self-flattery and think that my judgement of myself was more finical than fair.

No. 10 (Ep. XXIX)

(A.D. 395)

A LETTER FROM THE PRIEST OF HIPPO REGIUS TO ALYPIUS, BISHOP OF TAGASTE, CONCERNING THE ANNIVERSARY OF THE BIRTH OF LEONTIUS,[b] FORMERLY BISHOP OF HIPPO

In the absence of brother Macarius,[c] I can give 1 you no definite news meanwhile about that affair, which cannot fail to concern me. He is said to be returning soon, and what God's help will enable me to carry through, shall be carried through. Although the brethren, our fellow-townsmen, who were with you, could assure you of our zeal on their behalf, still a piece of news deserving of that epistolary con-

[c] Macarius is evidently one of Augustine's monks at Hippo, but his identity is otherwise uncertain.

epistulari conloquio quo nos invicem consolamur, a
domino praestita est, in quo promerendo multum nos
adiutos esse credimus ipsa vestra sollicitudine, quae
profecto sine deprecatione pro nobis esse non potuit.

2 Itaque non praetermittamus vestrae caritati narrare quid gestum sit, ut nobiscum deo gratias agatis
de accepto beneficio, qui nobiscum preces de accipiendo fudistis. Cum post profectionem tuam nobis
nuntiatum esset tumultuari homines et dicere se
ferre non posse, ut illa sollemnitas prohiberetur
quam laetitiam nominantes vinulentiae nomen frustra conantur abscondere, sicut etiam te praesente
iam iam nuntiabatur, opportune nobis accidit occulta
ordinatione omnipotentis dei, ut quarta feria illud
in evangelio capitulum consequenter tractaretur:
*Nolite dare sanctum canibus neque proieceritis margaritas
vestras ante porcos.* Tractatum est ergo de canibus
et de porcis, ita ut et pervicaci latratu adversus dei
praecepta rixantes et voluptatum carnalium sordi-
bus dediti erubescere cogerentur conclusumque ita
ut viderent quam esset nefarium intra ecclesiae
parietes id agere nomine religionis, quod in suis
domibus si agere perseverarent, sancto et marga-
ritis ecclesiasticis eos arceri oporteret.

---

a From the close of the second century Wednesday and
Friday were held as fast-days (*semi-ieiunia* or *dies stationum*,
Tert. *Orat.* 19, *Ieiun.* 13), but the observance of Wednesday
fell into disuse when Saturday was added to the weekly
fast-days.

b Not " chapter," for these modern divisions are due only
to the thirteenth century Hugo of St. Cher, though much
earlier the public reading of Scripture had necessitated the use
of sections (κεφάλαια, περικοπαί, *capitula*). In Augustine, for

verse which is a solace to us both has been provided by the Lord, in gaining Whose favour I believe I have been much assisted by that very anxiety of yours on my behalf, for it certainly must have been accompanied by intercession for me.

So let me not miss the chance of telling your 2 Charity what has happened, so that, as you joined me in pouring forth prayers for the bestowing of this boon, you may join me in giving God thanks for it, now that it has been bestowed. News was brought me after your departure, as it had been several times while you were here, that people were growing unruly and were saying they could not tolerate the prohibition of that festival, the drunken character of which they try in vain to disguise under the name of a "gaudy." Very appropriately, by a hidden dispensation of Almighty God, it happened that on the Wednesday [a] I was expounding in its due course that section [b] from the Gospel : " Give not that which is holy unto the dogs, neither cast ye your pearls before swine." [c] I discoursed about dogs and swine in such a way as to compel those to blush for very shame who were obstinately snarling and brawling against God's commandments and were abandoned to foul carnal pleasures. I ended up by showing them the heinousness of perpetrating within the four walls of the church, in the name of religion, what would necessitate their exclusion from " that which is holy " and the " pearls " of the church, if they persisted in doing it within their own homes.

example, Romans viii. 18-24 is a *capitulum*, as are the first five verses of St. John's Gospel.

[c] Matt. vii. 6.

3   Sed haec quamvis grate accepta fuerint, tamen
quia pauci convenerant, non erat satisfactum tanto
negotio.   Iste autem sermo cum ab eis qui aderant
pro cuiusque facultate ac studio foris ventilaretur,
multos habuit contradictores.   Postea vero quam
dies quadragesimae inluxisset et frequens multitudo
ad horam tractationis occurrit, lectum est illud in
evangelio, ubi dominus de templo expulsis venditori-
bus animalium et eversis mensis nummulariorum dixit
domum patris sui pro domo orationum speluncam
latronum esse factam.   Quod capitulum, cum eos
intentos proposita vinulentiae quaestione feci, et
ipse quoque recitavi adiunxique disputationem, qua
ostenderem, quanto commotius et vehementius dominus noster ebriosa convivia, quae ubique sunt
turpia, de templo expelleret, unde sic expulit concessa commercia, cum ea venderentur quae sacri-
ficiis illo tempore licitis essent necessaria, quaerens
ab eis quibus similiorem putarent speluncam latronum necessaria vendentibus an inmoderate biben-
tibus.

4   Et quoniam mihi praeparatae lectiones sug-
gerendae tenebantur, adiunxi deinde ipsum adhuc
carnalem populum Iudaeorum in illo templo ubi
nondum corpus et sanguis domini offerebatur, non
solum vinulenta sed nec sobria quidem umquam
celebrasse convivia nec eos publice religionis nomine
inebriatos inveniri in historia, nisi cum festa fabricato
idolo exsolverent.   Quae cum dicerem, codicem etiam
accepi et recitavi totum illum locum.   Addidi etiam
cum dolore, quo potui, quoniam apostolus ait ad dis-

ᵃ Matt. xxi. 12-13.
ᵇ *Historia*, the historical books of the Bible, which were
on a separate *codex*.   ᶜ Exod. xxxii. 6.

They took this in quite a good spirit, but as **3** the congregation was small, a matter so important demanded further treatment. When my hearers spread news of my sermon outside, each according to his ability and point of view, it found many to oppose it. But after the morning of Quadragesima had dawned and a considerable crowd had gathered at the time of Scripture exposition, we read that portion from the Gospel where the Lord drove from the Temple the sellers of animals and overthrew the tables of the money-changers, saying that His Father's house had been turned from a house of prayer into a den of thieves.[a] After securing their attention by announcing the subject of drunkenness, I read that section myself and followed it with an address designed to show that, if our Lord drove lawful trade from the Temple, since what was sold was requisite for the sacrifices permitted under that dispensation, He would with much greater indignation and violence drive from it drunken revels, which are abominable anywhere. And I asked them which they thought more like a den of thieves, those who sold necessaries or those who drank beyond measure.

The Scripture readings, turned up beforehand, **4** were being held ready to hand up to me, so I went on to say that the Jewish people, though yet carnal, never held even sober feasts, far less drunken ones, in that Temple in which as yet there was no offering up of the body and blood of the Lord, and that as a people they were never found in the Bible [b] drunk in the name of religion, unless when they were celebrating a feast to the idol they had made.[c] So saying, I took the book and read all that passage. Reminding them that the Apostle, to distinguish

73

cernendum populum christianum a duritia Iudaeorum epistulam suam *non in tabulis lapideis* scriptam *sed in tabulis cordis carnalibus,* cum Moyses famulus dei propter illos principes binas lapideas tabulas confregisset, quo modo non possemus istorum corda confringere, qui homines novi testamenti sanctorum diebus celebrandis ea vellent sollemniter exhibere, quae populus veteris testamenti et semel et idolo celebravit.

5   Tunc reddito exodi codice crimen ebrietatis, quantum tempus sinebat, exaggerans sumpsi apostolum Paulum et inter quae peccata posita esset, ostendi legens illum locum : *Si quis frater nominetur aut fornicator aut idolis serviens aut avarus aut maledicus aut ebriosus aut rapax, cum eius modi nec cibum sumere,* ingemescendo admonens cum quanto periculo convivaremur cum eis qui vel in domibus inebriarentur. Legi etiam illud quod non longo intervallo sequitur : *Nolite errare ; neque fornicatores neque idolis servientes neque adulteri neque molles neque masculorum concubitores neque fures neque avari neque ebriosi neque maledici neque raptores regnum dei possidebunt. Et haec quidem fuistis, sed abluti estis, sed iustificati estis in nomine domini Iesu Christi et spiritu dei nostri.* Quibus lectis, dixi ut considerarent quo modo possent fideles audire *sed abluti estis,* qui adhuc talis concupiscentiae sordes, contra quas clauditur regnum caelorum, in corde suo, id est in interiore dei templo esse patiuntur. Inde ventum est ad illud capitulum : *Con-*

---

^a 2 Cor. iii. 3.   ^b Exod. xxxii. 19.
^c 1 Cor. v. 11.   ^d 1 Cor. vi. 9-11.

the Christian people from the obdurate Jews, speaks
of his letter as written " not in tables of stone, but
in fleshy tables of the heart," [a] I went on to ask
with all the sorrow I could how it was that, though
God's servant, Moses, had broken those two tables of
stone [b] because of the rulers of Israel, we found it
impossible to break their hearts ; they were men of
the new covenant, yet they chose, in celebrating
their saints' days, to practise such rites as the people
of the old covenant had practised only once, and
that before an idol.

Then I gave back the book of Exodus and enlarged, 5
as far as time permitted, on the sin of drunkenness,
taking the apostle Paul and showing in what class
of sins he placed it. I read that passage, " If any
man that is called a brother be a fornicator or covetous
or an idolater or a railer or a drunkard or an extor-
tioner, with such an one no, not to eat," [c] reminding them with groanings what a risk we ran in
carousing with those who got drunk even at home.
I read that passage, too, which follows quite close
to the last, " Be not deceived : neither fornicators
nor idolaters nor adulterers nor effeminate nor
abusers of themselves with mankind, nor thieves
nor covetous nor drunkards nor revilers nor ex-
tortioners shall inherit the kingdom of God. And
such were some of you, but ye are washed, but ye are
justified in the name of the Lord Jesus Christ and
by the Spirit of our God." [d] After which, I bade them
consider how the faithful could bear to be told " But
ye are washed," when they still tolerated in their
heart, that is in the inward Temple of God, such
filthy lusts, against which the kingdom of heaven
is closed. Then I came to that section, " When

*venientibus ergo vobis in unum non est dominicam cenam
celebrare, unusquisque enim propriam cenam praesumit
in manducando et alius quidem esurit, alius ebrius est.
Numquid domos non habetis ad manducandum et bi-
bendum? an ecclesiam dei contemnitis?* Quo recitato,
diligentius commendavi ne honesta quidem et sobria
convivia debere in ecclesia celebrari, quando quidem
apostolus non dixerit : " Numquid domos non habetis
ad inebriandos vos," ut quasi tantum modo inebriari
in ecclesia non liceret, sed " *ad manducandum et biben-
dum*," quod potest honeste fieri sed praeter ecclesiam
ab eis qui domos habent ubi alimentis necessariis
refici possint. Et tamen nos ad has angustias cor-
ruptorum temporum et diffluentium morum esse
perductos, uti nondum modesta convivia sed saltem
domesticum regnum ebrietatis optemus.

6 Commemoravi etiam evangelii capitulum, quod
pridie tractaveram, ubi de pseudoprophetis dictum
est : *Ex fructibus eorum cognoscetis eos.* Deinde in
memoriam revocavi fructus eo loco non appellatos
nisi opera. Tum quaesivi inter quos fructus nomi-
nata esset ebrietas, et recitavi illud ad Galatas:
*Manifesta autem sunt opera carnis, quae sunt fornica-
tiones, inmunditiae, luxuriae, idolorum servitus, veneficia,
inimicitiae, contentiones, aemulationes, animositates, dissensiones, haereses, invidiae, ebrietates, comissationes et
his similia ; quae praedico vobis, sicut praedixi, quoniam
qui talia agunt, regnum dei non possidebunt.* Post quae

---

a 1 Cor. xi. 20-22.
b Matt. vii. 16.　　　　*c* Gal. v. 19-21.

ye come together into one place, that is not to eat
the Lord's Supper; for in eating every one taketh
before other his own supper, and one is hungry, and
another is drunken. What ? have ye not houses to
eat and to drink in ? or despise ye the Church of
God ? " *a* After reading that, I earnestly pressed
the point that it was not right that even decorous
and sober feasts should be held in church, for the
Apostle did not say, " Have ye not houses of your own
to get drunk in ? " as though it were only in church
that getting drunk was not allowed ; what he did say
was " to eat and to drink in," a seemly enough
action, provided it be done outside the church by
those who have houses in which they can be refreshed by the necessary food. And yet what
straits we had fallen into, what corrupt times and
lax morals, that we could not yet hope for decorous
feasts, but only that the dominion of drunkenness
should be confined to the home.

I mentioned, too, a passage in the Gospels which *b*
I had expounded the day before, in which it is said
of false prophets, " By their fruits ye shall know
them." *b* Then I reminded them that there " fruits "
meant only " works." Next I asked them what
fruits drunkenness was reckoned among, repeating to
them that passage in Galatians, " Now the works of
the flesh are manifest, which are these : adultery,
fornication, uncleanness, lasciviousness, idolatry,
witchcraft, hatred, variance, emulations, wrath,
strife, seditions, heresies, envyings, drunkenness,
revellings, and such like ; of the which I tell you,
as I have told you in time past, that they which
do such things shall not inherit the kingdom of
God." *c* After these words, I asked them how, when

E

verba interrogavi quo modo de fructu ebrietatis agnosceremur christiani, quos de fructibus agnosci dominus iussit. Adiunxi etiam legendum quod sequitur: *Fructus autem spiritus est caritas, gaudium, pax, longanimitas, benignitas, bonitas, fides, mansuetudo, continentia*, egique ut considerarent quam esset pudendum atque plangendum, quod de illis fructibus carnis non solum privatim vivere, sed etiam honorem ecclesiae deferre cuperent et, si potestas daretur, totum tam magnae basilicae spatium turbis epulantium ebriorumque complerent; de spiritalibus autem fructibus ad quos et divinarum scripturarum auctoritate et nostris gemitibus invitarentur, nolunt adferre deo munera et his potissimum celebrare festa sanctorum.

7 Quibus peractis, codicem reddidi et imperata oratione, quantum valui et quantum me ipsum periculum urguebat et vires subministrare dominus dignabatur, constitui eis ante oculos commune periculum, et ipsorum qui nobis commissi essent, et nostrum, qui de illis rationem reddituri essemus pastorum principi, per cuius humilitatem, insignes contumelias, alapas et sputus in faciem et palmas et spineam coronam et crucem ac sanguinem obsecravi ut, si se ipsi aliquid offendissent, vel nostri misererentur et cogitarent venerabilis senis Valerii circa me ineffabilem caritatem, qui mihi tractandi verba veritatis tam periculosum onus non dubitarit propter

---

[a] Gal. v. 22-23.

[b] A better rendering than "bidding the people pray." The congregation sometimes exercised the right of demanding a sermon.

[c] Probably this is the right meaning here, not "pierced

the Lord has enjoined that Christians be recognized by their fruits, we could ever be so recognized by the fruits of drunkenness. I added that we must read too the verse that follows, " But the fruit of the Spirit is love, joy, peace, long-suffering, gentleness, goodness, faith, meekness, temperance," [a] and I urged them to consider how shameful and lamentable it was that they were not satisfied with practising those fruits of the flesh at home, but actually wanted to honour the church with them and, if they were only allowed, to fill up all the space of a church of this great size with crowds of banqueters and drunkards ; yet they would not offer to God the tribute of those spiritual fruits, to which they were invited both by the authority of the Holy Scriptures and by our groanings, and with them rather than any others celebrate the saints' days.

After that, I handed back the manuscript and, [7] being asked to speak,[b] I set before their eyes, as far as I could and as far as the danger itself impelled me and the Lord was pleased to afford me strength, our common danger, theirs, who were entrusted to our care, as well as ours, who were to render an account of them to the Chief Shepherd. I implored them by His humiliation, the unequalled insults, buffetings, and spitting on the face that He endured, by the blows on His face [c] and His crown of thorns and cross and blood, to have pity at least for me, if they had any reason for personal displeasure, and to consider the inexpressible affection felt for me by the venerable Senior, Valerius, who for their sakes had not hesitated to lay upon me the dangerous burden of expounding

hands." *Cf.* Vulgate, Matt. xxvi. 67 " alii palmas in faciem ei dederunt."

eos inponere, eisque saepe dixerit quod orationes eius
exauditae essent de nostro adventu, quos non utique
ad communem mortem vel spectaculum mortis illorum
sed ad communem conatum in aeternam vitam ad
se venisse laetatus est. Postremo etiam dixi certum
esse me et fidere in eum qui mentiri nescit, qui per
os prophetae sui pollicitus est de domino nostro Iesu
Christo dicens : *Si reliquerint filii eius legem meam
et in praeceptis meis non ambulaverint, si iustificationes
meas profanaverint, visitabo in virga facinora eorum et
in flagellis delicta eorum ; misericordiam autem meam
non auferam*, in eum ergo me fidere, quod, si haec
tanta quae sibi essent lecta et dicta, contemnerent,
visitaturus esset in virga et in flagello nec eos per-
missurus cum hoc mundo damnari. In qua con-
questione sic actum ut pro negotii atque periculi
magnitudine tutor et gubernator noster animos facul-
tatemque praebebat. Non ego illorum lacrimas meis
lacrimis movi, sed cum talia dicerentur, fateor,
eorum fletu praeventus meum abstinere non potui.
Et cum iam pariter flevissemus, plenissima spe cor-
rectionis illorum finis sermonis mei factus est.

8   Postridie vero, cum inluxisset dies cui solebant
fauces ventresque se parare, nuntiatur mihi non-
nullos eorum etiam, qui sermoni aderant, nondum a
murmuratione cessasse tantumque in eis valere vim
pessimae consuetudinis, ut eius tantum voce ute-
rentur et dicerent : " Quare modo ? Non enim

---

[a] This was contrary to the custom of the western church :
in episcopal churches presbyters were forbidden to preach.
For his violation of this rule Augustine was severely criticized
by some of his colleagues, but Jerome describes the re-
striction as " a very bad practice " (Ep. lii.).

[b] Ps. lxxxviii. 31-34.

the words of truth [a] and had often said to them that my coming had been an answer to his prayers ; but his rejoicing was surely that I had come to him not to share or to behold their death, but to share their efforts towards eternal life. Finally, I told them that I had trust and confidence in Him who cannot lie, who made by the mouth of His prophet a promise concerning our Lord Jesus Christ, in the words, " If His children forsake My law and walk not in My judgements ; if they break My statutes and keep not My commandments ; then will I visit their transgression with the rod and their iniquity with stripes ; nevertheless My loving-kindness will I not utterly take from Him " [b]—I had confidence therefore in Him that if they despised the grave warnings that had been read and addressed to them, He would visit them with the rod and with stripes, but would not leave them to condemnation along with the world. Throughout this protest I acted as our Defender and Ruler, to meet the importance of the matter and the greatness of the danger, provided me with courage and ability. I did not move them to weep by first weeping myself, but while such remarks were being addressed to them, their own tears came first and I confess that I could not keep back my own. After we had thus wept together, I concluded my sermon in the full anticipation of their amendment.

But on the morrow, when the day dawned for 8 which it was the habit of their throats and stomachs to prepare, I was told that some of those who had been present at my sermon had not even then given over complaining, and were so much under the influence of that vile custom that they were speaking in terms of it alone and saying, " Why thus late in

antea, qui haec non prohibuerunt, Christiani non
erant." Quo audito, quas sicut maiores commovendi
eos machinas praepararem, omnino nesciebam; disponebam tamen, si perseverandum putarent, lecto
illo loco de propheta Ezechiele : "Explorator absol-
vitur, si periculum denuntiaverit, etiam si illi, quibus denuntiatur, cavere noluerint," vestimenta mea
excutere atque discedere. Tum vero dominus ostendit quod nos non deserat, et quibus modis, in se ut
praesumamus, hortetur ; namque ante horam, qua
exhedram ascenderemus, ingressi sunt ad me idem
ipsi, quos audieram de oppugnatione vetustae consuetudinis fuisse conquestos. Quos blande acceptos
paucis verbis in sententiam sanam transtuli. Atque
ubi ventum est ad tempus disputationis, omissa lectione quam praeparaveram, quia necessaria iam non
videbatur, de hac ipsa quaestione pauca disserui,
nihil nos nec brevius nec verius posse adferre adversus eos qui dicunt : " Quare modo ? " nisi et nos
dicamus : " Vel modo."

9 Verum tamen ne illi qui ante nos tam manifesta
inperitae multitudinis crimina vel permiserunt vel
prohibere non ausi sunt, aliqua a nobis affici contumelia viderentur, exposui eis, qua necessitate ista
in ecclesia viderentur exorta. Scilicet post persecu-

---

a Cf. Ezek. xxxiii. 9.

b *Exedrae*, ἐξέδραι, were originally recesses, rectangular or
semi-circular, opening out of the church, then, later, rooms
with seats. Here and elsewhere in Augustine the word seems
to mean that part of the church which had seats and projected
outwards, *i.e.* the portion later known as " choir " or " apse."
It was raised above the nave (see *Civ. Dei*, 22. 8, and *De
Gest. c. Emer.* 1. 1), and the clergy sat there during sermon,

the day? Those who allowed it in times past were
surely not unchristian." On hearing this, I was
quite at a loss what weapons to prepare that would
have a greater effect on them, but still, if they
decided to continue in that frame of mind, I was
intending to read that passage from the prophet
Ezekiel, "The watchman is absolved if he has
uttered a warning of the danger, even if those whom
he has warned have not cared to take precaution,"[a]
and to shake my garments and depart. But at that
point the Lord showed that He does not forsake us,
and taught me the means He takes to encourage
us to put our trust in Him, for before the time at
which I had to mount into the choir,[b] those same
individuals came in to me who, as I had learned, had
complained of my attack upon their long-established
custom. I received them graciously, and needed only
a few words to bring them round to a sound state of
mind. And when it came to the time for my dis-
course, I left out the reading I had prepared, since
it no longer appeared to be needed, and made a few
remarks about the very point they had raised, stating
that we could put forward against those who say
"Why thus late in the day?" no briefer and truer
reply than to imitate them and say, "Yes, thus late
in the day."

Yet to avoid the appearance of casting any slight 9
upon those who in earlier times either allowed, or
did not venture to forbid, the ignorant mob to
perpetrate these open sins, I explained to them the
critical circumstances in which those practices
apparently arose in the Church. When peace was

while the people stood. It was more commonly called the
βῆμα, bema, or suggestum.

tiones tam multas tamque vehementes cum facta
pace turbae gentilium in christianum nomen venire
cupientes hoc impedirentur, quod dies festos cum
idolis suis solerent in abundantia epularum et ebrietate consumere, nec facile ab his perniciosissimis sed
tamen vetustissimis voluptatibus se possent abstinere,
visum fuisse maioribus nostris ut huic infirmitatis
parti interim parceretur diesque festos post eos quos
relinquebant, alios in honorem sanctorum martyrum
vel non simili sacrilegio quamvis simili luxu cele-
brarent ; iam Christi nomine conligatis et tantae auctoritatis iugo subditis salutaria sobrietatis praecepta
traderentur, quibus iam propter praecipientis honorem ac timorem resistere non valerent. Quocirca
iam tempus esse, ut, qui non se audent negare
christianos, secundum Christi voluntatem vivere incipiant, ut ea quae, ut essent christiani, concessa
sunt, cum christiani sunt, respuantur.

10   Deinde hortatus sum, ut transmarinarum ecclesiarum, in quibus partim ista recepta numquam sunt,
partim iam per bonos rectores populo obtemperante
correcta, imitatores esse vellemus. Et quoniam de
basilica beati apostoli Petri cotidianae vinulentiae
proferebantur exempla, dixi primo audisse nos saepe
esse prohibitum, sed quod remotus sit locus ab epi-

---

^a The best-known example of this spirit of compromise is
that of Pope Gregory the Great, who wrote to St. Augustine
of Canterbury that the pagan practices of converts must be
checked only by degrees (Bede, *Hist. Eccl.* i. 30, with Plummer's
good note, and Bright, *Chapters in Early English Church
History*, pp. 78 ff.). Similar indulgence was common, although
opposition to all compromise was occasionally urged, for
example, by Vigilantius.

^b As at Milan, where the custom had been opposed by
St. Ambrose, as Monnica, the mother of Augustine, had dis-

made after many violent persecutions, crowds of pagans were anxious to come over to the Christian name but were hindered by the fact that they were accustomed to spend their feast-days with their idols in drunkenness and excessive banqueting and could not easily abstain from those baneful but long-established pleasures. So our predecessors thought it good to make concessions for the time being to those weaker brethren, and to let them celebrate in honour of the holy martyrs other feast-days, in place of those they were giving up, unlike them, at any rate, in profanation, though like them in excess. Now that they were bound together by the name of Christ and submissive to the yoke of His great authority, they must inherit the wholesome rules of sobriety, and these they could not oppose because of their veneration and fear for Him whose rules they were. It was now high time, therefore, for such as had not the courage to deny that they were Christians, to begin to live according to the will of Christ, casting behind them, now that they were Christians, the concessions made to induce them to become Christians.[a]

Then I urged them to undertake to follow the example of the churches overseas, in some of which those practices were never admitted, while in others they had already been corrected by the agency of good leaders and compliance on the part of the people.[b] And as examples of daily excess in drinking were produced to me from the Church of the blessed apostle Peter, I stated in the first place that I had heard that they had often been forbidden, but since

covered when she went to make the customary offerings on the martyrs' tombs. See the account in *Confessions*, bk. vi. 2.

scopi conversatione et in tanta civitate magna sit
carnalium multitudo peregrinis praesertim, qui novi
subinde veniunt, tanto violentius quanto inscitius
illam consuetudinem retinentibus, tam immanem
pestem nondum compesci sedarique potuisse. Verum
tamen nos si Petrum apostolum honoraremus, debere
praecepta eius audire et multo devotius epistulam
in qua voluntas eius apparet, quam basilicam in qua
non apparet, intueri ; statimque accepto codice recitavi ubi ait : *Christo enim passo pro nobis per carnem
et vos eadem cogitatione armamini, quia qui passus est
carne, desiit a carne, ut iam non hominum desideriis
sed voluntate dei reliquum tempus in carne vivat. Sufficit
enim vobis praeteritum tempus voluntate hominum per-
fecisse ambulantes in libidinibus, desideriis, ebrietate,
comissationibus et nefandis idolorum servitutibus.* Quibus gestis, cum omnes uno animo in bonam voluntatem
ire contempta mala consuetudine cernerem, hortatus
sum ut meridiano tempore divinis lectionibus et
psalmis interessent ; ita illum diem multo mundius
atque sincerius placere celebrandum et certe de
multitudine convenientium facile posse apparere,
qui mentem et qui ventrem sequeretur. Ita lectis
omnibus sermo terminatus est.

11   Pomeridiano autem die maior quam ante meridiem

---

^a His residence was on the other side of the city, in the
Lateran palace, presented to the Church by the Emperor
Constantine. There the Popes continued to reside until the
end of the fourteenth century.
    ^b 1 Pet. iv. 1-3.

the place was at a distance from the bishop's control [a]
and in a city of that size there was a great crowd
of carnally-minded people, the pilgrims especially,
of whom fresh batches were continually arriving,
clinging to that custom with a vehemence pro-
portionate to their unenlightenment, it had not yet
been possible to restrain and repress such a monstrous
disorder.   But yet, if we honoured the apostle Peter,
we personally should give ear to his counsels and
pay much more zealous attention to the Epistle
in which his intention is revealed, than to his
church, in which it is not, and straightway, taking
up the manuscript, I read the passage where he
says, "Forasmuch then as Christ hath suffered for
us in the flesh, arm yourselves likewise with the
same mind, for he that hath suffered in the
flesh hath ceased from sin, that he no longer
should live the rest of his time in the flesh to the
lusts of men, but to the will of God. For the
time past of our life may suffice us to have wrought
the will of the Gentiles, when we walked in lasciviousness, lusts, excess of wine, revellings, banquetings
and abominable idolatries." [b]   After that, when I
perceived that all with one mind were turning to
a right disposition and spurning their wretched
custom, I enjoined them to attend at mid-day for
Scripture reading and singing of psalms : it was our
purpose in that way to celebrate that day with
much more decency and purity, and it could easily
be seen, from the number of those who assembled,
who was following reason and who was the slave of
appetite.   So, when everything had been read, my
sermon concluded.

In the afternoon a greater crowd attended than 11

adfuit multitudo et usque ad horam qua cum episcopo egrederemur, legebatur alternatim et psalle-
batur ; nobisque egressis duo psalmi lecti sunt.
Deinde me invitum, qui iam cupiebam peractum esse
tam periculosum diem, iussum compulit senex ut
aliquid eis loquerer. Habui brevem sermonem, quo
gratias agerem deo, et quoniam in haereticorum
basilica audiebamus ab eis solita convivia celebrata,
cum adhuc etiam eo ipso tempore quo a nobis ista
gerebantur, illi in poculis perdurarent, dixi diei pulchritudinem noctis comparatione decorari et colorem
candidum nigri vicinitate gratiorem ; ita nostrum
spiritalis celebrationis conventum minus fortasse
futurum fuisse iucundum, nisi ex alia parte carnalis
ingurgitatio conferretur, hortatusque sum ut tales
epulas instanter appeterent, si gustassent quam
suavis est dominus ; illis autem esse metuendum, qui
tamquam primum sectantur quod aliquando de-
struetur, cum quisque comes efficiatur eius rei quam
colit, insultaritque apostolus talibus dicens : *Quorum
deus venter*, cum idem alio loco dixerit : *Esca ventri
et venter escis ; deus autem et hunc et illas evacuabit.*
Nos proinde oportere id sequi quod non evacuatur,
quod remotissimum a carnis affectu spiritus sanctifi-
catione retinetur. Atque in hanc sententiam pro
tempore cum ea quae dominus suggerere dignatus

---

a The Donatists.   *b* Phil. iii. 19.   *c* 1 Cor. vi. 13.

in the forenoon, and reading and singing went on
alternately until the hour when I was to come out
with the bishop. When we came out, two psalms
were read, then the Senior compelled me by express
injunction to say something to them, though it was
against my will, for by this time I was longing for
the end of so critical a day. I gave a short address
with the object of rendering thanks to God, and as
we heard in the church of the heretics [a] the noise of
the usual feasting that they were celebrating (for
even at the very time when we were so engaged
they were still lingering in their cups), I remarked
that the beauty of the day was enhanced by comparison with the night and that a white colour
was more pleasing alongside of a black; thus our
gathering for a spiritual celebration would perhaps
have been less gratifying without the contrast of
gluttonous carnality from other quarters. And I
exhorted them that such were the banquets that they
should eagerly seek after, if they had tasted how
sweet the Lord is, but that fear was to be the lot
of those who seek as the chief object of desire
anything that would some day be destroyed. For
each man is made to share the fate of that which he
worships, and such people had been mocked by the
Apostle in the words, " whose god is their belly," [b]
since in another place he has used the words : " Meats
for the belly and the belly for meats, but God shall
destroy both it and them." [c] It was therefore our
duty to follow after that which is not to be destroyed,
which through the sanctification of the spirit is kept
far removed from what befalls the flesh. And so,
when what the Lord was pleased to suggest had been
for the occasion spoken along those lines, the usual

est, dicta essent, acta sunt vespertina quae cotidie solent, nobisque cum episcopo recedentibus fratres eodem loco hymnos dixerunt non parva multitudine utriusque sexus[1] ad obscuratum diem manente atque psallente.

12 Digessi vobis, quantum breviter potui, quod vos audire desiderasse quis dubitaverit ? Orate ut a conatibus nostris omnia scandala et omnia taedia deus dignetur avertere. Magna sane ex parte vobiscum requiescimus cum alacritate fervoris, quia spiritalis ecclesiae Tagastensium tam crebra nobis dona nuntiantur. Navis cum fratribus nondum venit. Apud Asnam, ubi est presbyter frater Argentius, Circumcelliones invadentes basilicam nostram altare comminuerunt. Causa nunc agitur, quae ut pacate agatur et ut ecclesiam catholicam decet ad opprimendas linguas haereseos inpacatae, multum vos petimus ut oretis. Epistulam Asiarchae misimus. Beatissimi perseveretis in domino memores nostri. Amen.

[1] sexus *addidit Goldbacher.*

---

[a] Daily services had been the rule in Jerusalem until the fall of the city, but they were not practised from then until the fourth century, when the cessation of persecution and the influence of monastic use caused their revival.

[b] Apparently in the vicinity of Hippo, but the exact site is unknown.

[c] These were brigand companies of the Donatist party, who for long terrorized Numidia with their organized violence and bloodthirstiness. Some of their cruel deeds are described in later letters (see pp. 128 and 162).

daily evening service [a] was held and we retired with
the bishop, while the brethren repeated hymns there
and a considerable crowd of both sexes remained and
engaged in singing until darkness fell.

I have set forth for you, as briefly as I could, what 12
I am sure you were anxious to hear. Pray that God
will graciously protect my efforts from providing any
cause of offence or any distress.   In no small measure
we share with lively warmth of affection in your con-
tentment that such frequent gifts to us from the
spiritually-minded church of Tagaste are intimated.
The ship with the brethren has not yet arrived.   At
Asna,[b] where the priest is brother Argentius, the
Circumcellions[c] have broken into our church and
smashed the altar.   The case is at present being tried ;
we earnestly beg you to pray that the trial may
give no provocation, and may serve, as becomes the
Catholic Church, to check the tongue of provocative
heresy.   I have sent a letter to the Asiarch.[d]

May ye remain steadfast in the Lord, brethren,
in all blessedness, and forget us not !   Amen.

---

[d] The Asiarchs were originally the chief presidents of the
religious rites in the Roman province Asia, whose duties
consisted in giving every year games and theatrical amuse-
ments in honour of the Roman emperor and the gods.
The religious character of the office disappeared with the
establishment of Christianity.   The word occurs in Acts
xix. 31 and in the letter of the Church of Smyrna about the
martyrdom of Polycarp.   Here the presence of the word is
surprising, unless it be either a synonym for " pro-consul "
or a proper name.   There is an excellent account of the
pagan Asiarchate in Lightfoot, *Apostolic Fathers*, pt. ii.
vol. iii. pp. 404-415.

ST. AUGUSTINE

No. 11 (Ep. XXXIV)

DOMINO EXIMIO MERITOQUE SUSCIPIENDO ATQUE HONORABILI FRATRI EUSEBIO AUGUSTINUS

1 Scit deus, cui manifesta sunt arcana cordis humani, quantum pacem diligo Christianam, tantum me moveri sacrilegis eorum factis qui in eius dissensione indigne atque impie perseverant, eumque motum animi mei esse pacificum neque me id agere ut ad communionem catholicam quisquam cogatur invitus, sed ut omnibus errantibus aperta veritas declaretur et per nostrum ministerium deo iuvante manifestata se amplectendam atque sectandam satis ipsa persuadeat.

2 Quid enim execrabilius, quaeso te, ut alia taceam, quam id quod nunc accidit? Corripitur ab episcopo suo iuvenis crebris caedibus matris insanus et impias manus nec illis diebus cum etiam severitas legum sceleratissimis parcit, a visceribus unde natus est, revocans; minatur eidem matri se in partem Donati translaturum et eam quam incredibili furore solet caedere, perempturum; minatur ei, transit ad partem Donati, rebaptizatur furens et in maternum sanguinem fremens albis vestibus candidatur; constituitur intra cancellos eminens atque conspicuus

---

ᵃ At Easter, when, since the edicts of Valentinian in 367, the prisons were opened and all prisoners released, except those guilty of more serious crimes (*Cod. Theod.* lib. ix. tit. 38. 3).

No. 11 (Ep. XXXIV)

(A.D. 396)

AUGUSTINE TO BROTHER EUSEBIUS, MY DIS-
TINGUISHED LORD, WORTHY OF ALL
ESTEEM AND HONOUR

God knows (for to Him the secrets of the human **1**
heart are manifest) that, as I love Christian peace,
so I am disturbed by the profane deeds of those
who basely and impiously persist in dissenting from
it; He knows too that my indignation springs from
a desire for peace and that my object is not to drive
anyone into the Catholic communion against his will,
but to have the naked truth made known to all who
are astray and revealed by God's help through my
ministry, commending itself so well that they may
embrace and follow it.

I pass over other matters and ask you what could **2**
be more abominable than what has now happened?
A young man is rebuked by his bishop for repeatedly
thrashing his mother like a madman and for not with-
holding his unfilial hands from the body that gave
him birth even on those days when the very harshness of the law shows mercy to the vilest criminals.[a]
He threatens his mother to go over to the Donatist
party and to do her to death, used as he is to thrash
her with unbelievable ferocity. He makes this
threat, goes over to the Donatist party, receives re-
baptism while still in his frenzy, and is arrayed in
the white vestments of a candidate for baptism
while still raging for his mother's blood. Within
the altar-rails he is set up in a prominent and conspicuous position and, while planning matricide,

93

et omnium gementium oculis matricidii meditator tamquam renovatus opponitur.

3 Haecine tandem tibi placent, vir gravissime? Nequaquam hoc de te crediderim; novi considerationem tuam. Caeditur mater carnalis in membris, quibus genuit et nutrivit ingratum; prohibet hoc ecclesia, mater spiritalis; caeditur et ipsa in sacramentis, quibus genuit et nutrivit ingratum. Nonne tibi videtur dixisse parricidaliter frendens: "Quid faciam ecclesiae, quae me prohibet caedere matrem meam? Inveni quid faciam: iniuriis, quibus potest, etiam ipsa feriatur; fiat in me aliquid unde membra eius doleant; eundum[1] mihi ad eos qui noverunt exsufflare gratiam in qua ibi natus sum, destruere formam quam in utero eius accepi; ambas matres meas saevis cruciatibus torqueam; quae me posterior peperit, efferat prior; ad huius dolorem spiritaliter moriar, ad illius caedem carnaliter vivam." Quid aliud expectamus, vir honorabilis Eusebi, nisi ut in miseram mulierem senectute decrepitam, viduitate destitutam, a cuius caedibus in catholica prohibebatur, iam Donatista securus armetur? Quid enim aliud furibundo corde concepit, cum diceret matri: "Transferam me in partem Donati et bibam sanguinem tuum"? Ecce iam conscientia cruentus, veste dealbatus perficit partem pollicitationis suae; restat pars altera, ut matris sanguinem bibat. Si ergo

---

[1] eundum *scripsi*: vadam *mss.*

he is exhibited to the eyes of all the disgusted congregation as a regenerate man.

Do you, a man of sober judgement, really approve **3** of this ? I should never believe it of you ; I know how sensible a man you are. A mother after the flesh is beaten on the body which bore and nurtured her thankless son ; when the Church, his spiritual mother, forbids this, she too is beaten in her sacraments, by which she bore and nurtured her thankless son. Don't you think it is as if he had said in his rage for a parent's blood, " What shall I do to the Church, which forbids my beating my mother ? I know what I will do. I will wound her too with every possible insult ; I will commit anything that will cause her members pain ; I will betake me to those who are experienced in sneering at the grace in which she gave me birth, in destroying the form I received in her womb ; with cruel agonies let me rack both these mothers of mine. Let the one who gave me second birth be the first to give me burial ; for her grief I shall seek spiritual death, but for the other's death I shall continue my earthly life." What else can we expect, my esteemed Eusebius, than this, that the man who, while he was in the Catholic Church, was restrained from thrashing the unfortunate woman, crippled with age and a lonely widow, will be free to employ his weapons against her, now that he is a Donatist ? What other purpose was in his raving heart when he said to his mother, " I will go over to the Donatist party and will drink your blood " ? See now, with blood-stained conscience, but arrayed in white vestments, he has carried out one part of his threat ; the second part, the drinking of his mother's blood, awaits fulfilment.

placent ista, urgeatur a clericis et sanctificatoribus
suis ut intra octavas suas totum quod vovit exsolvat.

4   Potens est quidem dextera domini quae furorem
illius a misera vidua et desolata compescat et eum,
quibus modis novit, a tam scelerata dispositione
deterreat. Verum tamen ego tanto animi dolore
percussus quid facerem, nisi saltem loquerer? An
vero ista illi faciunt et mihi dicitur : Tace ? Avertat
a me dominus hanc amentiam, ut, cum ipse mihi
imperet per apostolum suum et dicat ab episcopo
refelli oportere docentes, quae non oportet, ego illorum
indignationibus territus taceam. Quod enim publicis gestis haerere volui tam sacrilegum nefas, ad
hoc utique volui, ne me quisquam maxime in aliis
civitatibus, ubi opportunum fuerit, ista deplorantem
fingere aliquid arbitretur, quando etiam apud ipsam
Hipponem iam dicitur non hoc Proculianum mandasse, quod publicum renuntiavit officium.

5   Quid autem modestius agere possumus, quam ut
tam gravem causam per te tamen agam, virum et
clarissima dignitate praeditum et considerantissima
voluntate tranquillum ? Peto igitur, sicut iam petivi
per fratres nostros, bonos atque honestos viros, quos
ad tuam eximietatem misi, ut quaerere digneris
utrum Proculiani presbyter Victor non hoc ab epi-

---

  a The eight days between Easter and the Sunday following, during which time neophytes wore their white garments.
These were put off on the first Sunday after Easter, which
was hence called *Dominica in albis* or *Dies neophytorum,*
and the newly baptized were then introduced to the Church
as full members.

  b Tit. i. 11.

  c Proculianus was the Donatist bishop of Hippo, a troublesome neighbour to Augustine until his death about 411. The

If that is the kind of thing you approve of, let your clergy and those who are to carry through his sanctification instigate him to fulfil all his vow within his eight days.[a]

But the Lord's right hand is strong to restrain his 4 rage from that unfortunate and lonely widow and, by means best known to Himself, to frighten him from his criminal purpose. Yet what was I to do, when I was so pained and indignant, but at least speak my mind ? Are they, indeed, to do such things and I be told to hold my peace ? The Lord deliver me from such folly, that when, by His apostle, He commands me and says that those who teach what they ought not, ought to be rebuked[b] by the bishop, I should be silent from dread of their indignation. In wanting this heinous crime to find permanent record in the public registers, my intention surely was to prevent anyone, especially in other towns where I may have a chance to deplore these deeds, from imagining that I am inventing any detail, for even here in Hippo it is already being said that Proculianus[c] did not issue the order which the public officials have recorded as his.

What more temperate course could we pursue 5 than to take action in a matter of such seriousness through you, a man invested with the most eminent rank and, at the same time, possessing great circumspection, goodwill and equanimity ? So I beseech you, as I have already done by our brethren, good and honourable men, whom I sent to your Excellency, to have the kindness to inquire whether it was not this order of Proculianus recorded by the

"order" is apparently that made by Proculianus to the priest Victor to receive the young man in question.

scopo suo mandatum acceperit, quod officio publico
renuntiavit, an forte, cum et ipse Victor aliud dixerit,
falsum illi apud acta prosecuti sint, cum sint com-
munionis eiusdem; aut, si consentit ut ipsam totam
quaestionem dissensionis nostrae placide pertracte-
mus, ut error qui iam manifestus est, manifestius
innotescat, libenter amplector. Audivi enim quod
dixerit, ut sine tumultu populari adsint nobiscum
deni ex utraque parte graves et honesti viri, et secundum scripturas quid in vero sit perquiramus. Nam
illud quod rursus eum dixisse nonnulli ad me per-
tulerunt, cur non ierim Constantinam, quando ibi
plures ipsi erant, vel me debere ire Mileum, quod
illic, sicut perhibent, concilium proxime habituri
sunt, ridiculum est dicere, quasi ad me pertineat
cura propria nisi Hipponiensis ecclesiae. Mihi tota
huius quaestionis ratio maxime cum Proculiano est.
Sed si forte inparem se putat, cuius voluerit collegae
sui inploret auxilium. In aliis enim civitatibus
tantum agimus quod ad ecclesiam pertinet, quantum vel nos permittunt vel nobis inponunt earundem
civitatium episcopi, fratres et consacerdotes nostri.

6 Quamquam et iste qui se tot annorum episcopum
dicit, quid in me tirone timeat quominus mecum
velit conferre sermonem, non satis intellego : si

ᵃ Better known under its earlier name, Cirta, capital of
the territory of King Syphax (Livy xxx. 12 and 44), and
associated with the names of Masinissa, Adherbal and
Micipsa. It suffered in a civil war in A.D. 308, but was
restored by the Emperor Constantine, who gave it his name.
It had a bishop since at least 256.

ᵇ Now Mila, about ten miles west of Constantine: the

public officials that the priest Victor received from
his bishop, or whether, since Victor himself has
denied it, they have fathered a lie upon him in the
public documents, although they belong to the same
religious body. Otherwise, if he agrees that we
should without heat discuss the whole question at
issue between us to the end that the error, which is
already clear, may be more clearly brought to light,
I gladly embrace the opportunity. I have heard of
his proposal that without any popular uproar we
should examine what is true according to the Scriptures, in the presence of ten weighty and honourable
men from each side. That alternative proposal,
which some reported to me as his, that I should
go to Constantine,[a] since his followers were more
numerous there, or that I ought to go to Milevis,[b]
because there, people say, they are going to hold a
council soon, it is absurd to make, as if any particular
charge concerned me except the church of Hippo.
The whole issue of this inquiry lies between me
and Proculianus above all, but if he considers himself unequal to it, let him implore the aid of any
colleague of his that he chooses. For in other towns
we deal with matters concerning the Church only so
far as the bishops of those towns, our brethren and
fellow-priests, allow us or enjoin upon us.

And yet, I do not quite see what he, who proclaims **6**
himself a bishop of such long standing, is afraid of
in a novice such as I am, to shrink from a conference

form of the name varies, the inscriptions having *Milev*
(indeclinable). Optatus, author of a work against the
Donatists, was a bishop there, and it was the birthplace of
the Donatist Faustus against whom Augustine wrote the
Contra Faustum.

doctrinam liberalium litterarum, quas forte ipse aut
non didicit aut minus didicit, quid hoc pertinet ad
eam quaestionem quae vel de sanctis scripturis vel
documentis ecclesiasticis aut publicis discutienda est,
in quibus ille per tot annos versatur, unde in eis
deberet esse peritior ? Postremo est hic frater et
collega meus Samsucius, episcopus Turrensis ecclesiae, qui nullas tales didicit quales iste dicitur
formidare ; ipse adsit, agat cum illo ; rogabo eum et,
ut confido in nomine Christi, facile mihi concedet
ut suscipiat in hac re vicem meam, et eum dominus
pro veritate certantem, quamvis sermone inpolitum,
tamen vera fide eruditum, sicut confidimus, adiu-
vabit. Nulla ergo causa est cur ad alios nescio quos
differat, ne inter nos quod ad nos pertinet per-
agamus. Nec tamen, ut dixi, etiam illos defugio, si
eorum ipse poscit auxilium.

No. 12 (Ep. XXXVII)

DOMINO BEATISSIMO ET VENERABILITER SIN-
CERISSIMA CARITATE AMPLECTENDO PATRI
SIMPLICIANO AUGUSTINUS IN DOMINO
SALUTEM

1   Plenas bonorum gaudiorum litteras, quod sis

ᵃ Before his conversion in 386, Augustine had been a
grammaticus at Tagaste (*Confess.* iv. 7), and a teacher of
rhetoric at Carthage (*ib.* iv. 12 ; *C. Acad.* ii. 2, 3) and Milan
(*Confess.* v. 23).

ᵇ The exact site of Turres is not known, but it was probably
near Hippo. Samsucius is mentioned again in No. 21 *infra*.

ᶜ Simplicianus succeeded St. Ambrose in the see of Milan
in 397. He was instrumental in converting Victorinus and
was a close and honoured friend of Ambrose's. Augustine
met him at Milan in 386, and was much influenced by his
account of Victorinus's conversion (*Confess.* viii. 5). To him

with me. If it is my learning in liberal studies,[a] in which he perhaps is uninstructed or less instructed than I am, what has this to do with an inquiry which is to be conducted about Holy Scripture and ecclesiastical or public records? In these he has so many years of experience, which should make him all the better equipped. In the last resort, my brother and colleague, Samsucius, bishop of the Church of Turres,[b] is here, and he has acquired no such learning as your man is said to be afraid of; let him come and conduct it with him. I shall ask him, and I trust in the name of Christ he will readily agree to undertake to be my substitute in this. Though he is without any grace of eloquence, yet he is learned in the true faith, and the Lord will help him, I feel sure, in his contest for the truth. There is then no reason why he should refer me to any others, instead of settling between ourselves a matter which concerns ourselves. But still, as I said before, I do not decline to meet those others, if he himself demands their aid.

No. 12 (Ep. XXXVII)

(A.D. 397)

TO MY DEAR LORD AND FATHER SIMPLICIA-NUS,[c] WHOM I CHERISH WITH REVERENCE AND VERY GENUINE DEVOTION, AUGUSTINE SENDS GREETING IN THE LORD

Your letter has reached me, containing the good 1

Augustine dedicated his work *De Diversis Quaestionibus,* alluded to below, and he mentions him with great respect in several of his other works (*De Praedest.* 8; *De Dono Persev.* 52; *Civ. Dei,* x. 29). Simplicianus died in 400 and is honoured on August 16.

memor mei meque, ut soles, diligas magnaeque
gratulationi tibi sit, quicquid in me donorum suorum
dominus conferre dignatus est misericordia sua, non
meritis meis, missas munere tuae sanctitatis accepi.
In quibus affectum in me paternum tuo benignis-
simo corde non repentinum et novum hausi, sed
expertum plane cognitumque repetivi, domine beatissime et venerabiliter sincerissima caritate amplec-
tende.

2   Unde autem tanta exorta est felicitas litterario
labori nostro quo in librorum quorundam conscrip-
tione sudavimus, ut a tua dignatione legerentur, nisi
quia dominus, cui subdita est anima mea, consolari
voluit curas meas et a timore recreare, quo me in
talibus operibus necesse est esse sollicitum, necubi
forte indoctior vel incautior quamvis in planissimo
campo veritatis offendam ?   Cum enim tibi placet,
quod scribo, novi cui placeat, quoniam quis te in-
habitet novi.   Idem quippe omnium munerum spiri-
talium distributor atque largitor per tuam sententiam
confirmavit oboedientiam meam.   Quicquid enim
habent illa scripta delectatione tua dignum, in meo
ministerio *dixit deus* : " *Fiat*," *et factum est* ; in tua
vero approbatione *vidit deus, quia bonum est.*

3   Quaestiunculas sane quas mihi enodandas iubere
dignatus es, etsi mea tarditate implicatus non in-
tellegerem, tuis meritis adiutus aperirem.   Tantum
illud quaeso ut pro infirmitate mea deprecaris deum
et sive in his quibus me exercere benigne paterneque

ᵃ Gen. i. 3-4.

and gladdening news that you have not forgotten me but regard me with your customary affection, and that you take great pleasure in whatever gifts the Lord has deigned in His mercy, and not for my deserving, to bestow on me. It was gracious of your Holiness to write to me, and in your letter, my dear lord whom I cherish with reverence and very genuine devotion, I discerned once more that fatherly feeling for me which is no new or sudden refreshment to me from your generous heart, but a joy already experienced and appreciated.

The literary efforts I expended in the composing **2** of some books have been well recompensed by your Grace's reading them. Surely that came from no other source than the Lord's desire (for my soul is subject to Him) to appease my anxieties and abate the fear that of necessity harassed me in such an undertaking, of stumbling, through my comparative inexperience and imprudence, even in the straight and level path of truth. For when my writings find favour with you, I know with whom it does find favour, for I know who it is that dwells in you : He who apportions and bestows all spiritual gifts has by your verdict ratified my obedience. For whatever my writings contained that merited your satisfaction, it was God who said " Let it be done, and it was done," by me as His instrument, while in your approval it is the Lord who " saw that it was good." [a]

If my own dullness has prevented me from grasping **3** those problems you were good enough to bid me solve, still I could unravel them with your valued assistance. But I do beg you to intercede with God for me in my weakness, and not only to give the careful attention of a reader, but also to adopt

103

voluisti, sive in aliis, quaecumque nostra in tuas
sanctas manus forte pervenerint, quia sicut dei data
sic etiam mea errata cogito, non solum curam legentis
inpendas, sed etiam censuram corrigentis adsumas.

No. 13 (Ep. XXXVIII)

FRATRI PROFUTURO AUGUSTINUS

1 Secundum spiritum, quantum domino placet atque
ipse vires praebere dignatur, recte sumus ; corpore
autem ego in lecto sum ; nec ambulare enim nec stare
nec sedere possum rhagadis vel exochadis dolore et
tumore. Sed etiam sic, quoniam id domino placet,
quid aliud dicendum est, nisi quia recte sumus ?
Potius enim, si id nolumus quod ille vult, nos cul-
pandi sumus, quam ille non recte aliquid vel facere
vel sinere existimandus est. Nosti haec omnia ; sed
quia mihi es alter ego, quid libentius tecum loquerer,
nisi quod mecum loquor ? Commendamus ergo
sanctis orationibus tuis et dies et noctes nostras, ut
oretis pro nobis, ne diebus intemperanter utamur, ut
noctes aequo animo toleremus, ut, etiam si *ambulemus
in medio umbrae mortis*, nobiscum sit dominus, ne
timeamus mala.

---

^a See above, p. 56 note *b*.
^b *Rhagades* (*rhagas, rhagadia, rhagadium*) is a "tear,"
"rent," "hack" of the skin (ῥαγάς, ῥαγάδια); *exochas*,

the critical attitude of a reviewer, to any works of mine that happen to come into your holy hands, both those on which it was your kind and fatherly desire that I should try my hand, and any others. For I am fully conscious of God's gifts, and no less of my own mistakes.

No. 13 (Ep. XXXVIII)

(A.D. 397)

AUGUSTINE TO BROTHER PROFUTURUS[a]

In spirit I am well, so far as it is the Lord's good 1 pleasure and as He deigns to grant me strength; in body, I am confined to bed. I can neither walk nor stand nor sit down because of the pain and swelling of piles or tumours.[b] Yet even so, since that is the Lord's good pleasure, what else should I say than that I am well? If we do not like what pleases Him, we ourselves are rather to assume the blame than to imagine that He is wrong in what He either does or allows. This is all familiar to you, but since you are my second self, what can I say to you with more pleasure than what I say to myself? To your holy prayers then I commend both my nights and my days; pray for me, that I may not squander my days and that I may endure my nights with patience; pray that even if I walk in the valley of the shadow of death, the Lord may be with me that I may fear no evil.[c]

(*exochadium*) is a " pile " (ἐξοχάς, ἐξοχάδιον). The words are rare save in the medical writers.

[c] Ps. xxii. 4.

2 Quod senex Megalius defunctus sit, iam vos audisse
quis dubitet ? Erant autem a depositione corporis
eius, cum haec scriberem, dies ferme viginti quattuor.
Utrum iam videris, disponebas enim, successorem pri-
matus eius, si fieri potest, nosse volumus. Non desunt
scandala sed neque refugium ; non desunt maerores
sed neque consolationes. Atque inter haec quam
vigilandum sit, ne cuiusquam odium cordis intima
teneat neque sinat, ut *oremus deum in cubili nostro
clauso ostio*, sed adversus ipsum deum claudat ostium,
nosti optime, optime frater ; subrepit autem, dum
nulli irascenti ira sua videtur iniusta. Ita enim
inveterescens ira fit odium, dum quasi iusti doloris
admixta dulcedo diutius eam in vase detinet, donec
totum acescat vasque corrumpat. Quapropter multo
melius nec iuste cuiquam irascimur, quam velut iuste
irascendo in alicuius odium irae occulta facilitate
delabimur. In recipiendis enim hospitibus ignotis
solemus dicere multo esse melius malum hominem
perpeti quam forsitan per ignorantiam excludi bonum,
dum cavemus, ne recipiatur malus. Sed in affectibus
animi contra est. Nam incomparabiliter salubrius
est irae etiam iuste pulsanti non aperire penetrale
cordis quam admittere non facile recessuram et per-

ᵃ Bishop of Calama and Primate of Numidia, who two
years before this had ordained Augustine as coadjutor to
Valerius at Hippo, although earlier he had opposed Augustine's election and made serious charges against him, which
he was afterwards compelled to withdraw. Probably the
remembrance of these charges suggested to Augustine's mind
what follows on ill-feeling. Megalius's successor in Calama,
about forty miles south-west of Hippo, was Augustine's
biographer, Possidius.

ᵇ Matt. vi. 6.

ᶜ *Cf.* Cic. *Tusc.* iv. 9. 21, and for the " vessel " metaphor

NO. 13 (Ep. XXXVIII)

You will have already heard, I am sure, of the **2**
death of the Senior Megalius [a] ; as I write, it is
almost twenty-four days since his body was laid to
rest. Let me know, if possible, whether you have
seen his successor in the primacy, as was your intention. We are not without our trials, yet not without our refuge ; we are not without our sorrows,
yet not without comfort either. And you are
excellently well aware, my excellent brother, how
carefully amid such vexations we must watch that
no ill-feeling towards anyone takes possession of
our inmost heart and prevents us from entering into
our chamber, closing the door and praying to God, [b]
and even closes the door against God Himself.
Although no angry person thinks his own anger is
unjustified, it grows upon him, and anger that becomes inveterate in this way passes into hatred, [c] since
the pleasureableness that accompanies an apparently
justified resentment keeps it longer in the vessel
until the whole thing grows sour and spoils the
vessel. For this reason it is much better to be
angry with no one, even when it is justifiable, than
from apparently justified anger to slip by the
stealthy tendency of passion into hatred of anyone.
We have a proverbial saying about welcoming unknown guests that it is much better to endure a bad
man than through ignorance to risk shutting out a
good one from fear of welcoming a bad one. But
with our passions the opposite is true : for it is beyond
comparison a more beneficial thing not to open the
shrine of our heart at the knock of even justified
anger than to yield it entrance ; once in, it will not

Hor. *Ep.* i. 2. 54 " sincerum est nisi vas, quodcumque in-
fundis acescit."

venturam de surculo ad trabem. Audet quippe inpudenter etiam crescere citius, quam putatur. Non enim erubescit in tenebris, cum super eam sol occiderit.[a] Recolis certe, qua cura et quanta sollicitudine ista scripserim, si recolis quid mecum nuper in itinere quodam locutus sis.

3 Fratrem Severum[b] et qui cum eo sunt salutamus. Etiam ipsis fortasse scriberemus, si per festinationem perlatoris liceret. Peto autem, ut apud eundem fratrem nostrum Victorem,[c] cui ago etiam apud tuam sanctitatem gratias, quod Constantinam cum pergeret indicavit, petendo adiuves, propter negotium quod ipse novit, de quo gravissimum pondus pro ea re multum deprecantis Nectarii maioris patior, per Calamam[d] remeare ne gravetur ; sic enim promisit mihi. Vale.

No. 14 (Ep. XLII)

DOMINIS LAUDABILIBUS IN CHRISTO SANCTISSIMIS FRATRIBUS PAULINO ET THERASIAE AUGUSTINUS IN DOMINO SALUTEM

Num etiam hoc sperari aut expectari posset, ut

---

[a] *Cf.* Eph. iv. 26.

[b] Probably the Severus who became bishop of Milevis about A.D. 400. He was born in the same town as Augustine, and was a member of the same monastic community, and a life-long friend. He is mentioned later in Nos. 22, 25 and 29, and probably died about 426.   [c] See note *a* on p. 98.

[d] See No. 24 *infra*, p. 150 note *a*. Calama lay about fifty miles from Hippo ; it was an old Punic town, under the name Malaca, and was later a Roman colony. The modern name is Guelma.

[e] Paulinus is, after Prudentius, the most notable Christian Latin poet of the patristic age. Sprung from a wealthy patrician family in Aquitania, he renounced the world and,

easily be expelled, and it will grow from a sapling to a sturdy tree, since it boldly and shamelessly develops at an even greater speed than people imagine, for it is not put to shame in the darkness, when the sun has gone down upon it.[a] You can at any rate bethink you of the care and anxiety with which I write this, if you bethink you of your remarks on a recent journey we made together.

Give my greetings to brother Severus [b] and his company. I should perhaps be writing to them too, if the bearer's haste allowed it. I want, however, to express my thanks through your Holiness to our brother Victor for letting me know when he was going to Constantine.[c] Please help me by asking him if he would mind making his return journey by Calama, as he promised me he would, because of that business he knows of ; it is weighing very heavily on me, for the elder Nectarius [d] is very insistent about it. Good-bye.

No. 14 (Ep. XLII)

(A.D. 397)

TO PAULINUS AND THERASIA,[e] MY HOLY BROTHER AND SISTER IN CHRIST, WORTHY OF HONOUR AND PRAISE, AUGUSTINE SENDS GREETING IN THE LORD

Who could have expected or anticipated that I

with his wife, Therasia, a Spanish lady, established himself in 394 at Nola in Campania, where he lived a monastic life, built a church in honour of his patron saint, Felix, and spent his life and substance in good works, dying in 431. His extant works consist of 51 letters and 36 poems, marked by grace and fluency and revealing a pious and humble mind, already medieval in its outlook.

per fratrem Severum rescripta flagitaremus tam diu
tam ardentibus nobis a vestra caritate non reddita?
Quid est, qui duas aestates easdemque in Africa sitire
cogamur? Quid amplius dicam? O qui res vestras
cotidie donatis, debitum reddite. An forte, quod
adversus daemonicolas te scribere audieram atque
id opus vehementer desiderare me ostenderam, volens
perficere ac mittere tanto tempore ad nos epistulas
distulisti? Utinam saltem tam opima mensa iam
annosum ab stilo tuo ieiunium meum tandem accipias!
Quae si nondum parata est, non desinemus conqueri,
si nos, dum illud perficis, non interim reficis.

Salutate fratres, maxime Romanum et Agilem.
Hinc, qui nobiscum sunt, vos salutant et parum nobiscum irascuntur, si parum diligunt.

No. 15 (Ep. XLVIII)

DOMINO DILECTO ET EXOPTATISSIMO FRATRI
ET CONPRESBYTERO EUDOXIO ET QUI
TECUM SUNT FRATRIBUS AUGUSTINUS ET
QUI MECUM SUNT FRATRES IN DOMINO
SALUTEM

1   Quando quietem vestram cogitamus, quam habetis
in Christo, etiam nos, quamvis in laboribus variis
asperisque versemur, in vestra caritate requiescimus.

---

a Eudoxius was abbot of the monastery on the island of
Capraria, now Capraja, between Corsica and Tuscany, which
lies thirty miles away. In 398, after Gildo's rebellion, the
Roman punitive force embarked at Pisa and put in at
Cagliari in Sardinia; its leader, Gildo's brother, visited
Capraria and took on board some monks, who probably
brought a letter to Augustine and were now to take back his
reply (cf. Claudian, Bell. Gild. 415-424; Oros. Hist. vii.
36. 5).

should be demanding by brother Severus the replies
that you, my dear friends, have failed to send, though
I have waited for them so long and so eagerly?
What have I done, to be compelled to endure this
thirst for news for two whole summers, and that
too in Africa? What more shall I say? You are
making daily distribution of what wealth you have—
why not pay your debt to me? Can it be that you
have so long postponed writing to me from the desire
to finish and send the work which I had heard you
were writing against devil-worshippers and which I
had shown myself very anxious to peruse? I do hope
that it will at least be a groaning table at which you
eventually receive my hungry appetite, so long denied
the products of your pen. But if as yet it be not set and
ready, my complaints will give you no respite if, while
your book is finishing, you still leave me famishing.

Greet the brethren, especially Romanus and
Agilis. Those who are with me here greet you. If
they are less exasperated than I am, it is because their
affection for you is less than mine.

No. 15 (Ep. XLVIII)

(A.D. 398)

TO MY BELOVED LORD AND MOST LONGED
    FOR BROTHER AND FELLOW-PRIEST, EU-
    DOXIUS,[a] AND THE BRETHREN WHO ARE
    WITH YOU, AUGUSTINE AND THE BRETH-
    REN WHO ARE WITH ME SEND GREETING
    IN THE LORD

When we think of the peace that you enjoy in 1
Christ, we too, though harassed by manifold irksome
tasks, find peace in your affection. For we are one

Unum enim corpus sub uno capite sumus, ut et vos
in nobis negotiosi et nos in vobis otiosi simus, quia, *si
patitur unum membrum, compatiuntur omnia membra
et, si glorificatur unum membrum, congaudent omnia
membra.* Admonemus ergo et petimus et obsecramus
per Christi altissimam humilitatem et misericordis-
simam celsitudinem, ut nostri memores sitis in sanctis
orationibus vestris, quas vos vigilantiores et magis
sobrias habere credimus ; nostras enim saepe sauciat
et debilitat caligo et tumultus saecularium actionum.
Quas etsi nostras non habemus, eorum tamen, qui nos
angariant mille passus et iubemur *ire cum eis alia duo*,
tanta nobis ingeruntur, ut vix respirare possimus,
credentes tamen, quod ille, *in cuius conspectu intrat
gemitus compeditorum*, perseverantes nos in eo ministerio, in quo conlocare dignatus est cum promissa
mercede, adiuvantibus orationibus vestris ab omni
angustia liberabit.

2   Vos autem, fratres, exhortamur in domino, ut
propositum vestrum custodiatis et usque in finem
perseveretis ac, si qua opera vestra mater ecclesia
desideraverit, nec elatione avida suscipiatis nec blan-
diente desidia respuatis, sed miti corde obtemperetis
deo, cum mansuetudine portantes eum qui vos regit,
qui dirigit mites in iudicio, docebit mansuetos vias suas.
Nec vestrum otium necessitatibus ecclesiae prae-
ponatis, cui parturienti si nulli boni ministrare vellent,
quo modo nasceremini, non inveniretis.   Sicut autem
inter ignem et aquam tenenda est via, ut nec exuratur
homo nec demergatur, sic inter apicem superbiae et
voraginem desidiae iter nostrum temperare debemus,

---

[a] 1 Cor. xii. 26.
[b] Matt. v. 41. [c] Ps. lxxviii. 11.

body under one head, so that you share our occupation
and we share your relaxation, since " if one member
suffer, all the members suffer with it, and if one
member be honoured, all the members rejoice with
it."[a] So we exhort and beg and beseech you by
Christ's profound humility and compassionate exaltation to remember us in your holy prayers; yours are,
we are confident, more watchful and composed, for
ours are often crippled and weakened by the gloom
and bustle of worldly affairs. Not that we have any
of our own, but those who compel us to go a mile and
we are bidden to go with them other twain[b] impose so
many burdens on us that we have scarcely time to
draw our breath; yet we are confident that He
"before whom comes the sighing of the prisoner"[c]
will deliver us, by the help of your prayers, from every
distress, while we endure in that ministry in which He
has pleased to place us with the promise of reward.

We exhort you in the Lord, brethren, to maintain 2
your purpose and to persevere unto the end,[d] and if the
Church, your mother, seeks any service from you, not
to undertake it with eager elation nor to refuse it
under the solicitation of indolence, but submit to God
with lowly heart, suffering with meekness Him who
governs you, "who guides the meek in judgement and
will teach them His ways."[e] And do not place your
own ease before the Church's needs, for if no good
men were willing to minister to her in her travail,
you would find no means of being born yourselves.
But just as a man must hold the path between fire and
water if he would avoid either burning or drowning,
so should we regulate our way between the peak of
pride and the gulf of sloth, as it is written " declining

[a] Matt. xxiv. 13; x. 22.   [e] Ps. xxiv. 9.

sicut scriptum est : *Non declinantes neque ad dexteram neque ad sinistram.* Sunt enim, qui, dum nimis timent, ne quasi in dexteram rapti extollantur, in sinistram lapsi demerguntur, et sunt rursus, qui, dum nimis se auferunt a sinistra, ne torpida vacationis mollitia sorbeantur, ex altera parte iactantiae fastu corrupti atque consumpti in fumum favillamque vanescunt. Sic ergo, dilectissimi, diligite otium, ut vos ab omni terrena delectatione refrenetis et memineritis nullum locum esse, ubi non possit laqueos tendere, qui timet, ne revolemus ad deum, et inimicum omnium bonorum, cuius captivi fuimus, iudicemus, nullamque esse nobis perfectam requiem cogitetis, *donec transeat iniquitas et in iudicium iustitia convertatur.*

3 Item cum aliquid strenue atque alacriter agitis et inpigre operamini sive in orationibus sive in ieiuniis sive in elemosynis vel tribuentes aliquid indigentibus vel *donantes* iniurias, *sicut et deus in Christo donavit nobis,* sive edomantes perniciosas consuetudines *castigantesque corpus et servituti subicientes* sive sufferentes tribulationem et ante omnia vos ipsos invicem in dilectionem—quid enim sufferat, qui fratrem non suffert ?—sive prospicientes astutiam atque insidias temptatoris et *scuto fidei iacula* eius *ignita* repellentes et *extinguentes* sive *cantantes et psallentes in cordibus vestris domino* vel vocibus a corde non dissonis : *omnia in gloriam dei facite, qui operatur omnia in omnibus,* atque ita *ferventes spiritu,* ut *in domino laudetur anima vestra.* Ipsa est enim actio recti itineris, quae *oculos*

---

[a] Deut. xvii. 11 ; Prov. iv. 27.
[b] Ps. lvi. 2 ; xciii. 15.   [c] Eph. iv. 32.   [d] 1 Cor. ix. 27.
[e] Eph. vi. 16.   [f] Eph. v. 19.   [g] 1 Cor. x. 31.
[h] 1 Cor. xii. 6.   [i] Rom. xii. 11.   [j] Ps. xxxiii. 3.

114

neither to the right hand nor to the left." [a] For there are some who, over-afraid of being snatched up and borne, as it were, to the right hand, slip and sink down upon the left ; and there are some again who, while withdrawing too far from the left hand from fear of being engulfed in the slothful weakness of indolence, are corrupted and destroyed on the other side by the arrogance of boastfulness and vanish away into smoke and ashes. So then, beloved, do you love ease in such fashion as to restrain yourselves from every earthly delight, and remember that there is no spot free from a possible snare laid by him whose fear it is that we may take our flight back to God ; let us reckon him whose prisoners we once were to be the foe of all good men, and bear in mind that there is no perfect rest for us " until iniquity has ceased and judgement shall return unto righteousness." [b]

Likewise, when you do anything with vigour and **3** fervour and are unweariedly labouring in prayer or in fasting or in almsgiving or bestowing something on the needy or forgiving injuries, " as God also for Christ's sake hath forgiven us," [c] or subduing evil habits and " chastening the body and bringing it into subjection," [d] or bearing tribulation and (before anything else) " bearing one another in love "—for what can he endure, who does not endure his brother ?—or looking out for the craftiness and guile of the tempter and " with the shield of faith " averting and " quenching his fiery darts," [e] or " singing and making melody to the Lord in your heart " [f] or with voices in harmony with your heart : " do all to the glory of God, [g] who worketh all in all," [h] and be so " fervent in spirit " [i] that " your soul may make her boast in the Lord." [j] For on the straight path that is the behaviour of those

semper habet *ad dominum, quoniam ipse evellet de laqueo pedes.*[a] Talis actio nec frigitur negotio nec frigida est otio nec turbulenta nec marcida est nec audax nec fugax nec praeceps nec iacens. *Haec agite et deus pacis erit vobiscum.*[b]

4 Nec importunum me existimet caritas vestra, quia vobiscum loqui vel per epistulam volui. Non enim hoc vos monui, quod vos non arbitror facere ; sed credidi me non parum commendari deo a vobis, si ea quae munere illius facitis, cum adlocutionis nostrae memoria faciatis. Nam et ante iam fama et nunc fratres, qui venerunt a vobis, Eustasius et Andreas bonum Christi odorem de vestra sancta conversatione ad nos adtulerunt. Quorum Eustasius in eam requiem praecessit, quae nullis fluctibus sicut insula tunditur, nec Caprariam desiderat, quia nec cilicio[c] iam quaerit indui.

No. 16 (Ep. L)

DUCTORIBUS AC PRINCIPIBUS VEL SENIORIBUS COLONIAE SUFETANAE AUGUSTINUS EPISCOPUS

Immanitatis vestrae famosissimum scelus et in-

---

[a] Ps. xxiv. 15.   [b] Phil. iv. 9 ; 2 Cor. xiii. 11.

[c] The goat's-hair garment, the chief article of manufacture on Capraria, "the goat-island." It was a rough garment used by the poor, by penitents as a sign of grief, and by monks.

[d] Sufes, now Sbiba, is in Tunisia, near the Algerian border. It was a *castellum* under the early Empire, but became a colony about the time of Marcus Aurelius, as the name indicates (*colonia Aurelia Sufetana*). It had been a bishopric since at least A.D. 255, but Augustine's language shows that the majority of its inhabitants were still pagan. In consequence, apparently, of the legislation of 399, by which Honorius ordered the closing of pagan temples and the destruction of idols (*Cod. Theod.* xvi. x. 16, 17, 18), the

" whose eyes are ever upon the Lord, for He shall pluck their feet out of the net." [a] Such behaviour is neither parched by business nor chilled by ease, neither boisterous nor enervated, neither reckless nor runaway, neither headstrong nor supine. " These things do, and the God of peace shall be with you." [b]

Let your Charity not think me troublesome in 4 wishing to have converse with you even by letter. I have given you these admonishments, not with the idea that you are failing to perform them, but in the belief that if what you do by His favour you do in remembrance of my exhortation, I have no slight commendation to God from you. For a good savour of Christ from your holy conduct had already reached me, first through rumour and now through the brethren, Eustasius and Andrew, who have come from you. Of these Eustasius has gone before us to that rest, which no waves beat upon as they do upon your island, nor does he long for Caprera, for in its hair-cloth he seeks no more his raiment.[c]

No. 16 (Ep. L)

(A.D. 399)

BISHOP AUGUSTINE TO THE LEADERS AND MAGISTRATES OR ELDERS OF THE COLONY OF SUFES [d]

Earth quakes and the heavens shake at the most

Sufetan statue of Hercules had been destroyed, and in retaliation the townspeople had massacred sixty Christians. The cult of Hercules at Sufes is attested by an inscription to that god found among the ruins (*C.I.L.* viii. no. 262). The martyred Christians are commemorated on August 30 (*Martyrol. Rom.* III. Kal. Sept.; *Acta Sanctorum*, Aug. vi. 553). The letter is unusually difficult and the style makes it doubtful that Augustine is actually the writer.

opinata crudelitas terram concutit et percutit caelum,
ut in plateis ac delubris vestris eluceat sanguis et
resonet homicidium. Apud vos Romanae sepultae
sunt leges, iudiciorum rectorum calcatus est terror,
imperatorum certe nulla veneratio nec timor. Apud
vos sexaginta numero fratrum innocens effusus est
sanguis et, si quis plures occidit, functus est laudibus
et in vestram curiam tenuit principatum. Age nunc
principalem veniamus ad causam. Si Herculem
vestrum dixeritis, porro reddemus ; adsunt metalla,
saxa nec desunt ; accedunt et marmorum genera,
suppeditat artificum copia. Ceterum deus vester
cum diligentia sculpitur, tornatur et ornatur ; addi-
mus et rubricam, quae pingat ruborem, quo possint
vota vestra sacra sonare. Nam si vestrum Herculem
dixeritis, conlatis singulis nummis ab artifice vestro
vobis emimus deum. Reddite igitur animas, quas
truculenta vestra manus contorsit, et, sicuti a nobis
vester Hercules redhibetur, sic etiam a vobis tantorum animae reddantur.

No. 17 (Ep. LX)

DOMINO BEATISSIMO ET DEBITA OBSERVANTIA
VENERABILI SINCERITERQUE CARISSIMO
FRATRI ET CONSACERDOTI PAPAE AURELIO
AUGUSTINUS IN DOMINO SALUTEM

1   Litteras nullas tuae venerabilitatis, ex quo ab

glaring criminality and shocking barbarity of your fiendish conduct, which has made your streets and shrines run red with blood and resound with cries of murder. Among you the laws of Rome have been consigned to oblivion, the fear of righteous judgement has been trampled under foot, and for the Crown you have assuredly neither respect nor awe. Among you the innocent blood of exactly sixty Christian brethren has been spilt, and he who has the more murders to his credit has enjoyed various honours and been appointed to the chief post in your assembly. See now, let us come to the chief point. If you mention your Hercules, we shall straightway restore it to you ; we have quarries at hand, and there is no lack of stone ; there are in addition various kinds of marble and a sufficient supply of craftsmen. Moreover, your god will be chiseled, smoothed off and ornamented : we shall even add red ochre to paint the blush with which your holy prayers may be uttered. For if you say the Hercules is your own, we shall contribute a penny each and buy a god for you from your own craftsman. Restore then the souls that your ferocious hand has destroyed, and as we give back your Hercules, so do you restore these many souls.

No. 17 (Ep. LX)

(A.D. 401)

TO FATHER AURELIUS, MY LORD MOST BLESSED AND WITH DUE RESPECT REVERED, MY BROTHER AND COLLEAGUE, MOST SINCERELY BELOVED, AUGUSTINE SENDS GREETING IN THE LORD

Since we parted from each other in body, I have l

invicem corporaliter digressi sumus, accepi. Nunc vero legi epistulam benignitatis tuae de Donato et fratre eius et, quid responderem, diu fluctuavi. Sed tamen etiam atque etiam cogitanti, quid sit utile saluti eorum quibus nutriendis in Christo servimus, nihil mihi aliud occurrere potuit nisi non esse istam viam dandam servis dei, ut facilius se putent eligi ad aliquid melius, si facti fuerint deteriores. Et ipsis enim facilis lapsus et ordini clericorum fit indignissima iniuria, si desertores monasteriorum ad militiam clericatus eliguntur, cum ex his, qui in monasterio permanent, non tamen nisi probatiores atque meliores in clerum adsumere soleamus, nisi forte, sicut vulgares dicunt, "malus choraula bonus symphoniacus est," ita idem ipsi vulgares de nobis iocabuntur dicentes "malus monachus bonus clericus est." Nimis dolendum, si ad tam ruinosam superbiam monachos subrigimus et tam gravi contumelia clericos dignos putamus, in quorum numero sumus, cum aliquando etiam bonus monachus vix bonum clericum faciat, si adsit ei sufficiens continentia et tamen desit instructio necessaria aut personae regularis integritas.

2 Sed de istis, credo, arbitrata sit beatitudo tua, quod nostra voluntate, ut suis potius conregionalibus utiles essent, de monasterio recessissent. Sed falsum est; sponte abierunt, sponte deseruerunt nobis,

received no letter from your Holiness, but now I have read a letter of your Grace about Donatus and his brother. For a considerable time I could not settle what answer to make, but after repeated consideration of what would further the welfare of those whose nurture in Christ is the aim of our service, I could reach no other conclusion than this : we must not put God's servants in the way of thinking that the worse their behaviour, the easier their advancement to better posts. For it would only make backsliding easier for them and lay a quite undeserved slight on the regular clergy, if we selected for clerical service monks who had run away from their monastery, seeing that our usual practice is to select for adoption to the ranks of the clergy only those of higher merit and character from among the monks who stay on in their monastery. The common people say that a bad accompanist makes a good singer ; do we want these same common people to laugh at us in the same way and say that a bad monk makes a good clergyman ? It is a great pity if we encourage monks to such demoralizing pride and think fit to lay so serious a slight on the clergy, to whose ranks we ourselves belong. Sometimes even a good monk hardly makes a good clergyman, if he possesses sufficient self-control and yet has not the necessary education or the finish of a man who has gone through the normal training.

In the case we are discussing, your Holiness may, 2 I think, have assumed that it was with my consent that they abandoned monastic life for a more desirable sphere of service among the men of their own district. That, however, is not so ; they left of their own accord, of their own accord they deserted

quantum potuimus, pro eorum salute renitentibus.
Et de Donato quidem, quia iam factum est, ut, antequam de hac re aliquid in concilio statueremus, ordinaretur, si forte a superbiae perversitate correctus
est, quod vult, faciat prudentia tua. De fratre vero
eius, in cuius vel maxime causa de monasterio etiam
ipse Donatus abscessit, cum intellegas quid sentiam,
nescio quid respondeam. Contradicere tamen prudentiae tuae, honori caritatique non audeo et sane
spero id te facturum quod membris ecclesiae salubre
perspexeris. Amen.

No. 18 (Ep. LXV)

DOMINO BEATISSIMO ET VENERABILITER SUS-CIPIENDO PATRI ET CONSACERDOTI SENI XANTHIPPO AUGUSTINUS IN DOMINO SALU-TEM

1 Officio debito meritis tuis salutans dignationem
tuam tuisque me orationibus valde commendans
insinuo prudentiae tuae Abundantium quendam in
fundo Strabonianensi pertinente ad curam nostram
ordinatum fuisse presbyterum. Qui cum non am-
bularet vias servorum dei, non bonam famam habere
coeperat. Qua ego conterritus non tamen temere aliquid credens sed plane sollicitior factus operam dedi,
si quo modo possem ad aliqua malae conversationis
eius certa indicia pervenire. Ac primo comperi eum

ᵃ The Council held at Carthage in June 401.

ᵇ Xanthippus was bishop of Thagura (Taoura, near Souk Ahras). He is mentioned again in Ep. lix. as one of those on whom devolved the duty of summoning a Council.

ᶜ The site of this *fundus* and of Gippi have not been identified, but they must have been near Hippo.

their vocation, notwithstanding the most strenuous efforts I could make to oppose them, for their own best good. With Donatus, who has already managed to get himself ordained before we could decide any-thing in the Council[a] about this matter, just do in your wisdom as you will, if he happens to have been cured of his obstinate pride. But since you under-stand what I feel, I am at a loss what to say about his brother, for whose sake most of all Donatus himself left his monastery. Yet I do not presume to oppose one of your wisdom, rank and kindliness, and I do hope that you will do what you see to be bene-ficial for the members of the Church. Amen.

No. 18 (Ep. LXV)

(A.D. 402)

TO THE SENIOR XANTHIPPUS,[b] MY SAINTLY LORD AND REVERENTLY CHERISHED FATHER AND FELLOW-PRIEST, AUGUSTINE SENDS GREETING IN THE LORD

I greet your Honour with the respect due to your 1 merits and earnestly commend myself to your prayers. I have to report to your Wisdom that a man by the name of Abundantius was ordained priest on the manor of Strabonian,[c] which belongs to my diocese, but, as he did not walk in the paths of God's servants, he began to acquire a bad reputation. This alarmed me, but yet I did not lightly give it any credence ; yet, my worry clearly increasing, I made an effort to reach, if it were at all possible, some incontrovertible proofs of his evil conduct. And my first discovery was that he had embezzled money

pecuniam cuiusdam rusticani divino apud se com-
mendato intervertisse, ita ut nullam inde posset pro-
babilem reddere rationem. Deinde convictus atque
confessus est die ieiunii natalis domini, quo etiam
Gippitana ecclesia sicut ceterae ieiunabant, cum
tamquam perrecturus ad ecclesiam suam "vale"
fecisset collegae suo presbytero Gippitano, hora ferme
quinta, et cum secum nullum clericum haberet, in
eodem fundo restitisse et apud quandam malae famae
mulierem et prandisse et cenasse et in eadem domo
mansisse. In huius autem hospitio iam quidam
clericus noster Hipponiensis remotus erat; et hoc
quia iste optime noverat, negare non potuit, nam quae
negavit, deo dimisi, iudicans quae occultare permissus non est. Timui ei committere ecclesiam praesertim inter haereticorum circumlatrantium rabiem
constitutam. Et cum me rogaret, ut ad presbyterum
fundi Armenianensis in campo Bullensi, unde ad nos
devenerat, causa eius insinuata litteras darem, ne
quid de illo atrocius suspicaretur, ut illic vivat, si
fieri potest, sine officio presbyterii correctior, misericordia commotus feci. Haec autem me praecipue
prudentiae tuae intimare oportebat, ne aliqua tibi
fallacia subreperet.

2   Audivi autem causam eius, cum centum dies essent
ad dominicum paschae, qui futurus est VIII Id. Aprilis.
Hoc propter concilium insinuare curavi venerabilitati
tuae, quod etiam ipsi non celavi, sed ei fideliter, quid

---

    [a] For this late use of *nam* see Stolz-Schmalz, *Lat. Gramm.*[5]
p. 679; Löfstedt, *Peregr. Aeth.* p. 34; Linderbauer, *S. Bened.
Reg.* p. 174.
    [b] There were at least two places called Bulla: Bulla Regia,
the modern Derradji, five miles from Souk El Arba, and

belonging to a certain countryman, entrusted to him for religious purposes, and could give no satisfactory account of it. The next charge proved against him and admitted by himself was that, on the fast-day of Christmas, when the church of Gippi was fasting like all the others, he took leave of his colleague, the priest of Gippi, about 11 o'clock in the day, on the pretext of departing for his own church ; and although he had no clergyman with him, he remained in the same manor and dined and supped and stayed in the same house with a woman of ill fame. But one of our clergy of Hippo was already living from home in the local inn, and since Abundantius was very well aware of this, he could not deny the charge, but[a] what he did deny I left to God, passing sentence upon the facts he was not allowed to conceal. I was afraid to trust him with a church, especially one situated in the very midst of frenzied and snarling heretics. And when he asked me to give him letters explaining his case to the priest of the manor of Armenian in the district of Bulla,[b] from which he had come to us, so that no worse suspicion might be conceived against him and that there he might live, if possible, a reformed life with no duties as a priest, I was moved by pity to do so. But it was my duty to report these facts particularly to your Wisdom, lest any misrepresentation be practised upon you.

I heard his case one hundred days before Easter Sunday, which will fall on the 6th April. This fact I have been careful to mention to your Reverence because of the Council, and I have not concealed it from him either, but have revealed to him exactly what

Bulla Minor, doubtfully identified with Embarek, not far from Bulla Regia.

institutum esset, aperui. Et si intra annum causam
suam, si forte sibi aliquid agendum putat, agere ne-
glexerit, deinceps eius vocem nemo audiat. Nos
autem, domine beatissime et venerabiliter suscipiende
pater, si haec indicia malae conversationis clericorum,
maxime cum fama non bona eos coeperit comitari,
non putaverimus nisi eo modo vindicanda quo in
concilio constitutum est, incipimus cogi ea quae sciri
non possunt, velle discutere et aut incerta damnare
aut vere incognita praeterire. Ego certe presbyterum, ut qui die ieiunii, quo eiusdem loci etiam
ecclesia ieiunabat, " vale " faciens collegae suo eiusdem loci presbytero apud famosam mulierem nullum
secum clericum habens remanere et prandere et
cenare ausus est et in una domo dormire, removen-
dum ab officio presbyterii arbitratus sum timens ei
deinceps ecclesiam dei committere. Quod si forte
iudicibus ecclesiasticis aliud videtur, quia sex episcopis causam presbyteri terminare concilio statutum
est, committat illi, qui vult, ecclesiam suae curae
commissam ; ego talibus, fateor, quamlibet plebem
committere timeo, praesertim quos nulla bona fama
defendit, ut hoc eis possit ignosci, ne, si quid perniciosius eruperit, languens inputem mihi.

was decided. And if he thinks fit to take some action and fails to present his case within a year, let no one thereafter hearken to his plea. But for my part, my saintly lord and reverently cherished father, if I thought that these evidences of evil conduct on the part of the clergy, especially when a bad reputation has begun to attend them, deserved no punishment except in the manner prescribed by the Council, I should now be compelled to agree to the discussion of things that cannot be ascertained, and either to condemn things that are unproved or to pass over things that are really unknown. For my own part, at any rate, I have decided that a priest who, on a fast-day which was actually being observed by the local church, took leave of his colleague, the local priest, dared to stay, unaccompanied by a clergyman, with a woman of ill fame, to dine and sup and sleep in the same house, ought to be deposed from the office of priest, since I was afraid thereafter to entrust to his care a church of God. If the ecclesiastical judges happen to take a different view, because the Council decreed that six bishops should pronounce the final verdict in a case affecting a priest, let who will entrust him with a church situated within his own jurisdiction; personally, I confess my own fear of entrusting any congregation to people of that kind, especially when they have no good reputation to urge in defence as a reason for condoning this delinquency ; otherwise, if any more heinous disorder broke out, I should with pain feel responsible for it myself.

No. 19 (Ep. LXVI)

INCIPIT LIBELLUS SANCTI AUGUSTINI EPISCOPI CATHOLICI CONTRA CRISPINUM SCHISMATICUM

1 Deum quidem timere debuisti ; sed quia in rebaptizandis Mappaliensibus sicut homo timeri voluisti, cur non valeat iussio regalis in provincia, si tantum valuit iussio provincialis in villa ? Si personas compares, tu possessor, ille imperator ; si loca compares, tu in fundo, ille in regno ; si causas compares, ille ut divisio resarciatur, tu ut unitas dividatur. Sed nos te de homine non terremus. Nam possemus agere ut decem libras auri secundum imperatoria iussa persolveres. An forte propterea non habes unde reddas quod dare iussi sunt rebaptizatores, dum multum erogas, ut emas quos rebaptizes ? Sed nos, ut dixi, de homine te non terremus ; Christus te potius terreat. Cui volo scire quid respondeas, si tibi dicat : "Crispine, carum fuit pretium tuum ad emendum timorem Mappaliensium et vilis mors mea ad emendum amorem omnium gentium ? Plus valuit rebaptizandis colonis tuis, quod numeratum est de sacculo tuo, quam baptizandis populis meis quod manavit de latere meo ?" Scio te plura audire posse, si Christo aurem praebeas, et ex ipsa tua

---

^a Crispinus was Donatist bishop of Calama ; to him Ep. li. is addressed. He had acquired the property of Mappalia, on the imperial domain near Hippo, and had compelled eighty Christian slaves to undergo re-baptism. Later, one of his priests, of the same name, broke into the house of Augustine's friend, Possidius, and severely beat him, but Crispinus refused to punish the offender, and was himself convicted and fined.

No. 19 (Ep. LXVI)

(A.D. 402)

[THE BEGINNING OF THE NOTE OF ST. AUGUS-
TINE, CATHOLIC BISHOP, AGAINST CRIS-
PINUS[a] THE SCHISMATIC]

You should have feared God at least, but since 1
it was your desire to be feared like a man in your re-
baptizing of the Mappalians, why is a royal command
of no avail in the province, if a provincial command
has been of such avail on a private property ? If you
compare the persons concerned, you are the possessor,
he is emperor ; if you compare the positions of both,
you are on an estate, he is on a throne ; if you compare the motives of both, he aims at mending what is
rent, you at rending what is one whole. But we are
not seeking to make you afraid of a man, for we could
make you pay up ten pounds of gold, according to the
imperial decrees. Or perhaps you have no money
with which to pay the fine imposed on those who re-
baptize, after your great expenses in bribing people to
accept re-baptism ? But, as I said, we are not seeking to make you afraid of a man ; let Christ rather
make you afraid. I want to know what answer you
would make to Him, if He were to say to you : " Crispinus, was it a high price you paid for the fear of the
Mappalians, and was my death a small price to pay for
the love of all the nations ? Was the money that was
counted out from your purse of greater value for the
re-baptizing of your serfs than the blood which flowed
from my side for the baptizing of my nations ? " I
know that if you were to give ear to Christ, you could

though the fine was remitted at Possidius's request (Aug. *C.
Cresc.* iii. 46-47; *C. Litt. Petil.* ii. 83 ; Possid. *Vit. Aug.* 12).

possessione admoneri quam impia contra Christum loquamini. Si enim humano iure praesumis firme te possidere quod emisti argento tuo, quanto firmius divino iure possidet Christus quod emit sanguine suo! Et ille quidem inconcusse possidebit totum, de quo dictum est: *Dominabitur a mari usque ad mare et a flumine usque ad terminos orbis terrae.* Sed certe quo modo confidis non te perditurum, quod in Africa videris emisse, qui Christum dicis toto orbe perdito ad solam Africam remansisse?

2 Quid multa? Si voluntate sua Mappalienses in tuam communionem transierunt, ambos nos audiant, ita ut scribantur quae dicimus, et a nobis subscripta eis Punice interpretentur, et remoto timore dominationis eligant quod voluerint. Ex his enim quae dicimus, apparebit utrum coacti in falsitate remaneant, an volentes teneant veritatem. Si enim haec non intellegunt, qua temeritate traduxisti non intellegentes? Si autem intellegunt, ambos, ut dixi, audiant et quod voluerint, faciant. Si quae etiam plebes ad nos transierunt, quas putas a dominis coactas, hoc et ibi fiat; ambos nos audiant et eligant quod placuerit. Si autem non vis hoc fieri, cui non appareat non vos de veritate praesumere? Sed

---

a Ps. lxxi. 8.

hear more such questions and be warned by your very property how impious are the words you and your like speak against Christ. For if you reckon that by human law you have a sure title to what you have bought with your own money, how much surer by divine law is Christ's title to what He has bought with His own blood! And yet He will have an unshakable title to everything, for it is written of Him : "He shall have dominion from sea to sea and from the river unto the ends of the earth." [a] But how do you expect with any assurance that you will not lose what you think you have bought in Africa, when you assert that Christ has lost the whole world and has been left for Africa alone ?

But why multiply words ? If it was of their own **2** free will that the Mappalians went over to your communion, let them hear us both, our statements being written down and, after being attested by our signatures, translated into Punic for them ; and without any fear of intimidation let them choose what they want. For from what we say it will be made clear whether they are abiding in falsehood from compulsion or are holding fast the truth of their own choice. For if they do not understand what is involved, how had you the boldness to take them over to your side with no understanding of the points at issue ? But if they do understand, let them, as I said, hear us both and do as they wish. Further, if there are any congregations who have come over to us and whom you believe to have done so under compulsion from their overlords, let the same course be followed there too : let them hear us both and choose what they please. But if you are unwilling to do this, who can fail to see that your party has no confidence in the truth ? Yet

cavenda est ira dei et hic et in futuro saeculo. Adiuro te per Christum, ut ad ista respondeas.

No. 20 (Ep. LXVII)

DOMINO CARISSIMO ET DESIDERANTISSIMO ET HONORANDO IN CHRISTO FRATRI ET CONPRESBYTERO HIERONYMO AUGUSTINUS IN DOMINO SALUTEM

1   Audivi pervenisse in manus tuas litteras meas; sed quod adhuc rescripta non merui, nequaquam inputaverim dilectioni tuae ; aliquid procul dubio impedimenti fuit. Unde agnosco a me dominum potius deprecandum, ut tuae voluntati det facultatem mittendi quod rescripseris, nam rescribendi iam dedit, quia, cum volueris, facillime poteris.

2   Etiam hoc ad me sane perlatum utrum quidem crederem, dubitavi, sed hinc quoque tibi aliquid utrum scriberem, dubitare non debui. Hoc autem breve est : suggestum caritati tuae a nescio quibus fratribus mihi dictum est, quod librum adversus te scripserim Romamque miserim. Hoc falsum esse noveris ; deum nostrum testor hoc me non fecisse. Sed si forte aliqua in aliquibus scriptis meis reperiuntur, in quibus aliter aliquid quam tu sensisse reperiar, non contra te dictum, sed quod mihi videbatur, a me scriptum esse puto te debere cognoscere aut, si cognosci non potest, credere. Ita sane hoc dixerim, ut ego non

---

^a Neither of Augustine's previous letters to Jerome, written in 394 and 397 (Ep. xxviii. and xl.), had till recently been delivered, but Ep. xl., in which the writer had repeated his objections to Jerome's account of the quarrel at Antioch (see No. 9 above), had been circulated without Augustine's knowledge and had eventually reached Bethlehem, where it had aroused much indignation, which the present letter seeks to dispel.

you must beware of the wrath of God both here and hereafter. I adjure you by Christ to reply to what I have written.

No. 20 (Ep. LXVII)

(A.D. 402)

TO JEROME, MY LORD DEARLY BELOVED AND MUCH LONGED FOR, AND MY HONOURED BROTHER IN CHRIST AND FELLOW-PRIEST, AUGUSTINE SENDS GREETING IN THE LORD [a]

I have heard that my letter has safely reached you, 1 but I would by no means make it a charge against your affection that as yet I have not been favoured with a reply ; no doubt something has come in your way. So I recognize that I must rather beseech the Lord to provide the opportunity of carrying out your intention to send the answer you have written, since He has already provided that of writing it, for you can very easily do so when you feel so disposed.

Further, I have hesitated whether indeed to give 2 credence to a report which has reached me, but it is my duty not to hesitate about writing something to you concerning it as well. Briefly, this is the point : I have been told that certain brethren have hinted to your Charity that I wrote a book against you and sent it to Rome. Rest assured that this statement is untrue : I call our God to witness that this I have not done. But if some remarks happen to be found in some of my writings, in which I am found taking a different view from you on any point, I think you ought to know, or if you have no means of knowing, to believe, that what I have written is not directed against you, but is an expression of my own opinion. And indeed, in so saying, I not only profess myself

tantum paratissimus sim, si quid te in meis scriptis moverit, fraterne accipere quid contra sentias, aut de correctione mea aut de ipsa tua benivolentia gavisurus, verum etiam hoc a te postulem ac flagitem.

3 O si licuisset etsi non cohabitante saltem vicino te in domino perfrui ad crebrum et dulce conloquium! Sed quia id non est datum, peto ut hoc ipsum quod in Christo, quam possimus, simul simus, conservare studeas et augeri ac perfici et rescripta quamvis rara non spernere. Saluta obsequio meo sanctum fratrem Paulinianum et omnes fratres, qui tecum ac de te in domino gaudent. Memor nostri exaudiaris a domino in omni sancto desiderio, domine carissime et desiderantissime et honorande in Christo frater.

No. 21 (Ep. LXXXIII)

DOMINO BEATISSIMO ET VENERABILITER CARISSIMO AC DESIDERANTISSIMO FRATRI ET COEPISCOPO ALYPIO ET QUI TECUM SUNT FRATRIBUS AUGUSTINUS ET QUI MECUM SUNT FRATRES IN DOMINO SALUTEM

1 Tristitia Thiavensis ecclesiae cor meum conquie-

---

a Jerome's younger brother, who left Rome with him in 385 and settled beside him in Bethlehem.

b A small town situated between Hippo and Tagaste; its site is unknown. Its priest, Honoratus, formerly a monk under Alypius at Tagaste, had died leaving property, which was claimed by both his church and his monastery. Augustine, as arbitrator, at first inclined to an equal division, but this decision greatly displeased the church-people at Thiava, who as recent converts from Donatism required conciliatory treatment. After further consideration and consultation, Augustine awarded them the whole, and writes now to Tagaste explaining and justifying his award. In spite of his decision to admit to monastic life in the future only those

134

quite prepared to accept in a brotherly spirit any objections you conceive to whatever you disapprove of in my writings and to feel glad either at having my faults corrected or at such evidence of your goodwill ; I even demand and claim it as a right.

O that it were possible to enjoy sweet and frequent 3 converse in the Lord with you ; if not by living with you, at least by living near you ! But since that is denied us, I beg you to do your best to maintain and increase and perfect this one object, that we should be together, as far as we can, in Christ, and not to disdain replying to me, even if it be only occasionally.

Greet with my respects your saintly brother Paulinianus [a] and all the brethren who rejoice in the Lord with you and because of you. May you, remembering us, be heard by the Lord in all your holy desires, beloved lord and much desired and honoured brother in Christ.

No. 21 (Ep. LXXXIII)

(A.D. 405)

TO ALYPIUS, MY SAINTLY LORD, MY BROTHER AND FELLOW-BISHOP, CHERISHED WITH MUCH REVERENCE AND LONGING, AND THE BRETHREN WHO ARE WITH YOU, AUGUSTINE AND THE BRETHREN WHO ARE WITH ME SEND GREETING IN THE LORD

The sorrow of the church at Thiava [b] prevents 1

who had surrendered their worldly possessions, he was later several times troubled by similar problems. The two sermons he preached to justify his acceptance of legacies to his monastery and to enunciate his determined adherence to the principle of monastic poverty were of considerable importance in making this principle indispensable to monastic life (*Serm.* 355, 356).

scere non permittit, donec eos tecum audiam in pristinum animum restitutos, quod cito faciendum est. Si enim de homine uno tantum sategit apostolus dicens: *Ne maiore tristitia absorbeatur, qui eius modi est*, ubi etiam ait: *Ut non possideamur a satana, non enim ignoramus mentes eius,* quanto magis nos oportet vigilanter agere ne hoc in toto grege plangamus et maxime in eis qui nunc catholicae paci accesserunt et quos nullo modo relinquere possum. Sed quia temporis non sivit angustia ut simul inde nobis diligenter deliberatam liceret eliquare sententiam, quid mihi post digressum nostrum diu cogitanti placuerit, accipiat sanctitas tua et si tibi quoque placet, iam litterae quas ad eos communi nomine scripsi, sine dilatione mittantur.

2 Dixisti ut dimidium habeant et alterum dimidium eis a me undecumque provideretur. Ego autem puto quia, si totum eis auferretur, esset quod diceremur non de pecunia nos sed de iustitia tantopere laborasse. Cum vero dimidium eis concedimus et eo modo cum eis pacem quandoque componimus, satis apparebit nostram curam nihil aliud quam pecuniariam fuisse et vides quae pernicies consequatur. Et illis enim videbimur alienam rem dimidiam tulisse

---

a 2 Cor. ii. 7.   *b* 2 Cor. ii. 11.

my heart from being at rest until I hear that they have been brought back to the same disposition towards you as before, and that must be done quickly. For if the Apostle was so much concerned about one individual when he said, " Lest such a one should be swallowed up with overmuch sorrow," [a] adding there the words, " Lest Satan should get an advantage of us ; for we are not ignorant of his devices," [b] it much more becomes us to act with circumspection so that we may not have the same thing to lament in a whole flock, and especially in those who have but recently come over to the peace of the Catholic Church, and whom I can in no wise abandon. But as the shortness of time did not allow us any opportunity to take careful counsel together on the matter and to clarify our opinions, may it please your Holiness to accept the decision I have reached after lengthy consideration since we parted, and, if you decide likewise, let the letter I have written them in our common name be dispatched to them without delay.

Your proposal was that they should have the one **2** half and that I should make up the other half to them from some other source. But it is my opinion that if they were deprived of the whole property, it might reasonably be said that we had so greatly exerted ourselves not for the sake of the money, but for the sake of justice. But when we yield them a half and on those terms arrange at some time a settlement with them, it will look pretty obvious that we were interested in only the financial aspect, and you see what a pernicious result would follow. For on one hand we shall be regarded by them as having taken one half to which we had no right, and they on the

et illi nobis videbuntur inhoneste et inique se passos fuisse, ut adiuvarentur de dimidio quod totum pauperum fuerat. Nam quod dixisti : " Cavendum est, ne cum rem dubiam emendari volumus, maiora vulnera faciamus," tantundem valebit, si eis dimidium concedatur. Propter ipsum quippe dimidium illi, quorum conversioni consulere volumus, ut hoc exemplo secum agatur, rerum suarum venditionem per moras illas excusatorias dilaturi sunt. Deinde mirum si de re dubia est totius plebis tam grande scandalum, cum episcopos suos, quos pro magno habent, sordida avaritia maculatos putant, dum maligna species non vitatur ?

3 Nam cum quisque ad monasterium convertitur, si veraci corde convertitur, illud non cogitat maxime admonitus quantum malum sit. Si autem fallax est et *sua quaerit, non quae Iesu Christi*, non habet utique caritatem et *quid ei prodest, si distribuerit omnia sua pauperibus et tradiderit corpus suum, ut ardeat?* Huc accedit quia illud, sicut iam conlocuti sumus, deinceps vitari potest et agi cum eo qui convertitur, si non potest admitti ad societatem fratrum, antequam se omnibus illis impedimentis exuerit et ex otio tendatur, cum eius res iam esse destiterit. Haec autem mors infirmorum et tantum impedimentum salutis eorum, pro quibus tantopere laboramus, ut eos catholicae paci lucremur, aliter vitari non potest, nisi ut apertis-

---

a Phil. ii. 21. *b* 1 Cor. xiii. 3.

other will be regarded by us as having unfairly and
dishonourably agreed to accept help from a half which
belonged entirely to the poor.   For your remark that
we must beware, while endeavouring to settle a
doubtful matter, of causing more serious wounds,
will have as much force if they be granted a half.
For because of this half, those whose conversion to
monastic life we wish to encourage will find excuses
for delaying and putting off the sale of their own
property so as to be dealt with under this precedent.
Moreover, is it surprising that by this doubtful matter
the whole Christian community is so much offended
when they imagine their bishops, whom they honour
so highly, to be smitten with sordid avarice, so long
as they do not avoid the appearance of evil ?

For when a man turns to monastic life and does so in **3**
a genuine spirit, he does not think of that, especially
when he has been warned of the great sinfulness of
such conduct.   But if he is a deceiver and is " seeking
his own, not the things which are Jesus Christ's," [a] he
certainly is without charity, and " what does it profit
him, if he bestow all his goods upon the poor and give his
body to be burned " [b] ? Further, as we already agreed
together, that difficulty may be avoided for the future,
and an arrangement made with any individual who
is turning monk, that he cannot be admitted to the
society of the brethren before he has rid himself of
all those encumbrances and throws off his life of ease,
his property having now ceased to belong to him.
There is, indeed, no other possible way of avoiding
this spiritual death of weak brethren and this grievous obstacle to the salvation of those for the winning
of whom to the peace of Catholicism we so strenuously
labour, unless by giving them very clearly to under-

sime intellegant nullo modo nos de pecunia satagere
in talibus causis, quod nullo modo intellecturi sunt,
nisi illam rem quam semper presbyteri esse putaverunt, eorum usibus relinquamus, quia et si eius non
erat, hoc ab initio scire debuerant.

4 Videtur itaque mihi haec regula esse in rebus
huiusce modi retinenda, ut, quicquid eo iure quo
talia possidentur, eius fuerit qui alicubi clericus
ordinatur, ad eam pertineat ecclesiam in qua ordinatur. Usque adeo autem eodem iure presbyteri
Honorati est illud, unde agitur, ut non solum alibi
ordinatus sed adhuc in Tagastensi monasterio constitutus si re sua non vendita nec per manifestam
donationem in quempiam translata moreretur, non
nisi heredes eius in eam succederent, sicut frater
Aemilianus in illos triginta solidos fratri Privato suc-
cessit. Haec ergo ante praecavenda sunt ; si autem
praecauta non fuerint, ea iura eis servare oportet,
quae talibus habendis vel non habendis secundum
civilem societatem sunt instituta, ut ab omni
non solum re sed etiam specie maligna, quantum
possumus, nos abstineamus et bonam famam custo-
diamus dispensationi nostrae multum necessariam.
Quam vero species maligna sit, advertat sancta prudentia tua. Excepta illorum tristitia, quam experti
sumus, ne quid forte ipse fallerer, sicut fieri solet,
dum in sententiam meam proclivior erro, narravi
causam fratri et collegae nostro Samsucio, nondum

---

^a 1 Thess. v. 22.

stand that we are in no way concerned about money in such cases; and this they will not understand unless we leave for their use the property which they always supposed to belong to their priest, because, if it did not belong to him, they ought to have known this from the beginning.

It seems to me, therefore, that in matters of this 4 kind we should abide by this rule, that whatever belonged by the law of possession to one who is ordained to be the clergyman of any place, is the appurtenance of that church over which he was ordained. Now, by the same law, the property in question so far belonged to the priest Honoratus that, had he still been, when he died, in the monastery of Tagaste, instead of being ordained to another post, and had neither sold his property nor transferred it to any other by an express deed of gift, no one but his heirs would have succeeded to it, just as brother Aemilianus succeeded to the thirty shillings left by brother Privatus. These precautions must then be taken beforehand, but if they have not been taken, we should in their case comply with those laws which were drawn up to regulate the possession or the disposal of property according to civil society, so that we may avoid as far as possible not only all reality, but even all appearance of evil,[a] and retain the untarnished reputation which is so necessary to our office as executors. And just how evil this appearance is, let your holy Wisdom observe. After hearing of their disappointment, which we fully realized, from fear that I might perchance be mistaken (as usually happens when I incline with the more partiality to my own opinion), I stated the case to our brother and colleague, Samsucius, without telling him at the

G

dicens quod mihi modo videtur, sed illud potius
adiungens quod utrique nostrum visum sit, cum illis
resisteremus. Vehementer exhorruit et nobis hoc
visum esse miratus est, nulla re alia permotus nisi
ipsa specie foeda, non nostra sed cuiuslibet vita ac
moribus indignissima.

5 Proinde obsecro, ut epistulam quam eis communi
nomine scripsi, subscriptam non differas mittere. Et
si forte illic illud iustum acutissime pervides, non
cogantur infirmi modo discere, quod ego nondum
intellego, ut hoc circa eos in hac causa servetur quod
dominus ait : *Multa habeo vobis dicere, sed non potestis
illa portare modo.* Tali quippe infirmitati parcens
etiam illud de tributo solvendo ait : *Ergo liberi sunt
filii ; sed ne scandalizemus eos* et cetera, quando Petrum
misit ut didrachmas quae tunc exigebantur, solve-
rent. Noverat enim aliud ius, quo nihil tale debe-
bat ; sed eo iure tributum ei ille solvebat, quo iure
diximus heredem presbyteri Honorati successurum
fuisse, si, antequam rem suam vel donaret vel ven-
deret, moreretur. Quamquam in ipso ecclesiae iure
Paulus apostolus parcit infirmis et debitum stipendium non exigit, certus conscientia quod rectissime
exigeret, sed nihil aliud quam suspicionem devitans
bonum odorem Christi turbantem et ab illa maligna
specie sese abstinens in eis regionibus, ubi hoc noverat

---

^a John xvi. 12.
^b Matt. xvii. 26-27.
^c 1 Cor. ix. 1-15.

time what I have now decided, but rather adding what we had both decided when we were resisting their claims. He was very much shocked and marvelled that we had so decided, and what disturbed him was nothing else than this very appearance of foul dealing, very unworthy not only of our life and character, but of anyone's.

I beseech you, therefore, not to postpone signing [5] and sending the letter I have written them in our common name. And if from it you very clearly realize that this course is just, let not those who are weak be compelled now to learn what I myself do not yet understand, so that in this affair we may observe towards them this saying of the Lord's : " I have many things to say to you, but ye cannot bear them now." [a] For He had compassion on such weakness and made the further remark about the payment of tribute : " Then are the children free ; notwithstanding, lest we offend them," [b] and so on, when He sent Peter to pay the half-shekel that was at that time exacted. He was acquainted with another law by which He had no such obligation, but Peter paid tribute for Him in accordance with that same law by which, as I have already said, the heir of the priest Honoratus would have succeeded, if he had died before either giving away or selling his property. And yet, under the law of the Church itself, Paul the Apostle had compassion on the weak and did not exact the subsidy due to himself, [c] though quite convinced in his own mind that he had every right to exact it, but with no other intention than to escape the suspicion which would spoil the sweet savour of Christ and to defend himself from that appearance of evil in those districts where he knew that such was his duty and

oportere, et forte antequam tristitiam hominum fuisset expertus. Sed nos tardiores vel experti corrigamus quod praevidere debuimus.

6 Postremo, quia omnia timeo et memini in digressu nostro quid proposueris, quod me fratres Tagastenses teneant debitorem in dimidio illius pretii, si hoc iustum esse liquido perspicis, ea dum taxat condicione non abnuo, ut, cum habuero, reddam, id est cum aliquid tantum obvenerit Hipponiensi monasterio, ubi hoc sine angustia fieri possit, ut tanta ibi summa detracta non minus quam aequalis pro numero cohabitantium pars ad nostros perveniat.

No. 22 (Ep. LXXXIV)

DOMINO BEATISSIMO ET VENERABILI AC DE-
  SIDERABILI FRATRI ET CONSACERDOTI
  NOVATO ET QUI TECUM SUNT FRATRIBUS
  AUGUSTINUS ET QUI MECUM SUNT FRATRES
  IN DOMINO SALUTEM

1 Et ego sentio quam durus videar, et me ipse vix fero, quod filium meum diaconum Lucillum germanum tuum sanctitati tuae non mitto atque permitto. Sed cum ipse quoque aliquos ex tuis nutrimentis valde carissimos atque dulcissimos necessitatibus ecclesiarum longe abs te positarum concedere coeperis, tunc senties quibus desideriorum stimulis fodiar, quod quidam mihi maxima et dulcissima

---

* Novatus is probably the bishop of Sitifi (Sétif), from about 403 to 440. He occurs again in Ep. ccxxix.

in fact before he had experienced men's disappointment. But now, though we are somewhat behindhand, let us even profit by our experience and put right what we ought beforehand to have guarded against.

Finally, since I am completely a prey to fear and 6 recall the proposal you made when we parted, that the brethren at Tagaste should hold me responsible for the half of the sum named, if you clearly view this proposal as fair, I do not reject it, but on this condition, that I pay the amount when I have it, that is, when so great a sum falls to our monastery at Hippo that it may be done without unduly straitening us, so that, after subtracting the large amount owing them, our people may acquire no less than an equal share in proportion to the number of resident brethren.

No. 22 (Ep. LXXXIV)

(A.D. 405)

TO MY SAINTLY AND REVERED LORD AND
  LONGED FOR BROTHER AND FELLOW-
  PRIEST, NOVATUS[a] AND THE BRETHREN
  WHO ARE WITH YOU, AUGUSTINE AND THE
  BRETHREN WHO ARE WITH ME SEND
  GREETING IN THE LORD

I myself feel how hard-hearted I must appear, 1 and I can scarcely excuse myself for not sending and lending to your Holiness my son the deacon Lucillus, your brother. But when you yourself begin to surrender some of the very dearest and sweetest of those you have nurtured to the needs of churches situated far from you, then you will understand the pangs of regret that stab me at losing the bodily com-

familiaritate coniuncti non sunt etiam corporaliter
mecum. Nam ut longe mittam cognationem tuam,
quantum libet valeat germanitas tui sanguinis, non
vincit amicitiae vinculum quo nobis invicem ego et
frater Severus inhaeremus ; et tamen nosti quam
raro mihi eum videre contingat. Atque hoc fecit
non utique voluntas vel mea vel illius, sed dum
matris ecclesiae necessitates propter futurum saeculum quo nobiscum inseparabiliter convivemus,
nostri temporis necessitatibus anteponimus. Quanto
ergo aequius te tolerare oportet pro utilitate ipsius
matris ecclesiae eius fratris absentiam cum quo non
tam diu cibum dominicum ruminas, quam diu ego
cum dulcissimo concive meo Severo, qui mecum
tamen nunc vix et interdum per exiguas chartulas
loquitur et eas quidem plures aliarum curarum et
negotiorum refertas quam portantes aliquid nostrorum in Christi suavitate pratorum !

2   Hic forsitan dicas : " Quid enim ? Et apud nos
germanus meus ecclesiae non erit utilis aut propter
aliud eum mecum habere desidero ? " Plane si tantum ibi, quantum hic mihi eius praesentia lucrandis
vel regendis ovibus domini utilis videretur, non dico
duritiam sed iniquitatem meam nemo non iure culparet. Sed cum Latina lingua, cuius inopia in nostris
regionibus evangelica dispensatio multum laborat,

---

^a See p. 108, note *b*.

^b As the text stands, with no variant, there is an anaco-
luthon, and the sense demands " Punic " instead of " Latin."
Even in Hippo, a coast town long Romanized, there were
many who spoke Punic, and in inland districts it was often
the only language spoken (see note *b* on p. 24). The true
reading probably lies hid in *Latina* or *cum Latina*, and
perhaps there was no adjective present (*cum illam [calleat?]
linguam*), *Latina* being an imported gloss.

panionship of individuals united to me in the closest
and most pleasing intimacy. For, to leave the fact
of your kinship quite out of account, the blood-bond
between you may be as strong as you please, yet it
is not superior to the bond of friendship that binds
brother Severus and me so closely to each other;
and yet you know how seldom I have the happiness
of seeing him. And it is not my wish or his that is
responsible for this, but the fact that the claims of
our mother, the Church, having regard to the world
to come, in which we shall live together and never
part, are more important than the claims of our own
time. Out of consideration, therefore, for the welfare
of that same mother, the Church, you ought with
all the greater equanimity to endure the absence of
the brother with whom you have not been browsing
upon the food of the Lord as long as I did with my
delightful fellow-townsman, Severus,[a] who yet holds
converse with me now with difficulty and at intervals
by means of meagre letters, and those indeed packed,
for the most part, with other cares and concerns
instead of bringing any evidence of our wanderings
in the sweet meadows of Christ.

At this point you may perhaps reply, "What 2
then? Here too, beside me, will my brother not be
of service to the Church, or is it for any other reason
that I want to have him with me?" Certainly, if his
being with you seemed as profitable for the winning
and directing of the Lord's flock as it is here to me,
there is no one who would not justly blame—I shall
not call it my hard-heartedness, but my unfairness.
But since he is familiar with a language [b] the lack of
which in our territories greatly hinders the administration of the Gospel, while where you are the same

illic autem eiusdem linguae usus omnino sit,—itane censes nos saluti plebium domini oportere consulere, ut hanc facultatem illuc mittamus et hinc auferamus, ubi eam magno cordis aestu requirimus ? Da itaque veniam quod non solum contra tuum desiderium, sed etiam contra sensum meum, facio quod me facere sarcinae nostrae cura constringit. Dabit tibi dominus in quo posuisti cor tuum, ut tales sint labores tui, ut pro isto beneficio remunereris ; sic enim regionum nostrarum ardentissimae siti diaconum Lucillum tu potius concessisti ; neque enim parum praestabis, cum de hac re nulla petitione me ulterius onerabis, ne nihil aliud quam durior appaream venerabili mihi et sanctae benivolentiae tuae.

No. 23 (Ep. LXXXVI)

DOMINO EXIMIO ET IN CHRISTI CARITATE VERE MERITOQUE HONORABILI AC SUSPICIENDO FILIO CAECILIANO AUGUSTINUS EPISCOPUS IN DOMINO SALUTEM

Administrationis tuae castitas et fama virtutum, pietatis quoque Christianae laudanda diligentia et fida sinceritas, quae tibi divina munera eo donante gaudes tributa a quo speras promittente potiora,

---

a Caecilianus was prominent in political life under Honorius. He was one of the legates sent by the senate to Honorius at Ravenna in 409 to deplore the misfortunes of Rome, where Alaric had broken his pledge. In 413 he was sent to Africa to examine the provincials' complaints and the adjustment of the corn-tax. On his arrival in Carthage, he bore letters from Pope Innocent to Augustine, who addressed to him Ep. cli. The edict mentioned is the vigorous legislation of 412 against the Donatists. The Benedictine editors, followed by Goldbacher, assign this letter to the year

language is in general use, do you think it is our duty so to provide for the welfare of the Lord's people that we send this ability to you and deprive ourselves of it here, where our need of it is so great and so heart-felt? Forgive me, then, for doing, not only in spite of your desire but also in spite of my own feelings, what my zeal for the office with which I am burdened compels me to do. The Lord, upon whom you have stayed your heart, will make your labours such that you will be rewarded for this kind service ; for it is kind of you to surrender the deacon Lucillus to the thirsty eagerness of our territories rather than claim him for yourself. And it will be no small favour if you will refrain from laying upon me any request concerning this matter in the future, so that I may not appear to your revered and holy Benevolence to be only too hard-hearted.

No. 23 (Ep. LXXXVI)

(A.D. 413)

TO MY DISTINGUISHED LORD, CAECILIANUS, MY SON TRULY AND DESERVEDLY HON- OURED AND CHERISHED IN CHRIST'S LOVE, BISHOP AUGUSTINE SENDS GREETING IN THE LORD

The purity of your administration and your virtu- ous reputation, as well as the praiseworthy zeal and genuine sincerity of your Christian devotion—gifts of God that you rejoice to have bestowed upon you by Him whose promise makes you hope for still better things—have stimulated me to share with your

405, but Monceaux (*Hist. litt. de l'Afrique chrétienne*, vii. 285) shows reasons for assigning it rather to early in 413.

excitaverunt me ut hoc epistulari alloquio aestus causarum mearum excellentia participaret tua. Quantum enim per alias Africae terras te unitati catholicae mirabili efficacia consuluisse gaudemus, tantum dolemus regionem Hipponiensium-Regiorum et ei vicinas partes confines Numidiae praesidali edicti tui vigore nondum adiuvari meruisse, domine eximie et in Christi caritate vere meritoque honorabilis ac suspiciende fili. Quod ne meae potius neglegentiae deputetur, qui episcopalem sarcinam Hippone sustineo, tuae magnificentiae non tacendum putavi. Quantum etiam in campo Hipponiensi haeretica praesumat audacia, si ex fratribus et collegis meis qui haec tuae sublimitati narrare potuerint, vel ex presbytero quem cum litteris misi, fueris audire dignatus, adiuvante domino deo nostro procul dubio providebis, ut tumor sacrilegae vanitatis terrendo sanetur potius quam ulciscendo resecetur.

No. 24 (Ep. XCI)

DOMINO EXIMIO MERITOQUE HONORABILI FRATRI NECTARIO AUGUSTINUS

1 Iam senio frigescentibus membris fervere animum

---

[a] Nectarius was a decurion of Calama, a pagan, though of Christian descent. In spite of the edict of Honorius forbidding any non-Christian celebrations, the Calamans had held pagan festivals which resulted in the destruction of life and property. Fearing the legal consequences, Nectarius wrote asking Augustine to use his influence on the Calamans' behalf (Ep. xc.). Augustine's reply points out the enormity of the offence, argues that paganism must of necessity lead to excess and immorality, and urges Nectarius and the people to adopt Christianity. After eight months Nectarius answered in Ep. ciii., and Augustine in turn replied in Ep. civ., covering much the same ground as here.

Excellency by means of this epistolary converse the
anxieties arising from my controversies. For in proportion as we have been gladdened by the surprising
success of your measures in favour of catholic unity
throughout the other parts of Africa, so do we regret,
my distinguished lord and son truly and deservedly
honoured and cherished in Christ's love, that the
district of Hippo Regius and the territories adjoining
it on the borders of Numidia have not yet been
honoured with the vigorous support of your edict as
governor. I have thought it better to mention this
fact to your Excellency, so that it may not be
attributed rather to negligence on my part, since
I bear the burden of episcopal office at Hippo. If
you condescend to ascertain from my brethren and
colleagues, who are in a position to recount the facts
to your Highness, or from the priest whom I am
sending with this letter, how far the heretics have had
the boldness and effrontery to go in this same region
of Hippo, I am confident you will, with the help of the
Lord our God, take steps to have this puffed-up
irreverence and conceit healed by methods tending to
discourage it rather than cut away by measures that
are purely retaliatory.

No. 24 (Ep. XCI)

(A.D. 408)

AUGUSTINE TO MY DISTINGUISHED AND
DESERVEDLY HONOURED BROTHER, NEC-
TARIUS [a]

I find it admirable but not surprising that, though
age is beginning to chill your limbs, your heart still

151

tuum patriae caritate nec miror et laudo, teque non
tantum tenere memoriter verum etiam vita ac moribus demonstrare, quod nullus sit patriae consulendi
modus aut finis bonis, non invitus immo etiam libens
accipio. Unde supernae cuiusdam patriae, in cuius
sancto amore pro nostro modulo inter eos quibus ad
illam capessendam consulimus, periclitamur atque
laboramus, talem etiam te ipsum civem habere vellemus, ut eius portiunculae in hac terra peregrinanti
nullum consulendi modum finemque censeres, tanto
effectus melior, quanto melior vitati officia debita
praerogares, in eius aeterna pace nullum gaudendi
finem inventurus, cuius ad tempus laboribus nullum
tibi finem statueris consulendi.

2 Verum hoc donec fiat—neque enim desperandum
est illam te patriam posse adquirere vel iam ad-
quirendam prudentissime cogitare, ad quam te pater
etiam, qui in ista genuit, antecessit—hoc ergo donec
fiat, da nobis veniam, si propter patriam nostram,
quam cupimus numquam relinquere, contristamus
patriam tuam, quam cupis florentem relinquere. De
cuius quidem floribus si cum tua prudentia dispute-
mus, non est verendum ne tibi difficile persuadeatur
aut vero etiam non facile occurrat, quem ad modum
florere civitas debeat. Commemoravit poeta ille ve-
strarum clarissimus litterarum quosdam flores Italiae;

---

^a Virgil, *Aen.* vii. 643-644 " quibus Itala iam tum Floruerit
terra alma viris, quibus arserit armis." For the readiness
with which Augustine quotes Virgil compare No. 5, p. 21.
Earlier in life Augustine had been devoted to Virgil, and
at Cassiciacum he had spent much time reading the poet
(*C. Acad.* i. 15. 5, *De Ord.* ii. 20. 54), but later he tended to
despise all the pagan classics (*Conf.* i. 13. 20-22). Here,
Nectarius's use of the word *florere,* "flower," or "flourish,"
of his own province recalls to Augustine Virgil's use of the

glows with patriotic zeal, and I am not sorry, but rather delighted, to learn that you do not merely remember the maxim that " to good men there is no limit or end of devotion to their country," but actually exemplify it in your life and character. That is why we should like to have you enrolled in person as a citizen of a country which is above, in holy love for which we endure perils and toil, as far as in us lies, among those whose good we seek in urging them to make that country their own—and such a citizen that you would think there should be no limit or end to devotion to that fragment of it which is on pilgrimage in this land. So would you become a better man in proportion as you discharged here and now the duties due to that better country, in whose eternal peace you will find no end to rejoicing, if you prescribe for yourself no end to the devotion you bestow upon its temporal tasks.

But until you do so—for we must not surrender **2** the hope that it is in your power to gain, or that even already you must be wisely thinking how you should gain that country to which your own father, who begot you here, has gone before you—until you do so, you must forgive us if for the sake of our country, which we have no desire ever to leave, we inflict distress upon your country, which you desire to leave in the full flower of prosperity. Yet if I were to hold a discussion with your Wisdom about its flowering, I have every confidence that you would not be difficult to convince, or rather that you would easily discover for yourself, in what way a country ought to flower. That poet who enjoys the most renown in your literature has commemorated certain flowers of Italy [a] ; but in that word with reference to Italy, and throughout the letter he keeps playing upon the words *florere* and *flores.*

sed nos in vestra patria non tam experti sumus
"quibus floruerit" terra illa "viris," quam "quibus
arserit armis," immo vero non armis sed flammis nec
arserit, sed incenderit. Quod tantum scelus si fuerit inpunitum nulla digna correctione pravorum, florentem
te patriam putas relicturum? O flores non plane
fructuum sed spinarum! Compara nunc, utrum malis
florere patriam tuam pietate an impunitate, correctis
moribus an securis ausibus; compara ista et vide,
utrum in patriae tuae amore nos vincas, utrum eam
magis veriusque cupias florere quam nos.

3   Intuere paululum ipsos de re publica libros, unde
illum affectum amantissimi civis ebibisti, quod nullus
sit patriae consulendi modus aut finis bonis. Intuere,
obsecro te, et cerne quantis ibi laudibus frugalitas
et continentia praedicetur et erga coniugale vinculum
fides castique honesti ac probi mores, quibus cum
praepollet civitas, vere florere dicenda est. Hi
autem mores in ecclesiis toto orbe crescentibus tamquam in sanctis auditoriis populorum docentur atque
discuntur, et maxime pietas qua verus et verax cola-
tur deus, qui haec omnia quibus animus humanus
divinae societati ad inhabitandam aeternam caele-
stemque civitatem instruitur et aptatur, non solum
iubet adgredienda, verum etiam donat implenda.

---

^a Cicero's *De Republica*, quoted by Nectarius in his letter
to Augustine. The work itself survives only in fragments;
in *Civ. Dei* ii. 21 Augustine gives a summary of Book iii.

country of yours we have experienced not so much " with what men it has flowered " as " with what arms it has blazed," nay rather, not " arms," but " fires," and " not blazed," but " set on fire." If the heinous offence before us were left unpunished with no adequate chastisement of the miscreants, do you think that you would leave your country in full flower? Flowers indeed, but promising thorns, certainly not fruit! Just make the comparison and see whether you prefer your country to flower by practising piety or by escaping punishment, by the discipline of character or by the protection of violence ; make the comparison and see whether in love for your country you outdo us, whether your desire to behold it in full flower is greater and more genuine than ours.

Look for a moment at those very books " On the 3 State " [a] from which you imbibed that sentiment of a loyal subject, that " to good men there is no limit or end of devotion to their country." Look at them, I pray you, and notice the praise with which frugality and self-control are extolled, and fidelity to the marriage-bond, and chaste, honourable, and upright character. When a country is distinguished for these qualities, it may truly be said to be in full flower. Now, it is in the churches that are springing up throughout the world, in the sacred lecture-rooms, one might say, of the nations, that these moral qualities are being taught and learned, and most especially the piety with which worship is paid to the true and truthful God, Who not only commands men to undertake, but also gives them the power to perform, all those things by which the human spirit is trained and fitted for fellowship with God and for dwelling in the everlasting heavenly country. It is for that

Inde est quod deorum multorum falsorumque simulacra et praedixit eversum iri et praecepit everti.
Nihil enim homines tam insociabiles reddit vitae
perversitate quam illorum deorum imitatio, quales
describuntur et commendantur litteris eorum.

4   Denique illi doctissimi viri qui rem publicam
civitatemque terrenam, qualis eis esse debere videbatur, magis domesticis disputationibus requirebant
vel etiam describebant, quam publicis actionibus in-
stituebant atque formabant, egregios atque lauda-
biles quos putabant homines potius quam deos suos
imitandos proponebant erudiendae indoli iuventutis.
Et re vera Terentianus ille adulescens qui spectans
tabulam pictam in pariete, ubi pictura inerat de
adulterio regis deorum, libidinem qua rapiebatur,
stimulis etiam tantae auctoritatis accendit, nullo
modo in illud flagitium vel concupiscendo laberetur
vel perpetrando inmergeretur, si Catonem maluisset
imitari quam Iovem ; sed quo pacto id faceret, cum
in templis adorare cogeretur Iovem potius quam
Catonem ?   Verum haec ex comoedia quibus impiorum luxus et sacrilega superstitio convinceretur,
proferre forsitan non debemus.   Lege vel recole
in eisdem libris quam prudenter disseratur nullo
modo potuisse scriptiones et actiones recipi co-
moediarum, nisi mores recipientium consonarent.
Ita clarissimorum virorum in re publica excellentium

---

a Lev. xxvi. 30 ; Ezek. vi. 4, xxx. 13; Hos. x. 2 ; 3 Kings
xv. 11-13 ; 2 Chron. xxiii. 17, xxxi. 1, xxxiii. 15, xxxiv. 3-4.
  b Ter. *Eun.* 584-591.
156

reason that He predicted the future overthrow **of** the images of the many false gods and enjoined that that overthrow should begin now.[a] For there is nothing that makes men so unsuited for fellowship by reason of their depraved lives as does the imitation of those gods, such as they are described and commended by pagan literature.

In short, those learned men who in private dis- **4** cussion sought after and even portrayed what seemed to them the model republic and earthly state instead of bringing it into being and giving it shape by public service, usually put forward as examples for the training of the youthful character those men they deemed famous and praiseworthy rather than their own gods. And, in fact, that young man in Terence [b] who, on gazing upon a painted wall-panel which represented the adultery of the king of the gods, felt fuel added to the fire of passion that was consuming him by the encouragement given by an authority so eminent, would certainly not have fallen into that sin through desire nor have been overcome by it through bringing it to pass, if he had chosen Cato as his model rather than Jove. But how could he do that when in the temples he was compelled to reverence Jove instead of Cato? And yet perhaps I should not put forward these scenes from comedy to confute the wantonness and the sacrilegious superstition of the ungodly. Read or recall how carefully it is argued in those same books that the writing or acting of comedies could by no means have received public approbation if they had not harmonized with the character of those who approved of them. So the authority of the most outstanding men, both those who are prominent in the State and those who discuss

et de re publica disputantium auctoritate firmatur
nequissimos homines fieri deorum imitatione peiores,
non sane verorum sed falsorum atque fictorum.

5　At enim illa omnia quae antiquitus de vita deorum
moribusque conscripta sunt, longe aliter sunt in-
tellegenda atque interpretanda sapientibus. Ita
vero in templis populis congregatis recitari huiusce
modi salubres interpretationes heri et nudiustertius
audivimus. Quaeso te, sicine caecum est humanum
genus adversus veritatem, ut tam aperta et manifesta non sentiat ? Tot locis pingitur, funditur, tunditur, sculpitur, scribitur, legitur, agitur, cantatur,
saltatur Iuppiter adulteria tanta committens ; quantum erat, ut in suo saltem Capitolio ista prohibens
legeretur ? Haec mala dedecoris impietatisque
plenissima si nemine prohibente in populis ferveant,
adorentur in templis, rideantur in theatris, cum his
victimas immolant, vastetur pecus etiam pauperum,
cum haec histriones agunt et saltant, effundantur
patrimonia divitum, civitates florere dicuntur ?
Horum plane florum non terra fertilis, non aliqua
opulens virtus sed illa dea Flora digna mater inventa
est, cuius ludi scenici tam effusiore et licentiore turpi-
dine celebrantur, ut quivis intellegat quale daemo-
nium sit, quod placari aliter non potest nisi illic non

---

a Perhaps a reference to the attempt made by the Emperor
Julian to allegorize the myths of paganism.

b With this heaping up of verbs *cf. In Ps.* lvi. 16 " (caro)
esuriat, sitiat, dormiat, teneatur, flagelletur, irrideatur,
crucifigatur, sepeliatur."

c Flora was supposed to preside over the blossoming of
plants in spring. The floral games (*Floralia*), which have
been asserted to be the source of the May-day games, were
held from April 28 to May 3, and were accompanied by
such licence that the Church Fathers name them with

the nature of the State, establishes our point that by imitating the gods—not, to be sure, true gods, but false and fabricated gods—the most depraved of men become still worse.

But it may be objected that all those ancient tales 5 about the life and character of the gods are to be understood and interpreted far differently by men of wisdom. Thus, in fact, we heard just the other day harmless interpretations of this kind read to the people gathered in the temples.[a] Tell me, is the human race so blind to truth as not to perceive facts so evident and open ? In so many places Jove is exhibited committing his numerous adulteries by painters, founders, smiths, sculptors, writers, reciters, actors, singers and dancers ; what was the use of reciting, in his own Capitol at any rate, decrees forbidding such sins ? If, with no one to forbid them, these foul deeds that are the culmination of turpitude and ungodliness are enthusiastically acclaimed by the people, worshipped in the temples, applauded in the theatres[b] ; if, when victims are sacrificed to their perpetrators, even the poor are despoiled of their flock, and when actors represent them in dance and action, the rich lavish their fortunes on them—are countries to be described as in flower ? Such flowers as these certainly do not owe their birth to fruitful soil or to any bounteous virtue ; they have found a worthy parent in that goddess Flora,[c] whose theatrical games are celebrated with such unusually abandoned and shameless vileness that anyone may understand what is the nature of a divinity that cannot be conciliated unless there perish as victims on her altars

abhorrence (Min. Felix xxv. 8 ; Cypr. *Idol.* 4 ; Lact. i. 20. 5 ; Arnob. vii. 33 ; Prud. *C. Symm.* i. 266).

aves, non quadrupedes, non denique sanguis humanus,
sed multo scelestius pudor humanus tamquam im-
molatus intereat.

6   Haec dixi, propter quod scripsisti, quantum tibi
aetas fini proxima est, cupere te ut patriam tuam
incolumem ac florentem relinquas. Tollantur illa
omnia vana et insana, convertantur homines ad
verum dei cultum moresque castos et pios ; tunc patriam tuam florentem videbis non opinione stultorum
sed veritate sapientium, cum haec patria carnalis
generationis tuae portio fuerit illius patriae, cui non
corpore sed fide nascimur, ubi omnes sancti et fideles
dei post labores velut hiemales vitae huius intermina
aeternitate florebunt. Nobis itaque cordi est neque
Christianam amittere mansuetudinem neque pernicio-
sum ceteris imitationis exemplum in illa civitate relinquere. Quo modo id agamus, aderit deus, si eis
non ita graviter indignetur. Alioquin et mansuetudo
quam servare cupimus, et disciplina qua uti moderate
nitimur, impediri potest, si deo aliud in occulto placet
sive iudicanti hoc tantum malum flagello acriore
plectendum sive etiam vehementius irascenti, si non
correctis nec ad se conversis ad tempus esse voluerit
inpunitum.

7   Praescribit nobis quodam modo prudentia tua de
persona episcopali et dicis patriam tuam non levi

not birds or beasts or even human bodies, but (a much viler scandal) human modesty and shame.

I have spoken of these things because of the 6 statement in your letter that the nearer you come to the end of your life, the more strongly you desire to leave your country in sound condition and full flower. Take away all those frivolous and unwholesome practices and let men turn to the genuine worship of God and to purity and godliness of character, then you will see your country in full flower, not in the empty opinion of the foolish, but in the sober judgement of the wise, when this country that gave you birth after the flesh has become a part of that country to which we are born not by the body, but by faith. There, after the wintry labours of this life, all God's saints and faithful people will flower in an endless eternity. Therefore is it our dear desire neither to put away Christian meekness nor to leave your country as a baleful example for others to follow. In our attempt to realize this hope, God will be at hand to help, provided He be not too grievously wroth with them. Otherwise both the meekness that we desire to preserve and the punishment that it is our aim to impose in moderation may be arrested, if God in His hidden wisdom ordaineth differently, whether He appoint that this immeasurable evil be punished with a keener chastisement, or whether, should the guilty fail to repent and to turn to Him, He shall will in still more vehement wrath to leave it in this world unpunished.

Your Wisdom lays down for me certain principles 7 for the conduct of my episcopal office and pleads that your native place has been brought to a serious pass by a grave misdemeanour on the part of its in-

populi sui errato prolapsam. "Quod quidem si iuris
publici rigore metiamur, debet plecti severiore censura ; sed episcopum," inquis, " fas non est nisi salutem hominibus impertire et pro statu meliore causis
adesse et apud omnipotentem deum veniam aliorum
mereri delictis." Hoc omnino servare conamur, ut
severiore censura nemo plectatur neque a nobis
neque ab alio ullo intercedentibus nobis, et salutem
hominibus cupimus impertire, quae posita est in recte
vivendi felicitate, non in male faciendi securitate.
Veniam quoque non tantum nostris verum et aliorum
instamus delictis mereri, quod impetrare nisi pro
correctis omnino non possumus. Adiungis etiam et
dicis : "Quanta possum supplicatione deposco, ut
si defendenda res est, innoxius defendatur, ab innocentibus molestia separetur."

8   Accipe breviter quae commissa sint, et noxios
ab innocentibus ipse discerne. Contra recentissimas
leges Kalendis Iuniis festo paganorum sacrilega
sollemnitas agitata est, nemine prohibente, tam in-
solenti ausu, ut, quod nec Iuliani temporibus factum
est, petulantissima turba saltantium in eodem prorsus
vico ante fores transiret ecclesiae. Quam rem in-
licitissimam atque indignissimam clericis prohibere
temptantibus, ecclesia lapidata est. Deinde post
dies ferme octo, cum leges notissimas episcopus ordini

---

a In addition to the regular duty of the bishop to hear
and decide clerical cases, the Emperor Constantine allowed
either party in a civil suit to appeal to the bishop, but
episcopal intercession for those accused, all along looked
upon as a duty and regarded with favour, received legal
sanction only under Justinian. These avocations occupied
great portions of the bishop's time, as Augustine frequently
complains (Ep. xxxiii. 5, ccxiii. 5, etc.).

habitants. "Should we estimate it by the severity of the public law, it deserves to be punished with a harsher sentence, but a bishop "—you say—" may not do aught but contribute to men's welfare, and attend court *a* to improve conditions there, and win before Almighty God pardon for other men's sins." It is certainly our endeavour to secure greater mercy, either from ourselves or from any other through our intercession, in the sentencing of those who are punished, and it is our desire to contribute to men's welfare. But that welfare consists in the happiness that comes from righteous living, not in the impunity that may attend evil-doing. And as for pardon, we earnestly endeavour to win it not merely for our own sins, but for those of others as well, but we certainly cannot obtain it except for those who have repented. You go on then to say, " I entreat you with all possible urgency not to prosecute the guiltless, if the matter must come to a prosecution, but to ward off any trouble from the innocent."

Let me briefly remind you of the offence, then 8 draw the distinction for yourself between the innocent and the guilty. In defiance of quite recent legislation a sacrilegious celebration was held on the first of June, a pagan feast-day, with no prohibition from anyone and with such insolent effrontery that an impudent crowd of dancers actually passed along the same street in front of the church-doors—a thing that never happened even in Julian's time. When the clergy attempted to stop this most illegal and insulting procedure, the church was stoned. Then, almost a week later, when the bishop had drawn the attention of the magistrates to the well-known laws

replicasset, et dum ea quae iussa sunt velut implere
disponunt, iterum ecclesia lapidata est. Postridie
nostris ad inponendum perditis metum, quod videbatur, apud acta dicere volentibus publica iura negata
sunt, eodemque ipso die, ne vel divinitus terrerentur,
grando lapidationibus reddita est ; qua transacta continuo tertiam lapidationem et postremo ignes ecclesiasticis tectis atque hominibus intulerunt, unum
servorum dei, qui oberrans occurrere potuit, occi-
derunt, ceteris partim ubi potuerant latitantibus,
partim qua potuerant fugientibus, cum interea con-
trusus atque coartatus quodam loco se occultaret
episcopus, ubi se ad mortem quaerentium voces audie-
bat sibique increpantium quod eo non invento gratis
tantum perpetrassent scelus. Gesta sunt haec ab
hora ferme decima usque ad noctis partem non
minimam. Nemo compescere, nemo subvenire temp-
tavit illorum quorum esse gravis posset auctoritas,
praeter unum peregrinum, per quem et plurimi
servi dei de manibus interficere conantium liberati
sunt et multa extorta praedantibus. Per quem
clarum factum est quam facile illa vel omnino non

on the subject, and they were, to all intents and purposes, preparing to put the legal prescriptions into effect, the church was stoned again. Next day, when our people wanted to lodge a complaint in court, with the object, apparently, of inspiring those abandoned characters with fear, their rights were denied them, and on the very same day, to see if menaces from heaven might not dismay them, their stonings were answered by a shower of hail; but when it was over, they immediately cast another shower of stones and finally fire upon the roofs of the church and the people within. One servant of God who was wandering about and may have run into them, they put to death, the others partly taking shelter wherever they could, partly escaping wherever they could. In the meantime the bishop was hiding in a certain spot into which he had thrust himself to lie all cramped, and from which he kept hearing the voices of those who were seeking him to put him to death and were reproaching themselves for letting him escape and so for perpetrating such a heinous crime to no effect. This went on from almost four o'clock until a late hour of night. No attempt at repression, no attempt at rescue was made by any of those who could have exercised some weight of authority. Only one person interfered, a stranger, by whom a considerable number of God's servants were delivered from the hands of those who were seeking to slay them, and much property as well was recovered from looters. His example made it clear how easily those outrages might have been wholly prevented, or have been arrested if they had actually begun, provided only that the inhabitants and, most of all, the leading

fierent vel coepta desisterent, si cives maximeque primates ea fieri perficique vetuissent.

9 Proinde in universa illa civitate non innocentes a nocentibus sed minus nocentes a nocentioribus poteris fortasse discernere. Nam in parvo peccato illi sunt qui metu deterriti maximeque, ne offenderent eos quos in illo oppido plurimum posse et inimicos ecclesiae noverant, opem ferre non ausi sunt ; scelerati autem omnes, quibus etsi non facientibus neque inmittentibus tamen volentibus ista commissa sunt ; sceleratiores, qui commiserunt ; sceleratissimi, qui inmiserunt. Sed de inmissione suspicionem putemus esse, non veritatem, nec ea discutiamus, quae nisi tormentis eorum per quos inquiruntur, inveniri omnino non possunt. Demus etiam veniam timori eorum, qui potius deum pro episcopo et servis eius deprecandum quam potentes inimicos ecclesiae offendendos esse putaverunt. Quid eos qui restant, nullane censes disciplina cohercendos et proponendum aestimas inpunitum tam immanis furoris exemplum ? Non praeterita vindicando pascere iram nostram studemus, sed misericorditer in futurum consulendo satagimus. Habent homines mali ubi et per Christianos non solum mansuete verum etiam utiliter salubriterque plectantur ; habent enim quod corpore incolumi vivunt, habent unde vivunt, habent unde

citizens had forbidden them, either from the very first or after they had started.

Accordingly you will hardly be able to draw a **9** distinction in the whole community between the innocent and the guilty, but only perhaps between the less guilty and the more guilty. For slight is the sin of those who were deterred by fear (and especially by fear of offending those known to them to be men of great influence in the town and hostile towards the Church) from venturing to give any assistance; but all are guilty who, although not participating or instigating, were consenting to the outrage; more guilty are those who perpetrated it, and most guilty of all are those who instigated it. Let us assume that we have only suspicions who these instigators were, and no certain knowledge, and let us refrain from discussing facts which simply cannot be ascertained without the torturing of the witnesses. Let us, too, make allowance for the fear felt by those who thought it better to pray to God for the bishop and God's servants than to give offence to influential enemies of the Church. What about those who remain? Do you give it as your opinion that they should escape all punishment and censure? And do you think we should set the example of leaving so barbarous an outrage unpunished? We have no desire to gratify our anger by exacting retribution for past offences, but we are concerned to provide for the future in a spirit of compassion. Evil men have certain points in which they can be punished by Christians not only in gentleness, but also with profit and improvement to themselves. They have the life and health of the body; they have the means of sustaining that life;

male vivunt. Duo prima salva sint, ut quos paeniteat sint; hoc optamus, hoc, quantum in nobis
est, etiam inpensa opera instamus. Tertium vero
si deus voluerit tamquam putre noxiumque resecari,
valde misericorditer puniet; si autem vel amplius
voluerit vel ne hoc quidem permiserit, altioris et
profecto iustioris consilii ratio penes ipsum est; a
nobis curam officiumque oportet inpendi, quousque
videre conceditur, deprecantibus eum, ut animum
nostrum adprobet, quo cunctis volumus esse con-
sultum, nihilque fieri sinat per nos quod et nobis et
ecclesiae suae non expedire longe melius novit ipse
quam nos.

10 Modo cum apud Calamam essemus, ut nostri in tam
gravi dolore vel consolarentur afflicti vel sedarentur
accensi, quantum potuimus, quod in tempore opor-
tuisse existimavimus, cum Christianis egimus. Deinde
ipsos etiam paganos, mali tanti caput et causam,
petentes ut ab eis videremur, admisimus, ut hac
occasione admoneremus eos, quid facere deberent,
si saperent, non tantum pro removenda praesenti
sollicitudine verum etiam pro inquirenda salute perpetua. Multa a nobis audierunt, multum etiam ipsi
rogaverunt; sed absit ut tales servi simus, quos ab
eis rogari delectet, a quibus noster dominus non
rogatur. Unde pervides pro vivacitate mentis tuae
ad hoc esse nitendum servata mansuetudine et
moderatione Christiana, ut aut ceteros deterreamus
eorum imitari perversitatem aut ceteros optemus

they have the means of living a wicked life. Let the first two be untouched so that there may be some who repent ; this is our prayer, this, as far as in us lies, we spare no effort to secure. But for the third, if it be God's will to take it away like some foul and virulent growth, He will inflict punishment in great compassion ; but if it be His will to go farther and to allow not even this, the reason for this higher and certainly more just design rests with Himself. Our duty is to devote our zeal and efforts, according to the light that is granted us, to praying God for His approval of our intention to promote the welfare of all and to let nothing be done through us that is not for the good both of ourselves and of the Church ; for He knows that much better than we do.

Recently when I was at Calama with the purpose of 10 consoling the distress, or else appeasing the indignation, of our people in their grievous sorrow, I used all my influence with the Christians to bring about what I thought was at the moment expedient. Then when the pagans themselves, the fount and cause of this great outrage, besought me for an interview, I received them, with the object of advising them on this occasion of the course of action that they ought to pursue if they were wise, not only to banish the present anxiety but also to seek for everlasting salvation. They listened to many things that I said, and even made many petitions themselves ; but far be it from me to be such a servant as to take delight in petitions by those who make no petitions to my Master. So with your quick mind you will clearly see that, while preserving our meekness and Christian moderation, we must direct our efforts either to deterring others from imitating their ob-

eorum imitari correctionem. Damna, quae inlata
sunt, vel tolerantur a Christianis vel resarciuntur
per Christianos. Animarum nos lucra, quibus ad-
quirendis cum periculo etiam sanguinis inhiamus, et
in loco illo quaestuosius provenire et aliis locis illo
exemplo non impediri desideramus. Dei misericordia nobis praestet de tua salute gaudere.

No. 25 (Ep. XCVII)

DOMINO EXIMIO ET MERITO PRAESTANTISSIMO MULTUMQUE IN CHRISTI CARITATE HONO-RANDO FILIO OLYMPIO AUGUSTINUS IN DOMINO SALUTEM

1 Quamvis mox ut audivimus te merito sublimatum,
cum ipsa fama nondum certissima nobis esset, nihil
aliud de animo tuo credidimus erga ecclesiam dei,
cuius te veraciter filium esse gaudemus, quam quod
tuis litteris mox aperuisti, tamen etiam illis lectis,
quibus ultro dignatus es, etiam si pigri et cunctantes

ª The *Edictum quod de Unitate* of March 5, 405 (*Cod.
Theod.* xvi. xi. 2), promulgated by the Emperor Honorius
to make Donatism a penal offence, had only succeeded
in producing in Numidia fresh outbreaks of Donatist fury,
of which previous letters have provided examples. On the
downfall of Stilicho the Donatists believed for a moment
that persecution would end, but Olympius, Stilicho's betrayer, who became Master of the Offices on November 14,
408 (the " promotion " mentioned by Augustine), confirmed
the anti-Donatist legislation by a rescript of November 24
addressed to the African Proconsul, whom Augustine besought in No. 27 (Ep. c.) to exercise coercion upon the
Donatists but not to impose the penalty of death. Before
news of Olympius's confirmation had reached Africa, a
deputation was sent by the African bishops to beg the
Emperor to put in force the laws against disturbers of peace

stinacy or to praying that others may imitate their
repentance. The losses that were inflicted are either
being borne by Christians or are being made good
by Christians. As for the gain of souls, which we
long to secure even at the peril of our own body, we
hope that your district will furnish an unusually
precious harvest and that other districts will not be
kept back by that example. May God in His mercy
grant us to rejoice over your salvation !

No. 25 (Ep. XCVII)

(A.D. 408)

TO OLYMPIUS,[a] MY EXCELLENT AND JUSTLY
DISTINGUISHED LORD AND SON WORTHY
OF MUCH HONOUR IN THE LOVE OF CHRIST,
AUGUSTINE SENDS GREETING IN THE LORD

As soon as we heard of your well-deserved promotion, although the report that reached us was still
very indefinite, we were confident that your attitude
towards the Church of God, of which we rejoice that
you are truly a son, is no other than what you have
now revealed in your letter. Nevertheless, I write
to you, my excellent and justly distinguished lord and

and religion. To secure Olympius's support Augustine sends
this letter by a priest passing through Hippo on his way
from Mileum to Rome. The letter is important too because,
according to Zosimus, Olympius merely used Christianity
as a cloak for his evil-doing, but Augustine's warm and
appreciative language here gives quite another view of his
character. If allowance must be made for Zosimus's ill-will
to all Christians, it must equally be made for Augustine's
want of personal knowledge of Olympius and the exaggeratedly deferential tone of epistolary address.

essemus, exhortationem benivolentissimam mittere,
ut instruente humilitate nostra per religiosam oboedientiam tuam dominus, cuius munere talis es, ecclesiae suae iam iamque subveniat, maiore fiducia
tibi scribimus, domine eximie et merito praestantissime multumque in Christi caritate honorande fili.

2   Et fratres quidem multi sancti collegae mei graviter
ecclesia perturbata profecti sunt paene fugientes ad
gloriosissimum comitatum, quos sive iam videris sive
litteras eorum ab urbe Roma opportunitate cuiusquam occasionis acceperis, ego tamen, licet nullum
consilium cum eis communicare potuerim, non potui
praetermittere per hunc fratrem et conpresbyterum
meum, qui urgenti necessitate pro salute civis sui
etiam media hieme quomodocumque ad illas partes
venire compulsus est, et salutare et admonere caritatem tuam, quam habes in Christo Iesu domino nostro,
ut opus tuum bonum diligentissima acceleretur in-
stantia, quo noverint inimici ecclesiae leges illas quae
de idolis confringendis et haereticis corrigendis vivo
Stilichone in Africam missae sunt, voluntate im-
peratoris piissimi et fidelissimi constitutas ; quo
nesciente vel nolente factum sive dolose iactant
sive libenter putant atque hinc animos inperitorum
turbulentissimos reddunt nobisque periculose ac
vehementer infestos.

3   Hoc autem quod petendo vel suggerendo admoneo
praestantiam tuam, non dubito omnium per Africam

---

* Stilicho, son of a Vandal captain, became one of
Theodosius I.'s most distinguished generals, and under
Honorius was the virtual ruler of the West. He defeated
Alaric and Radagaisus, but was assassinated in 408. He
was the patron of the poet Claudian, who dedicated to him
the panegyric *De Consulatu Stilichonis.*

son worthy of much honour in the love of Christ, with all the greater confidence after reading that letter in which of your own accord you deigned to send us, even if we were hesitant and backward, a very kind invitation to use our humble efforts to point out to you how, through your pious obedience, the Lord, by whose gift you have become what you are, may at this juncture come to the assistance of His Church.

And indeed, many of the brethren, my holy col-2 leagues, have by reason of the Church's serious troubles started out almost as fugitives for the imperial court; you may have seen them or by some fortunate encounter have received a letter of theirs from Rome. But for my part, although I was unable to talk over any plans with them, I could not miss the opportunity provided by this brother and fellow-priest of mine, who is driven by the urgent peril of a fellow-citizen to make the journey as best he can, even though it is mid-winter, to your part of the world, of greeting and exhorting you by that affection you have in Christ Jesus our Lord, to hasten on your good work with the most pressing attention. So shall the enemies of the Church know that those laws about the demolition of idols and the correction of heretics, which were sent to Africa while Stilicho [a] was still alive, were drawn up at the desire of our most godly and faithful emperor. They deceitfully allege or fondly imagine that this action was taken without his knowledge or against his will, and thus they incite the mind of the ignorant to the utmost pitch of violence and to a vehemence of hostility that is fraught with peril to us.

But I am quite sure that in submitting this petition 3 or suggestion for your Eminence's consideration, I

collegarum meorum fieri voluntate. Arbitror quacumque primitus exorta occasione facillime posse
ac debere maturari, ut noverint, sicut dixi, homines
vani, quorum et adversantium salutem requirimus, et
leges quae pro ecclesia Christi missae sunt, magis
Theodosii filium quam Stilichonem curasse mittendas.
Propterea quippe memoratus presbyter harum perlator, cum de regione sit Milevitana, ab episcopo
suo venerabili fratre meo Severo, qui tuam mecum
sincerissimam dilectionem multum salutat, per
Hipponem-Regium, ubi ego sum, transire iussus est,
quia, cum forte simul essemus in magnis ecclesiae
tribulationibus et perturbationibus, quaerebamus
occasionem scribendi ad eximietatem tuam et non
inveniebamus. Iam quidem unam epistulam miseram
in negotio sancti fratris et collegae mei Bonifatii
episcopi Cataquensis ; sed nondum ad nos per-
venerant graviora, quae nos vehementius agitarent,
quibus comprimendis vel corrigendis quem ad modum
meliore secundum viam Christi consilio succurratur,
commodius episcopi qui propterea navigaverunt,
cum tanta benignitate tui cordis acturi sunt, qui
potuerunt communi consilio diligentius deliberatum
aliquid ferre, quantum temporis permittebat angustia. Illud tamen quo animum clementissimi et
religiosissimi principis erga ecclesiam provincia
noverit, nullo modo esse differendum, sed etiam

---

^a The emperor Honorius.   ^b For Severus see p. 108, n. b.
^c This business of Boniface forms the subject of Ep.
xcvi. ; it concerned the possession of a piece of land
acquired by Boniface's predecessor, which Boniface wanted
to have regularly granted to himself. Cataquas was probably
near Hippo, for Boniface is frequently found in correspondence and on business with Augustine (Epp. xcvi.,
cxxxix., cxliii., cxlix., clii.).

am acting agreeably to the desire of all my colleagues throughout Africa. My opinion is that steps very easily could and should be taken at the first opportunity that arises to let those vain men, whose welfare we seek even though they are our opponents, know, as I said already, that it was due to the care of Theodosius's son [a] rather than of Stilicho that the laws that were sent to Africa for the Church of Christ were sent at all. For this reason, then, the above-mentioned priest, the bearer of this letter, being from the district of Mileve, was ordered by his bishop, my revered brother Severus, [b] who joins me in sending hearty greetings to your genuine affection, to pass through Hippo Regius, where I am stationed, because, as we happened to be together in the great tribulations and anxieties of the Church, we were seeking an opportunity of writing to your Excellency and found none. I have already sent one letter about the business of my holy brother and colleague, Boniface, [c] the bishop of Cataquas, but this more serious news had not yet reached us to trouble us more keenly. As to the way in which you may come to our assistance in suppressing and punishing those offences with a wiser plan according to the method of Christ, that will more suitably form the subject of negotiation between the bishops who have made the voyage with that end in view, and yourself in your great and heartfelt benevolence. They have been able to bring with them some scheme that has been carefully thought out in mutual consultation, as far as the shortness of time allowed. But this other point, how to let the province know the attitude of our most gracious and godly sovereign towards the Church, should on no account be post-

antequam episcopos qui profecti sunt, videas, quam primum tua praestantissima pro Christi membris in tribulatione maxima constitutis vigilantia potuerit, accelerandum suggero, peto, obsecro, flagito. Neque enim parvum in his malis solatium dominus obtulit, quod te voluit multo amplius posse quam poteras, quando iam de tuis multis et magnis bonis operibus gaudebamus.

4 Multum sane de quorundam neque paucorum fide firma et stabili gratulamur, qui ex occasione legum ipsarum ad Christianam religionem vel catholicam pacem conversi sunt, pro quorum salute sempiterna nos in hac temporali etiam periclitari delectat. Propterea enim maxime ab hominibus nimium durumque perversis nunc inimicitiarum graviores impetus sustinemus, quos nonnulli eorum nobiscum patientissime sustinent; sed plurimum infirmitati metuimus, donec discant et valeant adiuvante misericordissima gratia domini saeculum praesens et hominum diem robore cordis valentiore contemnere. Commonitorium quod misi, fratribus episcopis, si, ut puto, nondum ibi sunt, ab eximietate tua illis tradatur, cum venerint. Tantam quippe tui sincerissimi pectoris habemus fiduciam, ut adiuvante domino deo nostro non solum impertitorem auxilii te velimus verum etiam consilii participem.

---

[a] *Hominum dies* apparently occurs only here in Augustine, but compare Ep. cxl. 12 "humanus dies et vitae huius prolixitas concupiscitur," and Seneca, Ep. lxxxiii. 2 "observabo me . . . et . . . diem meum recognoscam. Hoc nos

poned; I recommend, beg, beseech, implore you to hurry it on, even before you see the bishops who are on their way, as soon as is possible for you in your most earnest watchfulness for the members of Christ who are undergoing this very heavy trial. Amid these evils the Lord has given us no small comfort by being pleased to extend your sphere of influence much beyond what it was before, for even then we were rejoicing in the number and magnitude of your good works.

We have indeed much cause for rejoicing in the 4 firm and steadfast faith of some, and they are not a few, who were converted to the Christian religion and to Catholic peace by the opportuneness of those laws; for their eternal welfare we are glad even to risk our temporal welfare. For on this account we are enduring more violent outbreaks of hostility especially from men of excessive and obdurate perversity; and these some of the converts endure most patiently with us. But we have very great fears for their weakness until by the help of the Lord's compassionate favour they acquire the wisdom and the strength to despise the present age and the day of men[a] with sturdier and stouter spirit. The letter of instructions I am sending with this for my brother-bishops will your Excellency hand to them when they arrive, if, as I imagine, they have not yet come? Such confidence we place in your most unfeigned devotion that with the help of the Lord our God we wish to have you not only bestow assistance, but also take a share in our counsels.

pessimos facit, quod nemo vitam suam respicit." The Christian use of the phrase is no doubt suggested by the Scriptural "day of the Lord."

ST. AUGUSTINE

No. 26 (Ep. XCIX)

RELIGIOSISSIMAE ATQUE IN CHRISTI MEMBRIS
MERITO SANCTEQUE LAUDABILI FAMULAE
DEI ITALICAE AUGUSTINUS IN DOMINO
SALUTEM

1 Tres epistulas tuae benignitatis acceperam, cum
ista rescripsi : unam quae adhuc meas litteras exige-
bat, alteram quae ad te iam pervenisse indicabat,
tertiam quae benivolentissimam pro nobis curam
tuam etiam de domo clarissimi et egregii iuvenis
Iuliani, quae nostris adhaeret parietibus, continebat.
Qua accepta, continuo respondere non distuli, quia
procurator eximietatis tuae cito se Romam posse
mittere scripsit. Cuius litteris graviter contristati
sumus, quod ea quae illic in urbe vel circa urbem
geruntur, non nobis insinuare curavit, ut certum apud
nos fieret quod incertae famae credere nolebamus.
Fratrum quippe litteris ante transmissis quamvis
molesta et dura multo tamen leviora nuntiata sunt.
Plus sane quam dici potest, miratus sum, quod nec
tanta occasione hominum tuorum fratres sancti episcopi scripserint nec epistula tua quicquam nobis de
tantis tribulationibus vestris insinuaverit, quae utique
per viscera caritatis et nostrae sunt, nisi forte faciendum non putasti, quod nihil prodesse duxisti aut

---

a Probably identical with the Italica to whom Augustine
wrote Ep. xcii. to console her on the death of her husband.
She is probably also the Italica to whom Chrysostom wrote
in 406 (Ep. clxx.), and appears to have enjoyed both wealth
and position. The calamity to which Augustine refers is
the capture of Rome in 408 by Alaric.

No. 26 (Ep. XCIX)

(A.D. 409)

TO THE VERY DEVOUT HANDMAID OF GOD,
ITALICA,[a] DESERVEDLY AND PIOUSLY
PRAISED AMONG THE MEMBERS OF CHRIST,
AUGUSTINE SENDS GREETING IN THE LORD

Three letters from your Grace have reached me up 1
to the moment of my writing this reply ; the first
still demanded a letter from me, the second intimated
that you had by then received it, and the third
contained the assurance of your most kind solicitude
on my behalf, especially in the matter of the house
belonging to that illustrious and distinguished young
man, Julian, which adjoins my own walls. On receiving it I lost no time in replying promptly, since your
Excellency's agent wrote that he was in a position
to send to Rome at an early date. His letter caused
me grievous disappointment, in that he did not take
the trouble to let me know what is happening in and
around Rome, so that we might know for certain
what we were reluctant to believe on uncertain
rumour. The letters of the brethren that were sent
to us before his, conveyed news that was vexatious
and affecting enough, but still none too serious, but
I was more surprised than I can tell you that my
brethren, the holy bishops, did not seize such an excellent opportunity to write to me as that provided
by your bearers, and that your letters gave me no
news at all about the great trials that you are passing
through, though they are ours too by reason of our
heart-felt affection. But perhaps you decided not to
mention them, because you thought it would do no

179

nos tuis litteris maestificari noluisti. Prodest aliquid, quantum ego arbitror, etiam ista cognoscere, primo quia iniustum est *gaudere* velle *cum gaudentibus et flere* non velle *cum flentibus*, deinde quia *tribulatio patientiam operatur, patientia probationem, probatio spem, spes autem non confundit, quia caritas dei diffusa est in cordibus nostris per spiritum sanctum, qui datus est nobis.*

2 Absit itaque ut recusemus audire etiam quae amara et tristia sunt erga carissimos nostros. Nescio quo enim modo minus fit quod *patitur unum membrum*, si *compatiuntur alia membra.* Nec ipsa mali relevatio fit per communionem cladis sed per solatium caritatis, ut, quamvis alii ferendo patiuntur, alii cognoscendo compatiuntur, communis sit tamen tribulatio, quibus probatio, spes, dilectio spiritusque communis est. Omnes autem nos dominus consolatur, qui et haec temporalia mala praedixit et post haec bona aeterna promisit. Nec debet, cum proelietur, infringi, qui vult post proelium coronari, vires illo subministrante certantibus, qui praeparat ineffabilia dona victoribus.

3 Rescripta illa nostra non tibi ad nos auferant scribendi fiduciam, praesertim quia timorem nostrum non inprobabili defensione lenisti. Parvulos tuos resalutamus et in Christo tibi grandescere optamus,

---

ᵃ Rom. xii. 15.   *ᵇ* Rom. v. 3-5.   *ᶜ* 1 Cor. xii. 26.

good or because you did not want your letter to sadden me. It does do some good, in my humble opinion, to know even sad news, first because it is unfair to be willing to " rejoice with them that do rejoice " and to be unwilling to " weep with them that weep," [a] and then because " tribulation worketh patience, and patience experience, and experience hope ; and hope maketh not ashamed, because the love of God is shed abroad in our hearts by the Holy Ghost which is given unto us." [b]

Far be it from us, then, to refuse to hear even 2 the bitter and sorrowful things that befall those who are very dear to us. For somehow or other what one member suffers is mitigated if the other members suffer with it. [c] But this mitigation of affliction is effected not by participation in the calamity but by the consolation love provides, and so, although some bear the actual burden of sorrow and others share the burden with sympathetic understanding, the tribulation is yet common to both, since they have in common the same experience, the same hope, the same love and the same spirit. But all of us alike have the consolation of the Lord, who both foretold these temporal afflictions and promised eternal blessings after them. And he who after the battle would receive the crown ought not to be broken in spirit while the battle is on, for He Who prepares unspeakable gifts for the victors ministers strength to them when they are engaged in the conflict.

Do not let that reply of mine take away your 3 confidence in writing to me, especially since you have had a quite acceptable excuse for soothing my fears. I return the greetings of your little ones and pray that they may grow up for you in Christ.

qui iam in hac aetate cernunt quam sit amor huius
saeculi periculosus et noxius. Atque utinam, cum
magna et dura quatiuntur, parva et flexibilia corrigantur. De domo illa quid dicam, nisi benignissimae
tuae curae gratias agam ? Nam eam quam dare
possumus, nolunt, quam volunt autem dare non
possumus. Neque enim, sicut falso audierunt, a de-
cessore meo relicta est ecclesiae, sed inter antiqua
eius praedia possidetur et antiquae alteri ecclesiae
sic cohaeret quem ad modum ista qua de agitur,
alteri.

No. 27 (Ep. C)

DOMINO EXIMIO MERITOQUE HONORABILI IN-
SIGNITERQUE LAUDABILI FILIO DONATO
AUGUSTINUS IN DOMINO SALUTEM

1   Nollem quidem in his afflictionibus esse Africanam
ecclesiam constitutam, ut terrenae ullius potestatis
indigeret auxilio. Sed quia, sicut apostolus dicit,
non est potestas nisi a deo, procul dubio, cum per
vos sincerissimos catholicae matris filios eidem sub-
venitur, *auxilium nostrum in nomine domini est, qui
fecit caelum et terram.* Quis enim non sentiat in

---

^a It is uncertain which churches are here meant. In
addition to the Donatist church and *basilica Leontiana*
mentioned in Ep. xxix. 11 above (p. 89), there were at
Hippo other four churches : the *basilica maior* or *basilica
Pacis,* beside which was a chapel to St. Stephen (Ep. ccxiii.,
C.D. xxii. 8. 22, *Serm.* 318, 319, 356); the *basilica ad octo
martyres,* built by Augustine (*Serm.* 356. 10); a chapel *ad
viginti martyres* (*C.D.* xxii. 8. 9, *Serm.* 148, 325), and a
chapel dedicated to St. Theogenes (*memoria sancti Theogenis,
Serm.* 273. 7).

^b The name is of very frequent occurrence in Africa;
in Augustine's works there are about twenty-five different

Already, young as they are, they perceive how dangerous and harmful is the love of the present world. And would that, when the tall and sturdy things are shaken, the lowly and yielding may receive correction! What shall I say about that house, except to thank you for your very generous thought? For the house I can give they do not wish, and the one they wish, I cannot give, since it was not left to the Church by my predecessor, as they were wrongly informed, but is held among its ancient properties and adjoins the one ancient church just as the one now under consideration adjoins the other.[a]

No. 27 (Ep. C)

(A.D. 409)

TO DONATUS,[b] MY EXCELLENT LORD, WORTHY OF ALL HONOUR, AND EMINENTLY PRAISE-WORTHY SON, AUGUSTINE SENDS GREETING IN THE LORD

I should wish indeed that the African Church were 1 not placed in such afflictions as to require the aid of any earthly power, but since, as the Apostle says, "there is no power but of God,"[c] it is true that when you, a very whole-hearted son of our Catholic Mother, come to her aid, "our help is in the name of the Lord, Who made heaven and earth."[d] For amid such grievous afflictions who does not realize, my excellent lord, worthy of all honour, and eminently

individuals so called. This Donatus was proconsul of Africa, retiring from that post about 410, when Augustine addresses him in Ep. cxii.

[c] Rom. xiii. 1.   [d] Ps. cxx. 2.

tantis malis non parvam nobis consolationem divinitus missam, cum tu vir talis et Christi nominis amantissimus proconsularibus es sublimatus insignibus, ut ab sceleratis et sacrilegis ausibus inimicos ecclesiae bonae tuae voluntati potestas sociata cohiberet, domine eximie meritoque honorabilis insigniterque laudabilis fili ? Denique unum solum est quod in tua iustitia pertimescimus, ne forte quoniam, quicquid mali contra Christianam societatem ab hominibus impiis ingratisque committitur, profecto gravius est et atrocius, quam si in alios talia committantur, tu quoque pro immanitate facinorum ac non potius pro lenitatis Christianae consideratione censeas cohercendum. Quod te per ipsum Christum ne facias obsecramus. Neque enim vindictam de inimicis in hac terra requirimus aut vero ad eas angustias animi nos debent coartare quae patimur, ut obliviscamur quid nobis praeceperit, pro cuius veritate ac nomine patimur ; diligimus inimicos nostros et oramus pro eis. Unde ex occasione terribilium iudicum ac legum, ne in aeterni iudicii poenas incidant, corrigi eos cupimus, non necari ; nec disciplinam circa eos neglegi volumus nec supplicia, quae digna sunt, exerceri. Sic ergo eorum peccata compesce, ut sint quos paeniteat peccavisse.

2   Quaesumus igitur, ut, cum ecclesiae causas audis, quamlibet nefariis iniuriis appetitam vel afflictam esse cognoveris, potestatem occidendi te habere obliviscaris, petitionem nostram non obliviscaris.

ᵃ Luke vi. 27-28.

praiseworthy son, that no small consolation has been sent us from heaven, when a man of your character and great devotion to the name of Christ has been raised to the dignity of proconsul, so that your power seconded by your goodwill may restrain the enemies of the Church from their criminal and sacrilegious violence ? In short, there is only one thing that we fear in your administration of justice, namely, that perhaps, since whatever evil impious and irreverent men commit against the Christian community is surely more serious and more heinous than if the same evil were committed against others, you personally may decide to administer punishment in proportion to the enormity of the offence instead of in accordance with regard for Christian gentleness. We beseech you for Jesus' sake to refrain from doing so. For we exact no vengeance from our enemies on this earth, nor indeed should our sufferings drive us to such mental straits that we forget the injunctions of Him for Whose truth and name we suffer ; we love our enemies and pray for them.[a] So, in availing ourselves of the terror of judges and laws, we desire their repentance, not their death, so that they may be saved from falling into the penalties of the eternal judgement. We do not wish to see them quite absolved from punishment, nor, on the other hand, visited with the torments they deserve. Check their sins, therefore, in such a way as to produce repentance in at least a few.

I beg you then, when you are trying cases con- **2** cerning the Church, however outrageous the injuries with which you discover it has been assailed or distressed, to forget that you possess the power of life and death, but not to forget my entreaty. And do

185

Non tibi vile sit neque contemptibile, fili honorabiliter dilectissime, quod vos rogamus ne occidantur, pro quibus dominum rogamus ut corrigantur. Excepto etiam, quod a perpetuo proposito recedere non debemus *vincendi in bono malum*, illud quoque prudentia tua cogitet quod causas ecclesiasticas insinuare vobis nemo praeter ecclesiasticos curat. Proinde si occidendos in his homines putaveritis, deterrebitis nos, ne per operam nostram ad vestrum iudicium aliquid tale perveniat, quo comperto illi in nostram perniciem licentiore audacia grassabuntur, necessitate nobis impacta ut etiam occidi ab eis eligamus, quam eos occidendos vestris iudiciis ingeramus. Hanc admonitionem, petitionem, obsecrationem meam ne, quaeso, aspernanter accipias. Neque enim te arbitror non recolere magnam me ad te et multo quam nunc es altius sublimatum, etiam si episcopus non essem, fiduciam tamen habere potuisse. Cito interim per edicta excellentiae tuae noverint haeretici Donatistae manere leges contra errorem suum latas, quas iam nihil valere arbitrantur et iactant, ne vel sic nobis parcere aliquatenus possint. Plurimum autem labores et pericula nostra, quo fructuosa sint, adiuvabis, si eorum vanissimam et impiae superbiae plenissimam sectam non ita cures imperialibus legibus comprimi, ut sibi vel suis videantur qualescumque molestias pro veritate atque iustitia sustinere, sed

---

ᵃ Rom. xii. 21.

not think it an unimportant or contemptible thing,
my honoured and well-beloved son, that I ask you
to spare the lives of men whom we pray God to bring
to repentance. Even setting aside the fact that we
ought not to depart from the eternal principle of
overcoming evil with good,[a] let your Wisdom take
this other fact into account, that no one takes the
trouble to bring Church cases before you, except
churchmen themselves. So if in such cases you
think fit to put men to death, you will deter us from
having any such cases brought before your tribunal;
and when our opponents ascertain this, they will
proceed with all the more unrestrained effrontery
to destroy us, when the necessity is laid upon us
of choosing rather to die at their hands than to
hale them before your tribunal to suffer death
themselves. Do not receive with contempt, I beg
you, this exhortation, this request, this entreaty
of mine. For I do not think that you will forget
that, even if you were in a much more exalted position than the one you now occupy, and even were I
not a bishop, I might still have had great confidence
in addressing you. Meanwhile, let the heretical
Donatists quickly learn by your Excellency's edicts
that the laws passed against their error are still
in force, though they now think that they are of no
effect, and boast that, not even if they were, could
they to any extent spare us. But you will very
greatly assist our labours and perils to bear fruit, if
you strive to repress by the imperial laws that sect
of theirs which is so flaunting and so full of impious
pride, in such a way that they do not appear to
themselves or their supporters to be enduring hardships, no matter how slight, for the sake of truth

eos, cum hoc abs te petitur, rerum certarum mani-
festissimis documentis apud acta vel praestantiae tuae
vel minorum iudicum convinci atque instrui patiaris,
ut et ipsi qui te iubente adtinentur, duram, si fieri
potest, flectant in melius voluntatem et ea ceteris
salubriter legant. Onerosior est quippe quam utilior
diligentia, quamvis ut magnum deseratur malum et
magnum bonum teneatur, cogi tantum homines, non
doceri.

No. 28 (Ep. CI)

DOMINO BEATISSIMO ET VENERABILITER CA-
RISSIMO ET SINCERISSIMO DESIDERANTIS-
SIMO FRATRI ET COEPISCOPO MEMORIO
AUGUSTINUS IN DOMINO SALUTEM

1 Nullas debui iam reddere litteras sanctae caritati
tuae sine his libris quos a me sancti amoris iure
violentissimo flagitasti, ut hac saltem oboedientia
responderem epistulis tuis, quibus me magis onerare
quam honorare dignatus es. Quamquam ubi suc-
cumbo quia oneror, ibi etiam, quia diligor, sublevor.
Neque enim a quolibet diligor, sublevor, eligor, sed
ab eo viro et domini sacerdote, quem sic acceptum deo

---

^a Memorius was a bishop in Italy, perhaps at Capua.
An intimate friend of Augustine's, he is more notable as
the father of Julian of Eclanum (mentioned in § 4), the
Pelagian.

and righteousness; but allow them, when this is requested from you, to be convinced and instructed by the incontrovertible evidence of clearly ascertained facts either in your Excellency's own court or in that of inferior judges, to the end that those who are arrested at your command may themselves bend their stubborn will, if it can be bent at all, to the better side and profitably read those proofs to others. For the effort to make men abandon even a great evil and cleave to a great good produces more trouble than benefit, if they act merely under compulsion and not from conviction.

No. 28 (Ep. CI)

(A.D. 409)

TO MY LORD MOST BLESSED AND REVER-
ENTLY CHERISHED AND SINCERE, ME-
MORIUS,[a] MY BROTHER AND FELLOW-
BISHOP MOST LONGED FOR, AUGUSTINE
SENDS GREETING IN THE LORD

I should not now write any letter to your holy 1
Charity without sending those books that you demanded from me by the most urgent right of holy
affection, that by this act of obedience at least I
might make reply to those letters of yours with
which you were good enough to burden me rather
than to honour me. Yet where I am bent low by
the burden, even there I am raised up by your love.
For it is no ordinary person that loves me, upraises
me and makes me feel a picked man, but he can do
so, that priest of the Lord, whom I feel to be so

sentio, ut, cum animam tuam tam bonam levas ad
dominum, quoniam in illa me habes, leves et me.
Debui ergo nunc libros mittere, quos emendaturum
me esse promiseram et ideo non misi quia non
emendavi, non quia nolui, sed quia non potui, curis
videlicet multis et multum praevalentibus occupatus.
Nimis autem ingratum ac ferreum fuit, ut te, qui
nos sic amas, hic sanctus frater et collega noster
Possidius, in quo nostram non parvam praesentiam
reperies, vel non disceret vel sine nostris litteris disceret. Est enim per nostrum ministerium non litteris
illis quas variarum servi libidinum liberales vocant,
sed dominico pane nutritus, quantus ei potuit per
nostras angustias dispensari.

2   Quid enim aliud dicendum est eis, qui cum sint
iniqui et impii, liberaliter sibi videntur eruditi, nisi
quod in litteris vere liberalibus legimus : *Si vos filius
liberaverit, tunc vere liberi eritis* ? Per eum namque
praestatur, ut ipsae etiam quae liberales disciplinae
ab eis qui in libertatem vocati non sunt, appellantur,
quid in se habeant liberale noscatur. Neque enim
habent congruum libertati, nisi quod habent congruum veritati. Unde ille ipse filius : *Et veritas*,
inquit, *liberabit vos*. Non ergo illae innumerabiles et
impiae fabulae, quibus vanorum plena sunt carmina
poetarum, ullo modo nostrae consonant libertati,
non oratorum inflata et expolita mendacia, non

---

a Mentioned above on pp. 106 and 128. At a council held
in Carthage on June 14, 409, he was one of four African
bishops who were deputed to request the Emperor's protection from the fury of the Donatists. He conveyed a
letter from Augustine to Paulinus at Nola, but nothing
more is known of his journey or his mission.
  b John viii. 36.   *c* John viii. 32.
190

acceptable to God that when you lift up your good soul to the Lord, you lift me up too, since you hold me in it. I should then be now sending the books I had promised to revise, but I am not sending them for the reason that I have not revised them ; not because I did not want to, but because I had no chance to do so, being engrossed in a multitude of very cogent duties. But it would have been excessively ungrateful and hard-hearted to allow this holy brother and colleague of mine, Possidius,[a] in whom you will find no small traces of me, either to miss making your acquaintance, since you are so dear a friend of mine, or to make it without a letter from me. For by my efforts he has been brought up not on those studies which men who are enslaved to every kind of lust call liberal, but on the bread of the Lord, in so far as it could be supplied to him from my meagre store.

For what else can we say to those who, although 2 wicked and ungodly, believe themselves to be men of a liberal education, except what we read in the book that is truly liberal : " If the Son has made you free, then shall ye be free indeed "[b]? For it is by His gift that whatever even those disciplines that are termed liberal by men who have not been called unto liberty, contain that is liberal, can be known at all. For they contain nothing consonant with liberty, unless what they contain consonant with truth. That is why the Son Himself says, " And the truth shall make you free."[c] Those innumerable ungodly tales with which the verses of empty poets abound are in no wise consonant with the liberty that is ours, nor are the pompous, finely-turned falsehoods of the orators, nor even the long-winded subtleties of the

191

denique ipsorum philosophorum garrulae argutiae, qui vel deum prorsus non cognoverunt vel, *cum cognovissent deum, non sicut deum glorificaverunt aut gratias egerunt, sed evanuerunt in cogitationibus suis et obscuratum est insipiens cor eorum et dicentes se esse sapientes stulti facti sunt et inmutaverunt gloriam incorrupti dei in similitudinem imaginis corruptibilis hominis et volucrum et quadrupedum et serpentium* vel qui istis simulacris non dediti aut non nimis dediti *coluerunt* tamen *et servierunt creaturae potius quam creatori.* Absit omnino ut istorum vanitates et insaniae mendaces, ventosae nugae ac superbus error recte liberales litterae nominentur hominum scilicet infelicium, qui dei gratiam per Iesum Christum dominum nostrum, qua sola liberamur de corpore mortis huius, non cognoverunt nec in eis ipsis quae vera senserunt. Historia sane, cuius scriptores fidem se praecipue narrationibus suis debere profitentur, fortassis habeat aliquid cognitione dignum liberis, cum sive bona sive mala hominum tamen vera narrantur. Quamvis in eis cognoscendis, qui sancto spiritu non adiuti sunt rumoresque colligere ipsa humanae infirmitatis condicione compulsi sunt, quem ad modum non fallerentur in plurimis, omnino non video. Est tamen aliqua in eis propinquitas libertatis, si voluntatem mentiendi non habent nec homines fallunt, nisi cum ab hominibus humana infirmitate falluntur.

ᵃ Rom. i. 21-23.   ᵇ Rom. i. 25.
ᶜ Rom. vii. 24-25.

philosophers themselves, who were either completely without knowledge of God or else, "when they knew God, they did not glorify Him as God, neither were thankful, but became vain in their imaginations, and their foolish heart was darkened; professing themselves to be wise they became fools, and changed the glory of the uncorruptible God into an image made like to corruptible man and to birds and four-footed beasts and creeping things,"[a] or who, though not given, or not excessively given, to such images, yet "worshipped and served the creature more than the Creator."[b] Far be it, therefore, from us rightly to give the name of liberal studies to the lying conceits and follies, the empty trifles and complacent misrepresentations of those unhappy men who did not recognize the grace of God through our Lord Jesus Christ, by which alone we are delivered "from the body of this death,"[c] even in those things which they felt to be true. Their historical works, whose writers claim to be especially reliable in their narratives, contain something perhaps that may fitly be learned by the free, since what they narrate, whether the fortunes or the misfortunes of mankind, is at any rate true. And yet, I completely fail to see how men who were without the assistance of the Holy Spirit, and were compelled by the very nature of human infirmity to gather mere rumours together, were not in their search for facts mistaken in most of them. Yet in such writings there is an approximation to liberty, provided that the writers have no intention of deceiving and do not mislead men, except in so far as they themselves, through human infirmity, are misled by their informants.

193

3 Verum quia in omnibus rerum motibus, quid nu-
meri valeant, facilius consideratur in vocibus eaque
consideratio quibusdam quasi gradatis itineribus
nititur ad superna intima veritatis, *in* quibus *viis
ostendit se sapientia hilariter et in omni providentia
occurrit* amantibus, initio nostri otii, cum a curis
maioribus magisque necessariis vacabat animus, volui
per ista quae a nobis desiderasti scripta proludere,
quando conscripsi de solo rhythmo sex libros et de
melo scribere alios forsitan sex, fateor, disponebam,
cum mihi otium futurum sperabam. Sed postea
quam mihi curarum ecclesiasticarum sarcina inposita
est, omnes illae deliciae fugere de manibus, ita ut
vix nunc ipsum codicem inveniam, quoniam tuam
voluntatem nec petitionem sed iussionem contemnere
nequeo. Quod sane opusculum si potuero mittere,
non quidem me tibi obtemperasse, verum tamen te
hoc a me tanto opere flagitasse, paenitebit. Difficillime quippe intelleguntur in eo quinque libri, si
non adsit qui non solum disputantium possit separare
personas, verum etiam pronuntiando ita sonare
morulas syllabarum, ut eis exprimantur sensumque
aurium feriant genera numerorum, maxime quia in
quibusdam etiam silentiorum dimensa intervalla

---

^a Wisdom vi. 17, where the Septuagint reads ἐν πάσῃ
ἐπινοίᾳ and the English version " in every thought."
^b These are the six books *De Musica*, projected when
Augustine was in Milan but written only after he returned
to Africa in 388 and was living in monastic retirement
(" initio nostri otii " above) at Tagaste. They were intended
as part of an encyclopaedic work, *Libri disciplinarum*,
designed to include studies of dialectic, grammar, geometry,
arithmetic and philosophy, but the only part finished at

Now, since the power of rhythm in every kind of 3 movement is most easily studied in sounds, and since the study of those leads upwards to the highest secrets of truth by a kind of gradual ascent in following which Wisdom pleasantly reveals herself and in every act of providence[a] meets those who love her, I intended at the beginning of my retirement, when my mind was free from greater and more necessary tasks, to make those books you asked from me a preliminary trial of strength. I then wrote six books exclusively on rhythm,[b] and proposed, I confess, to write others, six perhaps, on music, as I was expecting to have leisure before me. But after the burden of ecclesiastical concerns was laid upon me, all those trifles vanished from my hands so completely that now, when I cannot but respect your desire, which is more a command than a request, I can hardly find my own manuscript copy. But if I actually am able to send the treatise to you, the regret will not be mine for submitting to your pressure, but yours for so eagerly demanding it from me. For five books of it are very difficult to follow, unless you have beside you someone who can not only distinguish the parts of the interlocutors, but also give by his enunciation the proper quantity to the syllables uttered, so that in them the character of the metre is expressed and strikes the sensitive ear, especially as some of the feet contain, besides, pauses of fixed length, which cannot

Milan was the *De Grammatica*. Posterity has endorsed Augustine's own opinion of the six books *De Musica* (*cf.* the beginning of Bk. VI: "satis diu paene atque adeo plane pueriliter per quinque libros in vestigiis numerorum ad moras temporum pertinentium morati sumus"), for while the first five have only an antiquarian interest, the sixth book was a favourite with medieval mystics.

miscentur quae omnino sentiri nequeunt, nisi audi-
torem pronuntiator informet.

4 Sextum sane librum, quem emendatum repperi,
ubi est omnis fructus ceterorum, non distuli mittere
caritati tuae ; fortassis ipse tuam non multum re-
fugiat gravitatem. Nam superiores quinque vix filio
nostro et condiacono Iuliano, quoniam et ipse iam
nobiscum commilitat, digni lectione vel cognitione
videbuntur. Quem quidem non audeo dicere plus
amo quam te, quia nec veraciter dico, sed tamen
audeo dicere plus desidero quam te. Mirum videri
potest, quem ad modum quem pariter amo, amplius
desiderem ; sed hoc mihi facit spes amplior videndi
eum ; puto enim quod si ad nos te iubente vel
mittente venerit, et hoc faciet quod adulescentem
decet, maxime quia nondum curis maioribus detinetur,
et te ipsum mihi expeditius adportabit. Quibus
numeris consistant versus Davidici, non scripsi, quia
nescio. Neque enim ex Hebraea lingua, quam ignoro,
potuit etiam numeros interpres exprimere, ne metri
necessitate ab interpretandi veritate amplius quam
ratio sententiarum sinebat, digredi cogeretur. Certis
tamen eos constare numeris credo illis qui eam
linguam probe callent. Amavit enim vir ille sanctus
musicam piam et in ea studia nos magis ipse quam
ullus alius auctor accendit. *Habitetis* omnes in
196

be sensed at all, unless the reader gives the hearer an idea of them by his method of enunciation.

But the sixth book, which I have found in a revised condition, contains the whole harvest of the others, and I am sending it to your Charity at once ; it perhaps will not so markedly shrink from the attentions of one of your sober-mindedness. For the earlier five will hardly appear to our son and fellow-deacon, Julian, to be worth reading or knowing, since he too is now engaged in the same warfare as ourselves. Of him I dare not say that he is dearer to me than you are, for it would not be true to say that, but still I do dare to say that I long for him more than I do for you. It may seem strange how I long for him more, for I love you both equally ; but this is the result of the greater hope I have of seeing him, for I think that if you were to send him or bid him come to me, he would both be doing what a young man should do, especially when he is not yet hindered by heavier responsibilities, and he would the more speedily bring you yourself to me.

I have not mentioned the nature of the verse in which the Psalms of David are composed, because I do not know, for the translator from the Hebrew tongue, which is unknown to me, could not reproduce the verse, for fear of being compelled by the needs of metre to depart from accuracy in his translation farther than was consistent with the meaning. But that they are composed in a definite metre I believe on the authority of those who have a thorough knowledge of that language ; for that holy man loved sacred music, and he more than any other writer kindled in me a zeal for its study.

May you all " dwell " for evermore " in the secret

aeternum *in adiutorio altissimi,* qui *habitatis unanimes in domo,* pater materque fratres filiorum et cuncti unius patris filii memores nostri.

No. 29 (Ep. CX)

DOMINO BEATISSIMO ATQUE DULCISSIMO VENERABILI NIMIUMQUE DESIDERABILI FRATRI ET CONSACERDOTI SEVERO ET QUI TECUM SUNT FRATRIBUS AUGUSTINUS ET QUI MECUM SUNT FRATRES IN DOMINO SALUTEM

1 Epistula mea, quam pervexit carissimus filius et condiaconus noster Timotheus, iam parata erat profecturo, quando filii nostri Quodvultdeus et Gaudentius ad nos venerunt cum litteris tuis. Inde factum est, ut continuo proficiscens non adferret responsionem meam, quoniam post illorum adventum quantulumcumque apud nos inmoratus est et profecturus per horas singulas videbatur. Sed etsi per eum respondissem, adhuc debitor forem. Nam et nunc, quod videor respondisse, debitor sum, non dico caritatis, quam tanto magis debemus quanto amplius inpenderimus, cuius nos perpetuos debitores ostendit apostolus dicens : *Nemini quicquam debeatis, nisi ut*

---

a Ps. xc. 1 (after the Septuagint).

b Ps. lxvii. 7 (after the Septuagint).

c See for Severus p. 108 note *b*.

d Probably the Timothy about whom Augustine had already written to Severus in Epp. lxii. and lxiii. In Ep. cclxiii. Augustine writes a consolatory letter on the death of a deacon Timothy, who may be the same.

e These two names are common in Africa at this time, and the individuals cannot be identified with certainty. Peculiar to Africa seems to have been the habit, best known

place[a] of the Most High," you who "in one house dwell together in oneness of heart,"[b] father and mother, of the same brotherhood as your children, and all of you children of one Father. Remember us.

No. 29 (Ep. CX)

(A.D. 409)

TO MY BLESSED AND DEAREST LORD, MY VENERABLE AND MUCH DESIRED BROTHER AND FELLOW-PRIEST, SEVERUS,[c] AND THE BRETHREN WHO ARE WITH YOU, AUGUSTINE AND THE BRETHREN WHO ARE WITH ME SEND GREETING IN THE LORD

This letter from me, which has been brought to you 1 by my very dear son and fellow-deacon, Timothy,[d] was ready for his departure, when my sons Quodvultdeus and Gaudentius[e] reached us with a letter from you. That is the reason why Timothy, who was departing forthwith, did not bring a reply from me, since after their arrival he waited with us here only a very short time and was apparently on the point of departure at any minute. But even if I had sent a reply by him, I should still be in your debt, for even now, though I seem to have replied, I am in your debt, I do not mean for affection, for the more we have paid of that, the more we owe (we are always in debt for it, as the Apostle's words show, "Owe

from the English Puritans, of employing these religious names : Augustine's own son was called Adeodatus, and there are many examples of such names as Deogratias, Deumhabet, Deusdedit, Habetdeus, Vincemalus, etc.

199

invicem diligatis, sed ipsius epistulae tuae ; quando enim sufficiam tuae suavitati tantaeque aviditati animi tui, quam mihi lecta nuntiavit ? Rem quidem in te mihi notissimam insinuavit ; verum tamen etsi non mihi rei novae insinuatrix, nova tamen re-scriptorum exactrix fuit.

2 Miraris fortasse cur me huius debiti persolutorem inparem dicam, cum tu de me tam multum sentias, qui me tamquam anima mea noveris. Sed hoc ipsum est, quod mihi magnam difficultatem facit respondendi litteris tuis, quia et quantus mihi videaris, parco dicere propter verecundiam tuam, et utique minus dicendo, cum tu in me tantam laudem contuleris, quid nisi debitor remanebo ? Quod non curarem, si ea quae de me ad me locutus es, non ex caritate sincerissima dicta scirem sed adulatione inimica amicitiae. Hoc quippe modo nec debitor fierem, quia talia rependere non deberem ; sed quanto magis novi quam fideli animo loqueris, tanto magis video quanto debito graver.

3 Vide autem quid mihi contigit, ut me quodam modo ipse laudaverim, qui me a te fideliter laudatum dixerim. Sed quid aliud dicerem quam id quod de te admonui, quam nosti ? Ecce mihi novam feci quaestionem, quam tu non proposuisti, et eam fortassis expectas ut solvam. Ita mihi parum erat quod debitor eram, nisi etiam me ampliore debito ipse

---

^a Rom. xiii. 8.

no man anything but to love one another " [a]), but for this letter of yours ; for when could I make a fair return for your graciousness and the great eagerness of your spirit conveyed to me in the reading of your letter ? Not that it told me anything in you that was not well known to me before, but yet, though not suggesting anything new, it was a new demand for a reply.

You perhaps wonder why I describe myself as un- **2** able to make an adequate repayment of this debt, when you, who know me as well as my own soul does, have conceived so great an opinion of me. But it is this very fact that makes it so difficult for me to reply to your letter, because I refrain for your modesty's sake from expressing the great esteem I entertain for you, and so by this restraint in express- ing myself, when you have heaped so much praise upon me, what can I do but remain in your debt ? This I should not mind, if I knew that your remarks to me about myself were inspired by flattery, that destroyer of friendship, and not by a very genuine affection, for in those circumstances I should not have been in debt at all, as it would have been no duty to pay back in the same coin. But the better I know the sincerity of mind with which you speak, the more I realize the burden of debt with which I am saddled.

Now just see what I have brought upon myself : in **3** saying that you were sincere in praising me, I have been in a way praising myself. Yet what else could I say than what I have suggested about yourself, what else than what you know ? But there I have put myself in another dilemma, one you did not set for me and which you perhaps expect me to resolve. Was it not enough for me to be in your debt without

cumularem. Quamquam hoc facile sit ostendere et, si non ostendam, facile tibi videre, et vera infideliter dici posse et non vera fideliter. Qui enim sic credit ut loquitur, etsi non vera loquitur, fideliter loquitur; qui autem non credit quae loquitur, etsi vera loquitur, infideliter loquitur. Numquid ergo dubito quod ea de me credas, quae scripsisti ? Quae cum in me non agnosco, potuisti fideliter de me non vera dicere.

4   Sed nolo te vel benivolentia sic falli. Cui benivolentiae debitor sum, quia et tam fideliter et tam benivole ea quae vera sunt, possem de te dicere, nisi, ut supra dixi, verecundiae tuae parcerem. Ego autem quando laudor a germanissimo et familiarissimo animae meae, velut a me ipso lauder, sic habeo. Quod cernis quam molestum sit, etiam si vera dicantur; quanto potius, quia etiam, cum sis altera anima mea, immo una sit anima tua et mea, sic in me falleris putando mihi adesse quae desunt, quo modo et de se ipse unus homo falli potest ! Quod non tantum ideo nolo, ne, quem diligo, tu fallaris, verum etiam ne minus ores, ut sim quod iam esse me credis. Nec in eo sum tibi debitor, ut eodem progressu benivolentiae credam et loquar de te bona quae adhuc et tu tibi deesse cognoscis, sed ut animo tam

burdening myself with a debt even greater? Still, it is easy to show (and if I do not show, it is easy for you to see) that the truth can be uttered with insincerity, and untruth with sincerity; for a man who believes what he says speaks with sincerity, even if what he says be untrue, while a man who does not believe what he says speaks with insincerity, even if what he says be true. Have I any doubt that you do believe what you wrote about me? Yet, when I fail to recognize in myself the things you praise, it is possible that in all sincerity you were saying about me what was not true.

But I do not want you to be so misled even in **4** your kindness of heart; to that kindness I am already in debt, since I could say with no less sincerity and no less kindness things that are true about you, if I were not anxious, as I said already, to spare your modesty. As for me, when praise is given me by one who is very near and very dear to my soul, I feel as if I were being praised by myself. So you see how embarrassing a position it is, even if what is said is true; how much more embarrassing since you, being my other soul—nay, we are but one soul, you and I—are just as misled in thinking I possess qualities that I do not possess, as a single individual can be misled about himself. And I do not want that to happen, not simply to keep you, so dear a friend of mine, from being misled, but also to keep you from slackening in your prayers that I may become what you believe I am already. I am not in your debt in such a way that with the same kindness and anticipation I should believe and speak favourably about qualities which you yourself are aware of not as yet possessing, but I am in debt

quidem benivolo ea tamen dicam bona tua, dona dei,
de quibus in te certus sum. Quod non ideo non
facio, ne fallar in eis, sed ne tu a me laudatus ipse
te laudasse videaris et propter illam iustitiae regulam,
quia mihi fieri nolo. Quod si fieri debet, eligo esse
debitor, quam diu puto non esse faciendum ; si
autem fieri non debet, nec debitor sum.

5   Sed novi, quid mihi ad haec respondere possis :
" Ita ista loqueris, quasi prolixam epistulam tuam
de laudibus meis desideraverim." Absit ut hoc de
te credam ; sed epistula tua nolo dicere quam veris
vel quam non veris plena tamen laudibus meis hoc
de me ut rependerem etiam te nolente flagitavit.
Nam si quid aliud volebas ut scriberem, largitorem
me desiderabas, non redditorem. Porro iustitiae
ordo sic habet, ut debitum prius reddamus, tum
deinde, cui reddimus, si hoc placet, aliquid et do-
nemus : quamquam etiam talia qualia desiderasti ut
scriberem, si diligentius praecepta dominica cogitemus, reddimus potius quam donamus, si nemini
quicquam debendum est, nisi ut invicem diligamus.
Ipsa quippe dilectio exigit debitum, ut fraternae
caritati servientes eum qui se adiuvari recte velit,
in quo possumus, adiuvemus. Sed, mi frater, et tu
credo quod noveris quanta sint in manibus meis,
quibus adversus curas quas nostrae servitutis neces-

---

a The " Golden Rule."
b John xiii. 34, xv. 12, 17 ; Rom. xii. 10, etc.

in this way, that with just the same kindliness of
intention I may describe you as possessing those good
qualities, sent from God above. which I am certain
are in you. And if I refrain from doing so, it is
not from fear that I may be misled. but from fear
that when I have been praising you, you may seem
to have been praising yourself, and because of that
principle of justice,[a] since I do not want this done
to myself. If this should be done, I prefer to be in
debt as long as I keep thinking that it should not
be done ; but if it should not be done, then am I not
in debt.

But I know the answer you may make to this : 5
"You speak as if I had wanted from you a
lengthy letter in my praise." Far be it from me
to think that of you : yet your letter, so full of my
praises (how true or untrue no matter), did demand
this repayment from me, even if you did not
intend it. For if you wished me to write in any
other way, it was not a repayment you wanted from
me but a fresh gift. Moreover, justice prescribes
this order, that we should pay our debt first, and
that only then we should, if we so decide, make
a gift to our creditor in addition; yet, even the
things you wanted me to write to you are, if we
more carefully consider the Lord's injunctions, a
repayment rather than a gift, if we are to owe no
man anything but to love one another[b] ; for love
requires the payment of our debt, to the end that,
in obedience to brotherly affection, we may, wherever
we can, help him who has the right desire to be
helped. But, my brother, I think you know how
full my hands are ; into them even the smallest drops
of time hardly trickle for my refreshment amid the

sitas habet, vix mihi paucissimae guttae temporis stillantur, quas aliis rebus si inpendero, contra officium meum mihi facere videor.

6 Quod enim vis, ut ad te prolixam epistulam scribam, et hoc quidem debeo, fateor ; debeo prorsus hoc tam dulci, tam sincerae, tam merae voluntati tuae. Sed quia bonus es amator iustitiae, inde te admoneo, ut de illa quam diligis, hoc a me libentius audias. Cernis prius esse quod et tibi et aliis quam quod tibi tantum modo debeo ; et tempus ad omnia mihi non sufficit, quando nec ad illa quae priora sunt. Unde omnes carissimi et familiarissimi mei, quorum in nomine Christi inter primos mihi es, rem facient officii sui, si non solum mihi alia scribenda ipsi non inponant, verum etiam ceteros quanta possunt auctoritate et sancta benignitate prohibeant, ne videar ego durus, cum a singulis petita non dedero, dum ea magis volo reddere, quae omnibus debeo. Denique cum, sicut speramus et promissum tenemus, ad nos venerit venerabilitas tua, scies quibus operibus litterarum et quantum occupatus sim, et instantius facies quod rogavi, ut et alios, quos potueris, mihi aliquid aliud scribendum volentes iniungere a me demoliaris. Dominus deus noster impleat cordis tui tam grandem et tam sanctum sinum, quem ipse fecit, domine beatissime.

anxieties that constitute the inevitable bondage of a servant of the Lord. If I squander those on other business, I seem to myself to be neglecting my duties.

Yet, when you want me to write you a lengthy 6 letter, I do indeed owe you that, I must confess; I surely do owe that to your sweet, sincere, and single-minded desire. But since you are a good lover of justice, I warn you to hear with the greater favour what I say about this object of your affection. You see that what I owe to you and others as well has a prior claim over what I owe to you alone; and time fails me for everything, when it fails me even for my first duties. So all those who are nearest and dearest to me (and in Christ's name you are among the first of these) will only be doing their duty if they not only lay no further burden of writing on me themselves, but with all the authority and holy kindness they can, forbid others also to do so, so that I may not seem hard-hearted when I fail to give what each one has asked, my own desire being all the time to pay the debt I owe to all. Finally, when your Reverence visits me, as I hope you will, for I have your promise, you will understand with what literary tasks so much of my time is taken up, and you will be more insistent in doing what I have asked, deterring any others you can from their desire to impose any more writing on me. May the Lord our God fill your spacious and holy breast and heart which He Himself has made, my most saintly lord!

ST. AUGUSTINE

No. 30 (Ep. CXV)

DOMINO BEATISSIMO ET VENERABILITER
CARISSIMO FRATRI ET CONSACERDOTI FOR-
TUNATO ET QUI TECUM SUNT FRATRIBUS
AUGUSTINUS IN DOMINO SALUTEM

Faventium bene novit sanctitas tua, qui Paratia-
nensis saltus conductor fuit. Is cum ab eiusdem
possessionis domino nescio quid sibi metueret, ad
Hipponiensem confugit ecclesiam, et ibi erat, ut
confugientes solent, expectans quo modo per intercessionem nostram sua negotia terminaret. Qui, ut
saepe fit, per dies singulos minus minusque sollicitus
et quasi adversario cessante securus, cum ab amico
suo de cena egrederetur, subito raptus est a Floren-
tino quodam, ut dicunt, comitis officiali per armatorum manum, quanta eis ad hoc factum sufficere visa

---

[a] Fortunatus was bishop of Cirta. He was present at the
Conference in Carthage in 411 and is elsewhere mentioned
by Augustine (Epp. liii., clxxvi.).

[b] The case of Faventius was the occasion of the writing
of Epp. cxiii., cxiv., and cxvi., as well as this letter. *Saltus*,
originally only wooded and pasture land (" saltus proprie
locus adhuc incultus et silvester dicitur," Aug. *In Ps.* cxxxi.
11), were vast estates as great as, sometimes larger than, the
territory of a city (*Grom.* ed. Lachmann, p. 53). At the centre
lay the *villa* of the owner, surrounded by the houses of the
workers, and this settlement was also called *villa*. All or
part of the *saltus* was let to a *conductor*, below whom were
the *coloni*, owing him certain services. The domain itself was
often called *fundus* or *lati fundi*, but the word *fundus* was
applied too to the smaller portions. See Reid, *Municipalities of the Roman Empire*, pp. 319 ff.; Boissier, *L'Afrique
Romaine*, p. 165.

[c] Paratianis has been identified with Medjez, on the coast

No. 30 (Ep. CXV)

(A.D. 410)

TO MY SAINTLY LORD AND REVERENTLY CHER-
ISHED BROTHER AND FELLOW-PRIEST,
FORTUNATUS[a] AND THE BRETHREN WHO
ARE WITH YOU, AUGUSTINE SENDS GREET-
ING IN THE LORD

Your Holiness is well acquainted with Faventius,[b]
the tenant of the estate at Paratianis.[c] Being apprehensive of something or other at the hands of the
proprietor of that same estate, he fled for refuge to
the Church of Hippo, where he remained, as those
who seek sanctuary[d] usually do, waiting to see if by
my interposition he could bring the affair to a satisfactory end. Becoming, as each day passed, less and
less vigilant — a usual occurrence — and lulled to
security by the delusion that his enemy was growing
remiss, he was leaving a friend's house after supper
when he was suddenly seized and abducted by one
Florentinus, said to be an officer of the Count,[e] aided
by what they thought to be for the purpose a suffi-

twenty-five miles from Rusicade. It has fairly extensive
ruins dating from Roman times.

[d] Since the time of Constantine, churches had been a
sanctuary for the innocent, the oppressed, and others who
sought episcopal intercession. Commonly thirty days' protection was granted. See *Cod. Theod.* IX. xv. 4 "de iis
qui ad ecclesias confugiunt." See also No. 61 *infra.*

[e] When Diocletian separated the military administration
of Africa from the civil, he appointed a *dux per Africam,*
but this title was changed about 330 to *comes.* In 393
Gildo was *comes et magister utriusque militiae*; he was
succeeded by Boniface, addressed by Augustine in Nos. 42
and 51.

est. Quod cum mihi nuntiaretur,[1] et adhuc quo vel a quibus raptus fuerit, nesciretur, suspicio tamen esset de illo quem metuens se per ecclesiam tuebatur, continuo misi ad tribunum, qui custodiendo litori constitutus est. Misit militares ; nemo potuit reperiri. Sed mane cognovimus, et in qua domo fuerit et quod post galli cantum cum illo abscesserit qui eum tenuerat. Etiam illuc misi, quo dicebatur abductus, ubi memoratus officialis inventus concedere presbytero quem miseram, noluit, ut eum saltem videret. Alio die misi litteras, petens ut ei concederetur quod iussit in causis talibus imperator, id est ut actis municipalibus interrogarentur, qui praecepti fuerint exhibendi, utrum velint in ea civitate sub custodia moderata triginta dies agere, ut rem suam ordinent vel praeparent sumptus, id utique existimans quod per ipsos dies possemus fortasse causam eius amica disceptatione finire. Iam vero cum illo officiali profectus ductus est. Sed metus est ne forte ad consularis perductus officium mali aliquid patiatur. Habet enim causam cum homine pecuniosissimo, quamvis iudicis integritas fama clarissima praedicetur. Ne quid tamen apud officium pecunia praevaleat, peto sanctitatem tuam, domine dilectissime et venerabilis frater, ut honorabili nobisque carissimo consulari digneris tradere litteras meas et has ei legere, quia bis eandem causam insinuare

---

[1] *The* MSS. *have simply* nuntiatum, *after which Goldbacher inserts* esset. *The correct reading is probably* nuntiaretur.

---

[a] The reference is to the laws of Theodosius, of December 30, 380, and of Honorius, of January 21, 409 (*Cod. Theod.* ix. tit. ii.).

ciently large band of armed men. This was reported
to me ; but since there was as yet no information who
his abductors were nor where they had taken him,
though suspicion fell on the man who had frightened
him into seeking protection from the Church, I at
once communicated with the tribune in command of
the coast-guards. He sent soldiers ; no one could be
found, but in the morning we discovered the house
in which he had been detained and found that his
keeper had left with him after cock-crow. I also
sent to the place to which it was said he had been
carried off. When the afore-mentioned officer was
found, he refused to grant to the priest I had sent
permission even to see him. Next day I sent a letter
requesting for him the privilege which the Emperor
appointed in such cases as this,*a* namely, that those
under summons to appear in court should be asked
at the municipal bench if they were willing to spend
thirty days in that town under lenient observation,
to put their affairs in order or to prepare their
finances. My expectation was that during that period
we could perhaps reach a settlement of his case by
friendly discussion. Already, however, he had gone
off with that officer and was taken to prison, but
there is some fear that if he be brought before the
governor's tribunal, he may suffer some hardship,
for although that judge has an excellent reputation
for rectitude, Faventius's opponent in the case is a
very wealthy man. So to prevent the exercise of any
undue influence in that court by his money, I beg
your Holiness, my dearest lord and venerable brother,
to hand my letter to the honourable magistrate, a
man very dear to me, and to read this one to him, for
I do not think it necessary to write a second account

necessarium non esse arbitratus sum : et eius causae
differat audientiam, quoniam nescio utrum in ea
nocens an innocens sit, et, quod circa eundem leges
non servatae sunt, ut sic raperetur neque, ut ab im-
peratore praeceptum est, ad acta municipalia per-
duceretur interrogandus utrum beneficium dilationis
vellet accipere, non contemnat, ut per hoc possimus
cum eius adversario rem finire.

No. 31 (Ep. CXXII)

DILECTISSIMIS FRATRIBUS CONCLERICIS ET UNIVERSAE PLEBI AUGUSTINUS IN DOMINO SALUTEM

1   In primis peto caritatem vestram et per Iesum
obsecro, ne vos mea contristet absentia corporalis.
Nam spiritu et cordis affectu puto vos non dubitare
nullo modo me a vobis posse discedere, quamvis me
amplius contristet quam forte vos ipsos, quod infirmitas mea sufficere non potest omnibus curis quas
de me exigunt membra Christi, quibus me et timor
eius et caritas servire compellit.   Illud enim noverit
vestra dilectio numquam me absentem fuisse licentiosa libertate sed necessaria servitute, quae saepe
sanctos fratres et collegas meos etiam labores marinos

ᵃ Written from the country, to which Augustine's ill-
health had made it necessary to retire (Ep. cxviii. 34 " me
post aegritudinem . . . aliquantum ab Hippone removeram,
quibus item diebus perturbatione valetudinis febribusque
repetitus sum "). For other indications of his poor health
cf. No. 13 above and *Serm.* 355. 7 "ego, sicut videtis, per
aetatem modo senui, sed per infirmitatem corporis olim sum
senex."

of the same case ; and let him postpone the hearing
of his case, since I do not know whether he is innocent or guilty. And let him not make light of the
fact that in dealing with him the legal procedure
was not observed, in that he was seized and abducted
and was not taken, as the Emperor enjoined, before
the municipal court to be questioned whether he
wished to avail himself of the concession of delay.
In this way we may be able to reach a settlement
with his opponent.

No. 31 (Ep. CXXII)

(A.D. 410)

TO HIS DEARLY BELOVED BRETHREN, THE
CLERGY, AND ALL THE LAITY AUGUSTINE
SENDS GREETING IN THE LORD [a]

I particularly beg you, my friends, and beseech 1
you for Jesus' sake, not to be grieved that I am
absent from you in the body, for I believe you are
confident that in no wise could I depart from you
in spirit and heart-felt affection. Yet I am more
grieved than perhaps you are yourselves that in the
weak state of my health I cannot adequately cope
with all the attentions required from me by the
members of Christ, whom love and fear of Him compel
me to serve. For you are well aware, my dear
friends, that I have never been absent because of
any selfish desire for a free time, but because of the
obligations imposed on me by my servitude, which
has often compelled my holy brethren and colleagues
to undertake tasks on the sea and over the sea,

et transmarinos compulit sustinere, a quibus me semper non indevotio mentis sed minus idonea valitudo corporis excusavit. Proinde, dilectissimi fratres, sic agite, ut, quod ait apostolus, *sive adveniens et videns vos sive absens, audiam de vobis quia statis in uno spiritu, uno animo conlaborantes fidei evangelicae.* Si vos aliqua molestia temporalis exagitat, ipsa vos magis admonere debet quem ad modum de illa vita cogitare debeatis, ubi sine aliquo labore vivatis, evadentes non molestas angustias temporis parvi sed horrendas poenas ignis aeterni. Nam si modo tanta cura, tanta intentione, tanto labore agitis ne in aliquos cruciatus transitorios incidatis, quantum vos oportet esse sollicitos, ut sempiternas miserias fugiatis ! Et si mors sic timetur, quae finit temporalem laborem, quo modo timenda est, quae mittit in aeternum dolorem ! Et si deliciae saeculi huius breves et sordidae sic amantur, quanto vehementius futuri saeculi gaudia pura et infinita quaerenda sunt ! Ista cogitantes, nolite esse pigri in operibus bonis, ut ad vestri seminis messem suo tempore veniatis.

2 Nuntiatum est enim mihi, quod morem vestrum de vestiendis pauperibus fueritis obliti, ad quam misericordiam, cum praesens essem, vos exhortatus sum et nunc exhortor, ne vos vincat et pigros faciat contritio mundi huius, cui talia videtis accidere

---

a Indevotio, a late word, means want of reverence, respect, dutifulness, to God, the emperor, or the laws, or want of conscientiousness in performance of duty. It is found fairly often in the legal writers with the meaning of failing to respect the last wishes of a testator (*Cod. Just.* vii. 2. 15. 2, *Novell.* i. 3). It is rare in literary language, but occurs in Ambrose (*Helia*, 17. 62, *In Ps.* cxviii. 16. 45), Salvian (*Gub.* 3. 2. 10, *Eccl.* 3. 45), and Alcim. Avit. (Ep. lxxxiv.).

b Phil. i. 27.

from which I have been excused not from want of conscientiousness,[a] but from imperfect bodily health. Accordingly, my brethren, let your behaviour be such that, as the Apostle says, "whether I come and see you or else be absent, I may hear of your affairs, that ye stand fast in one spirit, with one mind striving together for the faith of the gospel."[b] If you are harassed by some temporal vexation, it ought the more to remind you how you ought to think of that life which you are to live without any toil, escaping not the vexatious hardships of this fleeting age, but the terrible penalties of the everlasting fire. For if you now expend so much forethought, so much effort, so much toil, in saving yourselves from falling into any transitory torments, how anxious you should be to escape from everlasting miseries! And if the death which ends the toil of this life inspires such fear, how greatly that death is to be feared which casts men into everlasting pain! And if the vile and short-lived charms of this world are so loved, how much more eagerly are the undefiled and unending joys of the world to come to be sought after! Meditate upon these things and be not slothful in good works, that in due season you may come to the harvest of your sowing.

I have been informed that you have forgotten [2] your habit of clothing the poor; to that work of mercy I exhorted you when I was with you, and I now exhort you not to be overcome and made slothful by the trials of this present world, which you now see visited by such calamities[c] as our Lord and

---

[c] The reference is to the capture and sacking of Rome by the Goths under Alaric in 410.

qualia dominus et redemptor noster, qui mentiri non potest, ventura praedixit. Non solum ergo non debetis minus facere opera misericordiae, sed etiam debetis amplius quam soletis. Sicut enim ad loca munitiora festinatius migrant, qui ruinam domus vident contritis parietibus imminere, sic corda Christiana quanto magis sentiunt mundi huius ruinam crebrescentibus tribulationibus propinquare, tanto magis debent bona quae in terra recondere disponebant, in thesaurum caelestem inpigra celeritate transferre, ut, si aliqui humanus casus acciderit, gaudeat qui de loco ruinoso emigravit, si autem nihil tale fuerit subsecutum, non contristetur, qui quandoque moriturus inmortali domino ad quem venturus est, bona propria commendavit. Itaque, fratres mei dilectissimi, ex eo quod quisque habet, secundum suas vires, quas ipse novit, facite quod soletis, alacriore animo quam soletis, et inter omnes saeculi huius molestias apostolicam exhortationem corde retinete, ubi ait : *Dominus in proximo est ; nihil solliciti fueritis.* Talia mihi de vobis nuntientur, quibus noverim non propter meam praesentiam sed propter dei praeceptum, qui numquam est absens, vos solere facere quod multis annis me praesente et aliquando etiam me absente fecistis. Dominus vos in pace conservet, dilectissimi fratres ; orate pro nobis.

---

a Phil. iv. 5-6.

Redeemer, who cannot lie, foretold would come to pass. So far then from having any right to curtail your works of mercy, you ought to increase them beyond your usual measure. For just as they who see in the crumbling of its walls the impending downfall of their home, hasten to remove themselves to places more secure, so ought Christian hearts, the more they feel by the increase of its trials the approaching downfall of this present world, to be the more prompt and active in transferring to the treasury of heaven those goods they were proposing to store up on earth; in this way, if any human misfortune occurs, he who has removed from the place of destruction may rejoice, but if no such misfortune follows, he may not grieve, since, destined some day to die, he has committed his own possessions to his everlasting Lord, to Whom he will one day depart. Therefore, my beloved brethren, from what he has let each one of you according to his ability—and of that each man is the best judge—give his accustomed share with more than his accustomed cheerfulness, and cherish in your hearts amid all the vexations of this present world that admonition of the Apostle, in which he says : " The Lord is at hand ; be careful for nothing."[a] Let me have such reports of you that I may know that it is not because of my presence but because of God's command, Who is never absent from you, that you follow the practice you have followed for many years while I was present with you, and sometimes even when I was absent. The Lord preserve you in peace, my beloved brethren. Pray for us.

ST. AUGUSTINE

No. 32 (Ep. CXXIV)

DOMINIS IN DOMINO INSIGNIBUS ET SANCTITATE CARISSIMIS AC DESIDERANTISSIMIS FRATRIBUS ALBINAE, PINIANO ET MELANIAE AUGUSTINUS IN DOMINO SALUTEM

1 Cum habitu valitudinis vel natura frigus ferre non possim, numquam tamen maiores aestus quam ista hieme tam horrenda perpeti potui, quod ad vos, ad quos volatu maria transeunda fuerant, tam in proximo constitutos, tam de longinquo visendi nos gratia venientes, non dicam pergere sed volare non potui. Et forsitan sanctitas vestra eandem hiemalem asperitatem poenae meae tantum causam putaverit. Absit, carissimi. Quid enim grave ac molestum vel etiam periculosum habent imbres isti, quod non mihi subeundum ac ferendum fuit, ut ad vos venirem, tanta in tantis malis nostris solatia, in hac generatione tortuosa ac perversa tam ardenter accensa de summo lumine lumina suscepta humilitate sublimia et contempta claritate clariora ? Simul etiam fruerer carnalis patriae meae tam spiritali felicitate, quae

---

ᵃ Albina was a daughter-in-law of the famous convert, the elder Melania, who, though of noble birth and great wealth, became a devoted ascetic. At the age of thirteen Albina's daughter, the younger Melania here mentioned, married Pinianus, who was equally high-born and wealthy. The three left Rome after the sack by Alaric in 410 and settled at Tagaste (Augustine's *carnalis patria* of § 1). They desired to make Augustine's acquaintance, and the present letter is his apology for being unable to go to Tagaste to meet them, so they came to Hippo, where the curious scenes narrated in the following letter, so instructive for the church life of the period, took place. At Tagaste

No. 32 (Ep. CXXIV)

(A.D. 411)

TO ALBINA, PINIANUS, AND MELANIA,[a] HONOURED IN THE LORD, CHERISHED IN HOLINESS AND LONGED FOR IN BROTHERLY AFFECTION, AUGUSTINE SENDS GREETING IN THE LORD

Although from the state of my health, or from my natural constitution, I cannot endure cold, still I have never had a chance of suffering greater feverishness than I have done this dreadful winter because of my inability—I shall not say to go, but to fly, to you (for to see you I would have flown across the seas) now that you are settled so near, after coming so far to visit us. And perhaps you will think, my godly friends, that this same severity of the winter was the only cause of my affliction; far be it from me, beloved! For what difficulty or trouble or even danger lies in those storms that I would not have undergone and endured in order to be with you, our great comfort in our great troubles, who in this crooked and perverse generation are lights kindled into such brightness by the Light supreme, and are the loftier for the humility you have taken upon you and the more illustrious for the lustre you have scorned? At the same time I should have too such great spiritual enjoyment in my earthly birthplace, since it has had

the younger Melania acquired an estate of greater extent than the town itself. On it were many workers, a *balneum*, and two bishops, one Donatist and the other Catholic. This estate she presented to the church of Tagaste (*Anal. Bolland.* viii., 1889, p. 35).

vos etiam praesentes habere meruit, de quibus absentibus, cum id quod nati estis et quod gratia Christi facti estis, audiret, quamvis caritate crederet, tamen ne non crederetur, narrare forsitan verebatur.

2 Dicam igitur quare non venerim et quibus malis a tanto bono impeditus sum, ut non solum a vobis veniam, sed etiam vestris orationibus ab illo qui in vobis quod ei vivitis, operatur, merear misericordiam. Populus Hipponiensis, cui me dominus servum dedit, cum ex magna ac pene ex omni parte ita infirmus sit, ut pressura etiam levioris tribulationis possit graviter aegrotare, nunc tam magna tribulatione caeditur, ut etiam si non sic esset infirmus, vix eam cum aliqua salute animi sustineret. Eum autem, cum modo regressus sum, periculosissime scandalizatum comperi de absentia mea ; vestris autem de quorum spiritali robore gaudemus in domino, sanis utique faucibus sapit quo modo dictum sit : *Quis infirmatur et ego non infirmor? Quis scandalizatur et ego non uror?*, praesertim quoniam multi sunt hic qui detrahendo nobis ceterorum animas a quibus diligi videmur, adversus nos perturbare conantur, ut locum in eis diabolo faciant. Cum autem irascuntur nobis de quorum salute satagimus, magnum illis consilium vindicandi est libido moriendi non in corpore sed in corde, ubi funus occulte prius suo putore sentitur, quam nostra cogitatione prospicitur. Huic meae sollicitudini

2 Cor. xi. 29.

the honour of your presence; in your absence, it had heard what you were by birth and what by the grace of Christ you have become, yet though in love it believed this, yet it was perhaps afraid to tell it to others in case they might not believe it.

I shall tell you, then, my reasons for not coming **2** and the troubles that have kept me from so great a pleasure; thus I may gain not only pardon from you, but also, through your prayers, compassion from Him Who worketh in you to make you live unto Him. The people of Hippo, to whom the Lord gave me as a servant, are to a great extent, indeed to an almost complete extent, so feeble, that the infliction of even a trivial distress can seriously impair their well-being, and now they are smitten with such a great distress that, even were they not so feeble, they could scarcely endure it without a considerable risk of mental collapse. When I returned recently, I found them offended to a very dangerous degree at my absence. Now you, whose spiritual strength has given us such joy in the Lord, can certainly relish with wholesome palate the point of the saying: "Who is weak, and I am not weak? Who is offended, and I burn not?" [a] particularly since there are here many who by disparaging us attempt to stir up against us the minds of the others by whom we seem to be loved, in order to make room in them for the devil. But when those whose salvation is our concern are angry with us, their great method of taking revenge is to lust after death, not the death of the body, but of the soul, where the fact of dissolution is secretly perceived by the odour of corruption before we can guess at it and take measures against it. This anxiety of mine I am sure you will

procul dubio libenter ignoscitis, praesertim quoniam, si suscenseretis et velletis ulcisci, nihil fortasse gravius inveniretis, quam id quod patior cum vos Tagastae non video. Spero autem vestris adiutus orationibus, quod mihi ad vos, ubicumque in Africa fueritis, venire quantocius concedetur, cum hoc quo nunc detentus sum, praeterierit, si haec civitas in qua laboramus, digna non est, quia nec ego audeo dignam putare, quae nobiscum de vestra praesentia conlaetetur.

No. 33 (Ep. CXXVI)

DOMINAE SANCTAE AC VENERABILI FAMULAE DEI ALBINAE AUGUSTINUS IN DOMINO SALUTEM

1 Dolorem animi tui, quem te scribis explicare non posse, consolari aequum est, non augere, ut, si fieri potest, sanemus suspiciones tuas, non ut eis pro nostra causa suscensendo venerandum cor tuum et deo dicatum amplius perturbemus. Sancto fratri nostro filio tuo Piniano nullus ab Hipponiensibus metus mortis ingestus est, etiamsi forte ipse tale aliquid timuit; nam et nos metuebamus ne ab aliquibus perditis, qui saepe multitudini occulta con-

---

a When Albina, Melania, and Pinianus came to Hippo, the people there, allured by Pinianus's wealth, sought to have Pinianus forcibly ordained. Augustine was unable to restrain them from extracting from Pinianus an oath that he would not leave Hippo and would not receive ordination elsewhere, but the trio, despite the oath, returned next day to Tagaste. Letters cxxv.-cxxviii. then passed between Augustine, Alypius, and Albina, warmly discussing the validity of Pinianus's

gladly pardon, especially since you would perhaps find no heavier punishment, if you were angry and wanted to punish me, than what I have been enduring at not seeing you at Tagaste. But I hope that by the help of your prayers it may be granted me as soon as possible to pay you a visit, when this emergency that now detains me is past, wherever in Africa you may be, if this city that is the scene of my labours be unworthy, as I myself do not venture to consider it worthy, to share with me the joy of your presence.

No. 33 (Ep. CXXVI)

(A.D. 411)

TO THE HOLY LADY AND THE REVERED HAND-
MAID OF GOD, ALBINA,[a] AUGUSTINE SENDS
GREETING IN THE LORD

It is right that I should assuage, and not augment, **1** the grief of your spirit, which you describe in your letter as inexpressible ; in this way I may, if possible, heal your suspicions and not add to the agitation of your heart, so venerable and so devoted to God, by indignantly repudiating them for my own sake. The people of Hippo did nothing to make our holy brother, your son Pinianus, apprehensive of death, even though he himself perhaps entertained some fear of it. We ourselves, indeed, were afraid that some of the ruffians who often mix with a crowd from some

oath, which Augustine held to be valid, and repudiating the charge of covetousness. When Pinianus lost his property, the Hipponiensians quietly let the matter drop.

spiratione miscentur, in violentam prorumperetur
audaciam occasione seditionis inventa, quam velut
iusta indignatione concitaret. Sed, sicut post audire
potuimus, nihil tale a quoquam dictum est vel moli-
tum, sed vere in fratrem meum Alypium multa con-
tumeliosa et indigna clamabant, a quo tam ingenti
reatu utinam per illius orationes mereantur absolvi.
Ego autem post primos eorum clamores cum eis
dixissem de illo invito non ordinando, qua iam promissione detinerer, atque adiecissem quod, si mea fide
violata illum haberent presbyterum, me episcopum
non haberent, ad nostra subsellia relicta turba redie-
ram. Tum illi aliquantulum inopinata mea responsione
cunctati atque turbati velut flamma vento paululum
pressa, deinde coeperunt multo ardentius excitari,
existimantes fieri posse, ut vel mihi extorqueretur
illud non servare promissum vel me tenente promissi
fidem ab alio episcopo ordinaretur. Dicebam ego
quibus poteram, qui ad nos in absidem honoratiores
et graviores ascenderant, nec a promissi fide me posse
dimoveri nec ab alio episcopo in ecclesia mihi tradita
nisi me interrogato ac permittente posse ordinari ;
quod si permitterem, a fide nihilo minus deviarem.
Addebam etiam nihil eos velle, si ordinaretur invitus, nisi ut ordinatus abscederet. Illi hoc posse

---

^a The apse was the recess, usually semi-circular, in which
the eastern end of the church terminated. It was reserved
to the clergy, who had their seats or stalls (*subsellia*) there,
hence it was sometimes known as *presbyterium*, while, from
its shape, it also received the name *concha* (Paul. Nol. *Ep.*
xxxii. 12); the bishop's seat was usually provided with
curtains, so it was called *cathedra velata* (Aug. *Ep.* xxiii. 3).
This portion of the church was raised above the nave by

secret design might find an opportunity for rioting and produce an outburst of violence and outrage, stirring it up from apparently justified resentment; but we later had opportunity to ascertain that nothing of this kind was either suggested or attempted by anyone, although, to tell the truth, many insulting and opprobrious remarks were made against my brother Alypius—for which enormous offence I would that his prayers might win them pardon. But for my part, after their outcries began, I told them I could not ordain him against his will, being prevented by the promise I had already made, and I went on to say that if they made me break faith and had him as their priest, they would not have me as their bishop. I then left the crowd and returned to the clergy's stalls, whereupon, like a flame somewhat checked by the wind, they hesitated for a moment in consternation at my unexpected reply and then began to be much more afire with excitement, thinking that possibly they could wring from me the repudiation of my promise, or else that, if I stuck to my pledged word, he might receive ordination from another bishop. To those more notable and more venerable persons who came up to me in the apse [a] I kept saying, when possible, that I could not be deflected from keeping my pledged word, nor could any other bishop ordain in the church entrusted to me without my permission asked and given; even if I did allow that, I should none the less be departing from my pledge. I added, too, that if he were ordained against his will, they would only drive him away after his ordination. They

several steps (*absis gradata, ib.*), and before it stood the altar and the altar rails (*cancelli*).

fieri non credebant. Multitudo vero pro gradibus
constituta horrendo et perseverantissimo clamorum
fremitu in eadem voluntate persistens incertos animi
consiliique faciebant. Tunc illa in fratrem meum indigna clamabantur, tunc a nobis graviora timebantur.

2 Sed quamvis tanto motu populi et tanta perturbatione ecclesiae permoverer nec aliud constipationi
illi dixissem nisi eum me invitum ordinare non posse,
nec sic tamen adductus sum, quia et hoc promiseram
non me fuisse facturum, ut aliquid ei de suscipiendo
presbyterio suaderem ; quod si persuadere potuissem,
non iam ordinaretur invitus. Servavi utriusque promissionis fidem, non solum illius quam iam populo
patefeceram, verum etiam illius in qua uno teste,
quantum ad homines adtinet, detinebar. Servavi,
inquam, fidem promissionis, non iurationis, in tanto
periculo. Quod licet falso, sicut postea comperimus,
metuebatur, omnibus tamen, si quod esset, communiter inpendebat, et erat metus ipse communis, ac
propter ecclesiam, in qua eramus, maxime metuens
abscedere cogitabam. Sed metuendum fuit, ne
magis me absente tale aliquid faceret et reverentia
minor et dolor ardentior. Deinde, si cum fratre
Alypio discederem per populum constipatum, caven-

would not believe that this could possibly happen, but the crowd standing before the steps and expressing their unchanged and obstinate determination with the most persistent and hideous din and shouting made them irresolute and perplexed. It was then that those opprobrious outcries arose against my brother, and then that I was afraid of more serious consequences.

Yet, although I was much perturbed at the excitement among the people and the turmoil in the church, and assured the crowd only of my inability to ordain him against his will, even under those circumstances I was not induced to make any suggestion to him about accepting priestly orders, for that was just what I had promised I would not do ; if I could have succeeded in making him accept my suggestion, then he would not be ordained against his will. I remained faithful to both promises, not only the one I had revealed to the people, but also the other which, so far as men were concerned, had only one witness to bind me. I was faithful, I repeat, even in the face of such danger, to what was a promise, not an oath. We learned afterwards that our apprehensions of danger were without foundation, yet whatever danger there was threatened all of us alike, and the apprehension was shared by all, and I myself had thoughts of withdrawing, being chiefly apprehensive for the safety of the church in which we were gathered. But there was reason to fear that if I were not there, some such outrage might be more likely to result from the increase of their disrespect and the greater violence of their resentment. Further, if I did leave in company with brother Alypius through the crowded ranks of the people,

dum fuit, ne quisquam in eum manum mittere auderet; si autem sine illo, quae frons esset existimationis, si quid ei fortassis accideret et viderer eum propterea deseruisse, ut furenti populo traderetur.

3 Inter hos aestus meos gravemque maerorem et nullius consilii respirationem, ecce repente atque inopinate sanctus filius noster Pinianus mittit ad me servum dei, qui mihi diceret eum se velle populo iurare quod, si esset ordinatus invitus, ex Africa discederet omnino, credo, existimans eos, quando quidem peierare non posset, non iam ulterius infructuosa perseverantia clamaturos ad expellendum hinc hominem, quem saltem deberemus habere vicinum. Mihi autem quia videbatur vehementiorem eorum dolorem post hanc iurationem fuisse metuendum, apud me tacitus habui, et quia simul petierat ut ad eum venirem, non distuli. Cum mihi dixisset hoc ipsum, continuo et illud adiunxit eidem iurationi, quod mihi, dum ad eum pergo, per alium dei servum mandaverat, de praesentia scilicet sua, si ei clericatus sarcinam nolenti nullus inponeret. Hic ego in tantis angustiis quasi aura spirante recreatus nihil ei respondi, sed ad fratrem Alypium gradu concitatiore perrexi eique quid dixerit, dixi. At ille, ut existimo, devitans ne quid se auctore fieret, unde vos putabat offendi: " Hinc me," inquit, " nemo consulat." Quo

we should have had to see that no one ventured
to lay hands upon him; while if I left without
him, what a shameful reputation I should earn if
anything happened to him and I appeared to have
deserted him with the sole purpose of delivering him
over to the frenzy of the people.

Amid this feverish anxiety and oppressive anguish, **3**
when I was without a breath of any plan, lo!
our holy son Pinianus suddenly and unexpectedly
sends a servant of God to me to tell me that he
wanted him to swear to the people that, if he were
ordained against his will, he would leave Africa
altogether; his notion was, I imagine, that seeing
he could not break his oath, they would not go on
clamouring with such persistence, if it only resulted
in driving from the country a man whom we ought
at least to have as a neighbour. But since it appeared
to me that we had to fear a more violent outburst of
resentment from them in consequence of an oath of
this kind, I kept it to myself and said nothing about
it; and as he had asked at the same time that I should
go to him, I went at once. After telling me the same
thing, he immediately added to that oath a point that
he had sent another servant of God to put to me
while I was on my way to him, namely, about his
residence in Hippo, provided that no one compelled
him to undertake the burden of clerical office against
his will. At such an impasse, this refreshed me like
a breath of air, but I said nothing to him and went
with hurried step to brother Alypius and told him
what he had said. But he, seeking, I think, to avoid
responsibility for any occurrence that he thought
might give you offence, made answer, " Let no one
ask my advice about it." On hearing this, I returned

audito, ad populum tumultuantem perrexi, factoque
silentio, quid promissum esset, cum promissione etiam
iurationis aperui. Illi vero, qui solum eius presbyterium cogitabant atque cupiebant, non ita ut
putabam, quod oblatum fuerat, acceperunt, sed inter
se aliquantulum mussitantes petiverunt ut adderetur
eidem promissioni atque iurationi, ut, si quando illi
ad suscipiendum clericatum consentire placuisset,
non nisi in ipsa Hipponiensi ecclesia consentiret.
Rettuli ad eum ; sine dubitatione adnuit. Renun-
tiavi illis ; laetati sunt et mox iurationem pollicitam
poposcerunt.

4 Reverti ad filium nostrum eumque inveni fluctu-
antem quibusnam verbis comprehendi posset illa
cum iuratione promissio propter necessitates in-
ruentes, quae possent eum ut abscederet, cogere.
Simul etiam quid timeret ostendit, ne quis inruisset
hostilis incursus, qui esset discessione vitandus.
Volebat addi sancta Melania et aeris morbidi causa-
tionem, sed illius responsione reprehensa est. Ego
autem dixi gravem ab illo et non contemnendam
causam necessitatis ingestam, quae cives etiam
emigrare compelleret ; sed si haec populo dicerentur,
timendum esse ne male nos ominari videremur, si
autem sub generali necessitatis nomine fieret excusatio, non nisi fraudulentam necessitatem putari.
Placuit tamen ut de hac re populi animum ex-
periremur, et nihil aliud quam id quod putaveramus,
invenimus. Nam cum eius verba a diacono dicta

to the people, who were still in an uproar, and when silence had been obtained, I made them aware of the promise he had made and of the oath he had promised in addition. But as their mind and heart were set only on making him a priest, they did not accept his offer as I thought they would, but after a short time of muttering among themselves, demanded that he would add to his promise and oath the declaration that, if ever he decided to consent to undertake clerical office, he should do so only in the church of Hippo. I reported this to him; he agreed without hesitation; I returned to them with his answer; they were overjoyed, and presently demanded the oath he had promised.

I returned to our son, and found him at a loss for words in which to frame his promise confirmed by his oath, allowing for necessities that might occur to make his departure essential. At the same time, too, he revealed what it was he feared, namely, the occurrence of a hostile invasion, to avoid which it would be necessary to depart. The saintly Melania wanted to add to this the excuse of the unhealthy climate, but his reply to this reproved her. I stated that he had brought forward a ground of necessity that was grave and not to be despised, one which would compel the inhabitants as well to abandon the town; but if that reason were intimated to the people, it was to be feared that we might seem to be prophesying disaster, while if his excuse were stated in general terms of necessity, they would think that the necessity was only a make-believe. Yet he decided that we should test the mind of the people about it, and we found the result was exactly what we had anticipated. For when his words were read out to them

recitarentur et omnia placuissent, ubi nomen interpositae necessitatis insonuit, continuo reclamatum est promissioque displicuit, tumultu recrudescente et nihil aliud quam fraude secum agi populo existimante. Quod cum sanctus filius noster vidisset, iussit inde auferri nomen necessitatis rursumque ad laetitiam populus remeavit.

5 Et ut lassitudinem recusarem, sine me ad plebem accedere noluit; simul accessimus. Dixit ea quae a diacono audita erant, se mandasse, se iurasse, eaque se esse facturum, continuoque omnia eo tenore quo dictaverat, prosecutus est. Responsum est : " Deo gratias," et petitum ut totum scriptum subscriberetur. Dimisimus catechumenos continuoque scriptum subscripsit. Deinde peti coepimus nos episcopi, non vocibus populi sed tamen a populo per honestos fideles, ut nos quoque subscriberemus. At ubi coepi subscribere, sancta Melania contradixit. Miratus sum quare tam sero, quasi promissionem illam et iurationem nos non subscribendo facere possemus infectam ; sed tamen obtemperavi, ac sic remansit mea non plena subscriptio nec ultra nobis quisquam, ut subscriberemus, putavit instandum.

6 Qui autem alio die, posteaquam ipsum discessisse didicerunt, fuerint motus vel linguae hominum, quantum satis arbitratus sum, sanctitati vestrae per

---

by the mouth of a deacon and everything had been received with approbation, as soon as the word "necessity" that he had introduced fell on their ears, they immediately remonstrated and took exception to his promise, while the outcry was renewed, and the people jumped to the conclusion that the negotiations were meant only to deceive them. When our holy son perceived this, he ordered the word necessity to be struck out, and the people were restored to their condition of delight.

And although I pleaded weariness, he would not **5** approach the people without me, so we went together. He stated that it was his message they had heard the deacon recite, that he had confirmed it by oath and would carry out what he had promised, and straightway he repeated everything just as he had dictated it. The response was made, "Thanks be to God," and it was asked that the whole written statement should be subscribed. We dismissed the catechumens [a] and straightway he subscribed the statement. Then the people began to ask (not by shouting out, but still through some of the faithful of good report, commissioned by them) that I, as bishop, should subscribe it too. But when I began to subscribe it, the saintly Melania opposed it. I wondered why she intervened at that late hour, as if my refraining from subscribing could invalidate his promise and oath ; but yet I humoured her, and so my subscription remained unfinished, and no one thought of insisting any further on my subscribing.

But what the feelings and remarks of people were **6** on the following day, after they learned of his departure, I have taken the trouble to indicate to you, my saintly friend, as far as seemed to me necessary, in

commonitorium intimare curavi. Quisquis itaque
vobis contraria his quae narravi, forte narravit,
aut mentitur aut fallitur. Quaedam enim quae
mihi ad curam non pertinere visa sunt, praeter-
misisse me sentio, nulla tamen falsa dixisse. Proinde
sanctus filius noster Pinianus quod me praesente ac
permittente iuraverit, verum est ; quod autem me
praecipiente iuraverit, falsum est. Scit ipse, sciunt
servi dei quos ad me misit, primo sanctus Barnabas,
deinde Timasius, per quem etiam de promissione
praesentiae suae mihi mandavit. Ipse quoque
populus ad presbyterium, non ad ius iurandum cla-
mando cogebat ; sed oblatum sibi non respuit, ea
spe quo posset in eodem apud nos habitante voluntas fieri, quo consentiret ad ordinationem, ne,
sicut iuraverat, si invitus ordinaretur, abscederet.
Ac per hoc et illi propter opus dei clamaverunt —
neque enim sanctificatio presbyterii non est opus dei
— et, quod postea de promissa praesentia gratulati
non sunt, nisi adderetur quod, si quando ad suscipiendum clericatum consentire vellet, non nisi in
Hipponiensi ecclesia consentiret, satis in promptu
est quod etiam de ipsa eius apud se habitatione
speraverint, ideoque ab illo operis dei desiderio non
recesserunt.

7   Quo modo ergo dicis hoc eos fecisse turpissimo
appetitu pecuniae ? Primo quia ad plebem, quae
clamabat, omnino non pertinet ; sicut enim plebs
Tagastensis de his, quae contulistis ecclesiae Taga-

my official communication. Anyone, therefore, who happens to give you an account which contradicts the one I have given you is either lying or misinformed. I am conscious of having passed over certain points which seemed to me irrelevant to my purpose, but not of having made any false statement. Likewise, it is true that our holy son, Pinianus, took the oath in my presence and with my permission, but it is not true that he took it at my instigation. He knows this himself; the servants of God whom he sent to me know it, first the saintly Barnabas, then Timasius, by whom too he sent me the message about his promise to take up residence in Hippo. The people, too, were urging him by their cries to accept office as priest, not to take an oath; but when it was offered, they did not refuse it, in the hope that, if he came to live among us, he might become willing to agree to ordination, and that he would not take his departure, as he had sworn to do, if he were ordained against his will. And so even they were actuated in their outcries by concern for God's work—for the consecration to priesthood is surely God's work—and afterwards feeling dissatisfied with his promise of residence here without the further stipulation that if he eventually decided to agree to undertake clerical office he would do so only in the church of Hippo, it is quite evident that they were hopeful too of his taking up house among them, and so, here too, they did not depart from their zeal for God's work.

How then can you maintain that in so doing they **7** were impelled by a base love of money? In the first place, the people who raised the outcry have simply nothing to do with that; for just as the people of Tagaste derive from your gifts to the church of

stensi, non habet nisi gaudium boni operis vestri, sic et Hipponiensis et cuiuslibet alterius loci, ubi *de mammona iniquitatis* domini praecepta fecistis vel estis ubicumque facturi. Non ergo populus, ut de tanto viro ecclesiae consuleret suae, ardentissime flagitans suum pecuniarium commodum quaesivit a vobis, sed vestrum pecuniae contemptum dilexit in vobis. Nam si in me dilexerunt quod audierant paucis agellulis paternis contemptis ad dei liberam servitutem me fuisse conversum, neque in hoc inviderunt ecclesiae Tagastensi, quae carnalis patria mea est, sed, cum illa mihi clericatum non inposuisset, quando potuerunt, habendum invaserunt, quanto flagrantius in nostro Piniano amare potuerunt tantam mundi istius cupiditatem, tantas opes, tantam spem tanta conversione superatam atque calcatam ! Ego quippe secundum multorum sensum comparantium semet ipsos sibimet ipsis non divitias dimisisse, sed ad divitias videor venisse. Vix enim vigesima particula res mea paterna existimari potest in comparatione praediorum ecclesiae, quae nunc ut dominus existimor possidere. In qualibet autem maxime Africanarum ecclesiarum hic noster non dico presbyter sed episcopus sit, comparatus pristinis opibus suis, etiamsi animo dominantis egerit, pauperrimus erit. Multo ergo liquidius et securius in hoc amatur Christiana paupertas, in quo nulla rerum ampliorum potest putari cupiditas. Hoc accendit animos populi, hoc

---

^a Luke xvi. 9.   ^b 2 Cor. x. 12.

236

Tagaste only joy in your good deed, so, too, with
the people of Hippo and of any other place where you
have followed out the Lord's injunctions about the
"mammon of unrighteousness," [a] or wherever you
will do so. Thus, in demanding with such eagerness
that their own church should reap the advantage
of so outstanding a man, the people did not seek
their own monetary gain from you, but testified their
esteem for the scorn of money in you. For if because
they had heard that I had scorned my few paternal
acres and had turned to the willing bondage of
God, they testified their esteem for me and did
not grudge them to the church of Tagaste, which
is my earthly birthplace, but, since it had not
imposed clerical office upon me, laid violent hands
upon me when they had the opportunity to make
me their own, how much more ardently could they
esteem in our friend Pinianus his overcoming and
treading under foot such worldly ambitions, such
wealth, such prospects! I indeed appear in the
opinion of many who compare themselves with themselves [b] not to have forsaken a fortune but to have
come into a fortune, for my patrimony can scarcely be
reckoned to be a twentieth part in proportion to the
property of the church, which I am now considered to
possess as a master. But let our brother become—
I do not say a priest, but a bishop in any church,
especially in Africa, he will be extremely poor, in
comparison with his former wealthy condition, even
if he acts in the spirit of a proprietor. In one in
whom there can be no suspicion of coveting a position
of greater affluence, the love of Christian poverty is
therefore much more clearly apparent and certain.
It was that which inflamed the people's mind and

in illam violentiam perseverantissimi clamoris erexit. Non eos turpis cupiditatis insuper accusemus, sed magis bonum quod ipsi non habent, saltem in aliis diligere sine crimine permittamus. Nam etsi fuerunt illi multitudini permixti inopes vel mendici, qui simul clamabant et de vestra venerabili redundantia indigentiae suae supplementum sperabant, nec ista, ut arbitror, cupiditas turpis est.

8 Restat ergo ut iste pecuniae turpissimus appetitus ex obliquo in clericos et maxime in episcopum dirigatur. Nos enim rebus ecclesiae dominari existimamur, nos opibus frui. Postremo quicquid de istis nos accepimus, nos vel adhuc possidemus vel, ut placuit, erogavimus; nihil inde populo extra clericatum vel extra monasterium constituto nisi paucissimis indigentibus largiti sumus. Non ergo dico quia vel in nos maxime a vobis dici ista debuerunt, verum tamen in nos solos credibiliter dici potuerunt. Quid ergo faciemus? Qua nos, si apud inimicos non possumus, saltem apud vos ratione purgamus? Res haec animi est, intus est, procul ab oculis secreta mortalium deo tantum modo nota est. Quid ergo restat nisi deum testari, cui nota est? Cum ergo de nobis ista sentitis, non praecipitis quod multo melius est et quod mihi in epistula tua tamquam culpabile obiciendum putasti, sed omnino cogitis ut iuremus, non intentato metu mortis carnis nostrae,

238

stirred them up to that violent and most insistent clamour. Let us not accuse them in addition of sordid covetousness, but rather let us allow them, without imputation of base motives, to esteem in others at least the good they themselves do not possess. For even if that crowd had an admixture of poor persons or beggars who joined in the shouting and hoped for an addition to their meagre store from what your Honours could spare, even that, in my opinion, is not sordid covetousness.

It remains, then, that your charge of a most sordid 8 lust for money is indirectly levelled at the clergy, and especially at the bishop. For it is we who are thought to be lording it over the Church's property, and to be enjoying its resources. In short, whatever income we have received from those sources, it is we who either have it still in our possession or have expended it as we pleased; no portion of it have we distributed to the people who are outside the ranks of clergy or outside the monastery, except to a very few in want. I do not say, then, that the charges you made were necessarily uttered against us particularly, but that we are the only people against whom they could be credibly uttered. What then shall we do? If we cannot clear ourselves before our enemies, how at least shall we do so before you? It is a matter of conscience, it lies within, hidden from mortal eyes, and is known only to God. What then remains to us but to call as our witness upon God, to Whom it is all known? Since such is your feeling about us, you do not enjoin us to take the much better course which you have thought fit in your letter to cast up to me as blameworthy, but you absolutely force me to take an oath, not threatening me with the death

quod populus Hipponiensis fecisse putatus est, sed
intentato metu mortis existimationis nostrae, quae
propter infirmos quibus nos praebere ad exemplum
bonorum operum qualicumque conversatione conamur,
etiam vitae carnis huius utique praeponenda est.

9 Verum tamen vobis nos ita cogentibus ut iuremus,
non suscensemus, sicut vos Hipponiensibus sus-
censetis. Creditis enim, tamquam homines de hominibus, etsi ea quae in nobis non sunt, non tamen
ea quae in nobis esse non possunt. Sananda ista
in vobis, non accusanda sunt, et nostra purganda vobis
est fama, si est domino purgata conscientia. Qui
fortasse praestabit, sicut ante quam accidisset ista
temptatio ego et frater meus Alypius conlocuti sumus,
ut non solum vobis carissimis commembris nostris,
verum etiam ipsis inimicis notissimum fiat nulla nos
cupiditate pecuniae in rebus ecclesiasticis sordidari.
Quod donec fiat, si dominus donabit ut fiat, ecce nunc
interim, quod cogimur facimus, ne vestri cordis
medicinam in quantam libet moram temporis
differamus. Deus testis est istam omnem rerum
ecclesiasticarum procurationem, quarum credimur
amare dominatum, propter servitutem quam debeo
caritati fratrum et timori dei, tolerare me, non amare,
ita ut ea, si salvo officio possim, carere desiderem.
Nec aliud me de fratre meo Alypio sentire ipse deus

---

a Titus ii. 7.

of this body of mine, as the people of Hippo are supposed to have done, but threatening me with the death of my good reputation, which is surely to be reckoned more precious than even the life of this body, because of the weak brethren, to whom we strive by our conduct, such as it is, to show ourselves an example of good works.[a]

Yet, though you do in this way force me to take an oath, I am not indignant with you, as you are with the people of Hippo, for, like men judging other men, even if you believe the things which are not in us, still you do not believe the things that cannot be in us. That is a fault in you that is rather to be cured than to be censured, and, if our conscience is clear in the sight of the Lord, our character has to be cleared in your sight. It may be, as my brother Alypius and I said in conversation before that temptation occurred, that God will grant that not only you, our beloved fellow-Christians, but also our enemies, may know without a shadow of a doubt that no lust for money defiles us in our administration of the Church's business. Until that happen (if the Lord grants it to happen), just see, I am doing as a temporary expedient what you force me to do, in order to avoid the slightest possible delay in soothing your feelings. God is my witness that it is only because of the service I owe to the love of my brethren and the fear of God that I put up with all the administration of the Church's business over which I am supposed to love the exercise of lordship, and that I have so little liking for it that I should wish to do without it, if it could be done without unfaithfulness to my office. God Himself is my witness that I believe the same to be quite true about my brother Alypius. Neverthe-

testis est. Tamen et de illo aliter sentiendo populus
et, quod est gravius, Hipponiensis in tantas est illius
praecipitatus iniurias et de nobis vos sancti dei et
pleni visceribus misericordiae talia credendo nomine
eiusdem populi, qui ad causam huiusce modi cupiditatis omnino non pertinet, nos tangere atque admonere voluistis utique ad nos corrigendos, neque
enim odio, quod absit a vobis. Unde non irasci sed
gratias agere debeo, quod nec verecundius nec
liberius agere potuistis, ut episcopo non quasi
conviciose obiceretis quod sentiebatis, sed ex obliquo
intellegendum relinqueretis.

10   Nec molestum sit vobis ut vos velut gravatos
arbitremini, quia iurandum putavi. Neque enim
gravabat apostolus aut eos parum diligebat quibus
dicebat : *Non in sermone adulationis fuimus apud vos
neque in occasione cupiditatis; deus testis est.* Rei
quippe apertae ipsos testes adhibuit, rei autem
occultae quem nisi deum ? Si ergo ille merito est
veritus ne humana ignorantia de illo aliquid tale
sentiret, cuius labor in promptu omnibus erat, quod
nisi summa necessitate a populis quibus Christi
gratiam dispensabat, in usus suos aliquid non sume-
bat, cetera vero suo victui necessaria suis manibus
transigebat; quanto magis nobis laborandum est, ut
credatur, qui et merito sanctitatis et virtute animi
longe inpares sumus nec aliquid ad sustentacula vitae
huius operari nostris manibus possumus, et si posse-

---

less, because in his case the people (and what is worse, the people of Hippo) held a different belief, they rushed into that abuse of him, and in our case, because you believed such accusations, though nominally censuring the same people, who have simply nothing to do with this charge of covetousness, you, who are saints of God and full of tender compassion, tried to get at us and reprove us, though to be sure it was for our improvement, and not from dislike—far be that from you. And so I should not be angry, but grateful, since you could not have acted in a more respectful or a more courteous manner, not offensively hurling at the bishop the reproof you had in mind, but leaving it to be indirectly understood.

Do not be offended and think yourselves in a way ill-used, that I have thought it necessary to take an oath, for the apostle was not ill-using or ceasing to have affection for those to whom he said, "Neither used we at any time flattering words, as ye know, nor took any opportunity for covetousness; God is witness."[a] For the known fact he took them to witness themselves, but for the hidden fact, God alone. If he then was right in fearing that human ignorance might conceive some such opinion about himself, whose labours were open for all men to see and who only in extreme necessity took anything for his own benefit from the peoples to whom he ministered the grace of Christ, producing with his own hands everything necessary for his sustenance; how much more should we exert ourselves to secure men's confidence, for both in holy merit and in mental courage we are far inferior and are unable with our own hands to make anything that would support this life; even if we could, the

mus, tantis occupationibus, quas tunc illos non credo
fuisse perpessos, nequaquam sineremur! Non ergo
ulterius in hac causa populo Christiano, quae ecclesia
est dei, obiciatur pecuniae turpissimus appetitus.
Tolerabilius enim nobis obicitur, in quos huius mali
quamvis falsa, tamen verisimilis suspicio cadere potuit,
quam illis quos ab hoc appetitu et a suspicione
constat alienos.

11 Denegare autem iurationem qualibet fide prae-
ditas mentes, quanto magis fide Christiana, non dico
aliquid contrarium confirmare, sed omnino dubitare,
fas non est. De qua re quid sentiam, satis, ut
arbitror, in epistula quam ad fratrem meum scripsi,
planissime aperui. Scripsit mihi sanctitas tua: " Si
aut ego aut Hipponienses hoc censent, ut iuri iurando
violenter extorto satis fiat." Tu enim ipsa quid
censes? Placetne tibi, ut etiam certa morte imminente, quod tunc inaniter metuebatur, nomen
domini dei sui in fallaciam Christianus adsumat,
deum suum testem falsitati Christianus adhibeat?
Qui profecto si praeter iurationem ad falsum testimonium morte imminente cogeretur, maculare vitam
suam magis timere debuit quam finire. Hostiles
inter se acies et armatae certe apertissima mortis
intentione confligunt, et tamen, cum invicem iurant,
laudamus fidem servantes, fallentes autem merito
detestamur. Ut autem iurarent, quid utraeque ab
alterutris nisi occidi vel capi timuerunt? Ac per
hoc vel mortis vel captivitatis metu extortae iurationi

---

[a] His letter to Alypius, Ep. cxxv., discussing how far an
oath is binding.

many demands upon us, such as I do not think they in their day endured, would altogether prevent us. So in this matter let no further reproach of the base lust for money be made against the Christian people who constitute the Church of God. It is more tolerable that it should be made against us, for on us suspicion of that sin could fall, though without ground, yet not without probability, than upon those who are well known to be far removed from this lust and this suspicion.

For minds endowed with any faith—and how much 11 more Christian faith!—to deny an oath, I do not say to assert anything that contradicts it, but to waver in regard to it at all, this is utterly wrong. In the letter[a] I wrote to my brother I have, I think, revealed with sufficient clearness my opinion on this point. Your Holiness has written to me, asking whether the people of Hippo or I think that anyone should abide by an oath that was extorted by force. What do you think yourself? Does it meet with your approval that a Christian should call upon the name of the Lord his God with intent to deceive, that a Christian should make his God a witness to a falsehood, even under the menace of certain death, the fear of which was in this case unfounded? Surely if he were compelled by the menace of death to bear false witness besides his oath, he ought to fear the loss of honour more than the loss of life. Hostile armies confront each other with weapons and contend with the undoubted and avowed purpose of dealing death, and yet when they take an oath to each other, we praise those who keep their word and rightly execrate those who break it. What impelled them to take an oath, unless the fear on each side of being slain or captured? And so, unless the oath extorted by the fear of either

nisi parcatur, nisi fides quae ibi data est custodiatur, sacrilegii, periurii crimine detinentur etiam tales homines, qui magis metuunt peierare quam hominem occidere; et nos, utrum implenda sit extorta iuratio servorum dei munere sanctitatis praeminentium, monachorum ad perfectionem mandatorum Christi rerum etiam suarum distributione currentium, quasi disceptaturi ponimus quaestionem.

12 Nam quid exilii vel deportationis aut relegationis nomine promissa illa praesentia praegravatur, obsecro te? Puto quod presbyterium non est exilium. Hoc ergo noster eligeret quam illud exilium? Absit a nobis ut sic sanctus dei et nobis carissimus defendatur; absit, inquam, ut dicatur maluisse exilium quam presbyterium aut maluisse periurium quam exilium. Haec dicerem, si vere a nobis aut a populo iuratio ei fuisset extorta promittendae praesentiae; nunc vero non extorta est dum negaretur, sed, dum offerretur accepta, et hoc ea spe, sicut supra diximus, quia per illam praesentiam creditum est eum etiam ad clericatum suscipiendum posse desiderantibus consentire. Postremo, quodlibet de nobis vel de Hipponiensibus sentiatur, longe alia est eorum causa qui coegerint iurare, quam eorum qui non dicam coegerint, sed suaserint, peierare. Ipse etiam de quo agitur, considerare non renuat utrum sit peius

246

death or captivity be respected, unless the faith they
have pledged in it be kept, even men of that kind
are held back by the fear of being charged with
sacrilege and perjury, because they are more afraid
of breaking faith than of taking human life; and yet
we debate like splitters of hairs whether an oath
should be fulfilled that was extorted from servants of
God who are most notable by reason of their holiness,
from ascetics who even by the distribution of their
own property are swift to carry out Christ's commandments.

Is it that his promised residence here, I ask you, 12
is burdened with the name of exile or transportation
or banishment? I do not suppose that the office of
priest is an exile. Would our friend then choose it in
preference to that exile? Far be it from us to make
that excuse for one who is a saint of God and very
dear to ourselves; far be it from us, I repeat, to say
of him that he preferred exile to the priestly office,
or preferred perjury to exile. I might say that, if
the oath by which he promised to reside here had
been really extorted from him by us or by the people,
but in point of fact it was not extorted in spite of his
refusal, but accepted on being proffered, and that
in the hope and belief, as I said above, that by his
residence here he might possibly comply with their
desire that he should undertake clerical office. In
the last place, whatever opinion be entertained of the
people of Hippo or of us, there is a great difference
between the case of those who may have compelled
him to take the oath and that of those who may have
persuaded, not to say compelled, him to break it.
Further, let him of whom we speak not refuse to
consider whether an oath taken under the compulsion

sub quolibet timore ius iurandum, an remoto timore ipso periurium.

13 Deo gratias quia non aliter Hipponienses promissum circa se impleri sentiunt, quam ut adsit voluntate habitandi, et eat quo necesse fuerit, cum dispositione redeundi. Nam si verba iurationis adtenderent et exigerent, nullo modo servus dei recedere quam ullo modo debuit peierare. Sed quia crimen eorum esset non dico talem virum sed quemlibet hominem sic tenere, nec ipsi aliam expectationem se habuisse probaverunt, qui audientes quod rediturus abscesserit, gratulati sunt, nec aliud illis verax iuratio debet quam id quod ab illa expectaverunt. Quid est autem, quod dicitur eum iuratione ore suo expressa exceptionem fecisse necessitatis, quasi non ore suo rursus hoc iussit auferri ? Certe ad populum quando ipse locutus est, tunc etiam interponeret. Quod si fecisset, non utique responderetur : " Deo gratias," sed ad illam rediretur reclamationem quae facta fuerat quando sic a diacono recitatum est. Et numquid ad rem pertinet, sive interposita sit ad recedendum necessitatis excusatio sive non sit ? Nihil ab illo aliud expectatum est quam id quod supra diximus. Expectationem autem eorum quibus iuratur quisquis deceperit, non potest esse non periurus.

of any kind of fear is a worse thing than the breaking of that oath, when the actual fear has been removed.

Thanks be to God that the people of Hippo regard **13** his promise towards themselves as being fulfilled if he comes to the town with the intention of residing in it, and departs whither necessity calls him with the purpose of returning. If they were to regard the letter of his oath and demand its literal fulfilment, God's servant ought in no wise to depart rather than in any wise to break his word. Yet, since it would be criminal for them so to bind any individual, not to mention a man of his quality, they themselves have proved that they entertained no other expectation, for on hearing that he had departed with the promise of return, they manifested their satisfaction; and fidelity to an oath requires no more and no less than the performance of what was anticipated from it by those to whom it was made. What is the use of saying that in taking the oath that he framed with his own lips, he added a proviso about circumstances that might necessitate his leaving the town; the fact is that with his own lips he again ordered that clause to be struck out. To be sure, he might have put it in again when he spoke to the people, but if he had, they surely would not have made answer, "Thanks be to God!" but would have returned to that protest which they made when it was read out by the deacon with the proviso inserted. And does it really affect the point, whether the excuse of necessity for leaving the town was inserted or was not? Nothing more and nothing less was expected from him than what I mentioned above, and anyone who disappoints the expectations of those to whom he takes an oath cannot be anything but a perjurer.

14   Fiat ergo quod promissum est, et infirmorum corda
sanentur, ne tanto exemplo, quibus hoc placuerit,
ad imitandum periurium aedificentur, quibus autem
displicet, iustissime dicant nulli nostrum credendum
esse non solum promittenti aliquid sed etiam iuranti.
Hinc enim potius cavendae sunt linguae inimicorum, de quibus tamquam iaculis ad interficiendos
infirmos maior ille utitur inimicus.   Sed absit ut de
tali anima speremus aliud quam quod dei timor
inspirat et tanta quae in illa est excellentia sanctitatis hortatur.   Ego autem, quem dicis etiam prohibere debuisse, fateor, non potui sic sapere, ut tanto
vel tumultu vel offensione magis everti vellem ecclesiam cui servio, quam id quod a tali viro nobis
offerebatur, accipere.

No. 34 (Ep. CXXXIII)

DOMINO EXIMIO ET MERITO INSIGNI ATQUE
CARISSIMO FILIO MARCELLINO AUGUSTINUS
EPISCOPUS IN DOMINO SALUTEM

1   Circumcelliones illos et clericos partis Donati, quos

ᵃ Marcellinus, a tribune and notary, was brother to
Apringius, proconsul of Africa, and was appointed by the
Emperor Honorius to preside over an inquiry into the dispute between Catholics and Donatists. This conference took
place in June 411, and in spite of the impartiality and
moderation shown by Marcellinus, the Donatists accused
him of receiving bribes (Ep. cxli.; *Cod. Theod.* xvi. 11. 5).
In this letter, and in cxxxviii. and cxxxix., Augustine de-
plores the violence of the Circumcellions, but exhorts him
to show mercy to those misguided fanatics. Marcellinus
and Augustine were on terms of close friendship, and to him
Augustine dedicated his *De Peccatorum Meritis et Remissione,
De Spiritu et Littera,* and the first two books of the *De
Civitate Dei,* which he says were written at Marcellinus's

Therefore let his promise be fulfilled and the heart **14**
of the weak brethren be healed, so that this notable
precedent may not encourage those who approve of
it to commit similar perjury, or those who disapprove
of it to say with perfect justice that no one of us is
to be believed, not only on promise of anything, but
even on oath. In this connexion we ought rather
to safeguard ourselves against the tongues of our
enemies, which our greater enemy employs like
darts to slay the weak. But be it far from us to hope
for anything from a soul like his, other than what
the fear of God inspires, and its own great, native
excellence of holiness exhorts. As for myself, you
say I ought actually to have forbidden his oath, but
I confess I could not be so minded as to prefer seeing
the church I serve overthrown by such an uproarious
outbreak to accepting the offer made to me by a man
of his standing.

No. 34 (Ep. CXXXIII)

(A.D. 411)

TO MY NOBLE AND JUSTLY DISTINGUISHED
    LORD AND DEAREST SON, MARCELLINUS,[a]
    BISHOP AUGUSTINE SENDS GREETING IN
    THE LORD

Those Circumcellions and clergy of the Donatist **1**

suggestion. In 413, during the revolt of Heraclian, Marcellinus and his brother were seized, imprisoned, and, in spite
of a petition from several of the African bishops, put to
death. Ep. cli. narrates the circumstances of his death and
pays a noble tribute to his memory. The impartial conduct
of Marcellinus towards the Donatists was commemorated in
an imperial decree (*Cod. Theod.* xvi. 5. 55), and his memory
is honoured by the Church of Rome on April 6.

de Hipponiensi ad iudicium pro factis eorum publicae
disciplinae cura deduxerat, a tua nobilitate comperi
auditos et plurimos eorum de homicidio quod in
Restitutum, catholicum presbyterum, commiserunt,
et de caede Innocentii, alterius catholici presbyteri,
atque de oculo eius effosso et digito praeciso, fuisse
confessos. Unde mihi sollicitudo maxima incussa
est, ne forte sublimitas tua censeat eos tanta legum
severitate plectendos, ut qualia fecerunt, talia
patiantur. Ideoque his litteris obtestor fidem tuam,
quam habes in Christo, per ipsius domini Christi
misericordiam, ut hoc nec facias nec fieri omnino
permittas. Quamvis enim ab eorum interitu dissimulare possumus, qui non accusantibus nostris sed
illorum notoria, ad quos tuendae publicae pacis
vigilantia pertinebat, praesentati videantur exa-
mini, nolumus tamen passiones servorum dei quasi
vice talionis paribus suppliciis vindicari, non quo
scelestis hominibus licentiam facinorum prohibeamus
auferri, sed hoc magis sufficere volumus, ut vivi et
nulla corporis parte truncati vel ab inquietudine
insana ad sanitatis otium legum cohercitione diri-
gantur vel a malignis operibus alicui utili operi
deputentur. Vocatur quidem et ista damnatio, sed
quis non intellegat magis beneficium quam supplicium
nuncupandum, ubi nec saeviendi relaxetur audacia
nec paenitendi medicina subtrahatur?

party whom the guardians of public order had taken
from Hippo to be tried for their misdeeds, have been
heard, I am informed, by your Excellency, and the
majority of them have confessed to having murdered
Restitutus, a Catholic priest, and beaten Innocentius,
another Catholic priest, and gouged out his eye and
cut off a finger.   This news has plunged me into the
deepest anxiety, lest perchance your Highness may
decide that they must endure a legal sentence so
severe that their punishment shall be similar in kind
to their crime.   For that reason I implore you by the
faith you have in Christ, by the mercy of Christ the
Lord Himself, neither to do this nor to let it be done
at all.   For although we can disclaim responsibility
for the death of men who were clearly made to appear before the court on no accusation of ours, but
on the indictment of those officers who were concerned
with the safe-guarding of the public peace, still it is
not our desire that the sufferings of God's servants
shall be avenged by the infliction of similar punishments, as if by way of retaliation ; not that we refuse
to allow wicked men to be deprived of impunity
in crime, but that we rather desire that justice be
satisfied in such a way as to turn the wicked by
means of coercive measures from their mad frenzy
to the peaceableness of sane men, without taking
their life or crippling them in any part of the body,
and so set them to some useful work instead of
their works of malice.   That too is called a penal
sentence, but who can fail to see that it is to be termed
rather a benefit than a punishment, when, on the one
side, bold and frenzied violence is not allowed a free
hand, and, on the other, the remedy of repentance
is not withheld ?

2 Imple, Christiane iudex, pii patris officium, sic
suscense iniquitati, ut consulere humanitati memi-
neris, nec in peccatorum atrocitatibus exerceas ulcis-
cendi libidinem, sed peccatorum vulneribus curandi
adhibeas voluntatem. Noli perdere paternam dili-
gentiam, quam in ipsa inquisitione servasti, quando
tantorum scelerum confessionem non extendente
eculeo, non sulcantibus ungulis, non urentibus
flammis, sed virgarum verberibus eruisti,—qui modus
cohercitionis et a magistris artium liberalium et ab
ipsis parentibus et saepe etiam in iudiciis solet ab
episcopis haberi. Noli ergo atrocius vindicare quod
lenius invenisti. Inquirendi quam puniendi necessitas maior est ; ad hoc enim et mitissimi homines
facinus occultatum diligenter atque instanter exami-
nant, ut inveniant quibus parcant. Unde plerumque necesse est, exerceatur acrius inquisitio, ut
manifestato scelere, sit ubi appareat mansuetudo.
Omnia quippe bona opera amant in luce constitui
non propter humanam gloriam, sed *ut videant*, ait
dominus, *bona opera vestra et glorificent patrem vestrum,
qui in caelis est.* Et ideo non sufficit apostolo monere
ut mansuetudinem servaremus, sed ut eam etiam
notam omnibus faceremus : *Mansuetudo*, inquit,
vestra nota sit omnibus hominibus, et alio loco : *Mansuetudinem ostentantes ad omnes homines*, ut nec illa
sancti David, quando inimico sibi in manus tradito
clementer pepercit, praeclarissima lenitas emineret,

---

[a] Matt. v. 16. [b] Phil. iv. 5. [c] Titus iii. 2.

[d] The reference is to David's sparing the life of Saul in
the cave at En-gedi, when David cut off the skirt of Saul's
robe (1 Samuel xxiv. 1-8).

NO. 34 (Ep. CXXXIII)

Christian judge, fulfil the duty of a devoted father; **2**
be angry at wickedness, yet forget not humane considerations, and do not give rein to the desire to
seek revenge for the atrocity of their sinful deeds,
but exert your will to the curing of the sores of the
sinners. Do not lose that fatherly care that you
maintained at the inquiry, when you extracted the
confession of those heinous offences, not by stretch-
ing them on the rack, or by furrowing their flesh with
hooks, or by burning them with flames, but by beating them with rods—a method of coercion employed
by schoolmasters and by parents themselves, and
often by bishops as well in their courts. Do not then
punish with harsher sentence what you found out by
gentler methods. The need for finding out is greater
than that of punishment, for even the gentlest of men
investigate a hidden crime with care and insistence,
to the end that they may find out those whom
they are to spare. That is why it is usually necessary to pursue the investigation with greater harshness, so that, when the guilt has been brought to
light, there may be an opportunity for showing
moderation. For all good works delight in being
set in the light, not to gratify human vanity, but,
as the Lord says, that men " may see your good works
and glorify your Father which is in heaven." [a] And
for this reason the Apostle was not satisfied with
admonishing us to preserve our moderation, but urged
us further to make it known to all, saying, " Let your
moderation be known to all men," [b] and elsewhere,
" Showing moderation to all men." [c] So, too, that very
remarkable forbearance of the holy David, when in
his clemency he spared the enemy who was delivered
into his hands,[d] would not be so conspicuous, if his

255

nisi potestas pariter appareret. Non te ergo exasperet vindicandi potestas, cui lenitatem non excussit examinandi necessitas. Noli facinore invento quaerere percussorem, in quo inveniendo noluisti adhibere tortorem.

3 Postremo pro ecclesiae utilitate missus es. Hoc ecclesiae catholicae aut, ut modum dispensationis meae non supergredi videar, hoc ecclesiae ad Hipponiensium-Regiorum dioecesim pertinenti prodesse, hoc expedire contestor. Si non audis amicum petentem, audi episcopum consulentem, quamvis, quoniam Christiano loquor, maxime in tali causa non arroganter dixerim, audire te episcopum convenit iubentem, domine eximie et merito insignis atque carissime fili, unde scio quidem causas ecclesiasticas excellentiae tuae potissimum iniunctas; sed quia credo istam curam ad virum clarissimum atque spectabilem proconsulem pertinere, ad eum quoque litteras dedi, quas rogo ut ipse illi tradere et allegare, si opus est, non graveris. Atque ambos obsecro, ne importunam arbitremini vel intercessionem vel suggestionem vel sollicitudinem nostram, et passiones catholicorum servorum dei, quae infirmis ad aedificationem spiritalem utiles esse debent, haud reciproca inimicorum, a quibus passi sunt, poena decoloretis, sed potius refracta iudiciaria severitate et vestram fidem, quia filii estis ecclesiae, et ipsius matris mansuetu-

power to act otherwise were not equally apparent.
So then, do not let your power to exact punishment
drive you to harsh measures, when the need for
making an investigation did not make you discard
your clemency. Do not send for the executioner
after finding out the crime, when to find it out you
did not use the services of the torturer.

Finally, it is for the benefit of the Church that you 3
have been sent. I solemnly avow that such a line of
action is to the advantage of the Church as a whole
or, not to have the appearance of going beyond the
limits of my own stewardship, of the church belonging to the diocese of Hippo Regius. If you will not
give ear to the petition of a friend, give ear to
a bishop's advice; in fact, since I am addressing a
Christian, it would not be arrogant in me to say,
especially in a matter of this kind, that it is your duty,
my noble and justly distinguished lord and well-
beloved son, to give ear to a bishop's commands,
concerning that for which most of all, as I know, the
Church cases have devolved upon your Excellency;
but as I believe this responsibility belongs to that
illustrious and admirable man, the Proconsul, I have
written a letter to him too, which I beg you to take
the trouble to hand to him and, if need be, to recommend to his notice yourself. And I beseech
both of you not to think I am importunate with
either my intercession or advice or anxiety, and not
to let the sufferings of the Catholic servants of God,
which ought to be of benefit in the spiritual up-
building of the weak, be sullied by the retaliation of
punishment on the enemies at whose hand they
suffered ; rather, blunting the edge of judicial rigour,
exert every effort to commend your faith, since ye

dinem commendare minime neglegatis. Deus omni-
potens praestantiam tuam bonis omnibus augeat,
domine eximie et merito insignis atque carissime fili.

No. 35 (Ep. CXLIV)

DOMINIS HONORABILIBUS ET MERITO SUS-CIPIENDIS CARISSIMIS AC DESIDERANTIS-SIMIS FRATRIBUS IN OMNI HONORUM GRADU CIRTENSIBUS AUGUSTINUS EPI-SCOPUS

1 Si id quod in vestra civitate nos graviter con-
tristabat, absumptum est, si duritia cordis humani
resistens manifestissimae et quodam modo publicae
veritati eiusdem potentia veritatis evicta est, si
sapit dulcedo pacis unitatisque caritas non iam
reverberat oculos saucios, sed sanos inlustrat ac
vegetat, non sunt haec opera nostra sed dei, non
haec humanis opibus omnino tribuerem nec si, cum
apud vos essemus, tanta conversio multitudinis nobis
loquentibus et hortantibus proveniret. Hoc agit ille
et efficit, qui per ministros suos rerum signis ex-
trinsecus admonet, rebus autem ipsis per se ipsum
intrinsecus docet. Nec ideo pigrius moveri nos

---

^a For Cirta or Constantine see p. 98 n. *a*. That town was
apparently a stronghold of Donatism, and its Donatist bishop,
Petilianus, was addressed by Augustine in two treatises,
Contra litteras Petiliani and *De unico baptismo contra
Petilianum*; there, too, a Donatist council was held in 396
(Ep. xxxiv. 5). After the Conference of 411, Donatists
who refused to join the Catholic Church were exposed to the
full rigour of the law, and in January 412 Honorius an-
nulled all rescripts in their favour (*Cod. Theod.* xvi. 5. 52).
At Cirta itself a Council of Numidian bishops was held on

are sons of the Church, and at the same time the moderation of your Holy Mother.

May Almighty God enrich your Excellency with all good things, my noble and deservedly distinguished lord and well-beloved son.

No. 35 (Ep. CXLIV)

(A.D. 412)

BISHOP AUGUSTINE TO MY HONOURABLE AND JUSTLY ESTEEMED LORDS, MY DEAREST AND MUCH LONGED FOR BRETHREN, THE PEOPLE OF CIRTA *a* OF ALL RANKS

If that which greatly distressed me in your city [1] has been removed, if the hardness of the human heart, resisting the most evident and, as one might say, the most notorious truth, has been overcome by the power of that same truth, if there is relish for the sweet savour of peace, and the brotherly love that springs from unity no longer dazzles aching eyes, but fills with light and vigour eyes that are sound, this is not my doing, but God's; I would not in the least attribute it to human resources, even if the conversion of so great a multitude had taken place when I was among you, in response to my own addresses and exhortations. That is His doing, His achievement, Who uses his ministers to draw attention to the external signs of things, but teaches men by things themselves within, through none but Himself. Yet

June 14, 412, which addressed a letter (Ep. cxli.) to the Donatist laity. As a result of that Council the people of Cirta returned to the Church, whereupon Augustine wrote this letter of congratulation and exhortation.

oportet ad visendos vos, quoniam quicquid in vobis laudabile factum est, non a nobis sed ab illo factum est, *qui facit mirabilia solus*. Multo enim alacrius debemus accurrere ad spectanda opera divina quam nostra, quia et nos, si quid boni sumus, opus illius, non hominum sumus; unde apostolus dixit: *Neque qui plantat est aliquid, neque qui rigat, sed qui incrementum dat deus.*

2   Xenocrates Polemonem, ut scribitis et nos ex illis litteris recordamur, de fruge temperantiae disputando non solum ebriosum verum et tunc ebrium ad mores alios repente convertit. Quamquam ergo ille, sicut prudenter et veraciter intellexistis, non deo fuerit adquisitus sed tantum a dominatu luxuriae liberatus, tamen ne id ipsum quidem quod melius in eo factum est, humano operi tribuerim sed divino. Ipsius namque corporis, quod est infimum nostrum, si qua bona sunt sicut forma et vires et salus et si quid eius modi est, non sunt nisi ex deo creatore ac perfectore naturae; quanto magis animi bona donare nullus alius potest! Quid enim superbius vel ingratius cogitare potest humana vecordia, si putaverit, cum carne pulchrum deus faciat hominem, animo castum ab homine fieri? Hoc in libro Christianae sapientiae sic scriptum est: *Cum scirem*, inquit, *quia nemo esse potest continens, nisi deus det, et hoc*

---

^a Ps. lxxi. 18.   ^b 1 Cor. iii. 7.

^c Polemo was a profligate Athenian youth, who with a band of revellers burst one day into the school of Xenocrates the philosopher, and was so arrested by the discourse, which happened to be about temperance, that he tore off the garlands with which he was bedecked and remained an attentive listener. Adopting an abstemious life, he became a disciple of Xenocrates and succeeded him as head of the school in 315 B.C. The story was often told by the ancients (see

the fact that whatever praiseworthy change has been wrought in you has been wrought not by us, but by Him "Who alone doeth wonderful works," [a] is no reason why we should be less eager to stir ourselves to visit you. With much more eagerness ought we to hasten to behold the works of God than our own, for we too, in so far as we are good at all, are His work, not the work of men. That is why the Apostle says, "Neither is he that planteth anything, neither he that watereth, but God that giveth the increase." [b]

You mention in your letter an incident which I too 2 recall from classical literature, how by discoursing on the fruits of temperance Xenocrates suddenly converted Polemo [c] to another mode of life, though he was not only a drunkard but was actually drunk at the time. Now although he was not won for God, but was only delivered from the thraldom of self-indulgence, as you have wisely and truly apprehended, yet I would not ascribe even that change wrought in him for the better to the work of man, but to that of God, for from God alone, by Whom nature was created and made perfect, come whatever good qualities there are in the body itself, the lowest part of us, such as comeliness and strength and health and the like. How much more sure is it, therefore, that no other can bestow its good qualities upon the soul. Can human folly harbour a more arrogant or ungrateful thought than the notion that whereas God makes man beautiful in body, man makes himself pure in heart? In the book of Christian Wisdom it is written, "When I perceived that no one could have self-restraint, un-

Lejay on Horace, *Sat.* ii. 3. 254), and is frequently mentioned by Christian writers (Ambr. *Helia*, 12. 45; Aug. *C. Jul. Pelag.* i. 4. 12, 7. 35; Hier. *In Osee*, i. 1, etc.).

ipsum erat sapientiae scire cuius esset hoc donum.
Polemon ergo si ex luxurioso continens factus, ita
sciret cuius esset hoc donum, ut eum abiectis super-
stitionibus gentium pie coleret, non solum continens
sed etiam veraciter sapiens et salubriter religiosus
existeret, quod ei non tantum ad praesentis vitae
honestatem verum et ad futurae immortalitatem
valeret. Quanto minus igitur mihi adrogare debeo
conversionem istam vestram vel populi vestri, quam
nobis modo nuntiastis, quae me nec loquente nec
saltem praesente procul dubio divinitus facta est, in
quibus veraciter facta est ! Hoc itaque praecipue
cognoscite, hoc pie humiliterque cogitate. Deo,
fratres, deo gratias agite, deum timete, ne deficiatis,
amate, ut proficiatis.

3 Si autem adhuc quosdam amor hominis occulte
segregat et timor hominis fallaciter congregat,
observent, qui tales sunt, quoniam deum, cui nuda est
humana conscientia, nec testem fallunt nec iudicem
fugiunt. Si quid autem illos de quaestione ipsius
unitatis pro suae salutis sollicitudine permovet, hoc
sibi, quantum existimo, iustissimum extorqueant,
ut de catholica ecclesia, id est toto orbe diffusa, id
potius credant quod scripturae divinae dicunt, non
quod linguae humanae maledicunt. De ipsa vero
dissensione, quae inter homines orta est — qui quales

---

^a Wisdom viii. 21.
^b He is referring to those Donatists who had not yet joined
the Catholic communion.
^c Though much less frequent than *quod* and *quia, quoniam*
is occasionally found in Augustine introducing an oblique
statement after verbs of saying or thinking, and it is almost
always followed by the indicative. Usually such occurrences
are Scriptural ; the use is comparatively rare in Augustine's
own language.

less God give it him, and that this itself is a part of wisdom, to know whose gift it is." [a]   If, then, in being converted from dissipation to self-restraint, Polemo had known whose gift that was, and so had thrown over the superstitions of the heathen and worshipped Him in reverence, he would then have become not only self-restrained, but also truly wise and soundly religious, and that would have secured for him not only virtue in the present life, but also immortality in the life to come.   How much less, then, should I presume to claim for myself the credit for your conversion or that of your people, which you have just reported to me ; in those in whom it really was accomplished, it was unquestionably accomplished from above, without either my words or even my presence.   Recognize this fact, therefore, above everything else ; with humility and reverence keep it before your mind. To God, my brethren, to God render your thanks ; fear God, so that you may not fall back ; love Him, so that you may go forward.

If, however, there are some whom the love of man 3 keeps secretly apart and the fear of man keeps mistakenly united,[b] let all such take note that the human conscience lies naked to God and that they can neither deceive Him as witness nor escape Him as judge.[c]   But if, from anxiety to secure their own salvation, they are at all disturbed over this question of unity, let them force themselves to do what is, in my opinion, a thoroughly fair thing, namely, to accept the statements of Holy Scripture about the Church Catholic (that is, the Church spread abroad throughout the world) rather than the mis-statements of human tongues. With reference to this schism which has arisen among men (who, whatever they

libet fuerint, non utique praeiudicant promissis dei,
qui dixit ad Abraham : *In semine tuo benedicentur*
omnes gentes, quod creditum est cum audiretur prae-
dictum, et negatur cum videtur impletum,—hoc
tamen interim brevissimum et, nisi fallor, invictis-
simum cogitent, aut actam esse istam causam in
ecclesiastico transmarino iudicio aut non esse actam ;
si acta ibi non est, innocens est Christi societas
per omnes transmarinas gentes, cuius societatis nos
communione gaudemus, et ideo ab eis innocentibus
utique sacrilega diremptione separantur ; si vero
acta ibi est ista causa, quis non intellegat, quis non
sentiat, quis non videat eos in ea victos, quorum inde
communio separata est ? Eligant ergo utrum malint
credere quod pronuntiaverunt ecclesiastici cognitores
an quod murmurant victi litigatores. Adversus
istam complexionem dictu brevissimam, intellectu
facillimam, adtendite diligenter pro vestra prudentia
quam nihil sobrium responderi possit ; et tamen
malus Polemon magis ebrietate . . . inveterati erroris
evertitur.

Date veniam prolixiori fortassis epistulae quam
iucundiori verum tamen, ut arbitror, utiliori quam
blandiori, domini honorabiles et merito suscipiendi,
carissimi ac desiderantissimi fratres. De adventu
autem ad vos nostro utrorumque desiderium deus
impleat. Quanto enim caritatis ardore accen-
damur ad visendos vos, verbis explicare non pos-

---

a Gen. xxvi. 4 (*cf.* xii. 3).
b The Benedictine editors, followed by Goldbacher, indicate a lacuna here, but the sense must be something like
what is suggested.

264

may be, assuredly do not impair the promises of God,
Who said to Abraham, " In thy seed shall all the
nations of the earth be blessed," [a] a promise believed
when it was heard as a prophecy and denied when it is
seen as an accomplished fact), let them for the present meditate upon this very brief, but, unless I am
mistaken, very unanswerable argument, that the case
was either tried before a church court across the sea,
or was not tried ; if it was not tried there, the society
of Christians among all the overseas nations is guiltless ; we rejoice in communion with that society, and
so their separation from those guiltless brethren is
clearly an act of sacrilegious disruption. If, again,
the case was tried there, who can fail to understand,
and feel, and see, that those whose communion is
sundered from those others are the defeated party
in the case ? Let them have their choice then,
whether they prefer to accept the verdict of the
ecclesiastical judges or the insinuations of the
defeated plaintiffs. Notice carefully, as you are
wise enough to do, that no serious confutation can
be offered against this tersely expressed, yet easily
understood, dilemma ; and yet Polemo in his dissipation was more easily turned from his drunkenness than they from the folly of their deeply
rooted error. [b]

Grant me pardon, my noble and justly honoured
lords, my beloved and much longed for brethren,
for a letter which is perhaps more lengthy than
agreeable, but yet, in my opinion, more likely to
profit you than to flatter you. May God give fulfilment to the desire we both share, that I should visit
you ! Words fail me to express the great and fervent
love that inflames me to see you, but I have no doubt

sumus, sed vos benigne credere minime dubitamus.

No. 36 (Ep. CXLVI)

DOMINO DILECTISSIMO ET DESIDERANTISSIMO FRATRI PELAGIO AUGUSTINUS IN DOMINO SALUTEM

Gratias ago plurimum quod me litteris tuis exhilarare dignatus es et certum facere de salute vestra. Retribuat tibi dominus bona, quibus semper sis bonus, et cum illo aeterno vivas in aeternum, domine dilectissime et desiderantissime frater. Ego autem etsi in me non agnosco praeconia de me tua, quae tuae benignitatis epistula continet, benivolo tamen animo erga exiguitatem meam ingratus esse non possum, simul admonens ut potius ores pro me, quo talis a domino fiam, qualem me iam esse arbitraris.

[*Et alia manu*] Memor nostri incolumis domino placeas, domine dilectissime et desiderantissime frater.

---

a The heresiarch. Born in Britain, he was at Rome from about 401 to 409, when in consequence of the threatened invasion by Alaric, he withdrew to Sicily and afterwards to Africa. He visited Hippo when Augustine was absent, but they met later in Carthage. Pelagius soon sailed for Palestine, but his views were condemned by the Council of Carthage in 412. Augustine joined in the controversy, and between the Council and the writing of this letter wrote his treatises *De Peccatorum Meritis* and *De Spiritu et Littera*. Pelagius

at all that you will be good enough to recognize that
it is so.

No. 36 (Ep. CXLVI)

(A.D. 413)

TO PELAGIUS,ᵃ MY LORD GREATLY BELOVED AND MY MUCH LONGED FOR BROTHER, AUGUSTINE SENDS GREETING IN THE LORD

I am very grateful for your kindness in cheering
me by a letter from you and in giving me news of
your welfare. The Lord recompense you, my greatly
beloved lord and much longed for brother, with such
blessings that you may be ever blessed and may live
eternally with Him Who is eternal. Although I do
not recognize myself in those encomiums of me
contained in your Benevolence's letter, yet I cannot
be ungrateful for your goodwill towards one so in-
significant as I. At the same time I urge you rather
to pray for me, that the Lord may make me what you
imagine I already am.

[*In another hand*] May you abide in safety and be
well-pleasing unto the Lord, my greatly beloved lord
and much longed for brother. Forget us not!

wrote from Palestine, and the above reply is cordial enough
to show that Augustine was still hoping that Pelagius would
see and renounce his error. At the Synod of Diospolis in
415 Pelagius used this letter, among others, as evidence of
his good repute. Augustine was then led to defend himself
from the charge of favouring the heretic, and in his *De Gestis
Pelagii*, 50-53, he gives the text of his letter and discusses
the language he used in it.

No. 37 (Ep. CL)

DOMINARUM HONORE DIGNISSIMIS MERITO INLUSTRIBUS ET PRAESTANTISSIMIS FILIABUS PROBAE ET IULIANAE AUGUSTINUS IN DOMINO SALUTEM

Implestis gaudio cor nostrum tanto iucundius quanto carius, tanto gratius quanto citius. Vestrae namque stirpis sanctimoniam virginalem quoniam quacumque innotuistis, ac per hoc ubique, fama celeberrima praedicat, velocissimum volatum eius fideliore atque certiore litterarum nuntio praevenistis et prius nos fecistis exultare de cognito tam excellentissimo bono quam dubitare de audito. Quis verbis explicet, quis digno praeconio prosequatur, quantum incomparabiliter gloriosius atque fructuosius habeat ex vestro sanguine feminas virgines Christus quam viros consules mundus? Nam volumina temporum si magnum atque praeclarum est nominis dignitate signare, quanto est maius atque praeclarius cordis et corporis integritate transcendere! Magis itaque

[a] Proba was the wife of Sextus Anicius Petronius Probus, a member of one of the most illustrious families of Rome, consul in 371 and four times pretorian prefect. She is not to be identified with Falconia Proba, the compiler of a Virgilian cento which enjoyed great repute in the middle ages. Juliana was the wife of her son, Olybrius, and their daughter, Demetrias, mentioned in the text, delighted the Christian world in 413 by renouncing her worldly prospects and taking the vow of virginity. The family had left Rome shortly before the irruption of Alaric, but on arriving in Africa they fell into the hands of Count Heraclian, who seized a large part of their possessions. Augustine was not alone in offering congratulations and advice to the young

No. 37 (Ep. CL)

(A.D. 413)

TO THE LADIES PROBA AND JULIANA,ᵃ MOST
NOBLE IN RANK, DAUGHTERS JUSTLY DIS-
TINGUISHED AND EMINENT, AUGUSTINE
SENDS GREETING IN THE LORD

You have filled my heart with joy, the more
delightful because of your affection, and the more
welcome because of your promptitude. For while
the consecration of a daughter of your house to the
life of virginity is being proclaimed by busy rumour
wherever your fame is known, and that is everywhere,
you outstripped its speediest flight by the surer and
more trustworthy information in your letter and
made us exult at the news of so very excellent a
blessing before we had time to doubt the rumour
of it. What words are adequate to tell, what commendation worthy to commemorate, how incompar-
ably greater is the glory and the gain, that Christ
should have women from your family dedicated to
virginity than that the world should have men from
it elevated to the consulship? For if it is a great
and notable thing to leave the mark of an honoured
name upon the scrolls of time, how much greater and
more notable it is by unsullied innocence of mind and
body to rise above them! So let this maiden, noble in

ascetic: Jerome wrote to Demetrias a very lengthy letter
which is almost a treatise on the ascetic life, and Pelagius
too wrote a long epistle, *Ad Demetriadem*, into which he
insinuated some of his own errors, which Augustine sought
to confute in a later letter (Ep. clxxxviii.) addressed to
Juliana.

gaudeat puella nobilis genere, nobilior sanctitate,
quod sit per divinum consortium praecipuam in
caelis consecuta sublimitatem, quam si esset per
humanum conubium prolem propagatura sublimem.
Generosius quippe elegit Aniciana posteritas tam
inlustrem familiam beare nuptias nesciendo quam
multiplicare pariendo et in carne iam imitari vitam
angelorum quam ex carne numerum adhuc augere
mortalium. Haec est uberior fecundiorque felicitas
non ventre gravescere sed mente grandescere, non
lactescere pectore sed corde candescere, non visceribus terram sed caelum orationibus parturire. Dominarum honore dignissimae et merito inlustres et
praestantissimae filiae, perfruamini in illa quod defuit vobis, ut nasceretur ex vobis ; perseveret usque
in finem, adhaerens coniugio quod non habet finem.
Imitentur eam multae famulae dominam ignobiles
nobilem, fragiliter excelsae excelsius humilem ; virgines quae sibi optant Aniciorum claritatem, eligant
sanctitatem. Illud enim quanta libet cupiditate
quando adsequentur ? Hoc autem, si plene cupierint,
mox habebunt. Protegat vos incolumes et feliciores
dextera altissimi, dominae honore dignissimae et
praestantissimae filiae. Pignera sanctitatis vestrae,
praecipue ipsam sanctitate praecipuam debito vestris

ᵃ Of the Anicii Gibbon says (*Decline and Fall*, chap. 31):
" From the reign of Diocletian to the final extinction of the
Western Empire that name shone with a lustre which was
not eclipsed in the public estimation by the majesty of the
Imperial purple."

her race, nobler in her holiness, find more cause for joy that she is destined to obtain through this divine espousal an especial distinction in heaven than if she had been destined to become through an earthly marriage the mother of a distinguished line. It was a more noble-minded thing for a scion of the Anicii^a to prefer to magnify that illustrious family by repudiating marriage rather than to increase it by bearing children and now in the flesh to imitate the life of the angels rather than from the flesh still further to augment the number of mortals. It is a richer and more prolific happiness not to grow big with child but to grow great in mind, not to have milk in the breasts but to have purity in the heart, to bring forth not the earthly through travail, but the heavenly through prayer. May it be yours, ladies most worthy of honour and daughters deservedly famous and most distinguished, to enjoy in her what you surrendered to give her birth! May she be steadfast unto the end, cleaving to that union which has no end! May many low-born maids imitate her, the high-born mistress, and those whose eminence is perishable follow her who through humility has reached a higher eminence; may the virgins who covet the splendour of the Anician family choose to emulate its holiness! The one will always elude their grasp, however much they long for it; the other will soon be theirs, if their longing be whole-hearted. May the right hand of the Most High be your covering unto safety and fuller happiness, ladies most worthy of honour and daughters most distinguished! In the love of the Lord and with the respect due to your deservings, we greet the children of your holy house, especially her who is

271

meritis officio dilectione domini salutamus. Velationis apophoretum[a] gratissime accepimus.

No. 38 (Ep. CLIX)

DOMINO BEATISSIMO AC VENERABILI ET DESIDERABILI FRATRI ET CONSACERDOTI MEO EVODIO[b] ET TECUM FRATRIBUS AUGUSTINUS ET MECUM FRATRES IN DOMINO SALUTEM

1 Frater iste nomine Barbarus servus dei est iam diu apud Hipponem constitutus et verbi dei fervidus ac studiosus auditor. Desideravit ad tuam sanctitatem litteras nostras, in quibus tibi eum in domino commendamus tibique per eum salutem debitam dicimus. Litteris autem sanctitatis tuae quibus ingentes texuisti quaestiones, respondere operosissimum est etiam otiosis et multo maiore, quam nos sumus, praeditis facultate disserendi et acrimonia intellegendi. Duarum sane epistularum tuarum, quibus multa et magna conquiris, una nescio quo

---

[a] *Apophoreta* (ἀποφόρητα) were presents given to guests to take home with them after an entertainment (Suet. *Cal.* 55, *Vesp.* 19; Lamprid. *Heliog.* 21. 7; Ambr. *Ep.* 3. 5 "qui ad convivium magnum invitantur, apophoreta secum referre consueverunt"); in Symmachus it is used of gifts sent to friends by those who had just given games (*Ep.* 2. 81, 5. 56, 9. 59). With the present passage compare Paul. Nol. *Ep.* 5. 21 "misimus testimonialem divitiarum nostrarum scutellam buxeam ; ut apophoretum voti spiritalis accipies." The word is occasionally employed by the Fathers in a transferred sense, as Ambrosiaster, *Rom.* 1. 1, 49A "ad quod omnes invitati apophoreta duplicia consequuntur : remissam enim peccatorum accipiunt, et filii Dei fiunt."

[b] Evodius was bishop of Uzalis and a prominent figure among the clergy of Numidia. Born, like Augustine, at

outstanding in holiness. We have been very glad to receive the gift [a] commemorating her taking the veil.

No. 38 (Ep. CLIX)

(A.D. 415)

TO MY MOST SAINTLY LORD, MY VENERABLE AND LONGED FOR BROTHER AND FELLOW-PRIEST, EVODIUS [b] AND THE BRETHREN WHO ARE WITH YOU, AUGUSTINE AND THE BRETHREN WHO ARE WITH ME SEND GREETING IN THE LORD

The brother who brings this, Barbarus by name, 1 is a servant of God who has been settled for a long time now at Hippo and is an eager and diligent hearer of the word of God. He besought this letter from me to your Holiness, in which I commend him to you in the Lord and through him offer you my due greetings. To reply to your Holiness's letter, into which you have woven big questions, is a very considerable undertaking even for men of leisure, possessing much more skill in argument and greater acuteness of understanding than I do. Of the two letters from you, containing many extensive queries,

Tagaste, he had been converted shortly before him, and the two were in close fellowship at Milan and Cassiciacum, where he appears as interlocutor with Augustine in the *De Quantitate Animae* and the *De Libero Arbitrio*. After being present at Ostia when Monnica died, Evodius returned to Africa with Augustine and shared the monastic life of Tagaste. Four letters from him to Augustine are extant, full of abstruse questions. The present letter is a reply to one of his, *Ep.* clxxxviii., which had raised the problem of the reality and meaning of visions. Of Barbarus, the bearer of the letter, there is no other mention.

modo aberravit et diu quaesita non potuit reperiri;
altera vero, quae inventa est, habet commenda-
tionem suavissimam servi dei boni et casti adule-
scentis, quo modo ex hac vita migraverit et quibus
visionum fraternarum adtestationibus meritum eius
vobis insinuari potuerit. Deinde ex hac occasione
proponis et versas de anima obscurissimam quaestionem, utrum cum aliquo corpore egreditur e corpore,
quo possit ad corporalia loca ferri vel locis corporali-
bus contineri. Huius igitur rei tractatus, si tamen
ad liquidum a talibus, quales nos sumus, examinari
potest, curam atque operam negotiosissimam postulat
ac per hoc mentem ab his occupationibus otiosissimam.
Si autem breviter vis audire quid mihi videatur,
nullo modo arbitror animam e corpore exire cum
corpore.

2   Visiones autem illae futurorumque praedictiones
quo modo fiant, ille iam explicare conetur qui novit
qua vi efficiantur in unoquoque animo tanta, cum
cogitat. Videmus enim planeque cernimus in eo
fieri multarum rerum visibilium et ad ceteros sensus
corporis pertinentium innumerabiles imagines, quae
nunc non interest quam ordinate vel turbide fiant;
sed tantum, quia fiunt, quod manifestum est, qua
vi et quo modo fiant, quisquis potuerit explicare—
quae omnia certe cotidiana sunt atque continua,—
audeat praesumere aliquid ac definire etiam de illis
rarissimis visis. Ego autem tanto minus hoc audeo,

one, indeed, has somehow or other gone astray and after a long search has eluded discovery, but the other, which was found, contains a very charming commendation of a servant of God, a good and chaste young man, telling how he departed this life and by what testimony from the visions of brethren you were able to have assurance of his worth. Then you take the opportunity to set forth and discuss a very obscure question about the soul, whether, when it leaves the body, it is united with any other material body, so that it may be conveyed to material places or be enclosed in material places. The treatment of this problem, if indeed it can be clearly investigated by one such as myself, demands attention and the most laborious application, and therefore a mind quite free from such occupations as mine. But if you want to hear my opinion in a word or two, I certainly do not hold that the soul departs from the body with a material body.

How those visions and predictions of future events 2 come about is for him first to try to explain who knows what agency produces all those images that are in anyone's mind when he is thinking. For we see and clearly perceive that in it are found countless images of many objects that are discernible by the eye or by the other bodily senses ; it is of no importance for the moment whether they are produced in regular sequence or at random, but only that, since they do take place, as is obvious, anyone who can explain by what agency and in what way these phenomena are produced, all of which are of daily and repeated occurrence, may warrantably venture a conjecture or a definition about those very rare visions too. But for my part, the more I realize my incom-

quanto minus id quoque in nobis quod vita continua
vigilantes dormientesque experimur, quo pacto fiat,
explicare sufficio. Nam cum ad te dictarem hanc
epistulam, te ipsum animo contuebar, te utique
absente atque nesciente, et quo modo possis his
verbis moveri, secundum notitiam quae mihi de te
inest, imaginabar ; atque id quonam modo in animo
meo fieret, capere ac investigare non poteram certus
tamen non fieri corporeis molibus nec corporeis
qualitatibus, cum corpori simillimum fieret. Hoc
interim habeas ut ab occupato et festinante dictatum.
In duodecimo autem libro eorum quos de genesi
scripsi, versatur haec quaestio vehementer et multis
exemplis rerum expertarum atque credibiliter audi-
tarum disputatio illa silvescit. Quid in ea potuerimus
vel effecerimus, cum legeris, iudicabis, si tamen
dominus donare dignatur ut eos mihi libros, quantum
possum, congruenter emendatos iam liceat edere et
multorum fratrum expectationem non iam longa
disputatione suspendere.

3   Narrabo autem unum aliquid breviter, unde cogites.
Frater noster Gennadius, notissimus fere omnibus
nobisque carissimus medicus, qui nunc apud Carthaginem degit et Romae suae artis exercitatione prae-
polluit, ut hominem religiosum nosti atque erga

---

^a He is here referring to his twelve books *De Genesi ad
litteram*, begun about 401 but not published until 415, in
spite of repeated requests from friends that he should bring it
to an early completion (Ep. cxliii. 14 " periculosissimarum
quaestionum libros de Genesi . . . diutius teneo quam vultis
et fertis "). The twelfth book is a study of St. Paul's vision,
2 Cor. xii. 2-4, and of supernatural visions in general. He
had already before his ordination to the priesthood begun a
controversial exposition of Genesis directed against the
Manichees (*De Genesi contra Manichaeos*), but later he came
to the opinion that this treatise was too allegorical, so he

petence to account for the occurrence of the experience we have throughout life, asleep and awake, the more I shrink from attempting to explain these others. For while I am dictating this letter to you, I have a picture of you yourself in my mind, though naturally you are far away and unaware of my thoughts, and, in the light of my inward knowledge of you, I try to see how my words can affect you; and I fail to comprehend and discover how that process takes place in my mind, though I am sure that it is not caused by material particles or material qualities, although the actual picture is very like something material. For the present, accept this as a statement dictated in haste and under the pressure of work. However, in the twelfth book of my treatise on Genesis,[a] this problem is examined with thoroughness, and the discussion there is luxuriant with numerous examples drawn from personal experience and trustworthy report. When you read it, you will be able to judge of my competence or success in it, if the Lord is but pleased to grant me the opportunity of publishing those books suitably corrected and by concluding the discussion to end the suspense of anticipation in many of my brethren.

I shall give you a brief account, however, of one [3] such example, which I commend to your consideration. Our brother Gennadius,[b] the physician, very well known to almost everybody and very dear to us, who now lives at Carthage and was a leading figure in the practice of his art at Rome, is, as you know, a man of devout mind, unwearied compassion, most

undertook, first, about 393, a literal exposition (*De Genesi ad litteram imperfectus liber*), then the work mentioned here.
[b] Gennadius is not otherwise known.

pauperum curam inpigra misericordia facillimoque
animo benignissimum, dubitabat tamen aliquando,
ut modo nobis rettulit, cum adhuc esset adulescens
et in his elemosynis ferventissimus, utrum esset ulla
vita post mortem. Huius igitur mentem et opera
misericordiae quoniam deus nullo modo desereret,
apparuit illi in somnis conspicuus iuvenis et dignus
intendi eique dixit: "Sequere me." Quem dum
sequeretur, venit ad quandam civitatem, ubi audire
coepit a dextra parte sonos suavissimae cantilenae
ultra solitam notamque suavitatem; tunc ille intento
quidnam esset, ait hymnos esse beatorum atque
sanctorum; sinistra autem parte quid se vidisse
rettulit, non satis memini. Evigilavit et somnium
aufugit tantumque de illo quantum de somnio cogi-
tavit.

Alia vero nocte ecce idem ipse iuvenis eidem rursus
apparuit, atque ab illo utrum cognosceretur interro-
gavit; respondit iste quod eum bene pleneque
cognosceret. Tum ille quaesivit ubi se nosset.
Nec memoriae defuit quid iste identidem responderet,
totumque visum illum hymnosque sanctorum, ad
quos audiendos eo duce venerat, qua recentissimos
recordabatur facilitate, narravit. Hic ille percon-
tatus est utrumnam id quod narraverat, in somnis
vidisset an vigilans; respondit: "In somnis." At
ille: "Bene," inquit, "recolis; verum est, in somnis
illa vidisti; sed etiam nunc in somnis te videre scies."

278

gracious geniality, and great kindness to the afflicted poor. But at one time, as he told me recently, while he was still in the prime of life and most zealous in those works of charity, he was assailed by doubt of the existence of any life after death. As God would in no wise abandon a man so compassionate in temper and deeds, there appeared to him, accordingly, while he was asleep, a young man of striking appearance and imposing mien, and said to him, "Follow me." He followed him and came to a certain city, in which he began to hear on the right hand the strains of a song so very sweet that it surpassed the sweetness of known and ordinary music ; listening eagerly, he asked what it was and was told that it was the hymns of the blessed and the holy. What he reported he had seen on the left hand, I do not clearly remember. He awoke and his dream fled, and he thought only of it as one does of a dream.

Yet another night, lo, the same young man in 4 person appeared to him again and asked if he recognized him. Gennadius replied that he recognized him perfectly well. Then the young man asked where he had got to know him ; he had quite a clear recollection of the answer to that too, and he told all about that vision and the hymns of the saints which, under the other's guidance, he had gone to hear, with that readiness which marked the recollection of very recent experiences. At this point the other asked him whether he was asleep or awake when he saw what he had been telling of ; the answer was that he was asleep. The other replied, " Your memory is good ; you are right, you were asleep when you saw that, but you must know that even now you can

Hoc cum audisset iste, ita esse credidit atque id responsione firmavit. Tunc qui hominem docebat, adiecit et ait : " Ubi est modo corpus tuum ? " Ille respondit : " In cubiculo meo." " Scisne," inquit ille, " in eodem corpusculo nunc esse inligatos et clausos et otiosos oculos tuos nihilque illis oculis te videre ? " Respondit : " Scio." Tunc ille : " Qui sunt ergo," inquit, " isti oculi, quibus me vides ? " Ad hoc iste non inveniens quid responderet, obticuit. Cui haesitanti ille quod his interrogationibus docere moliebatur, aperuit, et continuo : " Sicut," inquit, " illi oculi carnis tuae utique in dormiente atque in lectulo iacente nunc vacant nec aliquid operantur et tamen sunt isti, quibus me intueris et ista uteris visione, ita cum defunctus fueris, nihil agentibus oculis carnis tuae, vita tibi inerit qua vivas, sensusque, quo sentias. Cave iam deinceps, ne dubites vitam manere post mortem." Ita sibi homo fidelis ablatam dicit huius rei dubitationem, quo docente nisi providentia et misericordia dei ?

5   Ista narratione dixerit aliquis tantae rei nos non solvisse sed auxisse quaestionem. Verum tamen cum his verbis credere vel non credere liberum cuique sit, se ipsum quisque habet, quo se avocet, profundissimam quaestionem. Et vigilat homo et dormit homo cotidie et cogitat homo. Dicat unde fiant ista similia formis, similia qualitatibus, similia motibus corporum nec tamen materie corporali. Dicat, si

see, though you are asleep." When Gennadius heard that, he accepted it as true and expressed his belief. Then his teacher went on to say, " Where is your body now ? " to which he made answer, " In my bed-chamber." " Do you know," said the other, "that in that puny body your eyes are at this moment bound down and shut and idle and that with those eyes you see nothing ? " He said, " I know." To which the other answered, "What eyes then are those with which you see me ? " Finding no reply to that question, Gennadius was silent, and when he hesitated, the young man revealed the lesson he was trying to teach by these questions and immediately replied, " Just as those eyes of your body that lies sleeping in bed are now inactive and do nothing and yet you have eyes with which you behold me and employ another power of sight, so when you are dead and the eyes of your flesh have ceased to do anything, you still will have a life by which you will live and perceptions by which you will perceive. Henceforth remember not to doubt the continuance of life after death." In this way that trustworthy man declares that his doubts concerning immortality were taken away. What taught him but the providence and mercy of God ?

Someone may say that by this story I have not 5 solved but complicated this great problem. But yet, since each man is free to believe what I have said or to disbelieve it, each one has a very deep problem in himself, and with that he may delight himself. Man wakes and sleeps each day and thinks. Let any man tell whence proceed those occurrences ; they are not material bodies, yet bear a likeness in shape, in properties and in motion, to material bodies ; let

potest; si autem non potest, quid se praecipitat
de rarissimis aut inexpertis quasi definitam ferre
sententiam, cum continua et cotidiana non solvat?
Ego autem, quamvis quo modo fiant ista veluti
corporea sine corpore, verbis prorsus explicare non
possim, tamen sicut scio non ea corpore fieri, utinam
sic scirem quo modo discernerentur, quae videntur
aliquando per spiritum et per corpus videri putantur,
quove modo distinguantur visa eorum, quos error vel
impietas plerumque deludit, quando visis piorum
atque sanctorum similia pleraque narrantur! Quorum
exempla si commemorare voluissem, tempus mihi
potius quam copia defuisset. Memor nostri in
domini misericordia vegeteris, domine beatissime et
venerabilis et desiderabilis frater.

No. 39 (Ep. CLXXIII)

DONATO PRESBYTERO PARTIS DONATI AUGU-
STINUS EPISCOPUS ECCLESIAE CATHOLICAE

1 Si posses videre dolorem cordis mei et sollicitudinem pro salute tua, fortasse *miserereris animae
tuae placens deo* in audiendo verbo non nostro, sed
ipsius, nec eius scripturas sic in memoria tua figeres,
ut contra eas cor clauderes. Displicet tibi quia

---

^a This Donatus, a priest of the Donatist party, who had
been compelled by law to join the Catholic Church and in
his resistance had done himself bodily harm, is not further
known. From § 7 it appears that he came from Mutugenna,
which lay in the vicinity of Hippo. This letter is very instructive for Augustine's arguments against toleration.
^b Ecclus. xxx. 24.

him tell, if he can, but if he cannot, why is he so hasty to pronounce a kind of final judgement about experiences he has very seldom or not at all, when he cannot explain matters that occur each day and every day? Though, for my part, words fail me to explain how those semblances of material bodies without a real body come to be, yet, just as I know that they are not produced by the body, so I should wish to know how we can separate those things that are seen at times by the spirit and are thought to be seen by the body, or how we can distinguish the things seen by those who are often deluded by error or by impiety, when the majority of the visions they tell of bear a likeness to those seen by the good and the holy. If I had wanted to give examples of these, I should have been short of time rather than material. Remember me, my saintly lord and revered and longed for brother, and may the mercy of the Lord be your refreshment!

No. 39 (Ep. CLXXIII)

(A.D. 416)

TO DONATUS,[a] PRIEST OF THE DONATIST PARTY, AUGUSTINE, BISHOP OF THE CATHOLIC CHURCH

If you could see my heart-felt grief and anxiety for 1 your salvation, you would perhaps "have pity on your own soul, doing what is pleasing unto God"[b] by giving ear to the injunction which is not ours, but His, and you would not impress His Scriptures on your memory only to close your heart against them. You

traheris ad salutem, cum tam multos nostros ad
perniciem traxeritis. Quid enim volumus, nisi te
comprehendi et praesentari et servari, ne pereas ?
Quod autem aliquantum in corpore laesus es, ipse
tibi fecisti, qui iumento tibi mox admoto uti noluisti
et te ad terram graviter conlisisti. Nam utique
alius qui adductus est tecum, collega tuus, inlaesus
venit, quia talia sibi ipse non fecit.

2 Sed neque hoc putas tibi fieri debuisse, quia
neminem aestimas cogendum esse ad bonum. Adtende quid apostolus dixerit : *Qui episcopatum desiderat, bonum opus concupiscit*, et tamen tam multi,
ut episcopatum suscipiant, tenentur inviti, perdu-
cuntur, includuntur, custodiuntur, patiuntur tanta
quae nolunt, donec eis adsit voluntas suscipiendi
operis boni ; quanto magis vos ab errore pernicioso,
in quo vobis inimici estis, trahendi estis et perdu-
cendi ad veritatem vel cognoscendam vel eligendam,
non solum ut honorem salubriter habeatis, sed etiam
ne pessime pereatis ! Dicis deum dedisse liberum
arbitrium, ideo non debere cogi hominem nec ad
bonum. Quare ergo illi, de quibus supra dixi,
coguntur ad bonum ? Adtende ergo quod considerare non vis. Ideo voluntas bona misericorditer

---

[a] 1 Tim. iii. 1.
[b] On forcible ordination see note on p. 35.

are angry because you are being dragged to salvation,
although you and your friends have dragged so many
of our people to destruction. What other intention
have we, but to arrest you and bring you before the
judge and preserve you from perishing? As for the fact
that you received a slight bodily injury, you are to
blame for that yourself, for you would not make use
of the mule that was at once brought for you, and
dashed yourself with violence to the ground ; for, as
you know, the other person who was taken away
with you, a colleague of yours, arrived uninjured,
since he did not cause any such injury to himself.

But even that, in your opinion, should not have
been done to you, for you hold that no one should
be forced to what is good. Mark the words of the
Apostle, "If a man desire the office of bishop, he
desireth a good work," [a] yet in spite of them, many
men are led to undertake the office of bishop only
by being detained against their will, brought from
one place to another, shut up and kept under supervision, subjected to treatment that they do not like,
until they acquire a willingness to undertake that
" good work." [b] How much more fitting it is that you
should be torn away from that pernicious error, by
clinging to which you are your own worst enemies,
and brought to either a knowledge or acceptance
of the truth, so that you may not only retain your
honour with safety to yourselves, but also escape the
great misery of destruction. You say that God has
given man free-will and that therefore no one should
be forced even to good. Why then are those men
I spoke of above compelled to good ? Mark well
then a point you refuse to take into consideration :
the reason why a good will expends itself in works

inpenditur, ut mala voluntas hominis dirigatur. Nam quis nesciat nec damnari hominem nisi merito malae voluntatis, nec liberari nisi bonam habuerit voluntatem ? Non tamen ideo, qui diliguntur, malae suae voluntati impune et crudeliter permittendi sunt, sed, ubi potestas datur, et a malo prohibendi et ad bonum cogendi.

3 Nam si voluntas mala semper suae permittenda est libertati, quare Israhelitae recusantes et murmurantes tam duris flagellis a malo prohibebantur et ad terram promissionis compellebantur ? Si voluntas mala semper suae permittenda est libertati, quare Paulus non est permissus uti pessima voluntate, qua persequebatur ecclesiam, sed prostratus est, ut excaecaretur, excaecatus, ut mutaretur, mutatus, ut mitteretur, missus, ut, qualia fecerat in errore, talia pro veritate pateretur ? Si voluntas mala semper suae permittenda est libertati, quare monetur pater in scripturis sanctis filium durum non solum verbis corripere sed etiam latera eius tundere, ut ad bonam disciplinam coactus et domitus dirigatur ? Unde idem dicit : *Tu quidem percutis eum virga, animam autem eius liberabis a morte.* Si mala voluntas semper suae permittenda est libertati, quare corripiuntur neglegentes pastores et dicitur eis : *Errantem ovem non revocastis, perditam non inquisistis ?*

---

[a] *Merito*, as often in late Latin, has the meaning of *propter*, "because of," "by reason of." So in No. 7 § 1 above (p. 32), "merito peccatorum meorum." See Butler-Owen on Apul. *Apol.* 8. 15 ; Bayard, *Le Latin de S. Cyprien*, p. 156 ; Roensch, *Itala u. Vulgata*, p. 398, and compare the similar use of *beneficio*, common in Seneca and the Jurists.

[b] In late Latin *tamen* often has a much weakened sense,

of mercy is to provide guidance for man's evil will. For who does not know that man is not damned unless for [a] his evil will, nor, on the other hand, granted deliverance, unless he has a good will? Still [b] it does not follow that those we love are to be cruelly left to enjoy their evil will without correction, but where the power is granted, they are to be both prevented from evil and forced to good.

For if an evil will is always to be left to enjoy its 3 liberty, why were such severe scourges employed to prevent the disobedient and querulous Israelites from evil and to compel them to the land of promise? [c] If an evil will is always to be left to enjoy its liberty, why was Paul not allowed the free use of his perverted will to persecute the Church, but was thrown to the ground to be blinded, and blinded to be transformed, and transformed to be made an apostle, and made an apostle to endure for the truth sufferings such as he had inflicted when in error? [d] If an evil will is always to be left to enjoy its liberty, why do the Holy Scriptures admonish a father not only to correct his obstinate son with rebukes, but also to punish his body with blows, so that, compelled and subdued, he may be led to habits of goodness? [e] That is why the same writer says, "Thou shalt beat him with a rod, and shalt deliver his soul from hell." [f] If an evil will is always to be left to enjoy its liberty, why are careless pastors rebuked with the words, "Ye have not brought back the wandering sheep, ye have not sought that which was lost" [g]? You too

becoming simply continuative. See Löfstedt, *Philol. Kommentar zur Peregrinatio Aetheriae*, pp. 27-33.

[c] Exod. xv. 22 *sqq.*   [d] Acts ix. 1-9.
[e] Ecclus. xxx. 12.   [f] Prov. xxiii. 14.   [g] Ezek. xxxiv. 4.

Et vos oves Christi estis, characterem dominicum
portatis in sacramento quod accepistis, sed errastis
et peristis. Non ideo vobis displiceamus, quia
revocamus errantes et quaerimus perditos ; melius
enim facimus voluntatem domini monentis ut vos
ad eius ovile redire cogamus, quam consentimus
voluntati ovium errantium, ut perire vos permittamus.
Noli ergo iam dicere, quod te assidue audio dicere :
" Sic volo errare, sic volo perire " ; melius enim nos
hoc omnino non permittimus, quantum possumus.

4   Modo quod te in puteum, ut morereris, misisti,
utique libera voluntate fecisti. Sed quam crudeles
essent servi dei, si huic malae tuae voluntati te
permitterent et non te de illa morte liberarent !
Quis eos non merito culparet ? Quis non impios
recte iudicaret ? Et tamen tu te volens in aquam
misisti, ut morereris, illi te nolentem de aqua levave-
runt, ne morereris ; tu fecisti secundum voluntatem
tuam sed in perniciem tuam, illi contra voluntatem
tuam sed propter salutem tuam. Si ergo salus ista
corporalis sic custodienda est, ut etiam in nolentibus
ab eis qui eos diligunt, servetur, quanto magis illa
spiritalis, in cuius desertione mors aeterna metuitur !
Quamquam in ista morte quam tibi tu ipse inferre
voluisti, non solum ad tempus sed etiam in aeternum

---

a Character, an Augustinian term, he defines (*Serm.* 302.
5. 3) thus : "characterem accipit Christianus, cum fit catechumenus." It is like the imprint on imperial money, or the
nota militaris of the soldier, or the mark a shepherd places
on his sheep (*C. Ep. Parm.* ii. 29), an indelible consecration.
It is linked up with Augustine's theory of the Church and
of Baptism, which once validly bestowed is not to be repeated, but is efficacious only when the baptized are joined
to the Church Catholic and are in grace.

are Christ's sheep; you bear the mark [a] of the Lord in the sacrament you have received, but you have wandered away and are lost. There is no reason why you should be angry with us for recalling you from wandering and seeking you when you were lost, for it is better for us to carry out the will of the Lord, Who gave us the injunction to compel you to return to His fold, than to acquiesce in the will of the wandering sheep and allow you to be lost. Do not then say what I hear you keep saying, " I want to wander in my own way; I want to be lost in my own way," for it is better that we should not allow that at all, as far as in us lies.

When lately you threw yourself into a well with **4** the intention of slaying your body, you certainly did that of your own free will. But how cruel the servants of God would have been if they had handed you over to your own evil will and not delivered you from that death! Who would not have justly blamed them? Who would not have been right in judging them inhuman? And yet you threw yourself into the water, intending to slay your body, of your own free will, and they lifted you out of the water, to defeat your intention, against your will; you acted according to your own will, but to your own destruction, while they acted against your will, but for your own preservation. If then the preservation of the body is to be safeguarded so that those who do not wish it are to be secured by their friends, how much more the preservation of the spirit, for the abandoning of which the fearsome consequence is eternal death! And yet the death you sought to deal yourself was not only a death for time but for eternity, for even if you

morereris, quia, etsi non ad salutem, non ad ecclesiae pacem, non ad Christi corporis unitatem, non ad sanctam et individuam caritatem, sed ad mala aliqua cogereris, nec sic tibi ipse mortem inferre debuisti.

5   Considera scripturas divinas et discute quantum potes, et vide utrum hoc fecerit aliquis aliquando iustorum atque fidelium, cum ab eis tanta mala perpessi sint qui eos ad aeternum interitum non ad vitam aeternam, quo tu compelleris, adigebant. Audivi quod dixeris apostolum Paulum significasse hoc fieri debere, ubi ait : *Et si tradidero corpus meum, ut ardeam.* Quia videlicet omnia bona dicebat, quae sine caritate nihil prosunt, sicut sunt linguae hominum et angelorum et omnia sacramenta et omnis scientia et omnis prophetia et omnis fides ita ut montes transferantur, et rerum suarum distributio pauperibus, ideo videtur tibi etiam hoc inter bona numerasse, ut sibi quisque inferat mortem. Sed adtende diligenter et cognosce quem ad modum dicat scriptura quod tradat quisque suum corpus ut ardeat, non utique, ut ipse se in ignem mittat, quando persequentem patitur inimicum, sed, quando ei proponitur ut aut mali aliquid faciat aut mali aliquid patiatur, eligat non facere mala quam non pati mala atque ita corpus suum tradat in potestatem interfectoris, sicut tres illi viri fecerunt qui auream statuam cogebantur adorare et, nisi facerent, minabatur eis ille qui cogebat, caminum ignis ardentem. Idolum adorare noluerunt, non ipsi se in ignem miserunt et tamen

---

were being compelled to some evil deed instead of to self-preservation, to the peace of the Church, to the unity of Christ's body, or to holy and indivisible charity, even so, you had no right to attempt to take your own life.

Examine the Holy Scriptures and scrutinize them 5 to the best of your ability, and see if at any time any one of the righteous and the faithful took this course, although they endured such great sufferings at the hands of those who sought to impel them to everlasting destruction, not to everlasting life, to which you are being forced. I have heard that you have said that the apostle Paul indicated that self-immolation was lawful, in the words, " Though I give my body to be burned,"^a on the supposition that, as he was there enumerating all the good things that are of no avail without charity, such as the tongues of men and of angels, and all mysteries, and all knowledge and all prophecy and all faith that could remove mountains, and the bestowal of one's property on the poor,^b he intended among these good things to count even self-immolation. But observe carefully and notice in what sense the Scripture says that a man may give his body to be burned: certainly not that he may throw himself into the fire when he is harassed by a pursuing enemy, but that when the proposal is made to him that he should do wrong or else suffer wrong, he should choose not to do wrong rather than not to suffer wrong and so give his body over to him who has power to slay it, as did those three men who were compelled to worship the golden statue, when he who applied the compulsion threatened them with the fiery furnace if they did not comply.^c They refused to worship the image ; they did not cast them-

etiam de illis scriptum est quod *tradiderunt corpora sua, ut neque servirent neque adorarent ullum deum sed deum suum.* Ecce quo modo dixit apostolus : *Si tradidero corpus meum, ut ardeam.*

6 Quod autem sequitur, vide : *Si caritatem non habeam, nihil mihi prodest.* Ad istam caritatem vocaris, ab ista caritate perire non sineris et putas tibi aliquid prodesse, si te ipse praecipites in interitum, cum tibi nihil prodesset, etiamsi alter te occideret caritatis inimicum. Foris autem ab ecclesia constitutus et separatus a compage unitatis et vinculo caritatis aeterno supplicio punireris, etiamsi pro Christi nomine vivus incendereris. Hoc est enim quod ait apostolus : *Et si tradidero corpus meum, ut ardeam, caritatem autem non habeam, nihil mihi prodest.* Revoca ergo animum ad sanam considerationem et sobriam cogitationem ; adtende diligenter utrum ad errorem et impietatem voceris, et patere pro veritate quaslibet molestias. Si autem tu potius in errore atque in impietate versaris, quo autem vocaris ibi est veritas et pietas, quia ibi Christiana unitas et sancti spiritus caritas, quid adhuc tibi esse conaris inimicus ?

7 Ideo praestitit misericordia dei, ut et nos et episcopi vestri tam frequenti numerosoque conventu Carthaginem veniremus atque inter nos de ipsa

---

ᵃ Dan. iii. 95. *ᵇ* 1 Cor. xiii. 3.

ᶜ The Conference of June 411, attended by 286 Catholic bishops and 279 Donatists. Its minutes, the *Gesta Collationis*, are printed in Mansi, iv., and in the appendix to the works of Optatus (*P.L.* xi. 1257-1420); they are summarized in Augustine's *Breviculus Collationis*, published soon after the Conference.

292

selves into the fire, and yet it was written even of
them that " they yielded their bodies that they might
not serve nor worship any god except their own
God."[a] That is the sense in which the Apostle
said, " If I give my body to be burned."

Notice, however, what follows : " If I have not 6
charity, it profiteth me nothing."[b] To that charity
you are summoned ; by that charity you are withheld from perishing, and yet you think that to throw
yourself headlong to destruction does to some degree
profit you, although even if you suffered death at
the hands of another person while you are still a foe
to charity, that would profit you nothing ; indeed,
as long as you remain outside the Church and severed
from the fabric of unity and the bond of charity,
you would be punished with everlasting chastisement, even if you were burned alive for Christ's
sake. That is what the Apostle means when he
says, " Though I give my body to be burned, and
have not charity, it profiteth me nothing." Bring
back your mind, then, to sane reflection and sober
thought ; consider carefully whether it is to error
and impiety that you are being summoned, and
endure any troubles you like for truth's sake. But if
you rather are living in error and in impiety, and
truth and piety rather exist in the place to which
you are summoned, for the reason that there are to
be found Christian unity and the charity of the
Holy Spirit, why do you keep on trying to be your
own worst enemy ?

It was with this end in view that God in His mercy 7
provided your bishops and us with an opportunity of
meeting at Carthage in a crowded and well-attended
conference[c] and of reasoning together in the most

dissensione ordinatissime conferremus. Gesta conscripta sunt, nostrae etiam subscriptiones tenentur.
Lege vel patere ut tibi legatur, et tunc elige quod
volueris. Audivi quod dixeris posse te nobiscum de
ipsis gestis aliquid agere, si omittamus verba episcoporum vestrorum, ubi dixerunt : " Nec causa
causae nec persona personae praeiudicat." Haec
verba vis omittamus, ubi per eos nescientes veritas
ipsa locuta est. Sed tu dicturus es hic eos errasse et
in falsam sententiam incautius cecidisse ; nos autem
dicimus hoc eos verum dixisse et hoc per te ipsum
facillime probamus. Si enim episcopi vestri electi
ab universa parte Donati, qui causam omnium
sustinerent et, si quid egissent, gratum et acceptum
ceteri haberent, tamen in eo quod illos temere et
non recte dixisse arbitraris, non vis ut tibi prae-
iudicent, verum ergo dixerunt, quia " nec causa
causae nec persona personae praeiudicat." Et ibi
debes agnoscere quia, si persona tot episcoporum
tuorum in illis septem constitutorum non vis ut prae-

---

^a The words were used by the Donatists at the Conference
of Carthage, " Quia ergo diximus eis sicut illud [concilium]
non obesse Caeciliano, quemadmodum hoc non obest Pri-
miano, quoniam contra absentes facta sunt ambo concilia ;
continuo non invenientes quae responderent, et horribiles
angustias passi, dixerunt nec causam causae, nec personam
praeiudicare personae " (*Ad Don. p. Coll.* 3. 3). His point
here is that, on this Donatist admission that one man's
guilt does not affect another, the crimes alleged by the
Council of Carthage in 312 against Caecilian in no way
affect his successors, still less the Church Universal. Seeing

orderly manner about this very question of separation. The minutes were written down ; further, our signatures are on record. Read them, or have them read to you, and choose then which you prefer. I have heard you have stated that you could have some discussion with us about those minutes, if we leave out the words of your bishops, in which it is said, " One case does not compromise another case, nor one person another person." [a] You want us to leave these words out, which truth itself spoke through them, though they knew it not. But you will say that in this point they were mistaken and through lack of foresight fell into a false opinion ; we say that what they said was true, and we very easily prove this by referring to yourself. For if you refuse to allow those bishops of yours, chosen by the entire Donatist party to represent the whole body in such wise that whatever they did, the rest should take as satisfactory and acceptable, to prejudice your case by what you hold to be a rash and incorrect statement on their part, by this refusal you admit the truth of their statement that one case does not compromise another case, nor one person another person. And at this point you ought to grant that, if you refuse to allow the person of so many of your bishops as represented in those seven [b]

the consequences of this argument, the Donatists declared that this admission by their leaders at the Conference of the intransmissibility of guilt was not " satisfactory and acceptable."

[b] At the Conference Catholics and Donatists each chose seven representatives to address the gathering, seven more as counsel, and four others to supervise the taking of the minutes. The reference here is to the seven speakers on the Donatist side.

iudicet personae Donati Mutugennensis presbyteri,
quanto minus non debet praeiudicare Caeciliani
persona, etiamsi mali aliquid in illo esset inventum,
universae unitati Christi, quae non in una villa
Mutugenna concluditur, sed toto terrarum orbe
diffunditur !

8   Sed ecce facimus quod voluisti ; sic tecum agimus,
ac si non dixerint vestri : " Nec causa causae nec
persona personae praeiudicat." Tu inveni quid illic
dicere debuerint, cum eis obiecta esset causa et
persona Primiani, qui damnatores suos et damnavit
cum ceteris et damnatos ac detestatos in suo rursus
honore suscepit, et baptismum quem mortui dederant
(quia de ipsis in illa praeclara sententia dictum erat

---

   a Caecilian was first archdeacon, then from 311 bishop, of
Carthage ; the question whether his ordination was valid or
not was the beginning of the Donatist schism.

   b Primianus was Donatist bishop of Carthage, appointed
in 391, the year which saw Aurelius elevated to the Catholic
see in Carthage and Augustine ordained to the priesthood
at Hippo. These two at once came to grips with the Donatist
problem, but that party had as well its own internal difficulties. Primianus became embroiled with a rival, Maximian,
and at a synod held in the province of Byzacena, Primianus
was deposed and Maximian appointed in his stead (June
393). Primianus rallied his supporters in Numidia, where the
original strength of Donatism lay, and at Bagai, in April
394, a synod of Primianist Donatists restored him. The
rebel Gildo, aided by the infamous Optatus, bishop of
Timgad, supported their cause, but when the rebellion was
put down in 398 the Donatists found themselves acutely
divided and in great disfavour. The Catholic party invoked

to compromise the person of Donatus, priest of
Mutugenna,[a] all the less ought the person of
Caecilian, even if some degree of evil had been
detected in him, to compromise Christian unity,
which is not confined to the single village of Mutugenna, but is spread abroad throughout the world.

But see, we shall do as you have desired; we **8**
shall treat with you as if your bishops had not said,
"One case does not compromise another case, nor
one person another person." Do you find out what
they ought to have replied to that point, when the
objection was made to them of the case and person
of Primianus,[b] who although he joined the others in
anathematizing those who had anathematized him,
nevertheless received back with their former honours
those whom he had anathematized and cursed, and
chose rather to recognize and accept, than to abolish
and breathe scorn upon,[c] the baptism given by
dead men (for of them it was said in that famous

in 404 the aid of the secular arm, and Primianus was dis-
possessed, but soon returned, playing a prominent part
in the Conference of 411. This marked a definite stage
in the history of Donatism, and Primianus's power was quite
broken.

[c] *Exsufflo* is a late word, properly "to breathe out,"
"blow out," as Cael. Aur. *Chron.* 4. 3 "exsufflatis omnibus
quae de se admiserint"; then, naturally, it came to imply
scorn (Iren.-Lat. i. 13. 4 "exsufflantes et catathemizantes
eum"). In the baptism of the young, exsufflation was part
of the ceremony of exorcism from very early in the Church's
history (Augustine calls it an "antiquissimam Ecclesiae tradi-
tionem," *De Nupt.* ii. 29. 51); then, since in re-baptizing
Catholic Christians the Donatists "exsufflated" the previous
baptism ("iterata baptismata, exsufflata sacramenta," Ep.
xliii. 24; "fidelis si veniat, exsufflant et rebaptizant," Ep.
lii. 2), it becomes almost a technical term to describe the
attitude of Donatists to the Catholic sacraments.

quod "mortuorum funeribus plena sint litora "), agnoscere potius et acceptare quam exsufflare et rescindere maluit, totumque dissolvit quod male intellegentes dicere soletis, quia *qui baptizatur a mortuo, quid ei prodest lavacrum eius?* Si ergo non dicerent : " Nec causa causae nec persona personae praeiudicat," rei tenerentur in causa Primiani ; cum autem hoc dixerunt, immunem fecerunt ecclesiam catholicam, sicut nos adserebamus, a causa Caeciliani.

9 Sed cetera lege, cetera discute. Vide utrum in ipsum Caecilianum, de cuius persona praeiudicare conabantur ecclesiae, aliquid mali probare potuerint. Vide utrum non potius etiam pro illo multa egerint et pluribus lectionibus, quas contra se protulerunt et recitaverunt, causam eius bonam omnino firmaverint. Lege ista vel legantur tibi. Considera omnia, retracta diligenter, et elige quid sequaris, utrum nobiscum in Christi pace, in ecclesiae catholicae unitate, in fraterna caritate gaudere, an pro nefaria dissensione, pro Donati parte, pro sacrilega divisione importunitatem nostrae circa te dilectionis diutius sustinere.

10 Adtendis enim et saepe repetis, sicut audio, quod in evangelio scriptum est recessisse a domino septua-

---

a The sentence is given in full in Augustine's *Contra Gaudentium*, i. 54, " Aegyptiorum admodum exemplo pereuntium funeribus plena sunt litora," the reference being to Exod. xiv. 31, when the Israelites "viderunt Aegyptios mortuos super litus maris," and the implication being that the Donatists behold the catholic successors of Caecilian, with the appearance of Christian life but a real absence of it, widespread in Africa, but quite ineffective. The "wrong interpretation " refers to the Donatist practice of adducing in support of their re-baptizing of Catholics the text from Ecclus. xxxiv. 25, "qui baptizatur a mortuo, et iterum **tangit**

decree[a] that "the shores were full of dead men"), and so gave a complete denial to that argument which you are wont to deduce from a wrong interpretation of the words, "He that washeth himself after touching a dead body, what availeth his washing?"[b] If then your bishops had not said, "One case does not compromise another case, nor one person another person," they would have been held to share the guilt in the case of Primianus; but in making that assertion they secured the Catholic Church, as we contended, from any guilt in the case of Caecilian.

But read all the rest and examine it well. Notice **9** whether they have succeeded in proving any evil against Caecilian himself, from whose person they attempted to compromise the Church; notice whether they have not rather achieved much in his favour and altogether confirmed the soundness of his case by the comparatively large number of extracts they produced and recited to the detriment of their own position. Read those, or have them read to you; consider the whole matter, give it a further careful investigation, and choose which you will follow, whether you will share our joy in the peace of Christ, in the unity of the Church Catholic, in brotherly affection, or, in the cause of wicked discord, the Donatist party and sacrilegious schism, will endure still further the importunity of our love for you.

I hear that you often quote and draw attention to **10** the fact recorded in the Gospels that seventy disciples withdrew from the Lord and were left to their

mortuum, quid ei prodest lavacrum eius?" with the omission of the middle clause, "if he touch it again," and a monstrous perversion of the meaning. The Catholics, the Donatists argued, being *mortui*, could not confer a valid sacrament.

[b] Ecclus. xxxiv. 30.

ginta discipulos et arbitrio suae malae atque impiae discessionis fuisse permissos, ceterisque duodecim qui remanserant, fuisse responsum : *Numquid et vos vultis ire?* Et non adtendis quia tunc primum ecclesia novello germine pullulabat nondumque in ea fuerat completa illa prophetia : *Et adorabunt eum omnes reges terrae, omnes gentes servient illi*, quod utique quanto magis impletur, tanto maiore utitur ecclesia potestate, ut non solum invitet, sed etiam cogat ad bonum. Hoc tunc dominus significare volebat, qui quamvis haberet magnam potestatem, prius tamen elegit commendare humilitatem. Hoc et in illa convivii similitudine satis evidenter ostendit, ubi misit ad invitatos et venire noluerunt ; et ait servo : *Exi in plateas et vicos civitatis et pauperes et debiles et caecos et claudos introduc huc. Et ait servus domino :* "*Factum est, ut imperasti, et adhuc locus est.*" *Et ait dominus servo : Exi in vias et saepes et compelle intrare, ut impleatur domus mea.* Vide nunc quem ad modum de his qui prius venerunt, dictum est : " *Introduc* " eos, non dictum est " compelle " ; ita significata sunt ecclesiae primordia adhuc crescentis, ut essent vires etiam compellendi. Proinde, quia oportebat eius iam viribus et magnitudine roborata etiam compelli homines ad convivium salutis aeternae, posteaquam dictum est : *Factum est, quod iussisti, et adhuc est*

---

* John vi. 67-68.   * Ps. lxxi. 11.   * Luke xiv. 21-23.

300

own choice in this wicked and undutiful desertion, and that to the other twelve who remained it was said, "Will ye also go away?"[a] But you neglect to draw attention to the fact that then the Church was just beginning to sprout with new shoots and that as yet that prophecy had not received fulfilment in her:" All kings shall fall down before him, yea, all nations shall serve him "[b]; it is in proportion to the more complete fulfilment of that prophecy that the Church enjoys greater authority, so that she not only invites, but actually compels, men to goodness. This is what our Lord intended in that incident to indicate, for although He possessed great authority, He chose rather to give the example of humility. This too He taught clearly enough in that parable of the feast, in which, after a message had been sent to the invited guests and they had refused to come, the servant was told, "'Go out into the streets and lanes of the city and bring in hither the poor and the maimed and the halt and the blind.' And the servant said to his lord, ' It is done as thou hast commanded, and yet there is room.' And the lord said to his servant, ' Go out into the highways and hedges, and compel them to come in, that my house may be filled.'"[c] Just notice the phrase used of those who came first: "bring them in," not the phrase, "compel them to come in "; that symbolized the incipient stage of the Church, still developing to the point where it would have the strength to compel men to it. Accordingly, since it was right that when it had grown stronger in power and extent men should actually be compelled to the feast of everlasting salvation, the words were afterwards added : "It is done as thou hast commanded, and still there is room. And the

M

locus, exi, inquit, *in vias et saepes et compelle intrare.*
Quapropter, si ambularetis quieti extra hoc convivium
sanctae unitatis ecclesiae, tamquam in viis vos in-
veniremus ; nunc vero, quia per multa mala et saeva
quae in nostros committitis, tamquam spinis et
asperitate pleni estis, vos tamquam in saepibus
invenimus et intrare compellimus. Qui compellitur,
quo non vult cogitur, sed, cum intraverit, iam volens
pascitur. Cohibe itaque iam iniquum et inpacatum
animum, ut in vera ecclesia Christi invenias salutare
convivium.

No. 40 (Ep. CLXXIV)

DOMINO BEATISSIMO ET SINCERISSIMA CARI-
TATE VENERANDO SANCTO FRATRI ET CON-
SACERDOTI PAPAE AURELIO AUGUSTINUS
IN DOMINO SALUTEM

De trinitate, quae deus summus et verus est, libros
iuvenis inchoavi, senex edidi. Omiseram quippe
hoc opus, posteaquam comperi praereptos mihi esse
sive subreptos, antequam eos absolverem et re-
tractatos, ut mea dispositio fuerat, expolirem. Non
enim singillatim, sed omnes simul edere ea ratione
decreveram, quoniam praecedentibus consequentes
inquisitione proficiente nectuntur. Cum ergo per

---

[a] The title *papa* was applied to all bishops indiscriminately
from the third century until the ninth, and only then was
reserved to the bishop of Rome (see P. de Labriolle in the
Bulletin Du Cange, t. iv. pp. 65-75). For Aurelius see note
on p. 40.

[b] The *De Trinitate* was begun about 400, but the first
twelve books having been published without his authority,
it was not until 416, in response to several urgent requests,

lord said, ' Go out into the highways and hedges and compel them to come in.' " Wherefore, if you were walking quietly outside this feast of the Church's holy unity, we should find you, so to speak, in the " highways "; but as it is, you are, so to say, full of thorns and sharpness, by reason of the many cruel sufferings you inflict on our people, so we find you, as it were, in the " hedges " and compel you to come in. He who is compelled is forced to go where he has no wish to go, but when he has come in, he partakes of the feast right willingly. So curb your hostile and rebellious spirit, that you may find the feast of salvation within the true Church of Christ.

No. 40 (Ep. CLXXIV)

(A.D. 416)

TO MY SAINTLY LORD, REVERED WITH VERY GENUINE LOVE, MY HOLY BROTHER AND FELLOW-PRIEST, POPE AURELIUS,[a] AUGUSTINE SENDS GREETING IN THE LORD

I was young when I began my work on the Trinity,[b] the supreme, true God; I am old now when it is published. I had indeed abandoned the task, after learning that someone had stolen it from me or at least stolen a march on me before I could finish and revise it and give it the final touch I had intended. For I had decided not to publish the books separately but all together, for the reason that the later books are linked up with the earlier in a progressive inquiry.

that he completed and published the whole fifteen books (*Retract.* ii. 15, *Epp.* cxx. 13, cxliii. 4, clxiv. 2, clxix. 1).

eos homines qui, priusquam vellem, ad quosdam
illorum pervenire potuerunt, dispositio mea nequi-
visset impleri, interruptam dictationem reliqueram
cogitans hoc ipsum in aliquibus scriptis meis conqueri,
ut scirent qui possent non a me fuisse eosdem libros
editos, sed ablatos priusquam mihi editione mea digni
viderentur. Verum multorum fratrum vehementis-
sima postulatione et maxime tua iussione compulsus,
opus tam laboriosum adiuvante domino terminare
curavi, eosque emendatos, non ut volui, sed ut potui,
ne ab illis, qui subrepti iam in manus hominum
exierant, plurimum discreparent, venerationi tuae
per filium nostrum condiaconum carissimum misi et
cuicumque audiendos, legendos describendosque per-
misi. In quibus si servari mea dispositio potuisset,
essent profecto, etsi easdem sententias habentes,
multo tamen enodatiores atque planiores, quantum
rerum tantarum explicandarum difficultas et facultas
nostra pateretur. Sunt autem qui primos quattuor
vel potius quinque etiam sine prooemiis habent et
duodecimum sine extrema parte non parva. Sed
si eis haec editio potuerit innotescere, omnia, si
voluerint et valuerint, emendabunt. Peto sane ut
hanc epistulam seorsum quidem sed tamen ad caput
eorundem librorum iubeas anteponi. Ora pro me.

NO. 40 (Ep. CLXXIV)

Seeing, then, that my intention was prevented from being carried out because of those persons who were able to have access to some of the books before I wanted them to, I broke off my dictation and abandoned it, thinking to voice my complaint in some other work of mine, so as to let those who could, know that those same books were not published by me, but were taken out of my hands before they seemed to me fit for publication by me. But compelled by the most urgent demands of many of my brethren and most of all by your command, I have taken the trouble to bring to completion, with the help of God, a work on which I have expended so much effort, and now by our son and dear fellow-deacon I am sending them to your Grace, and handing them over for anyone to hear, read, or copy, corrected as well as I could, not as well as I would, in case they might differ too much from those copies which were stolen from me and are already in circulation. If I could have stuck to what I intended in them, they should have contained the same opinions, but should certainly have been much less obscure and more easy to read, as far as the difficulty of explaining such weighty matters and my own ability allowed it. Now there are some people who possess the first four or rather five books without the introductions and the twelfth without the last portion, which is of a fair length; but if this edition happens to come to their notice, they will be able to make all the corrections, if they have the wish and the ability. I beg you by all means to give instructions for the placing of this letter at the head of those books, but apart from them. Pray for me.

ST. AUGUSTINE

No. 41 (Ep. CLXXIX)

DOMINO BEATISSIMO ET MERITO VENERA-BILI FRATRI ET COEPISCOPO IOHANNI AU-GUSTINUS IN DOMINO SALUTEM

1 Quod tuae sanctitatis scripta non merui, nihil audeo suscensere ; melius enim perlatorem credo defuisse, quam me suspicor a tua veneratione contemptum, domine beatissime et merito venerabilis frater. Nunc vero, quoniam servum dei Lucam, per quem ista direxi, cito comperi esse rediturum, agam domino et tuae benignitati uberes gratias, si me litteris fueris visitare dignatus. Pelagium vero fratrem nostrum, filium tuum, quem audio quod multum diligis, hanc illi suggero exhibeas dilectionem, ut homines, qui eum noverunt et diligenter audierunt, non ab eo tuam sanctitatem existiment falli.

2 Nam quidam ex discipulis eius adulescentes honestissime nati et institutis liberalibus eruditi spem, quam habebant in saeculo, eius exhortatione dimiserunt et se ad dei servitium contulerunt. In quibus tamen cum apparuissent quaedam sanae doctrinae adversantia, quae salvatoris evangelio

---

a This is John, bishop of Jerusalem from 386 to 417. When Pelagius and Coelestius reached Palestine in 415, John refused to accept the decrees of the Council of Carthage against them and held his own synod in 415. In 416 the Synod of Diospolis gave a decision favourable to Pelagius, but later this was reversed. Meantime Augustine writes warning John to beware of tolerating and encouraging the Pelagian heresy. For Augustine's earlier relations with Pelagius see No. 36.

b These young men were Timasius and Jacobus, who in 415 sent Augustine a copy of Pelagius's *De Natura*, to which

No. 41 (Ep. CLXXIX)

(A.D. 416)

TO MY SAINTLY LORD AND DESERVEDLY RE-
VERED BROTHER AND FELLOW - BISHOP,
JOHN,[a] AUGUSTINE SENDS GREETING IN
THE LORD

I would not for anything venture to cherish re- 1
sentment that I have not been honoured with letters
from your Holiness; for it is better for me to believe
that you, my saintly lord and deservedly revered
brother, were without anyone to convey them, than
to harbour the suspicion that your Grace was scorning
me. But now, as I have learned that Luke, the servant
of God by whom I am sending this letter to you, is
going to return very shortly, I shall give hearty thanks
to the Lord and to your Benignity, if you have the
kindness to visit me by letter. As for Pelagius, our
brother and your son, to whom I hear you show
much affection, I suggest that the affection you show
him be such that the people who know him and have
carefully listened to him may not imagine that your
Holiness is being deceived by him.

Some of his disciples, indeed, young men of very 2
noble birth and education in the liberal arts,[b] gave
up their worldly prospects at his persuasion and
betook themselves to the service of God. When,
however, they gave evidence of certain theories at
variance with sound doctrine as contained in the
Gospel of the Saviour and declared in the words of

Augustine replied in his *De Natura et Gratia*, dedicated to
the two young men; their letter of thanks on receiving the
reply is printed as Ep. clxviii.

307

continetur et apostolicis sermonibus declaratur, id
est cum invenirentur contra dei gratiam disputari,
propter quam Christiani sumus et in qua *spiritu ex
fide spem iustitiae expectamus*, et admonitionibus
nostris inciperent emendari, dederunt mihi librum,
quem eiusdem Pelagii esse dixerunt, rogantes ut ei
potius responderem. Quod posteaquam vidi me
facere debere, ut eo modo error ipse nefarius de
cordibus eorum perfectius auferretur, legi atque
respondi.

3   In hoc libro ille dei gratiam non appellat nisi
naturam, qua libero arbitrio conditi sumus. Illam
vero, quam innumerabilibus testimoniis sancta
scriptura commendat ea nos iustificari, hoc est iustos
fieri docens et in omni opere bono sive agendo sive
perficiendo dei misericordia iuvari, quod etiam
orationes sanctorum apertissime ostendunt, quibus
ea petuntur a domino, quae praecipiuntur a domino,
hanc ergo gratiam non solum tacet, sed ei contraria
multa loquitur. Adfirmat enim vehementerque con-
tendit per solum liberum arbitrium sibi humanam
sufficere posse naturam ad operandam iustitiam et
omnia dei mandata servanda. Unde quis non
videat, cum eundem librum legerit, quem ad modum
oppugnetur gratia dei, de qua dicit apostolus:
*Miser ego homo ! Quis me liberabit de corpore mortis
huius ? Gratia dei per dominum nostrum Iesum
Christum*, et nullus locus divino adiutorio relinquatur,
propter quod orantes dicere debeamus: *Ne nos
inferas in temptationem*, sine causa etiam dominus

ᵃ Gal. v. 5.   *ᵇ* Rom. vii. 24-25.
    ᶜ Matt. vi. 13 ; Luke xi. 4.

308

the apostles—that is, when they were discovered to be arguing against the grace of God, by means of which we become Christians and in which " we through the Spirit wait for the hope of righteousness by faith," [a] and were beginning to reject their errors under my strictures, they gave me a book which, they said, was by the same Pelagius, asking me instead to reply to him. After I saw that it was my duty to do so in order the more thoroughly to drive that wicked error from their hearts, I read it and composed an answer.

In that book he declares the grace of God to be 3 only nature, in which we are created with free-will. As for that grace, however, which Holy Scripture commends to us in countless texts, teaching that it is by it that we are justified, that is, made just, and assisted, by God's mercy, in doing or completing every good work (as is shown too very clearly by the prayers of the holy, in which those things are sought from the Lord which have been enjoined by the Lord)—this grace, then, he not only passes over in silence, but advances many statements opposed to it. For he asserts and urgently argues that through free-will alone human nature can be sufficient to do the works of righteousness and keep all God's commandments. From that anyone can see, on reading the same book, what an attack is made upon the grace of God, of which the apostle says, " O wretched man that I am ! Who shall deliver me from the body of this death ? The grace of God through our Lord Jesus Christ," [b] and how there is no place left for that divine assistance because of which it is our duty to say, when we pray, "Lead us not into temptation" [c]; further, the Lord seems to have had no reason for

apostolo Petro dixisse videatur: *Rogavi pro te, ne
deficiat fides tua*, si hoc totum in nobis nullo auxilio
dei sed potestate voluntatis impletur ?

4 His itaque disputationibus perversis et impiis non
solum contradicitur orationibus nostris, quibus a
domino petimus quicquid sanctos petisse legimus et
tenemus, verum etiam benedictionibus nostris re-
sistitur, quando super populum dicimus optantes eis
et poscentes a domino, ut eos *abundare faciat in
caritate invicem et in omnes* et *det* eis *secundum divitias
gloriae suae virtute corroborari per spiritum eius* et
impleat eos *omni gaudio et pace in credendo* et abundent
in spe et potentia spiritus sancti. Ut quid eis ista
petimus, quae populis a domino petisse apostolum
novimus, si iam natura nostra creata cum libero
arbitrio omnia haec sibi potest sua voluntate praestare ? Ut quid etiam dicit idem ipse apostolus:
Quotquot enim spiritu dei aguntur, hi filii sunt dei, si
spiritu naturae nostrae agimur, ut efficiamur filii dei ?
Ut quid dicit similiter : *Spiritus adiuvat infirmitatem
nostram,* si natura nostra sic creata est, ut spiritu
ad opera iustitiae non indigeat adiuvari ? Ut quid
scriptum est : *Fidelis autem deus, qui non permittet vos
temptari super id quod potestis, sed faciet cum temptatione etiam exitum, ut possitis sustinere,* si iam ita conditi
sumus, ut viribus liberi arbitrii universas tempta-
tiones sustinendo superare possimus ?

---

 a Luke xxii. 32.   *b* 1 Thess. iii. 12.
 c Eph. iii. 16.   *d* Rom. xv. 13.   *e* Rom. viii. 14.
     f Rom. viii. 26.   *g* 1 Cor. x. 13.

saying to the apostle Peter, " I have prayed for thee, that thy faith fail not," *a* if all this receives its fulfilment in us without any help from God, but by the power of our will alone.

So these perverted and sacrilegious arguments not **4** only give the lie to our prayers, in which we ask the Lord for anything that we read and believe that the holy have asked, but also are in conflict with the benediction we give, when over the people we utter the prayer and petition to God that He will " make them to increase and abound in love one towards another and towards all men," *b* and " grant them according to the riches of His glory to be strengthened with might by his Spirit," *c* and " fill them with joy and peace in believing and make them to abound in hope and in the power of the Holy Spirit." *d* Why do we ask these things for them which we know the apostle asked from the Lord for the nations, if even now our nature, created with free-will, can provide all of them for itself by its own will ? And why does this same apostle say too, " For as many as are led by the Spirit of God, they are the sons of God," *e* if we are led by the spirit of our nature to be made the sons of God ? And why does he likewise say, " The Spirit helpeth our infirmities," *f* if our nature is created such that it does not need any help from the Spirit to do the works of righteousness ? And why does Scripture say, " But God is faithful, who will not suffer you to be tempted above that ye are able, but will with the temptation also make a way to escape, that ye may be able to bear it," *g* if we have been created such that by the strength of our freewill we are able to overcome all temptations by simply enduring them ?

5   Quid pluribus agam apud sanctitatem vestram, quando quidem me onerosum sentio, maxime quia per interpretem audis litteras meas? Si diligitis Pelagium, diligat vos etiam ipse, immo magis se ipsum et non vos fallat. Cum enim auditis eum confiteri gratiam dei et adiutorium dei, putatis hoc eum dicere quod et vos, qui catholica regula sapitis, quoniam quid in libro suo scripserit, ignoratis. Propter hoc ipsum librum misi et meum, quo ei respondi ; unde perspiciat venerabilitas vestra quam gratiam vel adiutorium dei dicat, quando illi obicitur quod gratiae dei et adiutorio contradicat. Proinde ostende illi docendo et hortando et pro eius salute, quae in Christo esse debet, orando, ut eam dei gratiam confiteatur, quam probantur sancti dei fuisse confessi, cum a domino ea ipsi peterent, quae illis iubebat ut facerent, quoniam neque iuberentur, nisi ut nostra voluntas ostenderetur, neque peterentur, nisi ut voluntatis infirmitas ab illo, qui iusserat, iuvaretur.

6   Aperte interrogetur, utrum ei placeat orandum esse a domino, ne peccemus. Quod si ei displicet, legatur in auribus eius apostolus dicens : *Oramus autem ad deum, ne quid faciatis mali* ; si autem placet, aperte praedicet gratiam, qua iuvamur, ne ipse faciat multum mali. Hac enim gratia dei per Iesum Christum dominum nostrum omnes liberantur, quicumque liberantur, quoniam nemo praeter ipsam quolibet alio modo liberari potest. Propter hoc

---

NO. 41 (Ep. CLXXIX)

Why need I dilate upon the point to your Holiness, 5 when I already realize that I am wearying you, especially as you listen to my letter through an interpreter?[a] If you love Pelagius, may he too love you, or rather deceive himself and not you! For when you hear him confessing God's grace and God's help, you think he means the same as you do, who understand them in the light of the Catholic rule of faith, because you are unacquainted with what he has written in his book. For this reason I have sent the book itself and the reply I wrote to it; from these your Reverence may see what grace or help of God he speaks of, when the objection is made to him that he is speaking of something opposed to the grace and help of God. Open his eyes then by teaching and exhorting him and praying for the salvation he ought to have in Christ, so that he may confess that grace of God the saints are proved to have confessed, when they sought those things from the Lord which He commanded them to seek, for those things would have not been commanded unless to the end that our will should be revealed, nor would they be asked for, unless to the end that the weakness of our will should have the help of Him who commanded them.

Let the question be openly put to him whether he 6 approves of praying the Lord that we fall not into sin. If he disapproves of it, let the apostle be read in his ears, in the words, "Now I pray to God that ye do no evil"[b]; but if he does approve of it, let him openly preach that grace which assists us, so that he himself may be kept from doing much evil. For it is by this grace of God through Jesus Christ our Lord that all those who are delivered, are delivered, since no one can be delivered in any other way than through it.

313

scriptum est : *Sicut in Adam omnes moriuntur, sic ei*
in Christo omnes vivificabuntur, non quia nemo damna-
bitur, sed quia nemo aliter liberabitur, quia, sicut
nulli nisi per Adam filii hominis, ita nulli nisi per
Christum filii dei. Omnes itaque filii hominis nonnisi
per Adam et omnes ex eis filii dei nonnisi per Christum
fieri possunt. Aperte itaque etiam hinc exprimat
quid sentiat, utrum placeat ei etiam parvulos, qui
nondum iustitiam possunt velle vel nolle, tamen
propter unum hominem, per quem *peccatum intravit*
in mundum et per peccatum mors et ita in omnes homines
pertransiit, in quo omnes peccaverunt, per Christi
gratiam liberari, utrum etiam pro ipsis fusum credat
sanguinem Christi propter originale peccatum, qui
utique in remissionem fusus est peccatorum. De
his maxime ab illo volumus nosse quid credat, quid
teneat, quid certe confiteatur et praedicet. In
aliis autem, quae illi obiciuntur, etiamsi errare
convincitur, tamen, donec corrigatur, tolerabilius
sustinetur.

7   Peto etiam nobis transmittere, quibus perhibetur
esse purgatus, ecclesiastica gesta digneris. Quod ex
multorum episcoporum desiderio peto, quos mecum
de hac re fama incerta perturbat ; sed ideo solus
hoc scripsi, quia occasionem perlatoris festinantis a
nobis, quem cito ad nos audivi posse remeare, praetermittere nolui. Pro quibus gestis iam nobis misit

---

ᵃ 1 Cor. xv. 22.   ᵇ Rom. v. 12.   ᶜ Matt. xxvi. 28.

ᵈ Held at Diospolis, the ancient Lydda, in December 415.
When the minutes came into Augustine's hands, about the
end of 416 or early in 417, he found that Pelagius's summary
of the discussion was unfair, so he wrote the historical tract
De Gestis Pelagii, an account of the proceedings against
Pelagius in Palestine.

For that reason it is written, " For as in Adam all die, even so in Christ shall all be made alive," [a] not that no one will be damned, but that no one will be delivered in any other way ; for just as all those who are children of men are so through Adam, so all those who are children of God are so through Christ. So all children of men are able to become such only through Adam, and all of them who have become children of God, only through Christ. Let him therefore openly express his views on this further point, whether he accepts the fact that even little children, who have not yet reached the stage of willing righteousness or of refusing it, yet because of one man, by whom " sin entered into the world, and death by sin, and so death passed upon all men, for that all have sinned," [b] are delivered by the grace of Christ—whether even for them, because of original sin, he believes that the blood of Christ was shed, which was, to be sure, shed for the remission of sins.[c] About these points in particular I am anxious to know what he believes and holds, what he definitely confesses and preaches.   In the other points, however, that are raised against him, even if he be proved to be in error, none the less until he accepts correction, it is more tolerable to bear with him.

Further, I beg you to have the kindness to send to **7** me the minutes of the Church council [d] which declare him to be cleared of the charge of heresy. This I beg at the desire of many bishops who have, like me, been troubled by the indefinite rumour about this ; I have written, however, asking this in my own name for the reason that I did not want to miss the opportunity of the messenger, who is in a position, I understand, to return to us speedily.   In place of these

non quidem ullam partem gestorum sed quandam
a se conscriptam velut defensionem suam, qua se
dixit obiectis respondisse Gallorum. In qua, ut alia
omittam, cum ad illud responderet, quod ei obiectum
est, eum dixisse posse hominem esse sine peccato et
mandata dei custodire, si velit, " diximus," inquit ;
" hanc enim illi deus possibilitatem dedit ; non
diximus quoniam inveniatur quis, ab infantia usque
ad senectam qui numquam peccaverit, sed quoniam
a peccatis conversus labore proprio et gratia dei
adiutus potest absque peccato esse nec propter hoc
in posterum erit inconvertibilis."

8   In hac Pelagii responsione cernit reverentia tua
hoc eum fuisse confessum, priorem hominis vitam,
quae est ab infantia, sine peccato non esse, sed eum
ad vitam, quae sine peccato sit, labore proprio et
adiutus per gratiam dei posse converti. Cur ergo in
hoc libro, cui respondi, Abel ita hic vixisse dicit, ut
nihil omnino peccaverit ? Nam eius de hac re ista
sunt verba : " Hoc," inquit, " recte dici potest de
his, quorum neque bonorum neque malorum scriptura
sit memor ; de illis vero, quorum iustitiae meminit,
et peccatorum sine dubio meminisset, si qua eos
peccasse sensisset. Sed esto," inquit, " aliis temporibus turbae numerositate omnium dissimulaverit
peccata contexere, in ipso statim mundi primordio,
ubi nonnisi quattuor homines erant, quid," inquit,

---

a Pelagius had sent this to Augustine by Charus, a deacon
in Palestine, by birth a citizen of Hippo. See *De Gest. Pel.*
i. 57, 58. The Gauls are two bishops, Heros of Arles and
Lazarus of Aix, who had taken refuge in Palestine, after
undeserved ejection from their sees. They drew up a series

minutes Pelagius has already sent us not indeed any portion of the minutes, but a kind of defence of himself, written by his own hand, in which he says he has answered the objections of the Gauls.[a] In it, to leave other matters out, he replied to the objection made to him that he had said man could live without sin and keep God's commandments if he wished to ; his words are : " I maintained that this power was conferred upon him by God ; I did not maintain that any person would be found who had never committed a sin from his infancy to his old age, but that after turning from sin by his own effort and with the help of God's grace he can live without sin, and that the fact of having sinned does not prevent a man from turning from it at a future date."

In this reply of Pelagius your Reverence can dis- 8 cern that he has confessed that a man's earlier life, that is in infancy, is not without sin, but that he can be turned by his own effort, assisted by the grace of God, to the sinless life. Why then, in the book I have replied to, does he allege that Abel lived a life that was completely without sin ? These are his words about this point : " This can with justice be said of those of whose good deeds and evil deeds alike Scripture has no record ; but it would assuredly have recorded the sins of those whose righteousness it records, if it had perceived that they had sinned at all. But granted," he says, " that in other ages the great throng of men made Scripture neglect to weave an account of the sins of every one : right at the very beginning of the world, when there were only four people in existence, what reason," he

of formal charges against Pelagius, to consider which the Synod of Diospolis was called.

" dicimus, cur non omnium voluerit delicta memorare?
Utrumne ingentis multitudinis causa, quae nondum
erat ? An quia illorum tantum, qui commiserant,
meminit, illius vero, qui nulla commiserat, memi-
nisse non potuit ? Certe," inquit, " primo in tempore Adam et Eva, ex quibus Cain et Abel nati sunt,
quattuor homines tantum fuisse referuntur. Peccavit Eva, scriptura hoc prodidit ; Adam quoque
deliquit, eadem scriptura non tacuit ; sed et Cain
peccasse ipsa quoque scriptura testata est. Quorum
non modo peccata, verum etiam peccatorum indicat
qualitatem. Quod si et Abel peccasset," inquit,
" et hoc sine dubio scriptura dixisset ; si non dixit,
ergo nec ille peccavit."

9   Haec verba de libro eius decerpsi, quae in ipso
quoque volumine tua sanctitas poterit invenire, ut intellegatis quem ad modum et cetera neganti credere
debeatis, nisi forte dicat ipsum Abel nihil peccasse,
sed ideo non fuisse sine peccato et ideo non posse
domino comparari, qui in carne mortali solus sine
peccato fuit, quia erat in Abel originale peccatum
quod de Adam traxerat, non in se ipso ipse commiserat—utinam saltem hoc dicat, ut interim eius
de baptismo parvulorum certam sententiam tenere
possimus !—aut si forte, quoniam dixit " ab infantia
usque ad senectutem," ideo dicat Abel non peccasse,
quia nec senuisse monstratur. Non hoc indicant
verba eius ; ab initio priorem vitam dixit peccatricem,
posteriorem vero posse esse sine peccato. Ait enim

---

* This passage from Pelagius is again quoted and discussed by Augustine in *De Natura et Gratia*, §§ 43-45.

asks, " can we give for its failure to mention the sins
of every one ? Is it because of the great number of
people ? There was as yet nothing of the kind. Is
it because it remembered only those who had committed sin, and was unable to remember the one who
had not committed any ? To be sure," he says, " in
the first age of the world there were Adam and Eve,
from whom were born Cain and Abel—four people
only are mentioned as existing. Eve sinned ; the
Scripture has revealed that to us ; Adam also sinned ;
the same Scripture does not omit to mention it, and
that Scripture has testified too that Cain sinned as
well, and it points out not only their sins, but also the
nature of their sins. If Abel too had sinned, that too
would have been mentioned by Scripture ; but it is
not mentioned, so he did not sin." [a]

I have culled from his book these words, which 9
your Holiness will be able to find in the volume itself,
so that you may understand what manner of credence
you should afford him when he denies the other points
as well ; unless perhaps he says that Abel himself
committed no sin, but that he was not therefore without sin and could not therefore bear comparison with
the Lord, Who alone in mortal flesh was without sin,
since in Abel there was original sin inherited from
Adam, not committed by himself in his own person
(I wish he would at least make this assertion, so that
we might for the present obtain from him a definite
expression of opinion about infant baptism) ; or unless
he says perhaps, since he has used the words " from
infancy to old age," that Abel did not sin because he
is shown not to have lived to old age. This is not what
his words indicate : he said that from the beginning
the earlier period of life was given to sin, but that the

non se dixisse quoniam inveniatur quis ab infantia
usque ad senectutem qui non peccaverit, sed quoniam
a peccatis conversus labore proprio et gratia dei
adiutus potest absque peccato esse. Cum enim dicit
" a peccatis conversus," ostendit priorem vitam in
peccatis agi. Fateatur ergo quod peccaverit Abel,
cuius prima vita fuit in saeculo, quam fatetur non
carere peccatis, et respiciat librum suum, ubi eum
dixisse constat quod ait in hac defensione : " Non
diximus."

10　　Si autem et hunc librum vel hunc in eo libro locum
esse negaverit suum, ego quidem idoneos testes
habeo honestos et fideles viros et eius sine dubio
dilectores, quibus adtestantibus purgare me possum
quod eundem librum ipsi mihi dederint et ibi hoc
legatur eumque Pelagii esse dixerint, ut saltem hoc
mihi sufficiat, ne dicat a me fuisse sive conscriptum
sive falsatum. Iam inter illos eligat quisque cui
credat. Meum non est de hac re diutius disputare.
Rogamus, ut certe transmittas sibi, si[1] negaverit
se ista sentire, quae illi obiciuntur inimica gratiae
Christi. Tam quippe aperta est eius defensio, ut,
si vestram sanctam prudentiam, qui eius alia scripta
non nostis, nulla verborum ambiguitate fefellerit,

---

[1] *The Benedictine edition here reads* transmittas ipsi si, *the
manuscripts, two of the fifteenth century,* transmittas sibi si.
Goldbacher marks a lacuna, which is hardly necessary ; sibi
is probably a corruption of illi *or* ei.

---

[a] The reasoning here is a little involved. Pelagius has
been trying to prove the sinlessness of Abel, in order to
justify his own denial of the transmission of original sin and
his theory that even before Christ there had been sinless lives.
Augustine asks if he will maintain that Abel, whom he
declares to have committed no sin, is therefore to be put on
a level with Christ ; assuming Pelagius will hardly go so far,

later could be sinless; for he declares he did not state
that anyone would be found who from infancy to old
age had not committed sin, but that after turning
from sin by his own effort and with the help of God's
grace, he could live without sin. For when he says
" turning from sin," he shows that the earlier part of
life was lived in sin. Let him then admit that Abel
did sin, since his early life was lived in the world, and
it, according to his admission, is not without sin ; and
let him take another look at his own book, where it
is quite plain he did make the statement which in this
defence he denies having made.[a]

But if he asserts that this book, or this passage in 10
the book, is not from his pen, I on my side have
adequate witnesses, men of honour and reliability
and undoubted friends of his own, and I can acquit
myself by their testimony that they handed this same
book to me containing that sentence and that they
declared it was from the pen of Pelagius ; that evidence at any rate is sufficient to deter anyone from
saying that it was written or fabricated by me. Now
among these let each man choose whom to believe.
It is not my business to discuss the matter at any
greater length. I ask you to convey to him by a sure
hand, if he denies that those are his opinions, the
points to which objection is taken as being in conflict with the grace of Christ. So plausible is his defence, indeed, that we shall rejoice with exceeding
joy if he has not deceived your wise Holiness, unacquainted as you are with his other writings, by any

[a] he gives two alternatives: either Abel was not sinless in
character, even if he did no sinful deed, or else he turned
from sin—in either case, therefore, he was not without the
taint of original sin which Pelagius is seeking to deny.

magno gaudio gratulabimur non multum curantes,
utrum illa perversa et impia numquam senserit an
se ab eis aliquando correxerit.

No. 42 (Ep. CLXXXIX)

DOMINO EXIMIO ET MERITO INSIGNI ATQUE HONORABILI FILIO BONIFATIO AUGUSTINUS IN DOMINO SALUTEM

1 Iam rescripseram caritati tuae, sed, cum epistulae
dirigendae occasio quaereretur, supervenit dilectissimus filius meus Faustus pergens ad eximietatem
tuam. Qui cum ipsas litteras, quas iam feceram,
accepisset tuae benivolentiae perferendas, suggessit
mihi multum te desiderare ut aliquid tibi scriberem
quod te aedificet ad sempiternam salutem, cuius tibi
spes in Christo Iesu domino nostro. Et quamvis
mihi occupato tantum institit ut facere non differrem,
quantum scis quod te sinceriter diligat. Festinanti
ergo ut occurrerem, malui festinanter aliquid scribere
quam religiosum tuum desiderium retardare, domine
eximie et merito insignis atque honorabilis fili.

2 Quod ergo breviter possum dicere : *Dilige dominum deum tuum in toto corde tuo et in tota anima tua
et in tota virtute tua*, et : *Dilige proximum tuum tamquam*

---

a Count Boniface was governor of Africa under Honorius
and Placidia. Through the treachery of his perfidious rival
Aetius, he was unjustly disgraced and revenged himself by
making alliance with Genseric, king of the Vandals, who
at his invitation invaded Africa in 429. The duplicity of
Aetius being discovered, Boniface was restored to favour,
and set himself to oppose the invaders. He retired to Hippo,
which was besieged for fourteen months, during which time

ambiguous statement. For the rest we care not over-much whether those perverted and impious opinions were never his, or if at last he has renounced them.

No. 42 (Ep. CLXXXIX)

(A.D. 418)

TO BONIFACE,[a] MY NOBLE LORD AND JUSTLY DISTINGUISHED AND HONOURABLE SON, AUGUSTINE SENDS GREETING IN THE LORD

I had already written my reply to your Charity, 1 but when I was looking for an opportunity of transmitting my letter, my beloved son Faustus arrived on his way to your Excellency. After receiving the letter which I had already composed for conveyance to your Benevolence, he intimated to me your strong desire that I should write something to you that would build you up unto that eternal salvation of which your confidence is in Christ Jesus our Lord. And although I was busily occupied, he urged me with that instancy which, as you know, is proportioned to his affection for you, not to postpone the writing of it. To meet his haste, then, I have chosen rather to write something in haste than to keep your holy desire in suspense, my noble and justly distinguished lord and honourable son.

All then that I can say in the short time I have is this : 2 " Love the Lord thy God with all thy heart and with all thy soul and with all thy strength," and " love thy

Augustine's death took place, and was finally taken. Boniface returned to Italy, but was slain in battle with Aetius in 432. He is addressed in No. 51 *infra.*

te ipsum—hoc est enim verbum, quod breviavit
dominus super terram dicens in evangelio : *In his
duobus praeceptis tota lex pendet et prophetae,*—in hac
ergo dilectione cotidie profice et orando et bene
agendo, ut ipso adiuvante, qui tibi eam praecepit
atque donavit, nutriatur et crescat, donec haec te
perfecta perficiat. Ipsa est enim *caritas*, quae, sicut
dicit apostolus, *diffusa est in cordibus nostris per
spiritum sanctum, qui datus est nobis* ; ipsa est, de qua
item dicit : *Plenitudo legis caritas* ; ipsa est, per
quam fides operatur, unde iterum dicit : *Neque
circumcisio quicquam valet neque praeputium sed fides,
quae per dilectionem operatur.*

3   In hac omnes sancti patres nostri et patriarchae et
prophetae et apostoli placuerunt deo ; in hac omnes
veri martyres usque ad sanguinem contra diabolum
certaverunt et, quia in eis non refriguit nec defecit,
ideo vicerunt ; in hac omnes boni fideles cotidie
proficiunt, pervenire cupientes non ad regnum
mortalium, sed ad regnum caelorum, non ad temporalem, sed ad sempiternam hereditatem, non ad
aurum et argentum, sed ad divitias incorruptibiles
angelorum, non ad aliqua bona huius saeculi, in
quibus cum timore vivatur nec ea quisquam secum
potest auferre dum moritur, sed ad videndum deum ;
cuius suavitas et delectatio excedit omnem non
solum terrestrium, verum etiam caelestium corporum
pulchritudinem, excedit omnem decorem animarum
quantum libet iustarum atque sanctarum, excedit
omnem speciem supernorum angelorum atque virtutum, excedit quicquid de illo non solum dicitur,

---

a Luke x. 27, etc.   *b* Matt. xxii. 40.   *c* Rom. v. 5.
d Rom. xiii. 10.   *e* Gal. v. 6.   *f* Matt. xxiv. 12.
g Matt. vii. 21; Heb. ix. 15.   *h* Matt. v. 8.

neighbour as thyself."[a] These are the words in which
the Lord while upon earth summed up everything,
saying in the Gospel : " On these two commandments hang all the law and the prophets."[b] In this
love therefore make daily progress by both prayer
and good deeds, so that by the help of Him who
enjoined it upon you and granted you to possess it,
it may find nourishment and increase, until being
perfect it makes you perfect. For that is the love
which, in the words of the apostle, " is shed abroad
in our hearts by the Holy Ghost, which is given unto
us "[c] ; it is that love which he also describes as the
" fulfilling of the law "[d] ; it is that by which faith
worketh, of which he says again, " Neither circum-
cision availeth anything nor uncircumcision, but faith,
which worketh by love."[e]

In this love all our holy fathers and patriarchs and 3
prophets and apostles pleased God ; in it all true
martyrs contended against the devil even unto
blood,[f] and because in them it neither waxed cold nor
failed, they won the day : in it all good believers
make daily progress, seeking to attain not unto an
earthly kingdom, but unto the kingdom of heaven,
not unto a temporal, but unto an eternal inheritance,[g]
not unto gold and silver, but unto the incorruptible
riches of the angels, not unto any of this world's good
things, which make life full of fear and which no one
can take with him when he dies, but unto the vision
of God.[h] His sweetness and delight transcend all
beauty of form not only in earthly things, but even
in heavenly, transcend all loveliness of souls however
righteous and holy, transcend all the comeliness of
angels and powers above, transcend not only everything that language can express about Him, but also

verum etiam cogitatur. Neque hanc tam magnam promissionem, quia valde magna est, ideo desperemus, sed potius, quia valde magnus eam promisit, accepturos nos esse credamus. Sicut enim dicit beatus Iohannes apostolus, *filii dei sumus et nondum apparuit, quid erimus; scimus quia, cum apparuerit, similes ei erimus, quoniam videbimus eum sicuti est.*

4 Noli existimare neminem deo placere posse, qui in armis bellicis militat. In his erat sanctus David, cui dominus tam magnum perhibuit testimonium; in his etiam plurimi illius temporis iusti; in his erat et ille centurio, qui domino dixit: *Non sum dignus, ut intres sub tectum meum, sed tantum dic verbo et sanabitur puer meus. Nam et ego homo sum sub potestate constitutus habens sub me milites et dico huic: " Vade " et vadit, et alio : " Veni " et venit, et servo meo : " Fac hoc " et facit;* de quo et dominus: *Amen dico vobis; non inveni tantam fidem in Israhel.* In his erat et ille Cornelius, ad quem missus angelus dixit: *Corneli, acceptae sunt elemosynae tuae et exauditae sunt orationes tuae*; ubi eum admonuit, ut ad beatum Petrum apostolum mitteret et ab illo audiret quae facere deberet; ad quem apostolum, ut ad eum veniret, etiam religiosum militem misit. In his erant et illi, qui baptizandi cum venissent ad Iohannem, sanctum domini praecursorem et amicum sponsi, de quo ipse dominus ait: *In natis mulierum non exsurrexit maior Iohanne Baptista*, et quaesissent ab eo, quid facerent,

---

* 1 John iii. 2. *b* Matt. viii. 8-10; Luke vii. 6-9.
c Acts x. 1-8, 30-33 *d* Matt. xi. 11.

326

everything that the mind can imagine. And let us not despair of the fulfilment of a promise so great, since it is great indeed, but rather let us have faith that we shall obtain it, since He is great Who made the promise; as the blessed John the apostle says, " Now are we the sons of God, and it doth not yet appear what we shall be ; but we know that, when He shall appear, we shall be like Him, for we shall see Him as He is."[a]

Do not think that it is impossible for anyone to [4] please God while engaged in military service. Among such was the holy David, to whom the Lord gave so great a testimony, and among such were also many righteous men of that dispensation ; among such too was that centurion who said to the Lord, " I am not worthy that Thou shouldest come under my roof, but speak the word only and my servant shall be healed ; for I am a man under authority, having soldiers under me, and I say to this man, Go, and he goeth, and to another, Come, and he cometh, and to my servant, Do this, and he doeth it," and of whom the Lord said, " Verily, I say unto you, I have not found so great faith, no, not in Israel."[b] Among such too was that Cornelius to whom an angel said, " Cornelius, thine alms are accepted, and thy prayers are heard,"[c] by which words he signified that he should send to the blessed apostle Peter and hear from him what he should do ; to which apostle he sent a godly soldier, asking him to visit him. Among such too were those who came to be baptized by John, the holy forerunner of the Lord and the friend of the bridegroom, about whom the Lord Himself said, " Among them that are born of women there hath not arisen a greater than John the Baptist"[d]; they

respondit eis : *Neminem concusseritis, nulli calumniam feceritis, sufficiat vobis stipendium vestrum.* Non eos utique sub armis militare prohibuit, quibus suum stipendium sufficere debere praecepit.

5 Maioris quidem loci sunt apud deum, qui omnibus istis saecularibus actionibus derelictis etiam summa continentia castitatis ei serviunt. *Sed unusquisque,* sicut dicit apostolus, *proprium donum habet a deo, alius sic, alius autem sic.* Alii ergo pro vobis orando pugnant contra invisibiles inimicos, vos pro eis pugnando laboratis contra visibiles barbaros. Utinam una fides esset in omnibus, quia et minus laboraretur et facilius diabolus cum suis angelis vinceretur ! Sed quia in hoc saeculo necesse est, ut cives regni caelorum inter errantes et impios temptationibus agitentur, ut exerceantur et tamquam in fornace sicut aurum probentur, non debemus ante tempus velle cum solis sanctis et iustis vivere, ut hoc suo tempore mereamur accipere.

6 Hoc ergo primum cogita, quando armaris ad pugnam, quia virtus tua etiam ipsa corporalis donum dei est ; sic enim cogitabis de dono dei non facere contra deum. Fides enim quando promittitur, etiam hosti servanda est, contra quem bellum geritur ; quanto magis amico, pro quo pugnatur ! Pacem habere debet voluntas, bellum necessitas, ut liberet deus a necessitate et conservet in pace. Non enim

---

a Luke iii. 12-14.   *b* 1 Cor. vii. 7.
c Wisdom iii. 5-6.

asked of him what they should do, and he made
answer to them : " Do violence to no man, neither
accuse any falsely, and be content with your wages."[a]
To be sure, when he commanded them to be content
with their military wages, he did not forbid them to
serve as soldiers.

They have a greater place before God, who 5
abandon all these worldly employments to serve him
with the strictest self-discipline and chastity ; " but
everyone," as the apostle says, " hath his proper
gift of God, one after this manner and another after
that."[b] There are some, then, who by praying for you
fight against your invisible foes, while you by fighting
for them are striving against the visible barbarians.
Would that there were one faith in all, for there would
be less of striving and the devil with his angels would
be more easily overcome ! But as it is necessary in
this world that the citizens of the kingdom of heaven
should be harassed by temptations among erring
and irreverent men so that they may be exercised
and tried as gold in the furnace,[c] we ought not before
the appointed time to desire to live with the saints
and righteous alone, so that we may deserve to receive this blessedness in its own due time.

Think, then, of this point first of all when you are 6
arming for battle, that your strength, even that of the
body, is a gift from God ; in this way you will not
think of using God's gift against God. For when
faith is pledged, it is to be kept even with the enemy
against whom you are waging war ; how much more
with the friend, for whose sake you are fighting !
You ought to have peace as the object of your choice
and war only as the result of necessity, so that God
may deliver you from the necessity and preserve you

pax quaeritur, ut bellum excitetur, sed bellum
geritur, ut pax adquiratur. Esto ergo etiam bellando
pacificus, ut eos, quos expugnas, ad pacis utilitatem
vincendo perducas ; *beati* enim *pacifici*, ait dominus,
quoniam ipsi filii dei vocabuntur. Si autem pax
humana tam dulcis est pro temporali salute mortalium,
quanto est dulcior pax divina pro aeterna salute
angelorum ! Itaque hostem pugnantem necessitas
perimat, non voluntas. Sicut rebellanti et resistenti
violentia redditur, ita victo vel capto misericordia
iam debetur, maxime in quo pacis perturbatio non
timetur.

7 Ornet mores tuos pudicitia coniugalis, ornet
sobrietas et frugalitas ; valde enim turpe est, ut,
quem non vincit homo, vincat libido et obruatur vino,
qui non vincitur ferro. Divitiae saeculares si desunt,
non per mala opera quaerantur in mundo ; si autem
adsunt, per bona opera serventur in caelo. Animum
virilem et Christianum nec debent, si accedunt,
extollere nec debent frangere, si recedunt. Illud
potius cogitemus, quod dominus ait : *Ubi est thesaurus
tuus, illic erit et cor tuum*, et utique, cum audimus ut
cor sursum habeamus, non mendaciter respondere
debemus, quod nosti quia respondemus.

8 Et in his quidem bene studiosum te esse cognovi
et fama tua multum delector multumque tibi in

---

* Matt. v. 9.   ^b Matt. vi. 21 ; Luke xii. 34.
   ^c This is the usual preface before the Great Thanksgiving,
in the celebration of the Eucharist. Its use in public worship
is first mentioned by St. Cyprian, *De Dominica Oratione*,
31. It is frequently mentioned by Augustine (e.g. *Serm.*
227 "Tenetis sacramenta ordine suo. Primo post orationem,
admonemini sursum habere cor. . . . Respondetis, 'Habemus ad Dominum'").

in peace ; for peace is not sought in order that war may be aroused, but war is waged in order that peace may be obtained. So then be a peace-maker even when warring, that by overcoming those whom you conquer, you may bring them to the advantages of peace, for " blessed are the peace-makers," says the Lord, " for they shall be called the children of God."[a] Yet if human peace is so sweet for procuring the temporal salvation of men, how much sweeter is peace with God for procuring the eternal salvation of the angels! So let it be your necessity and not your choice that slays the enemy who is fighting against you. Just as violence is the portion of him who rebels and resists, so mercy is the due of him who has been conquered or captured, especially when a disturbance of the peace is not to be feared.

Let your character be adorned by chastity in the **7** marriage-bond, adorned by sobriety and moderation, for it is a very disgraceful thing that lust should overcome one whom man finds unconquerable, and that wine should overwhelm one whom the sword assails in vain. If you lack earthly riches, let them not be sought in the world by evil works ; but if you possess them, let them be laid up in heaven by good works. The manly Christian spirit ought neither to be elated by their accession nor depressed by their departure. Let us rather keep in mind what the Lord says, " Where your treasure is, there will your heart be also," [b] and certainly when we hear the exhortation to lift up our hearts, we ought unfeignedly to make the response which you know we do make.[c]

In such matters as this, however, I know that you **8** are very zealous, and I take great delight in your reputation and greatly congratulate you in the Lord

domino gratulor, ita ut haec epistula magis tibi sit
speculum, ubi qualis sis videas, quam ubi discas
qualis esse debeas. Verum tamen quicquid sive in
ista sive in scripturis sanctis inveneris quod tibi ad
bonam vitam adhuc minus est, insta ut adquiras et
agendo et orando, et ex his quae habes, gratias age
deo tamquam fonti bonitatis, unde habes, atque in
omnibus bonis actibus tuis illi da claritatem, tibi
humilitatem. Sicut enim scriptum est, *omne datum
optimum et omne donum perfectum desursum est descendens
a patre luminum.* Quantumcumque autem in dei et
proximi caritate atque in vera pietate profeceris,
quam diu in hac vita conversaris, sine peccato te esse
non credas ; de ipsa quippe legitur in litteris sanctis :
Numquid non temptatio est vita humana super terram?
Proinde quoniam semper quam diu es in hoc corpore,
necessarium est tibi in oratione dicere quod dominus
docuit : *Dimitte nobis debita nostra, sicut et nos dimitti-
mus debitoribus nostris,* memento cito ignoscere, si
quis in te peccaverit et a te veniam postulaverit, ut
veraciter possis orare et peccatis tuis veniam valeas
impetrare. Haec dilectioni tuae festinanter quidem
scripsi, quoniam me festinatio perlatoris urgebat.
Sed deo gratias ago, quoniam bono desiderio tuo
qualitercumque non defui. Semper te misericordia
dei protegat, domine eximie et merito insignis atque
honorabilis fili.

---

* James i. 17.   ᵇ Job vii. 1.   ᶜ Matt. vi. 12, etc.

upon it. This letter, then, may rather serve as a mirror to you, in which you can behold what manner of man you are, rather than as a lesson to you what manner of man you ought to be. And yet, whatever you find either in this letter or in Holy Scripture that you still lack for a good life, be instant in prayer and in deeds, so that you may acquire it; and from what you have, render thanks to God as the fount of goodness, from Whom you have received it, and in all your good deeds ascribe the glory to God and the humility to yourself, for, as it is written, "Every good and perfect gift is from above and cometh down from the Father of lights."*a* Yet whatever progress you make in the love of God and of your neighbour and in genuine godliness, do not imagine that you are without sin, as long as you are in this life, concerning which we read in Holy Writ, "Is not the life of man upon earth a life of temptation?"*b* And so, since it is necessary for you, as long as you are in this body, always to say in prayer what the Lord taught us, "Forgive us our debts, as we forgive our debtors,"*c* remember quickly to forgive anyone who has sinned against you and has asked for pardon, so that you may be able to pray with sincerity and succeed in obtaining pardon for your own sins.

I have written these exhortations to you, my dear friend, in haste, as the haste of the bearer compelled me, but I render thanks to God that I have in some degree been able to comply with your holy desire. May the mercy of God always be your protection, my noble lord and deservedly distinguished and honourable son!

ST. AUGUSTINE

No. 43 (Ep. CXCI)

DOMINO VENERABILI ET IN CHRISTI CARITATE SUSCIPIENDO SANCTO FRATRI ET CONPRESBYTERO SIXTO AUGUSTINUS IN DOMINO SALUTEM

1 Ex quo Hipponem litterae benignitatis tuae per
sanctum fratrem nostrum Firmum presbyterum
directae me absente venerunt, posteaquam illas,
cum remeassem, quamvis iam inde profecto earum
perlatore legere potui, haec prima eademque gratissima rescribendi occurrit occasio per dilectissimum
filium nostrum acolithum Albinum. Quod autem,
quibus simul scripsisti, tunc non eramus simul, ideo
factum est, ut singulorum singulas, non unam
amborum epistulam sumeres. A me quippe digressus est perlator huius, per venerabilem fratrem
et coepiscopum meum Alypium, qui tuae sanctitati
aliam rescriberet, transiturus. Ad quem etiam ipsas
quas ego iam legeram, litteras tuas ipse portavit.
Quae nos quanta laetitia perfuderint, quid homo nitatur loqui quod non potest eloqui ? Nec te ipsum

---

^a Sixtus was bishop of Rome from 432 to 440, when he
was succeeded by Leo the Great. He had taken a leading part in condemning Pelagianism, though some of the
Pelagians claimed that he was on their side (see § 1), and
had intervened too in the Nestorian dispute. Augustine also
addressed him in Ep. cxciv., a long theological discussion
of the errors of Pelagianism. Firmus, the letter-bearer,
appears several times in this capacity : visiting Jerome at
Bethlehem in 405, he was entrusted with letters for Augustine (Ep. cxv.) and ten years later he is again with
Jerome, later reaching Africa, where he is in communication
with Augustine (Ep. cxxiv.). He brings back an answer to
the present letter (Ep. cxciv. 1).

No. 43 (Ep. CXCI)

(A.D. 418)

TO SIXTUS,[a] MY VENERABLE LORD AND HOLY
BROTHER AND FELLOW-PRIEST, WORTHY
TO BE CHERISHED IN THE LOVE OF CHRIST,
AUGUSTINE SENDS GREETING IN THE LORD

Since the letter your Grace sent by the hands of 1
our holy brother, the priest Firmus, reached Hippo
during my absence, and on my return I had the
chance to read it only after the bearer of it had taken
his departure, this first opportunity of replying (and
it is a very welcome one too) is afforded by our well-
beloved son, the acolyte Albinus.[b] Your letter, addressed to Alypius and myself together, came at a time
when we were not together, so in consequence you
receive a letter from each of us, not one in the common name of us both, for the bearer of this letter, having left me, will on his way pass by my revered brother
and fellow-bishop, Alypius, so that he may write one
for himself in reply to your Holiness; that letter of
yours, after reading it, I sent on to him by the same
bearer. As for the great joy with which your letter
filled me, why should one attempt to utter feelings
that defy utterance? Indeed, I am not sure that

[b] Albinus is mentioned as bearer of Epp. cxcii., cxciii.
and cxciv. to Rome. The acolytes formed one of the minor
orders in the Church, introduced about the beginning of the
third century. Though the name is Greek (ἀκόλουθοι), the
office was peculiar to the Western Church; in the rituals of
the Greek Church, the word is only a synonym for sub-deacon.
As the name implies, the acolytes were the immediate
attendants and followers of the bishops; their specific duties
were to light the candles of the church and to attend the
officiating priest with wine for the Eucharist.

satis nosse arbitror, sed nobis crede, quantum boni
feceris talia nobis scripta mittendo. Sicut enim tu
testis es animi tui, ita nos nostri, quem ad modum sit
affectus illarum sinceritate luculentissima litterarum.
Si enim brevissimam epistulam tuam, quam de hac
ipsa re ad beatissimum senem Aurelium per Leonem
acolithum direxisti, exultanti alacritate descripsimus
et, quibus poteramus, magno studio legebamus,
ubi nobis exposuisti quid de illo perniciosissimo
dogmate vel quid contra de gratia dei, quam pusillis
magnisque largitur, cui est illud inimicissimum,
sentias, quanta nos putas ista tua prolixiora scripta
vel exultatione legisse vel cura, ut legantur, quibus
valuimus, aliis obtulisse atque adhuc, quibus valemus,
offerre ! Quid enim gratius legi vel audiri potest,
quam gratiae dei tam pura defensio adversus inimicos
eius ex ore eius, qui eorundem inimicorum magni
momenti patronus antea iactabatur ? Aut unde
uberiores deo debemus agere gratias, quam quod
eius sic defenditur gratia ab eis quibus datur, adversus eos quibus vel non datur vel ingratum est
quod datur, quia, ut eis gratum sit, occulto et iusto
iudicio dei non datur ?

2   Quapropter, domine venerabilis et in Christi caritate suscipiende sancte frater, quamvis optime facias
cum de hac re scribis ad fratres, apud quos se illi de
tua solent efferre amicitia, tamen haec cura maior

ᵃ This is very probably the Leo who afterwards became
pope and is known as " the Great."

you have any adequate conception yourself of the amount of good you have done to us in writing as you did, but take our word for it; for just as you can bear witness to your own soul, so we can to ours, of the extent to which we have been moved by the very transparent sincerity of your letter. For if we transcribed with exulting joy and with great fervour read to all we could that very short letter of yours on this same problem that you sent by the acolyte Leo *a* to our most saintly Senior, Aurelius—a letter in which you expounded to us your views about that most pernicious doctrine, and, on the other hand, about the grace of God bestowed by Him upon small and great, to which that doctrine is violently opposed,—how great do you think was the exultation with which we read that lengthier statement from your pen, and how great the care with which we have had it read by all we could offer it to and can still offer it to? For what more welcome document could be read or heard than so faultless a defence of the grace of God against its enemies, uttered by one whom those same enemies boasted of as an influential supporter of their cause? Or is there anything that should make us more abundantly grateful to God than this, that His grace is so well defended by those to whom it is given, against those to whom it is either not given or by whom it is so ungraciously received when given, since by the secret and righteous judgement of God it is not given them to accept it graciously?

Wherefore, my venerable lord and holy brother 2 cherished in the love of Christ, although you do an excellent service in writing on this question to the brethren before whom its supporters are in the habit of boasting of your friendship, yet this larger duty

tibi restat, ut non solum salubri severitate plectantur,
qui errorem illum Christiano infestissimum nomini
audent garrire liberius, sed etiam hi diligentissime
caveantur vigilantia pastorali propter infirmiores et
simpliciores dominicas oves, qui eum pressius quidem
atque timidius, sed tamen insusurrare non cessant,
penetrantes domos, sicut ait apostolus, et cetera
quae sequuntur, exercitata impietate facientes.
Nec illi neglegendi sunt, qui usque ad profundum
silentium supprimunt timore quod sentiunt, sed
tamen eandem perversitatem sentire non desinunt.
Nonnulli quippe eorum, antequam ipsa pestilentia
manifestissimo etiam sedis apostolicae iudicio damna-
retur, vobis innotescere potuerunt, quos nunc
repente reticuisse perspicitis nec, utrum sanati sint,
sciri potest, nisi cum non solum dogmata illa falsa
tacuerint, verum etiam illis vera contraria eo, quo
illa solent, studio defensaverint. Qui tamen lenius
sunt profecto tractandi ; quid enim eos terreri opus
est, quos satis territos ipsa taciturnitas monstrat ?
Nec ideo tamquam sani praetereundi sunt diligentia
medicinae, quorum vulnus in abdito est. Etsi enim
terrendi non sunt, tamen docendi sunt et, quantum
existimo, facilius possunt, dum in eis timor severitatis
doctorem adiuvat veritatis, ut opitulante domino

* 2 Tim. iii. 6-8.

awaits you of not only having punishment of wholesome severity administered to those who dare with
over-much freedom to rave about that error which is
such a dangerous challenge to the name of Christ, but
also for the sake of the Lord's weaker and more simple-
minded sheep of employing with all the vigilance of
a pastor the most careful safeguards against those who,
though in a stealthier and more covert manner, still
do not cease to whisper it, " creeping into houses," [a]
as the apostle says, and with practised ungodliness
doing the other things that he goes on to mention. Nor
should those be overlooked who under the restraint
of fear conceal their opinions under the deepest
silence, but yet do not cease to cherish the same perverted opinions. Some, indeed, of their party may
have attracted your attention before that pestilence
was denounced by the most explicit condemnation of
the Apostolic See itself, and may now, as you can
see, have suddenly become silent, so that it is impossible to ascertain whether they have been cured
of it unless they not only refrain from uttering those
false doctrines, but actually take up the defence of
the contrary doctrines with the same fervour they
showed in propounding error. These, however,
surely call for milder treatment : what need is there
to terrify them, when their very silence shows that
they are terrified enough ? At the same time, they
are not to be passed over and spared remedial attention, as though they were quite sound, because
their sore is hidden. For while they are not to be
terrified, yet they ought to be taught, and, in my
opinion, this process is easier while the fear they
have of severe measures assists him who teaches them
the truth. In this way, after they have learned

gratia eius intellecta atque dilecta etiam loquendo
expugnent, quod iam loqui non audent.

No. 44 (Ep. CXCII)

DOMINO VENERABILI NIMIUMQUE DESIDE-
RABILI SANCTO FRATRI ET CONDIACONO
CAELESTINO[a] AUGUSTINUS IN DOMINO
SALUTEM

1 Quamvis longe absens fuerim, quando per Proiec-
tum clericum ad me directa Hipponem sanctitatis
tuae scripta venerunt, tamen, posteaquam veni
eisque lectis rescriptorum debitorem me factum esse
cognovi, reddendi tempus opperiebar. Et ecce
subito profecturi a nobis carissimi fratris nostri
Albini acolithi gratissima occurrit occasio. De tua
igitur, quae mihi exoptatissima est, salute laetatus
sanctitati tuae salutationem debitam reddo. Semper
autem debeo caritatem, quae sola etiam reddita
semper detinet debitorem. Redditur enim, cum
inpenditur ; debetur autem, etiamsi reddita fuerit,
quia nullum est tempus, quando inpendenda iam non
sit. Nec, cum redditur, amittitur, sed potius reddendo multiplicatur ; habendo enim redditur, non
carendo. Et cum reddi non possit, nisi habeatur,
nec haberi potest, nisi reddatur ; immo etiam, cum

---

[a] Celestine was bishop of Rome from 422 to 432. He
took a prominent part in all the theological questions of the
time, and was especially active in opposing Pelagianism ;
in Britain the Pelagians had succeeded in winning much
support, so Celestine sent Germain of Auxerre and Palladius
to bring the Britons back to the orthodox faith. In 431,
the year after Augustine's death, he sent to the bishops of
Gaul a famous letter defining the Church's teaching on the

through the Lord's assistance to understand and
love His grace, they may by their utterance refute
the errors which they no longer dare to utter.

No. 44 (Ep. CXCII)

(A.D. 418)

TO CELESTINE,[a] MY REVERED LORD, MY HOLY
BROTHER AND FELLOW-DEACON GREATLY
LONGED FOR, AUGUSTINE SENDS GREETING
IN THE LORD

I was far away when the clerk Projectus brought the 1
letters your Holiness sent to me at Hippo, yet as soon
as I returned and read them and realized that I was
in your debt, I was awaiting a chance of paying my
debt, when lo ! the unexpected departure from us of
our well-beloved brother, the acolyte Albinus, has provided a most welcome opportunity. Rejoicing, therefore, in your good health, which is the object of my
earnest desire, I return your Holiness the salutation
I was owing you. But I always owe you love, the
only debt which, after being repaid, still keeps one a
debtor. For it is repaid when it is expended, but is
still owing even if it has been repaid, since there is no
time when it does not require to be expended. Nor
is it lost when it is repaid, but rather by repayment it is multiplied, for it is repaid by retaining
it, not by getting quit of it. And since it cannot be
repaid unless it be retained, so it cannot be retained
unless it be repaid—nay rather, when a man repays it,

question of grace. Augustine again addresses him in No. 47,
after his elevation to the papal chair.

redditur ab homine, crescit in homine et tanto maior
adquiritur, quanto plurius redditur. Quo modo
autem negatur amicis, quae debetur et inimicis?
Sed inimicis cauta inpenditur, amicis secura rependitur. Agit tamen, quantum potest, ut ab his
etiam, quibus pro malis bona retribuit, id recipiat,
quod inpendit. Optamus quippe fieri amicum, quem
veraciter diligimus inimicum, quia non eum diligimus,
nisi velimus bonum; quod utique non erit, nisi
amiserit inimicitiarum malum.

2   Non ergo sic inpenditur caritas ut pecunia. Excepto enim, quod illa inpendendo minuitur, haec
augetur, etiam illo inter se differunt, quod pecuniam
cui dederimus, tunc ei benivolentiores erimus, si
recipere non quaeramus, non autem potest esse verus
caritatis inpensor, nisi fuerit benignus exactor,
quoniam pecunia cum recipitur, accedit cui datur,
sed recedit a quo datur, caritas vero non solum apud
eum crescit qui hanc ab eo, quem diligit, exigit,
etiamsi non recipit, sed etiam ille, a quo eam recipit,
tunc incipit habere, cum reddit. Proinde, domine
frater, mutuam tibi caritatem libens reddo gaudensque
recipio; quam recipio, adhuc repeto, quam reddo,
adhuc debeo. Unum enim magistrum, apud quem
condiscipuli sumus, per eius apostolum dociles audire

---

[a] This and the next paragraph are characteristic of Augustine's fondness for seizing on one word or idea and pursuing
it through various arguments; for earlier examples see No.
24, where he plays on the words *flores* and *florere*, No. 28,
where he plays on the words " liberal studies " and " liberty,"
and No. 29, where he follows the same thought as here. The

it increases in him, and the more lavishly he expends it, the more of it he gains. But how can that be refused to friends which is owing even to enemies ? To enemies, however, it is paid out with hesitation, while to friends it is paid back with confidence. Nevertheless, it makes every possible effort to recover what it has expended, even from those to whom it renders good for evil. For we desire to have as a friend the man whom we truly love as an enemy, because we do not love him unless we wish him good, and that cannot be the case unless he gives up the evil of enmity.[a]

Love, then, is not expended like money, for in **2** addition to the fact that money is diminished by expenditure and love is increased, they differ in this too, that we give greater evidence of good-will towards anyone if we do not seek the return of money we have given him ; whereas no one can sincerely expend love unless he tenderly insist on being repaid ; for when money is received, it is so much gain to the recipient but so much loss to the donor ; love, on the other hand, is not only augmented in the man who demands it back from the person he loves, even when he does not receive it, but the person who returns it actually begins to possess it only when he pays it back.

Wherefore, my lord and brother, I willingly repay to you, and gladly receive back from you, the love we owe each other, and that which I receive back, I still claim ; that which I repay, I still owe. For it is our duty in all teachableness to hearken to our one Master, before Whom we are fellow-pupils, when He speaks

thought is a favourite with him ; *cf. In Ps.* xxxvi., *Serm.* 3. 18 "nos caritas debitores semper tenet ; illa enim una est quae, etsi quotidie redditur, semper debetur," etc.

debemus praecipientem ac dicentem : *Nemini quicquam debeatis, nisi ut invicem diligatis.*[a]

No. 45 (Ep. CC)

DOMINO INLUSTRI ET MERITO PRAESTAN-
TISSIMO ATQUE IN CHRISTI DILECTIONE
CARISSIMO FILIO VALERIO AUGUSTINUS
IN DOMINO SALUTEM[b]

1 Cum diu moleste haberem, quod aliquotiens
scripserim et nulla tuae sublimitatis rescripta
meruerim, repente epistulas tres tuae benignitatis
accepi, unam non ad me solum datam per coepiscopum meum Vindemialem et non longe post
per conpresbyterum Firmum duas. Qui vir sanctus
nobisque, ut ab illo scire potuisti, familiarissima
caritate coniunctus, multa nobiscum de tua excellentia conloquendo et veraciter insinuando, qualem
te *in Christi visceribus* noverit, non solum eas quas
memoratus episcopus vel quas ipse adtulit, sed etiam
illas quas non accepisse nos querebamur, litteras
vicit. Et ideo de te narratio eius suavior nobis erat,

---

[a] Rom. xiii. 8. With the preceding words compare *Disc.
Chr.* 14. 15 " Christus est qui docet. . . . Schola ipsius in
terra est "; *In Ps.* xxxiv., *Serm.* 1. 1 " in cuius schola condiscipuli sumus "; *In Ps.* 126. 3 " sub illo uno magistro in
hac schola vobiscum condiscipuli sumus "; *Serm.* 134. 1
" omnes nos unum Magistrum habere et sub illo condiscipulos
esse," 261. 2, 270. 1.

[b] Valerius was Count of Africa, an earnest Christian and a
firm supporter of orthodoxy against heretical error. He had
adopted the ascetic rule of conjugal continence, and of this
Augustine expresses warm approval, sending at the same time
the first book of his work *De Concupiscentia et Gratia.* To

through His apostle and bids us " owe no man anything but to love one another." [a]

No. 45 (Ep. CC)

(A.D. 418)

TO VALERIUS,[b] MY DISTINGUISHED AND JUST-
    LY RENOWNED LORD AND SON WELL-
    BELOVED IN THE LOVE OF CHRIST, AUGUS-
    TINE SENDS GREETING IN THE LORD

I have long been disappointed that, after writing 1
several times, I have not had the honour of receiving
any reply from your Excellency. Now quite unexpectedly I have received three letters from your
Benignity, one of them, not exclusively to me, by
the hands of my fellow-bishop Vindemialis,[c] and not
long afterwards two by the hands of my fellow-priest
Firmus.[d] That holy man, with whom I have ties of
the most intimate and affectionate nature, as you may
have heard from him, talked at length to me about your
Excellency and gave me such a true conception of you,
as he found you in " the tender mercies of Christ," [e] that
he outdid not only the letters brought to me by the
afore-mentioned bishop or by himself, but even those
I was complaining of not receiving. And his account
of you was all the more pleasant in that he told me

this book a reply was written by Julian of Eclanum (see p. 188
above), accusing Augustine of denying the divine institution
of marriage ; Augustine thereupon added a second book re-
futing the charge. Valerius is addressed also in Ep. ccvi., a
recommendation of a bishop called Felix.

   [c] Not otherwise known.
   [d] See above, p. 334.   [e] Phil. i. 8.

quia ea dicebat, quae ipse non possis ne quidem me inquirente rescribere, ne tuarum laudum, quod sancta scriptura prohibet, fieres praedicator.[a] Quamquam et ego verear haec ad te scribere, ne suspicionem adulantis incurram, domine inlustris et merito praestantissime atque in Christi dilectione carissime fili.

2   Laudes itaque tuas in Christo, sive magis in te laudes Christi, vide quid mihi delectationis et laetitiae fuit audire ab illo qui nec fallere me posset propter fidem suam, et eas ignorare non posset propter amicitiam tuam. Sed alia et ab aliis etsi non tam multa vel certa, verum tamen audivimus, fides tua quam sit sana et catholica, quam pia expectatio futurorum, quae dei fratrumque dilectio, quam non superbe sapias in excelsis honoribus nec speres in incerto divitiarum sed in deo vivo, et dives sis in operibus bonis,[b] quam sit domus tua requies solaciumque sanctorum et terror impiorum, quanta tibi cura sit, ne quis insidietur membris Christi coopertus velamine nominis Christi sive in veteribus eius sive in recentioribus inimicis, quamque sis eorundem inimicorum saluti providus, infestus errori. Haec atque huius modi, ut dixi, et ab aliis solemus audire, sed nunc ea per supra dictum fratrem plura et testatiora cognovimus.

3   Porro autem de pudicitia coniugali, ut eam quoque

---

[a] Prov. xxvii. 2 "Let another man praise thee, and not thine own mouth."
[b] 1 Tim. vi. 17-18.

those things which, for fear of becoming **addicted to** singing your own praises (which Holy Scripture forbids[a]), you yourself cannot write back to me even when I pointedly ask them.   In fact I myself am afraid to compliment you on them when I write to you, my distinguished and justly renowned lord and well-beloved son in the love of Christ, in case I incur the suspicion of flattering you.

So you can just imagine what a pleasure and delight it was to me to hear your praises in Christ, or rather the praises of Christ in you, from one whose own truthfulness prevents him from deceiving me and whose friendship with you provides him with a knowledge of them. Yet others too have furnished me with other information, which though not so full or so sure, was still worth hearing : how sound and catholic your faith is, how godly your hope of the world to come, what love you have towards God and towards the brethren, how humble-minded you are amid your high honours, and how your hope is not placed in the uncertainty of riches but in the living God,[b] how abounding you are in good works, and what a rest and consolation your home is to the holy and what a terror to the ungodly, what zeal you exhibit to keep any who skulk under the cloak of the name of Christ, whether they be His old or His newer enemies, from laying snares for the members of Christ ; and yet how careful you are to procure the salvation of these same enemies, while opposing their errors. These and such-like things, as I said, I am in the habit of hearing from others too, but now I have had much fuller and surer testimony to them through the above-mentioned brother.

Further, about your conjugal continence, what **3**

in te laudare et amare possimus, quid audiremus nisi
ab aliquo interiore familiari tuo, qui vitam tuam non
in superficie sed penitus nosset ? De hoc itaque tuo
bono, dei dono, me quoque delectat familiarius et
aliquanto diutius loqui tecum. Scio me non esse
oneri tibi, si aliquid prolixum mitto, quod legendo
diutius sis nobiscum. Nam et hoc comperi, quod
inter tuas multas magnasque curas facile ac libenter
legas, nostrisque opusculis, etiam quae ad alios con-
scripsimus, si qua in manus tuas venire potuerunt,
admodum delecteris ; quanto magis, quod ad te
scribitur, ubi tamquam praesenti loquar, et adver-
tere dignaris attentius et accipere gratius ! Ab hac
ergo epistula perge ad librum, quem simul misi, qui
tuae reverentiae, et cur conscriptus sit et cur ad te
potissimum missus, ipse suo principio commodius
intimabit.

No. 46 (Ep. CCIII)

DOMINO INSIGNI ET PRAESTANTISSIMO AC DESIDERANTISSIMO FILIO LARGO AUGUSTINUS IN DOMINO SALUTEM

Accepi litteras eximietatis tuae, quibus me ad te
petis ut scriberem. Quod quidem non desiderares,
nisi et hoc, quod me posse scribere existimasti,

---

[a] This jingle with *bonum* and *donum* is a favourite one
with Augustine: *Conf.* i. 20. 31 "Dei mei dona sunt . . . et
bona sunt"; *ib.* x. 4. 5; *In Ps.* 118, *Serm.* 17. 1 "quando
ergo delectat bonum, magnum est Dei donum"; *Civ. Dei*,
xv. 4 "haec bona sunt et sine dubio Dei dona sunt"; *ib.*
xv. 22 ; *Grat. et Arb.* 6. 15 "si autem bona sunt, Dei dona
sunt"; *Epp.* cx. 4 and ccxi. 3.

[b] Largus is probably the proconsul of that name in Africa,
415, 418, and 419.

information could I have to be in a position to praise and love that too in you, save from someone intimately familiar with you, who knew your life not on the surface, but within ? So, since you are thus, by God's blessing, good possessing,[a] I too take pleasure in talking with you more intimately and at rather greater length. I know I shall not weary you if I send you something comprehensive, the reading of which will keep you all the longer in my company. For I have learned too that among your many arduous duties you are ready and glad to read my little books, and take considerable delight in them, when they happen to come into your hands, even if they are addressed to others ; how much greater should be your pleasure in receiving one addressed to yourself, in which I speak to you as though you were present, and how much more thorough the attention you kindly bestow upon it ! From this letter, then, pass on to the book that accompanies it ; why it was written and why it was especially sent to you, your Reverence will more conveniently find out from the opening chapter.

No. 46 (Ep. CCIII)

(A.D. 420)

TO MY NOBLE AND MOST DISTINGUISHED LORD, LARGUS,[b] MY SON MUCH LONGED FOR, AUGUSTINE SENDS GREETING IN THE LORD

I have received your Excellency's letter, in which you ask me to write to you. This you would not desire, did you not believe that what you thought I would write to you would be acceptable and pleasant

349

gratum haberes atque iucundum, id autem est, ut
vana saeculi huius, si inexperta concupisti, experta
contemnas. Fallax est enim in eis suavitas et in-
fructuosus labor et perpetuus timor et periculosa
sublimitas, initium sine providentia et finis cum
paenitentia. Ita se habent omnia, quae in ista
mortalitatis aerumna cupidius quam prudentius ap-
petuntur. Alia est autem spes piorum, alius laboris
fructus, alia periculorum merces. Nam in hoc mundo
non timere, non dolere, non laborare, non periclitari
inpossibile est ; sed plurimum interest, qua causa,
qua expectatione, quo termino quisque ista patiatur.
Ego quidem cum amatores saeculi huius intueor,
nescio quando possit esse ad eorum animos sanandos
opportuna sapientia. Quando enim res velut pro-
speras habent, fastu respuunt salubres monitus et
quasi anilem reputant cantilenam ; quando autem
in adversis anguntur, magis cogitant evadere unde
ad praesens anguntur, quam capere unde curentur
et unde perveniant ubi angi omnino non possunt.
Aliquando tamen quidam cordis aures admovent
atque adhibent veritati rarius inter prospera, crebrius inter adversa, sed tamen pauci sunt, ita enim
praedicti sunt, inter quos te esse cupio, quia veraciter diligo, domine insignis et praestantissime ac
desiderantissime fili. Haec admonitio tibi sit mea
resalutatio, quia, etsi te deinceps talia perpeti qualia

---

a The phrase *cordis aures* occurs first in Tertullian (*De
An.* 9), then in Juvencus, 2. 812. It is not uncommon in
Augustine (*Conf.* i. 5, iv. 5. 10, *In Ps.* 48, *Serm.* 1, 2 ; *In
Ioan. Ev.* 1. 15, etc.), from whom it passes into the Benedic-
tine Rule and Gregory the Great's writings. Similarly
Augustine often speaks of the *oculus cordis* (*Serm. Dom. in
Monte,* ii. 1. 1, *In Ioan. Ev.* 14. 12, 17. 1, 18. 6, etc.).
350

—in other words, if you longed for the vanities of this world while they were unknown to you, you scorn them now they are known, for the charm in them is illusory, the toil unrewarded, the anxiety unremitting, the uplifting dangerous ; man seeks them at first without reflection and abandons them at last with remorse. So it is with all the things that are sought in the tribulation of this mortal life with more eagerness than reflection, but it is far different with the hope of the godly; different with the reward of their toil, different too with the outcome of their perils. For in this world fear and grief, toil and peril, are unavoidable, but it is of the utmost importance for what cause, with what hope, and to what end a man endures those things. For my part, when I look upon those who love this world, I know not at what moment wisdom can most opportunely undertake the healing of their souls, for when things apparently are prosperous with them, they scornfully disdain her wholesome warnings and deem them but a kind of old wives' song ; but when they are in the pangs of adversity, they rather think of escaping the source of their present pangs than of seizing the things that may provide a cure and a haven of refuge, in which their pangs will be completely prevented. At times, however (though these are less frequent in prosperity and more frequent in adversity), some of them turn the ears of their heart [a] to apply them to the truth, yet these are few, for so it was foretold. [b] Among them I desire you to be, my noble and most distinguished lord and son much longed for, because I love you truly. Let this counsel to you be my answer to your letter. for, though I

[b] Matt. vii. 13 " narrow is the way . . . and few there be that find it."

pertulisti, plus tamen nolo haec ipsa te sine aliqua
in melius vitae mutatione fuisse perpessum.

No. 47 (Ep. CCIX)

DOMINO BEATISSIMO ET DEBITA CARITATE
VENERANDO SANCTO PAPAE CAELESTINO
AUGUSTINUS IN DOMINO SALUTEM

1   Primum gratulationem reddo meritis tuis, quod te
in illa sede dominus deus noster sine ulla, sicut
audivimus, plebis suae discissione constituit. Deinde
insinuo sanctitati tuae quae sint circa nos, ut non
solum orando pro nobis, verum etiam consulendo
et opitulando subvenias. In magna quippe tribulatione positus haec ad tuam beatitudinem scripta
direxi, quoniam volens prodesse quibusdam in nostra
vicinitate membris Christi, magnam illis cladem
inprovidus et incautus ingessi.

2   Fussala dicitur Hipponiensi territorio confine

ᵃ See above, p. 340.

ᵇ For the word *papa* see note a on p. 302.

ᶜ Augustine here appeals to Celestine to reconsider a case
on which his predecessor Boniface had earlier pronounced
judgement. Later, the African bishops decided not to allow
appeals from Africa to Rome, and when in 426 Celestine
wrote on behalf of a priest deposed from office, they pointed
out that the African Church retained the right of judging its
own causes (*Cod. Eccl. Cath.* cxxv. " non provocent nisi ad
Africana concilia vel ad primates provinciarum suarum ; ad
transmarina autem qui putaverit appellandum, a nullo intra
Africam in communionem suscipiatur ").

ᵈ The exact site of Fussala is unknown, but it probably lay
to the south or south-east, for on that side the boundary of
the commune of Hippo extended to about 40 miles. A later
letter (Ep. ccxxiv.) speaks of a priest of Fussala. It was still
a bishopric in 484, and a passage of Procopius mentions the

should not wish you to endure henceforward such sufferings as you have endured in the past, my wish is yet greater that you may not have endured them without some change of your life for the better.

No. 47 (Ep. CCIX)

(A.D. 423)

TO CELESTINE,[a] MY LORD MOST SAINTLY AND HOLY FATHER [b] REVERED WITH ALL DUE AFFECTION, AUGUSTINE SENDS GREETING IN THE LORD

First of all I pay my tribute of congratulation to 1 your merits that the Lord our God has placed you in that apostolic chair with (as we are informed) no division among His people. In the next place, I lay before your Holiness the state of affairs with us, so that you may come to our assistance not only by praying for us, but also by giving us your counsel and assistance,[c] for I am writing to your Holiness under deep affliction : by my lack of foresight and caution I have brought a great disaster upon certain members of Christ in our neighbourhood, though I had intended only their benefit.

Fussala [d] is the name of a small town not far from 2

construction of a fortress there under Justinian. In *Civ. Dei* xxii. 8. 6 is mention of a private estate near Fussala, on which the owner had built a chapel in which he placed soil from the Holy Sepulchre. The bishop mentioned below, Antoninus, was present at the Council of Mileve in 416 (Ep. clxxvi., title), but in view of his misdeeds Augustine assumed control himself (§ 5, *cf.* Ep. ccxxiv.), and retained it till his death. *Castellum* is defined by Augustine himself in *De Consensu Evang.* iii. 25. 71 : " castellum . . . non absurde accipimus etiam villam potuisse appellari."

castellum. Antea ibi numquam episcopus fuit, sed
simul cum contigua sibi regione ad parochiam
Hipponiensis ecclesiae pertinebat. Paucos habebat
illa terra catholicos ; ceteras plebes illic in magna
multitudine hominum constitutas Donatistarum error
miserabiliter obtinebat, ita ut in eodem castello
nullus esset omnino catholicus. Actum est in dei
misericordia, ut omnia ipsa loca unitati ecclesiae
cohaererent ; per quantos labores et pericula nostra,
longum est explicare, ita ut ibi presbyteri qui eis
congregandis a nobis primitus constituti sunt, ex-
poliarentur, caederentur, debilitarentur, excaeca-
rentur, occiderentur. Quorum tamen passiones
inutiles ac steriles non fuerunt, unitatis illic securitate
perfecta. Sed quod ab Hippone memoratum castellum milibus quadraginta seiungitur, cum in eis
regendis et eorum reliquiis licet exiguis colligendis,
quae in utroque sexu oberrabant non minaces ulterius
sed fugaces, me viderem latius quam oportebat
extendi, nec adhibendae sufficere diligentiae, quam
certissima ratione adhiberi debere cernebam, episcopum ibi ordinandum constituendumque curavi.

3 Quod ut fieret, aptum loco illi congruumque
requirebam, qui et Punica lingua esset instructus.
Et habebam, de quo cogitabam, paratum presbyterum, propter quem ordinandum sanctum senem qui
tunc primatum Numidiae gerebat, de longinquo ut
veniret, rogans litteris impetravi. Quo iam praesente omniumque in re tanta suspensis animis, ad

---

a *Parochia* continues to mean a " diocese " and not a
" parish " at least as late as the time of Bede, although the
Greek word is used even for a country congregation as early
as the Council of Chalcedon, A.D. 451 (see Bright, *Notes on
the Canons of the first four General Councils*, pp. 51-53).

b That is, the Donatists.

the district of Hippo ; formerly there was never a bishop there, but along with the adjoining country it belonged to the diocese *a* of the church of Hippo. Of Catholics that region had but few ; all the other congregations there, located among a fairly dense population, were under the wretched influence of the Donatist error, so that in this town there was no Catholic at all. In the mercy of God it came about that all those districts became attached to the unity of the Church ; it would take too long to tell you what toil and danger that involved us in, such that the priests there, who were originally appointed by us to gather them *b* together, were robbed, beaten, maimed, blinded, and killed ; yet their sufferings were not ineffectual or unfruitful, for by them unity was there securely achieved. But since the aforesaid town is forty miles distant from Hippo, and in the superintendence of the people and the gathering together of the remnants, however small, of the wandering bands, composed of both sexes, who were no longer threatening others but fleeing for their own safety, I saw myself drawn farther afield than was fitting, and unable to exercise that careful oversight which I perceived and was thoroughly convinced should be exercised, I arranged that a bishop should be ordained and appointed there.

For this purpose I needed a man fitted and suitable 3 for the place, one, too, possessing a knowledge of Punic, and I had in my mind a priest ready for the post, for whose ordination I wrote asking the holy Senior who at the time held the office of Primate of Numidia to make the long journey to us, and he agreed. When he was already with us and the minds of all were exalted in expectation of the solemn cere-

horam nos ille, qui mihi paratus videbatur, omni modo
resistendo destituit. Ego autem, qui utique, sicut
exitus docuit, differre potius debui quam periculosum
praecipitare negotium, dum nolo gravissimum et
sanctissimum senem ad nos usque fatigatum sine
effectu propter quem venerat tam longe, ad propria
remeare, obtuli non petentibus quendam adulescentem Antoninum, qui mecum tunc erat, in monasterio
quidem a nobis a parvula aetate nutritum, sed
praeter lectionis officium nullis clericatus gradibus
et laboribus notum. At illi miseri, quod futurum
fuerat ignorantes, offerenti eum mihi oboedientis-
sime crediderunt. Quid plura ? Factum est ; esse
illis episcopus coepit.

4   Quid faciam ? Nolo apud tuam venerationem
gravare quem nutriendum collegi, nolo deserere
quos colligendos timoribus et doloribus parturivi, et
quo modo utrumque agam, reperire non possum.
Res quippe ad tantum scandalum venit, ut cum eo
hic apud nos causas dicerent, qui de illius episcopatu
suscipiendo tamquam bene sibi consulentibus ob-
temperaverant nobis. In quibus causis cum stupro-
rum crimina capitalia, quae non ab ipsis quibus

ᵃ *Ad horam,* " in our hour of need," " at the critical
moment," sometimes simply " at the time," as in the next
letter, § 2 " ad horam contristetur," *Ep.* lxxi. 3 " mihi ad
horam codex defuit," *Cat. Rud.* ii. 4 " hilaritas ad horam
ut adsit," *Civ. Dei* i. 31 " [subselliis] ad horam congestis,"
etc.

ᵇ It will be observed that this Antoninus was ordained *per
saltum,* elevated to the rank of bishop from being merely a
reader, responsible for the sacred books, without passing
through the intermediate ranks. This was forbidden in the
Eastern Church at the Council of Sardica, A.D. 343, but it
continued in the Latin Church until about the ninth century.
Further, it is to be noticed that Augustine did not himself

mony, at the last minute [a] the man who had appeared to me to be ready left me in the lurch by absolutely opposing our plans. As the event proved, I ought certainly to have postponed a matter fraught with such dangers, instead of hurrying it on ; however, not wanting the very eminent and holy Senior, after being at the trouble of coming all the way to us, to go back home without accomplishing the purpose for which he had made such a long journey, I put forward, without waiting to be asked, a certain young man Antoninus, who was with me at the time. He had been brought up by me in the monastery from his earliest years, but beyond holding the office of reader, he had no experience of any of the ranks or labours of clerical life ; yet those unfortunate people, not knowing what lay before them, very dutifully acquiesced in my offer of him. Why say more ? The deed was done ; he began his career as their bishop.[b]

What am I to do ? I do not want to charge before 4 your Reverence one whom I gathered in and fostered, nor do I want to abandon those for whose in-gathering I travailed with anxiety and pain ; and how I am to do both I cannot discover. The matter has indeed come to such a scandalous pass that those who yielded to my wish to have him undertake episcopal office, in the belief that it was to their own best interest, have approached me here and laid charges against him. Among these charges the most serious offence of gross immorality made against him, not by those over whom

consecrate Antoninus, but sought the services of his Primate. The co-operation of other bishops in episcopal consecration was expressly enjoined by the Council of Nicaea, which prescribes three as a general rule (Canon IV.).

episcopus erat, sed ab aliis quibusdam obiecta fuerant,
probari minime potuissent, atque ab eis quae in-
vidiosissime iactabantur, videretur esse purgatus,
tam miserandus factus est et nobis et aliis, ut,
quicquid a castellanis et illius regionis hominibus de
intolerabili dominatione, de rapinis et diversis op-
pressionibus et contritionibus obiciebatur, nequaquam nobis tale videretur, ut propter hoc vel propter
simul cuncta congesta episcopatu eum putaremus
esse privandum, sed restituenda quae probarentur
ablata.

5 Denique sententias nostras sic temperavimus, ut
salvo episcopatu non tamen omnino inpunita re-
linquerentur, quae non deberent vel eidem ipsi
deinceps iterumque facienda vel ceteris imitanda
proponi. Honorem itaque integrum servavimus iu-
veni corrigendo, sed corripiendo minuimus potestatem, ne scilicet eis praeesset ulterius, cum quibus
sic egerat, ut dolore iusto eum sibi praeesse ferre
omnino non possent et cum suo illiusque periculo in
aliquod scelus forsitan erupturam inpatientiam sui
doloris ostenderent. Quorum talis animus etiam
tunc, quando cum eis de illo episcopi egerunt, evidenter apparuit, cum iam vir spectabilis Celer, de
cuius adversum se praepotenti administratione con-
questus est, nullam gerat vel in Africa vel uspiam
potestatem.

6 Sed quid multis morer? Conlabora, obsecro,
nobiscum, pietate venerabili domine beatissime et

    ᵃ Celer became proconsul of Africa in 429, but he is
known from Augustine's works from soon after 400. He
is addressed in Epp. lvi. and lvii., which show him to have been
a Donatist. In Ep. cxxxix. 2 mention is made of the opening
of Donatist churches on Celer's estates near Hippo.

he was bishop, but by certain others, was found to be quite unproved, and, apparently cleared of the most malicious of the imputations made against him, he was reduced to what we and others thought such a pitiful state that whatever complaint the town's-people and those of the district made about his intolerable tyranny, his rapacity and oppression and abuses of various kinds, seemed to me by no means so grievous that, because of it or of all of them put together, we should reckon it necessary to deprive him of his office as bishop; it seemed enough to make him restore the things that were proved to have been taken away.

In short, I so tempered my judgement with mercy **5** that he was not deprived of office, although his faults were yet not left altogether unpunished; they were not of a kind either to be repeated by him in the future or held up to others as a model. In correcting the young man, we therefore left him his rank unimpaired, but as a punishment we limited his authority, so that he should no longer be over those whom he had treated in such a way that from justified resentment it might have been impossible for them to endure having him over them at all; they might perhaps show their impatience and resentment by breaking out into some misdeed fraught with danger to themselves and to him. That this was the state of their mind even at the time when the bishops were discussing his case with them appeared very clearly, although by now the eminent Celer,[a] of whose very influential interference against him he complained, exercises no authority either in Africa or anywhere else.

But why make a long story of it? I beseech you **6** to lend me your assistance, my saintly lord venerable

debita caritate venerande sancte papa, et iube tibi
quae directa sunt, omnia recitari. Vide episcopatum qualiter gesserit, quem ad modum iudicio nostro
usque adeo consenserit communione privatus, nisi
prius Fussalensibus omnia redderentur, iam postea
citra acta aestimatis rebus solidos seposuerit, ut ei
communio redderetur, quam versuta suasione sanctum
senem primatem nostrum gravissimum virum, ut ei
cuncta crederet, quem velut omni modo inculpatum
venerando papae Bonifatio commendaret, induxerit,
et cetera quae a me quid opus est recoli, cum
memoratus venerabilis senex ad tuam sanctimoniam
universa rettulerit ?

7   In illis autem multiplicibus gestis, quibus de illo
nostrum iudicium continetur, magis deberem vereri
ne tibi minus severe, quam oporteret, iudicasse
videamur, nisi scirem vos tam propensos ad misericordiam, ut non solum nobis, quia illi pepercimus,
verum etiam ipsi existimetis esse parcendum. Sed
ille, quod a nobis aut benigne aut remisse factum
est, in praescriptionem vertere atque usurpare
conatur ; clamat : " Aut in mea cathedra sedere
debui aut episcopus esse non debui," quasi nunc
sedeat nisi in sua. Propter hoc enim loca illa eidem
dimissa atque permissa sunt, in quibus et prius episcopus erat, ne in alienam cathedram contra statuta

---

for your piety and holy father revered with all due affection, and give orders that all the documents sent you be read to you. See how he conducted himself in his office as bishop, how, when deprived of communion until after everything had been restored to the people of Fussala, he so far accepted our decision, then later set aside a sum in compensation for the things, quite apart from the legal decision, so that he might regain the privilege of communion ; see too with what crafty persuasion he led the holy Senior, that very excellent man our Primate, to believe all his statements and to recommend him to the revered Pope Boniface as one in every way blameless. What need is there for me to rehearse all the rest, since the venerable Senior afore-mentioned will have reported the affair to your Holiness in all its details ?

From the numerous minutes, however, that contain **7** our judgement upon him, I should rather fear to appear to you less severe in judging him than I ought to have been, if I did not know that you are so prone to mercy as to reckon it your duty to spare the man himself and us as well for sparing him. But what we did, either from kindness or from carelessness, he is now trying to turn to account and employ as a legal objection. His cry is, " Either I ought to be sitting in my own episcopal chair or else I ought not to be a bishop at all," as if he were now sitting in any chair [a] but his own. For it was for this very reason that those districts in which he was bishop before were set apart and set under his care that he might not be said to have been illegally transferred to another

the word came to mean the building in which the bishop's throne stood.

patrum translatus inlicite diceretur. Aut vero quisquam ita esse debet sive severitatis sive lenitatis exactor, ut, qui non visi fuerint episcopatus honore privandi, nullo modo in eis aliquid vindicetur, aut in quibus aliquid visum fuerit vindicandum, episcopatus honore priventur ?

8 Existunt exempla ipsa sede apostolica iudicante vel aliorum iudicata firmante quosdam pro culpis quibusdam nec episcopali spoliatos honore nec relictos omnimodis inpunitos. Quae ut a nostris temporibus remotissima non requiram, recentia memorabo. Clamet Priscus, provinciae Caesariensis episcopus : " Aut ad primatum locus sicut ceteris et mihi patere debuit aut episcopatus mihi remanere non debuit." Clamet alius eiusdem provinciae Victor episcopus, cui relicto in eadem poena in qua etiam Priscus fuit, nusquam nisi in dioecesi eius ab aliquo communicatur episcopo, clamet, inquam : " Aut ubique communicare debui aut etiam in meis locis communicare non debui." Clamet tertius eiusdem provinciae Lauren-

---

a Translation from one see to another was definitely forbidden by the Council of Nicaea (Canon XV.) and later Councils.

b His point is that there should be some form of punishment for offenders, midway between the extremes of complete immunity and complete deposition.

c Priscus was bishop of Quiza in 411. Victor's see is not known, but Laurentius was bishop of Icosium, the modern town of Algiers, and as such he appears at the Synod of Carthage in 419. Further particulars of their cases are wanting. One or other of them is probably the case which took Augustine to Mauretania about 418 ("litteras . . . quas ad Mauretaniam Caesariensem misisti, me apud Caesaream praesente venerunt, quo nos iniuncta nobis a venerabili papa Zosimo apostolicae sedis episcopo ecclesiastica necessitas traxerat," Ep. cxc. 1).

see contrary to the statutes of the Fathers.[a] Or
should anyone be so extreme an advocate of severity or
of gentleness as either to exact absolutely no punishment from those who do not seem to merit deprivation
of the honour of the bishop's office, or on the other
hand to deprive of the honour of that office those who
have been judged to deserve some punishment ?[b]

There are on record among the judgements given **8**
by the Apostolic See itself, or its confirmations of the
judgements of others, precedents for not depriving
certain bishops, tried for certain offences, of their
episcopal rank, and yet for not leaving them altogether unpunished. Not to seek out examples that
are far from our own day, I shall mention some of
recent date. Hear the protest of Priscus,[c] a bishop
of the province of Caesarea[d] : " Either the office of
Primate ought to be open to me too, or else I ought
not to retain my episcopal office." Let the protest
be heard of another bishop of the same province,
Victor, who when left in the same fault as Priscus, is
not allowed to receive communion from any bishop
unless within his own diocese—let his protest, I
repeat, be heard : " Either I ought to communicate
anywhere, or else I ought not to communicate even
in my own district." Let the protest be heard of a
third bishop of the same province, Laurentius, and

---

[d] Caesarea was one of the two portions of Mauretania,
which was incorporated in the Empire by Caligula in A.D. 40.
About 292 Diocletian divided Caesarea into two, giving the
new portion the name of *Mauretania Sitifiensis*, roughly
corresponding to the western part of modern Algeria, while
the other, Caesarea, corresponds to the eastern part of
Morocco. Caesarea takes its name from the town of Iol, a
Phoenician colony, which Juba II. called Caesarea in honour
of Julius Caesar. The modern name is Cherchel.

tius episcopus et prorsus huius vocibus clamet : " Aut
in cathedra, cui ordinatus sum, sedere debui aut
episcopus esse non debui." Sed quis ista vituperet,
nisi qui parum adtendit nec inulta omnia relinquenda
nec uno modo omnia vindicanda ?

9 Quia ergo pastorali vigilique cautela beatissimus
papa Bonifatius in epistula sua posuit de Antonino
loquens episcopo et ait : " Si ordinem rerum nobis
fideliter indicavit," accipe nunc ordinem rerum,
quem ille in suo libello reticuit, ac deinde, quae post
eius sanctae memoriae viri in Africa lectas litteras
gesta sunt, et subveni hominibus opem tuam in
Christi misericordia multo avidius quam ille poscenti-
bus, a cuius inquietudine desiderant liberari. Iudicia
quippe illis et publicas potestates et militares impetus tamquam executuros apostolicae sedis sententiam sive ipse sive rumores creberrimi comminantur,
ut miseri homines Christiani catholici graviora
formident a catholico episcopo, quam, cum essent
haeretici, a catholicorum imperatorum legibus for-
midabant. Non sinas ista fieri, obsecro te per
Christi sanguinem, per apostoli Petri memoriam, qui
Christianorum praepositos populorum monuit, ne
violenter dominentur in fratres. Ego Fussalenses
catholicos filios in Christo meos et Antoninum epi-

ª These rumours were encouraged by the fact that the
representations of the African bishops to Pope Celestine were
not yet made or known. Besides asking the Pope not to
allow appeals from Africa or to receive those excommunicated
in Africa, the bishops asked him not to send his clerks to
carry out his sentences, lest the Church should appear to
be introducing " the smoky vanity of the world " (" fumosum
typhum saeculi ") (*Cod. Eccl. Afr.* No. cxxxviii). The letter
of an African Council to Pope Celestine: " deinceps ad
vestras aures hinc venientes non facilius admittatis, nec a
nobis excommunicatos ultra velitis excipere; . . . executores

heard indeed in the very words of Antoninus: "Either I ought to sit in the see to which I was ordained, or else I ought not to be a bishop at all." But who would find fault with those sentences, except one who does not reflect that, on the one hand, all these offences must not be left unpunished, and on the other, that they are not all to be punished in the same way?

In his letter about Antoninus, addressed to his 9 bishop, the saintly Pope Boniface, with the vigilance and caution of a true pastor, put the words, " Provided that he has faithfully revealed the sequence of events to us." So now accept this statement of the sequence of events which he in his memorandum passed over in silence, and further, of what happened after the letter of that man of blessed memory was read in Africa ; do you come to the aid of men who implore your aid in Christ's mercy more earnestly than did he, from whose harassment they seek deliverance. For threats are being made to the people, either by Antoninus himself or by oft-repeated rumours,[a] of legal processes and public officials and military attacks that are to enforce the decision of the Apostolic See ; in consequence, those unfortunate people, though Catholic Christians, are in dread of heavier punishment from a Catholic bishop than what they feared from the laws of Catholic emperors when they were heretics. Do not let that be so, I implore you by the blood of Christ, by the memory of the apostle Peter who warned those placed in authority over Christian peoples not to lord it over their brethren.[b] For myself, I commend to the gracious love of your Holiness both the Catholics of Fussala, my children

etiam clericos vestros quibuscumque petentibus nolite mittere, nolite concedere."   [b] 1 Pet. v. 3.

scopum filium in Christo meum benignitati caritatis
sanctitatis tuae, quia utrosque diligo, utrosque
commendo. Neque Fussalensibus suscenseo, quia
iustam de me querimoniam ingerunt auribus tuis,
quod eis hominem nondum mihi probatum, nondum
saltem aetate firmatum, a quo sic affligerentur, inflixi,
neque huic noceri volo, cui quanto magis sinceram
habeo caritatem, tanto magis pravae cupiditati eius
obsisto. Utrique misericordiam mereantur tuam,
illi, ne mala patiantur, iste, ne faciat, illi, ne oderint
catholicam, si a catholicis episcopis maximeque ab
ipsa sede apostolica contra catholicum non eis sub-
venitur episcopum, iste autem, ne se tanto scelere
obstringat, ut, quos molitur invitos facere suos, a
Christo faciat alienos.

10   Me sane, quod confitendum est beatitudini tuae,
in isto utrorumque periculo tantus timor et maeror
excruciat, ut ab officio cogitem gerendi episcopatus
abscedere et me lamentis errori meo convenientibus
dedere, si per eum cuius episcopatui per inprudentiam
suffragatus sum vastari ecclesiam dei, et quod ipse
deus avertat, etiam cum vastantis perditione perire
conspexero. Recolens enim quod ait apostolus : *Si
nosmet ipsos diiudicaremus, a domino non iudicaremur,*
iudicabo me ipsum, ut parcat mihi *qui iudicaturus est
vivos et mortuos.* Si autem et membra Christi, quae
in illa regione sunt, ab exitiabili timore ac tristitia

---

^a *Catholica* for *catholica ecclesia* is very frequent in
Augustine. See Rottmanner, " Catholica," in *Geistesfrüchte
aus der Klosterzelle,* pp. 74-84.

^b 1 Cor. xi. 31.   ^c 2 Tim. iv. 1.

in Christ, and bishop Antoninus, my son in Christ, for both are dear to me. And I do not blame the people of Fussala for pouring into your ears their just complaint against me that I imposed upon them a man whom I had not tested and who was in age at least, immature, to cause them such afflictions; nor do I wish any harm to Antoninus, whose vile greed I oppose all the more stubbornly because I hold him in such genuine affection. Let your compassion be extended to both—to them, so that they may suffer no harm, to him, that he may do none; to them, so that they may not hate the Catholic Church,[a] if Catholic bishops and especially the Apostolic See itself fail to come to their defence against a Catholic bishop; to him, so that he may not involve himself in such great wickedness as to alienate from Christ those whom he is striving to win for Him against their will.

As for myself, however, I must confess to your 10 Holiness that in the danger that threatens both I am racked by such great fear and grief that I contemplate retiring from the responsibility of carrying on my episcopal office and giving myself over to lamentation befitting my fault, if I see the Church of God despoiled through one whose election as bishop I supported through lack of foresight and even (which may God forbid) brought to destruction along with the destruction of the despoiler himself. For in remembrance of the Apostle's words, " If we would judge ourselves, we should not be judged by the Lord,"[b] I shall judge myself, so that I may be spared by Him "Who shall judge the quick and the dead."[c] But if you secure the recovery of the members of Christ in that district from their deadly fear and sorrow and

recreaveris et meam senectutem hac misericordi
iustitia fueris consolatus, retribuet tibi et in praesenti
et in futura vita bona pro bonis, qui per te nobis in
ista tribulatione succurrit et qui te in illa sede
constituit.

No. 48 (Ep. CCX)

DILECTISSIMAE ET SANCTISSIMAE MATRI FELI-
CITATI ET FRATRI RUSTICO ET SORORIBUS
QUAE VOBISCUM SUNT AUGUSTINUS ET
QUI MECUM SUNT IN DOMINO SALUTEM

1 *Bonus est dominus* et misericordia eius ubique
diffusa, quae nos de vestra caritate in suis visceribus
consolatur. Quantum enim diligat credentes et
sperantes in se et illum atque invicem diligentes et
quid eis in posterum servet, hinc maxime ostendit,
cum infidelibus et desperatis et perversis, quibus in
mala voluntate usque in finem perseverantibus ignem
cum diabolo aeternum minatur, in hoc tamen saeculo
bona tanta largitur, *qui facit oriri solem suum super
bonos et malos et pluit super iustos et iniustos.* Breviter
enim aliquid dictum est, ut plura cogitentur ; quam
multa enim habeant impii in hac vita munera et dona

---

^a Felicitas was probably the prioress of the nunnery at
Hippo in which Augustine's own sister had held office until
her death. It seems likely that the development of monasticism among women in North Africa was due to Augustine,
for while Tertullian and Cyprian give evidence of the honour
in which consecrated widows and virgins were held, the
first notice of their monastic life is given by the Council of
Carthage in 397, and Possidius declares that when Augustine
died in 430 he left " a sufficient body of clergy and monasteries of men and women " (*Vit.* 31). Of monasteries for
men at Hippo, one was built on ground provided by Bishop
Valerius (*Serm.* 355. 2), and on succeeding Valerius, Augus-

at the same time comfort my old age by administering justice tempered with mercy, He Who through you brings us deliverance in this trial and Who has set you in your See will recompense unto you good for good, both in this life and in the life to come.

No. 48 (Ep. CCX)

(A.D. 423)

TO THE WELL-BELOVED AND SAINTLY MOTHER FELICITAS *a* AND BROTHER RUSTICUS AND THE SISTERS WHO ARE WITH YOU, AUGUSTINE AND THE BRETHREN WHO ARE WITH ME SEND GREETING IN THE LORD

The Lord is good *b* and everywhere His mercy is **1** shed abroad, which comforts us with your love in Him. How greatly He loves those who believe and hope in Him and who love both Him and one another, and what blessings He stores up for them to enjoy hereafter, He shows most of all by this, that upon the unbelieving and the abandoned and the perverse, whom He threatens with eternal fire in company with the devil if they persist in their evil disposition unto the end,*c* He nevertheless in this present world bestows so many benefits, making "His sun to rise on the evil and on the good and sending rain on the just and on the unjust." *d* That is a brief sentence, meant to suggest further thoughts to the mind, for who can count up how many benefits and unearned

tine made another of his episcopal house, and during his life-time two more were founded near Hippo (*Serm.* 356. 10, 15).

b Lam. iii. 25.   *c* Matt. xxv. 41.   *d* Matt. v. 45.

gratuita ab illo quem contemnunt, enumerare quis
potest ? Inter quae illud magnum, quod exemplis
interpositarum tribulationum, quas huius saeculi
dulcedini tamquam bonus medicus miscet, admonet
eos, si adtendere velint, fugere ab ira ventura,[a] et
cum in via sunt, id est in hac vita, concordare cum
sermone dei, quem sibi adversarium male vivendo
fecerunt.[b] Quid ergo non misericorditer praestatur
hominibus a domino deo, a quo etiam tribulatio
beneficium est ? Nam res prospera donum est con-
solantis, res autem adversa donum est admonentis
dei. Et si haec praestat, ut dixi, etiam malis, quid
praeparat sustinentibus se ?[c] Quorum in numero vos
per illius gratiam congregatos esse gaudete, *sus-
tinentes invicem in dilectione, studentes servare unitatem
spiritus in vinculo pacis.*[d] Non enim deerit quod in
vobis invicem sufferatis, nisi cum vos ita portaverit
dominus absorpta morte in victoriam, *ut sit deus
omnia in omnibus.*[e]

2 Dissensiones autem numquam debent amari. Sed
aliquando tamen aut caritate nascuntur aut caritatem
probant. Quis enim facile invenitur, qui velit
reprehendi ? Et ubi est ille sapiens, de quo dictum
est : *Corripe sapientem et amabit te ?*[f] Numquid tamen
ideo non debemus reprehendere et corripere fratrem,

---

[a] Matt. iii. 7.   [b] Matt v. 25.

[c] A Scriptural phrase: Ps. xxvi. 14 "confortetur cor tuum
et sustine Dominum "; Isaiah xxv. 9 "iste Dominus; susti-
nuimus eum," etc. Augustine plays on the two meanings of
sustinere, "to wait for (God)," and "to endure (one's fellow-
men)."   [d] Eph. iv. 2-3.   [e] 1 Cor. xv. 54, 28.

[f] *Ubi est . . . ?* a common rhetorical formula in late
Latin, perhaps derived from the *controversiae,* serving to
introduce against an opponent a final and unanswerable
argument, almost always from Scripture. See an example

gifts the wicked receive in this life from Him whom they despise ? Among these is this great blessing, that by the instances of intermingled tribulation with which, like a good physician, He blends the charm of this world, He warns them, if they but pay heed, to " flee from the wrath to come " [a] and to " agree, while they are in the way " [b] (that is, in this life) with the word of God, which by their wicked lives they have made their " adversary." What, then, is not sent to men by the Lord God in His compassion, when even tribulation is a blessing sent by Him ? For prosperity is God's gift when He comforts us, while adversity is God's gift when He is warning us. And if, as I said, He furnishes these even to the wicked, what does He prepare for those who wait for Him [c] ? Among this number rejoice ye that by His grace you have been gathered, " forbearing one another in love, endeavouring to keep the unity of the Spirit in the bond of peace." [d] For there will not fail to be occasion for your bearing with one another, until the Lord has borne you hence and " death is swallowed up in victory " and " God shall be all in all." [e]

Yet in strife we ought never to take pleasure, though **2** from time to time it is either born of love or puts love to the test. For who is easily found that is willing to endure reproof? And, what about [f] that wise man of whom it is said, " Rebuke a wise man, and he will love thee " [g] ? Surely then we ought not to refrain from reproving and correcting a brother in

on p. 44, " Quamquam ubi est illud ... quod ... apostolus ... ita conclusit ut diceret ... ? " Fastid. *Vit. Chr.* 13 " si Deus peccatorum non punit, ubi est illud propheticum ... ? " My note in *Bulletin Du Cange*, i. (1924) p. 51, first recorded this use. [g] Prov. ix. 8.

ne securus tendat in mortem ? Solet enim fieri et
frequenter accidit, ut ad horam contristetur, cum re-
prehenditur, et resistat et contendat et tamen postea
consideret secum in silentio, ubi nemo est nisi deus et
ipse nec timet displicere hominibus, quia corripitur, sed
timet displicere deo, quia non corrigitur, et deinceps
non faciat illud, quod iuste reprehensus est, et, quantum odit peccatum suum, tantum diligat fratrem, quem
sensit hostem peccati sui. Si autem de illo numero
est, de quo dictum est : *Corripe stultum et adiciet ut
oderit te,* non de caritate illius dissensio nascitur, sed
tamen caritatem reprehensoris sui exercet et probat,
quia non ei rependitur odium, sed dilectio, quae
cogit reprehendere, inperturbata perdurat, etiam
cum ille qui reprehensus est, odit. Si autem ille
qui corripit, reddere vult malum pro malo ei qui
corripienti indignatur, non fuit dignus qui corriperet,
sed dignus plane, qui etiam ipse corripi deberet.
Haec agite, ut aut non inter vos existant indignationes
aut exortae statim celerrima pace perimantur.
Maiorem date operam concordandis vobis quam
redarguendis, quia, sicut acetum corrumpit vas, si
diutius ibi fuerit, sic ira corrumpit cor, si in alium
diem duraverit. *Haec* ergo *agite, et deus pacis erit
vobiscum,* orantes simul et pro nobis, ut ea quae
bene monemus, alacriter impleamus.

---

[a] *Ad horam* : see note *a* on p. 356.
[b] *Cf.* note on *arbitraris tecum*, p. 6.
[c] Prov. ix. 8.   [d] *Cf.* p. 106.   [e] Phil. **iv. 9.**

case he go down to death in false security ? It is a usual experience and a common occurrence for one who is reproved to be mortified at the time [a] and to wrangle and be recalcitrant, yet afterwards to reflect within himself [b] in silence, alone with God, where he is not afraid of displeasing men by being reproved, but is afraid to displease God by refusing correction, and thenceforward to refrain from doing the thing for which he was justly rebuked, and in proportion as he hates his sin, to love the brother whom he realizes to have been the enemy of his sin. But if he belongs to the number of those of whom it is written, "Rebuke a fool and he will go on to hate thee," [c] the contention is not born of his love, but yet it tries and tests the love of his reprover, since he does not repay hatred with hatred, but the love which prompted his rebuke endures undisturbed, even when he who was rebuked requites it with hatred. If the reprover, however, choose to render evil for evil to the man who takes offence at being reproved, he was not fit to reprove another, but clearly fit to be reproved himself. Act upon these principles, so that occasions of provocation may either not arise among you, or, when they do occur, be immediately quenched in speedy peace. Strive more earnestly to disseminate harmony among yourselves than to encourage fault-finding, for just as vinegar corrodes a vessel if it remain too long in it, so anger corrodes the heart if it linger on to another day.[d] "These things, therefore, do, and the God of peace shall be with you." [e] At the same time pray for us, that we may with cheerful mind carry out the good advice we have given you.

ST. AUGUSTINE

No. 49 (Ep. CCXI)

1   Sicut parata est severitas peccata quae invenerit, vindicare, ita non vult caritas quod vindicet, invenire. Haec causa fecit, ut non venirem ad vos, cum meam praesentiam quaereretis, non ad pacis vestrae gaudium, sed ad dissensionis vestrae augmentum. Quo modo enim contemnerem et inpunitum relinquerem, si et me praesente tantus vester tumultus existeret, quantus me absente etsi oculos meos latuit, tamen aures meas vestris vocibus verberavit ? Nam fortassis etiam maior esset vestra seditio in praesentia mea, quam necesse esset vobis non concedi, quod in perniciosissimum exemplum contra sanam disciplinam, quod vobis non expedit, petebatis ; ac sic non quales volo, invenirem vos et ipse invenirer a vobis qualem non volebatis.

2   Cum ergo scribat apostolus ad Corinthios dicens : *Testem deum facio super animam meam, quia parcens vobis nondum veni Corinthum, non quia dominamur fidei*

---

a This famous letter is the source of the Augustinian Rule, which from the eleventh century to the Renascence was the standard of canons regular, preaching friars, knights of the military orders, and the hospital brethren and sisters—of the active, as opposed to the contemplative religious orders, which were nearly all Benedictine. In this its original form, it was part of a letter addressed to a convent of nuns in Hippo, probably that to which the last letter was written, although the circumstances do not appear to be quite identical. The Rule itself, the first actual monastic legislation in Western Europe, was early adapted to communities of men, but it is not a complete system of rules for monastic observance, requiring expansion and elucidation from Augustine's other ascetic writings, especially the *De Opere Monachorum* and *De Sancta Virginitate*. Here, for ex-

No. 49 (Ep. CCXI) ^a

(A.D. 423)

Just as severity is ready to punish the sins it dis- 1
covers, so love is anxious not to discover sins to punish.
That was the motive which withheld me from coming
to you, when you besought my presence, not to
rejoice in your peacefulness, but to increase your
strife. For how could I have made light of your
wrangling or left it unpunished, if even in my presence
it had arisen to the same pitch as that which in my
absence, though it was hidden from my eyes, yet
assailed my ears with your clamour? Perhaps
your rebelliousness would have been even greater
in my presence, which it was necessary for me to
withhold from you since you were demanding, to
the detriment of sound discipline, things inexpedient
for you and furnishing a most dangerous precedent.
Thus I should not have found you such as I desire, and
you would have found me such as you did not desire.

The Apostle writes to the Corinthians and says, "I 2
call God for a record upon my soul, that to spare you
I came not as yet unto Corinth. Not for that we

ample, Augustine passes over the great monastic counsel
of silence and touches but lightly on the subject of labour,
yet the Rule became essentially that of the religious orders
with an active mission. Nor, again, does he speak in detail
of the liturgical offices, perhaps because in the Africa of his
day there was no uniformity (Ep. lv. 34 " de hac re varia
consuetudo est ") and no great enthusiasm for it (*ib.*, "pleraque
in Africa ecclesiae membra pigriora sunt "), except among
the Donatists. Yet such as it is, the " Rule " had all the
authority of his name and all the mingled severity and
kindness of his nature to make it imposing to the medieval
mind.

vestrae, sed cooperatores sumus gaudii vestri, hoc ego etiam dico vobis quia *parcens vobis* non ad vos veni. Peperci etiam mihi, *ne tristitiam super tristitiam de vobis haberem,* et elegi non exhibere faciem meam vobis, sed effunderem cor meum deo pro vobis, et causam magis periculi vestri non apud vos verbis sed apud deum lacrimis agerem, ne convertat in luctum gaudium meum, quo soleo gaudere de vobis et inter tanta scandala, quibus ubique abundat hic mundus, aliquantulum consolari, cogitans copiosam congregationem et castam dilectionem et sanctam conversationem vestram et largiorem gratiam dei, quae data est vobis, ut non solum nuptias carnales contemneretis, verum etiam eligeretis societatem in domo habitandi unanimes, ut sit vobis anima una et cor unum in deum.

3   Haec in vobis bona, haec dei dona considerans inter multas tempestates, quibus ex aliis malis quatitur, cor meum solet utcumque requiescere. *Currebatis bene. Quis vos fascinavit? Suasio illa non est ex deo, qui vocavit vos. Modicum fermenti* — nolo dicere quod sequitur ; hoc enim magis cupio et oro et hortor, ut ipsum fermentum revertatur in melius, non tota massa, sicut paene iam fecerat, convertatur in peius. Si ergo repullulastis sanum sapere, *orate, ne intretis in temptationem,* ne iterum in *contentiones, aemulationes, animositates, dissensiones, detractiones, seditiones, susurrationes.* Non enim sic plantavimus et rigavimus

---

ª 2 Cor. i. 23-24.   ᵇ Phil. ii. 27.
ᶜ Lam. ii. 19.   ᵈ Acts iv. 32.
ᵉ 1 Cor. v. 6 "modicum fermenti totam massam corrumpit."
ᶠ Matt. xxvi. 41 ; Mark xiv. 38 ; Luke xxii. 46.
ᵍ 2 Cor. xii. 20.

have dominion over your faith, but are helpers of
your joy." [a] I too say the same to you: to spare
you I came not unto you; further, I spared myself,
" lest I should have sorrow upon sorrow" [b] from you,
and preferred not to show my face before you but
to pour out my heart to God for your behoof and to
conduct this perilous case of yours, not by speech
before you, but rather by tears before God,[c] lest He
turn to mourning the joy wherewith I am wont to
rejoice in you and to find some little comfort, amid
the great offences with which this world everywhere
abounds, in the remembrance of your large community and your chaste love and holy conversation
and the more abundant grace of God that has been
given you, whereby you have not only renounced
carnal wedlock, but have also chosen to dwell with
one accord in fellowship together under the same
roof, to have "one soul and one heart" unto God.[d]

When I consider these excellences you show, **3**
which God did bestow, my heart is wont to find
some sort of peace amid the many storms that arise
through evils elsewhere to agitate it. "Ye did run
well; who did hinder you that ye should not obey
the truth? This persuasion cometh not of God that
called you. A little leaven" [e]—what follows I prefer
to leave unsaid, for it is rather my desire and prayer
and exhortation that the leaven itself may return
to something better, not that "the whole lump" may
turn (as it had almost done already) to something
worse. If then you have blossomed again into
soundness of mind, "pray that ye enter not into
temptation," [f] nor fall once more into "debates,
envyings, wraths, strifes, backbitings, tumults,
whisperings." [g] For we did not so plant and water

hortum dominicum in vobis, ut spinas istas metamus
ex vobis. Si autem adhuc vestra tumultuatur infirmitas, orate ut eruamini de temptatione. Quae
autem conturbant vos, si adhuc conturbant, nisi
correxerint, portabunt iudicium, quaecumque illae
fuerint.

4   Cogitate quid mali sit, ut, cum de Donatistis in
unitate gaudeamus, interna schismata in monasterio
lugeamus. Perseverate in bono proposito et non
desiderabitis mutare praepositam, qua in monasterio
illo per tam multos annos perseverante et numero et
aetate crevistis, quae vos mater non utero sed animo
suscepit. Omnes enim quae illuc venistis, ibi eam
aut sanctae praepositae sorori meae servientem,
placentem aut etiam ipsam praepositam, quae vos
susciperet, invenistis ; sub illa estis eruditae, sub illa
velatae, sub illa multiplicatae ; et sic tumultuamini,
ut vobis eam mutemus, cum lugere deberetis si eam
vobis mutare vellemus. Ipsa est, quam nostis ;
ipsa est, ad quam venistis ; ipsa est, quam per tot
annos habendo crevistis. Novum non accepistis nisi
praepositum ; aut si propter illum quaeritis novitatem
et in eius invidia contra matrem vestram sic rebel-

---

[a] 1 Cor. iii. 6-8 ; Hier. xii. 13.

[b] This intransitive use of *corrigere* is peculiar to late Latin,
as is the similar use of *emendo* and *reformo*. It is often corrected in texts by the poorer manuscripts, as it is here, and
probably occurs more frequently than the texts show. See
Thes. Ling. Lat. s.v., and Souter, *A Study of Ambrosiaster*,
p. 96, and *cf*. Aug. *In Ps.* 93. 3 "utinam corrigant et non
dicant sic."

[c] Gal. v. 10.

[d] The reading *Donatistis* is a conjecture of the Maurist
editors, all the manuscripts giving *deo natis*, but *Donatistis*
is almost certainly right. The phrase *in unitate gaudere* is
always used by Augustine with reference to the Donatists ;

the garden of the Lord among you as to reap these thorns from you [a]; yet if your weakness still causes turmoil, pray to be delivered from temptation. Yet unless those sisters that trouble your peace reform [b] (if they still trouble it), they shall bear their judgement, whosoever they be.[c]

Consider what an evil thing it is that we should **4** have to bewail internal discords in your monastery, when we are rejoicing over the Donatists [d] in unity. Be steadfast in the good purpose you have set before you and you will not desire to change your superior; steadfastly abiding in that monastery for so many years, she begot you not of the body, but of the soul, and you have grown both in numbers and in age. All of you, when you came to it, found her either doing service that was well-pleasing to the holy superior my sister, or else acting as superior herself and adopting you. Under her you received your training, under her you took the veil, under her you have been increased; and yet you demand with all this clamour that we should replace her for you, when you ought to be lamenting if we proposed to replace her for you. She is the one you have learned to know; she is the one to whom at first you came; she is the one under whom for so many years you have grown. No new official has been given you except the priest-superior; or if it be because of him that you seek some new thing and through jealousy for him that you have thus rebelled

deo nati is too vague to be an adequate contrast to *interna schismata*, and the reading *deo natis* is easily explained as derived from *Donatistis* by the wrong expansion of *do-* to *Deo* and the dropping of the second *-tis*. See my note in *Journal of Theological Studies*, xxiii. (1922), p. 188.

lastis, cur non potius hoc petistis, ut ipse vobis mutetur ? Si autem hoc exhorretis, quia novi quo modo eum in Christo venerabiliter diligatis, cur non potius illud ? In vobis namque regendis sic praepositi rudimenta turbantur, ut magis velit vos ipse deserere, quam istam ex vobis famam et invidiam sustinere, ut dicatur non aliam vos quaesituras fuisse praepositam, nisi ipsum coepissetis habere praepositum. Tranquillet ergo deus et componat animos vestros ; non in vobis praevaleat opus diaboli, sed *pax Christi vincat in cordibus vestris*[b] ; nec dolore animi, quia non fit quod vultis, vel quia pudet voluisse quod velle non debuistis, erubescendo curratis in mortem, sed potius paenitendo resumatis salutem nec debeatis paenitentiam Iudae traditoris[c] sed potius lacrimas Petri pastoris.[d]

5 Haec sunt, quae ut observetis praecipimus in monasterio constitutae.[e] Primum propter quod estis in unum congregatae, ut unanimes habitetis in domo et sit vobis *anima una et cor unum*[f] in deum et non dicatis aliquid proprium, sed sint vobis omnia communia, et distribuatur unicuique vestrum a praeposita vestra victus et tegumentum non aequaliter omnibus, quia non aequaliter valetis omnes, sed

---

[a] 1 John iii. 8. [b] Col. iii. 15.
[c] Matt. xxvii. 3-5. [d] Matt. xxvi. 75.

[e] The " Rule " proper begins here. In the version adapted to male use the previous sections are omitted and in their place is a short introduction, comprising, among other things, liturgical injunctions, passed over very lightly in the " Rule."

[f] Acts iv. 32. Goldbacher reads with one family of manuscripts *cor unum et anima una*, which follows the order of the Greek and the Vulgate. But not only is the reading *anima una et cor unum* attested by a better family ; it is frequent and almost invariable in Augustine. Similarly Goldbacher lower down reads *singulis prout*, a Vulgate form,

against your mother, why did you not rather ask to have him changed for you ? But if you shrink from that (since I know with what reverence and affection you regard him in Christ), why not the more shrink from the other course ? For in ruling you the efforts of the priest-superior are so thwarted by your disorderliness, that he himself is the rather minded to abandon you than to endure such an invidious reputation from you as to have it said that you would not have demanded another mother-superior, if you had not begun to have him as priest-superior. May God then calm and compose your hearts ! May the work of the devil not gain the upper hand within you,[a] but may " the peace of Christ rule in your hearts[b] "! And do not rush headlong unto death, either from mortification that your desire is not granted or from the shame that you experience from desiring what you ought not to have desired. Rather by repentance renew your salvation, nor ought it to be the repentance of Judas the betrayer,[c] but rather the tears of Peter the shepherd.[d]

These are the rules we lay down for your observ- 5 ance, who have entered upon monastic life.[e]

Firstly, to fulfil the end for which you have gathered into one community, dwell together in the house as single-minded sisters, and have " one mind and one heart "[f] towards God. And call not anything your own, but let everything be common property ; and let there be a distribution made to each of you by your superior of food and raiment, not in equal portions to all, since you are not all of

which probably never occurs in Augustine, his usual form being that here read on the authority of the same better class of manuscripts.

unicuique sicut opus fuerit. Sic enim legitis in actibus apostolorum, quia *erant illis omnia communia et distribuebatur unicuique sicut cuique opus erat.* Quae aliquid habebant in saeculo, quando ingressae sunt monasterium, libenter illud velint esse commune; quae autem non habebant, non ea quaerant in monasterio, quae nec foris habere potuerunt, sed tamen earum infirmitati, quod opus est, tribuatur, etiam si pauperies earum, quando foris erant, nec ipsa necessaria poterat invenire; tantum non ideo se putent esse felices, quia invenerunt victum et tegumentum quale foris invenire non potuerunt.

6 Nec erigant cervicem, quia sociantur ad quas foris accedere non audebant, sed sursum cor habeant et terrena bona non quaerant, ne incipiant monasteria esse divitibus utilia non pauperibus, sed divites illic humiliantur et pauperes illic inflantur. Sed rursus etiam illae quae aliquid esse videbantur in saeculo, non habeant fastidio sorores suas quae ad illam sanctam societatem ex paupertate venerunt; magis autem studeant non de parentum divitum dignitate sed de pauperum sororum societate gloriari. Nec extollantur, si communi vitae de suis facultatibus aliquid contulerunt, ne de suis divitiis magis superbiant quia eas monasterio partiuntur, quam si eis in saeculo fruerentur. Alia quippe quaecumque

---

[a] Acts iv. 32, 35.

[b] That there were many of low degree who entered monastic life appears too from *De Opere Monachorum*, 25: "nunc autem veniunt plerumque ad hanc professionem servitutis Dei et ex condicione servili vel etiam liberti, vel propter hoc ex dominio liberati seu liberandi et ex vita rusticana et ex opificum exercitatione et plebeio labore."

equal importance, but to each one according as she has need. For in the Acts of the Apostles you read that " they had all things common, and distribution was made to every man according as he had need."[a] Let those of you who had any possessions in the world before you entered the monastery willingly consent that they become common property ; let those, on the other hand, who had none, not seek in the monastery for things they could not have outside it, but yet let what is needful be conceded to their weakness, even if their poverty, while they were outside, was such that they could not procure even the bare necessities of life. Nevertheless, let them not think themselves fortunate only because they have procured such food and raiment as they were unable to procure outside.

And let them not go about with head erect because **6** they are associating with those whom they did not dare to approach outside, but let them lift up their hearts and not seek earthly goods, in case the monasteries become of service to the rich and not to the poor, while in them the rich are bowed down with humility and the poor in them puffed up with vanity. But again, let not those who in the world considered themselves something, hold in scorn their sisters who have come to that holy fellowship from poverty[b] ; let them endeavour to take greater pride in the fellowship of their poor sisters than in the rank of their wealthy parents. And let them not exalt themselves, if they have made some contribution from their own resources to the common life, lest they grow more vain of their wealth because they are sharing it with the monastery, than if they were enjoying the use of it in the world ; for every other kind of iniquity

iniquitas in malis operibus exercetur, ut fiant;
superbia vero etiam in bonis operibus insidiatur, ut
pereant. Et quid prodest dispergere dando pauperibus et pauperem fieri, cum anima misera superbior
efficiatur divitias contemnendo, quam fuerat possi-
dendo? Omnes ergo unanimiter et concorditer vivite
et honorate in vobis invicem deum, cuius templa
factae estis.

7 Orationibus instate horis et temporibus constitutis.
In oratorio nemo aliquid agat, nisi ad quod est
factum, unde et nomen accepit, ut, si aliquae etiam
praeter horas constitutas, si eis vacat, et orare
voluerint, non eis sint impedimento, quae ibi aliquid
agendum putaverunt. Psalmis et hymnis cum oratis
deum, hoc versetur in corde quod profertur in voce,
et nolite cantare, nisi quod legitis esse cantandum;
quod autem non ita scriptum est, ut cantetur, non
cantetur.

8 Carnem vestram domate ieiuniis et abstinentia
escae et potus, quantum valitudo permittit. Quando
autem aliqua non potest ieiunare, non tamen extra
horam prandii aliquid alimentorum sumat, nisi cum
aegrotat. Cum acceditis ad mensam, donec inde
surgatis, quod vobis secundum consuetudinem legitur,
sine tumultu et contentionibus audite nec solae vobis
fauces sumant cibum, sed et aures esuriant dei
verbum.

9 Quae infirmae sunt ex pristina consuetudine, si
aliter tractantur in victu, non debet aliis molestum
esse nec iniustum videri, quas fecit alia consuetudo
fortiores. Nec illas putent feliciores, quia sumunt

---

^a 1 Cor. iii. 16.   ^b Coloss. iv. 2.

prompts the doing of evil deeds, but pride lurks even in good deeds to their undoing. And what does it avail to scatter wealth in alms to the poor and to become poor oneself, when the wretched soul is rendered prouder by despising wealth than it was by possessing it? Live, then, all of you, in singlemindedness and harmony, and in each other honour God, Whose temples you have become.[a]

Be instant in prayer [b] at the appointed hours and **7** seasons. In the oratory let no one do anything but that for which it was made and from which it received its name, so that if any of you have leisure and wish to pray outside the appointed hours, you may not be hindered by others who think they should be doing something else in it. When you pray to God with psalms and hymns, meditate in your heart upon that which you utter with your voice, and do not sing anything unless what you read is to be sung; what is not written to be sung, is not to be sung.

Subdue your flesh by fasting and abstinence **8** from meat and drink, as far as the health allows. When, however, anyone is unable to fast, let her not take any nourishment outside of the hour of repast, unless when ill. From the time of your coming to table until you rise from it, hearken without din and wrangling to what according to the custom is read to you; let not your mouths alone take food, but let your ears too hunger for the word of God.

If those who are of weaker health from their **9** former mode of life are treated differently with regard to food, this ought not to be vexatious or to seem unfair to others whom a different mode of life has made stronger. And let them not imagine

quod non sumunt ipsae, sed sibi potius gratulentur, quia valent quod non valent illae. Et si eis quae venerunt ex moribus delicatioribus ad monasterium, aliquid alimentorum, vestimentorum, stramentorum, operimentorum datur, quod aliis fortioribus et ideo felicioribus non datur, cogitare debent, quibus non datur, quantum de sua saeculari vita illae ad istam descenderunt, quamvis usque ad aliarum, quae sunt corpore fortiores, frugalitatem pervenire nequiverint. Nec velle debent, quod eas vident amplius, non quia honorantur, sed quia tolerantur, accipere, ne contingat detestanda perversitas, ut in monasterio, ubi, quantum possunt, fiunt divites laboriosae, fiant pauperes delicatae. Sane, quem ad modum aegrotantes necesse habent minus accipere, ne graventur, ita post aegritudinem sic tractandae sunt, ut citius recreentur, etiam si de humillima saeculi paupertate venerunt, tamquam hoc illis contulerit recentior aegritudo, quod divitibus anterior consuetudo. Sed cum vires pristinas reparaverint, redeant ad feliciorem consuetudinem suam, quae famulas dei tanto amplius decet, quanto minus indigent, nec ibi eas teneat

these weaker sisters more fortunate than themselves because they enjoy a fare which is denied to themselves, but let them rather congratulate themselves that they have strength which is denied to the others. And if they who have come to the monastery from a more delicate upbringing are granted any food, clothing, bedding, or covering, that is not granted to others who are stronger and therefore more fortunate, those to whom it is not granted should consider how great a descent the others have made from their sphere of life in the world to this one, even although they have been unable to attain to the severe simplicity of those who are stronger in body. Nor should they hanker after what they see others receiving (not as a mark of higher favour, but as a mark of patient long-suffering) to a greater degree than they do themselves, lest there arise the abominable travesty of monastic life whereby the rich, as far as possible, are to be compelled to toil, and the poor allowed to live in luxury. Certainly, just as those who are ill have of necessity to take less food so as not to aggravate their disease, so after their illness they must receive such treatment as will help them to a speedier recovery, even although the worldly station from which they have come was one of the deepest poverty ; just as if the illness they have just passed through had bestowed on them the privileges allowed to the wealthy because of their previous mode of life. But when they have made up their former strength, let them return to their own more fortunate mode of life, which is all the more befitting the handmaidens of God as it involves fewer wants ; and let not their choice keep them, when they are well, in the privi-

voluntas iam vegetas, quo necessitas levarat infirmas.
Illae se aestiment ditiores, quae fuerint in sus-
tinenda parcitate fortiores; melius est enim minus
egere quam plus habere.

10 Non sit notabilis habitus vester nec affectetis
vestibus placere, sed moribus; non sint vobis tam
tenera capitum tegmina, ut retiola subter appareant.
Capillos ex nulla parte nudos habeatis nec foris vel
spargat neglegentia vel componat industria. Quando
proceditis, simul ambulate; cum veneritis quo itis,
simul state. In incessu, in statu, in habitu, in omnibus motibus vestris nihil fiat, quod inliciat cuiusquam
libidinem, sed quod vestram deceat sanctitatem.
Oculi vestri etsi iaciuntur in aliquem, figantur in
neminem. Neque enim, quando proceditis, viros
videre prohibemini, sed appetere aut ab ipsis appeti
velle. Nec tactu solo et affectu sed aspectu quoque
appetitur et appetit femina. Nec dicatis vos habere
animos pudicos, si habeatis oculos inpudicos, quia
inpudicus oculus inpudici cordis est nuntius et,
cum se invicem sibi etiam tacente lingua conspectu mutuo corda nuntiant inpudica et secundum
concupiscentiam carnis alterutro delectantur ardore,
etiam intactis ab inmunda violatione corporibus,
fugit castitas ipsa de moribus. Nec putare debet,
quae in masculo figit oculum et illius in se ipsa

ᵃ In Egyptian and Syrian monasteries, according to Jerome,
it appears to have been the custom for nuns to have the
hair cut short (" moris est in Aegypti et Syriae monasteriis
ut tam virgo quam vidua quae Deo se voverint . . . crinem
monasteriorum matribus offerant desecandum, non intecto
postea . . . capite, sed ligato pariter ac velato," Hier. *Ep.*
147. 5), but in the Western church they were allowed to wear
the hair long (Optatus, vi. 4; Ambr. *Laps. Virg.* 8. 35).

leged position to which necessity had raised them, when they were ill. Let those reckon themselves richer who in enduring frugality have been stronger ; it is better to want less than to receive more.

Let not your apparel be conspicuous, and aspire to please, not by your attire, but by your conduct ; let the covering of your head not be so thin that the nets appear under it. Do not let any part of your hair be uncovered, and, when you are outside the monastery, do not let it fly loose through carelessness or be arranged with fastidiousness.[a] When you go in procession, walk together ; when you reach the place you are going to, stand together. In walking, in standing, in deportment, in all your movements, let nothing be done that might attract the desire of anyone, but let everything be in keeping with your holy character. Though your eyes may be cast upon anyone, let them be fixed upon no one ; for when you are in procession, you are not forbidden to look upon men, but to desire to make approaches to them or to have them make approaches to you. It is not by touch only and by bearing that a woman solicits approaches or makes them, but by look as well. And do not say that you have chaste minds if you have unchaste eyes, because an unchaste eye is the messenger of an unchaste heart, and when unchaste hearts send messages to each other, even though the tongue is silent, by the exchange of a look and agreeably to the lust of the flesh find pleasure each in the other's ardour, the body may actually remain uncontaminated by any unclean violation and yet purity may take its departure from the character. And she who fixes her eye upon a man and takes delight in having his fixed upon herself, must not

diligit fixum, non se videri ab aliis, cum hoc facit;
videtur omnino, et a quibus videri non arbitratur.
Sed ecce lateat et a nemine hominum videatur, quid
faciet de illo desuper inspectore, quem latere nihil
potest? An ideo putandus est non videre, quia
tanto videt patientius quanto sapientius? Illi ergo
timeat sancta femina displicere, ne velit viro male
placere; illum cogitet omnia videre, ne velit virum
male videre. Illius namque et in hac causa com-
mendatus est timor, ubi scriptum est: *Abominatio
est domino defigens oculum.* Quando ergo simul estis
in ecclesia et ubicumque ubi et viri sunt, invicem
vestram pudicitiam custodite; deus enim, qui habitat
in vobis, etiam isto modo vos custodit ex vobis.

11   Et si hanc, de qua loquor, oculi petulantiam in
aliqua vestrum adverteritis, statim admonete, ne
coepta progrediantur, sed e proximo corrigantur. Si
autem et post admonitionem iterum vel alio quocumque die id ipsum eam facere videritis, iam velut
vulneratam sanandam prodat quaecumque hoc potuit
invenire, prius tamen et alteri vel tertiae demon-
stratam, ut duarum vel trium possit ore convinci et
competenti severitate coherceri. Nec vos iudicetis
esse malivolas, quando hoc indicatis; magis quippe

    a Prov. xxiv. 12.
    b Prov. xxvii. 20, after the Septuagint: βδέλυγμα Κυρίῳ
στηρίζων ὀφθαλμόν.
    c 1 Cor. iii. 16; 2 Cor. vi. 16.
    d Deut. xix. 15; Matt. xviii. 16; 2 Cor. xiii. 1.

imagine that, when she does so, she is not observed by others ; she assuredly is observed, and observed by those she wots not of. But just suppose she does escape detection and is not observed by any human being, what will she do about that observer from above, Whose detection nothing can escape ? [a] Is He to be considered to observe nothing, because He observes with as much long-suffering as wisdom ? Let each holy woman therefore cherish the fear of displeasing Him, so as to avoid the desire of sinfully pleasing man ; let her keep in mind that He observes everything, so that she may avoid the desire of sinfully observing man. For it is fear of Him, and that in this self-same matter, that is commended to us by the passage, " One that fixeth the eye is an abomination to the Lord." [b] So then, when you are together in church and in any place where men too are present, keep mutual guard upon your chastity, for in that way too God, " Who dwelleth in you," [c] makes you His guards upon yourselves.

And if in anyone of your number you perceive 11 this frowardness of eye of which I am speaking, at once admonish her, so that what has begun may go no farther, but may be remedied straightway. But if, even after admonishment, you notice her doing the same thing again on any other day, whoever has had the opportunity of noticing this should report her for treatment, as one afflicted with a sore, but not before she has been pointed out to a second or a third, so that she may be convicted from the mouth of two or three witnesses [d] and be punished with becoming severity. And do not judge yourselves to be acting from malice when you point out anything of this kind ; for the truth rather is that you share

innocentes non estis, si sorores vestras, quas indicando
corrigere potestis, tacendo perire permittitis. Si
enim soror tua vulnus haberet in corpore, quod
vellet occultare, cum timeret secari, nonne crudeliter
abs te sileretur et misericorditer indicaretur?
Quanto ergo potius eam debes manifestare, ne
perniciosius putrescat in corde! Sed antequam aliis
demonstretur per quas convincenda est, si negaverit,
prius praepositae debet ostendi, si admonita ne-
glexerit corrigi, ne forte possit secretius correpta
non innotescere ceteris. Si autem negaverit, tunc
mentienti adhibendae sunt aliae, ut iam coram
omnibus possit non ab una teste argui, sed a duabus
tribusque convinci; convicta vero secundum praepositae vel etiam presbyteri arbitrium debet emenda-
toriam sustinere vindictam; quam si ferre recusaverit
et si ipsa non abscesserit, de vestra societate proiciatur. Non enim et hoc fit crudeliter, sed misericorditer, ne contagione pestifera plurimas perdat. Et
hoc quod dixi de oculo non figendo, etiam in ceteris
inveniendis, prohibendis, indicandis, convincendis
vindicandisque peccatis diligenter observetur, cum
dilectione hominum et odio vitiorum. Quaecumque
autem in tantum progressa fuerit malum, ut occulte
ab aliquo litteras vel quaelibet munuscula accipiat,
si hoc ultro confitetur, parcatur illi et oretur pro illa;

---

a A favourite thought of Augustine's: *In Ps.* 138. 22
"nec propter vitia homines oderis, nec vitia propter homines
diligas"; *In Ps.* 118. 5. 24, 1-2: *ib.* 139. 2, etc. So, too, in
the Benedictine Rule, 64 "oderit vitia, diligat fratres."

the guilt if you allow your sisters to perish by keeping silence, when it lies in your power to correct them by pointing them out. For if your sister had a sore on the body that she wanted to conceal from fear of the surgeon's knife, would it not be cruel on your part to say nothing about it, and compassionate to point it out? How much rather, then, are you bound to expose her, so that she may not incur greater risk from the canker in her heart? But before she be pointed out to the others whose witness is to convict her if she deny her guilt, she ought first to be reported to the superior, if on being warned she has neglected to reform so that through the more private rebuke she may not escape the others' knowledge. If, however, she denies her guilt, then she should, on making this false assertion, be confronted with the others, so that in the presence of all she may be convicted by two or three witnesses, and not charged simply by one. After conviction she ought to be visited with corrective punishment at the discretion of the superior or the priest-in-charge; if she refuses to undergo that and does not of herself take her departure, let her be expelled from your community. This extreme step is taken not out of cruelty, but out of compassion, as a precaution against the destruction of many others through deadly contamination. And let my remarks about wanton looks be carefully observed, with love of the sinner and hatred of the sin,[a] in the discovery, prohibition, denunciation, trial and punishment of the other sins. But if anyone of you has gone to such lengths in sin that she is secretly receiving from a man letters or any kind of gifts, let her be pardoned and prayer be made for her, if she confesses it of her own accord; but if she is detected

ST. AUGUSTINE

si autem deprehenditur atque convincitur, secundum
arbitrium presbyteri praepositi vel aliorum simul
presbyterorum vel etiam episcopi gravius emendetur.

12 Vestes vestras habete sub una custode vel duabus
vel quot sufficere potuerint ad eas excutiendas,
ne tinea laedantur, et, sicut pascimini ex uno
cellario, sic induamini ex uno vestiario. Et si
fieri potest, non ad vos pertineat quid vobis in-
duendum pro temporis congruentia proferatur, utrum
hoc recipiat unaquaeque vestrum quod deposuerat,
an aliud quod altera habuerat, dum tamen unicuique
quod opus est, non negetur. Si autem hinc inter vos
contentiones et murmura oriuntur, cum queritur
aliqua deterius aliquid se accepisse quam prius
habuerat, et indignam se iudicat esse quae ita
vestiatur, sicut alia soror eius vestiebatur, hinc vos
probate, quantum vobis desit in illo interiore *sancto
habitu* cordis, quae pro habitu corporis litigatis.
Tamen si vestra toleratur infirmitas, ut hoc recipiatis
quod posueratis, in uno tamen loco sub communibus
custodibus habete quod ponitis, ita sane ut nulla
sibi aliquid operetur, sive unde induatur sive ubi
iaceat sive unde cingatur vel operiatur vel caput
contegat ; sed omnia opera vestra in commune fiant,
maiore studio et frequentiori alacritate quam si vobis
propria faceretis. Caritas enim, de qua scriptum est
quod *non quaerit quae sua sunt*, sic intellegitur, quia
communia propriis, non propria communibus ante-
ponit. Et ideo, quanto amplius rem communem quam

ᵃ Titus ii. 3.   ᵇ 1 Cor. xiii. 5.

and it be proved against her, let more serious punishment be inflicted on her at the discretion of the priest-superior or the other priests in a body or even the bishop.

Keep your clothes under the care of one or two or 12 as many as may be necessary to shake them out for protection against moths ; and just as your food is supplied from one store-room, so let your clothing come from one wardrobe. And whatever is brought forth for you to wear according to the weather, let it not concern you, if you can attain this, whether each of you receives the garment she put off, or another that someone else had been wearing, so long as each is not denied what she needs. But if this gives occasion for strife and murmuring among you, and someone complains that she has received a worse garment than she was wearing before and considers herself too good to be clad in the same way as her sister was, let that be evidence to you how far deficient you are in that inward holy apparel[a] of the heart, when you quarrel about the apparel of the body. Nevertheless, if your weakness is so far indulged that you are granted the dress you had put off, let what you put off be, nevertheless, kept in one place in charge of the ordinary keepers of the wardrobe ; thus no one will work at anything for her own use, whether it be clothing or bedding or underclothing or covering or head-dress ; but let everything you make be for the common stock, with greater zeal and more cheerful urgency than if you were making anything for yourself. For the love about which it is written that it " seeketh not its own "[b] is to be understood as that which prefers the common good to personal good, not personal good to the common good. And so, the more attention you

395

propriam vestram curaveritis, tanto vos amplius pro-
fecisse noveritis, ut in omnibus quibus utitur transitoria necessitas, superemineat quae permanet caritas.
Consequens ergo est, ut etiam illud quod suis vel
filiabus vel aliqua necessitudine ad se pertinentibus
in monasterio constitutis aliquis vel aliqua contulerit
sive vestem sive quodlibet aliud inter necessaria
deputandum, non occulte accipiatur sed sit in potestate praepositae, ut in rem communem redactum, cui
necessarium fuerit, praebeatur. Quod si aliqua rem
sibi conlatam celaverit, furti iudicio condemnetur.

13   Indumenta vestra secundum arbitrium praepositae
laventur sive a vobis sive a fullonibus, ne interiores
animae sordes contrahat mundae vestis nimius appetitus. Lavacrum etiam corporum ususque balnearum
non sit assiduus, sed eo, quo solet, intervallo temporis
tribuatur, hoc est semel in mense. Cuius autem
infirmitatis necessitas cogit lavandum corpus, non
longius differatur ; fiat sine murmure de consilio
medicinae, ita ut etiam si nolit, iubente praeposita
faciat quod faciendum est pro salute. Si autem
velit et forte non expedit, suae cupiditati non
oboediat ; aliquando enim, etiamsi noceat, prodesse creditur quod delectat. Denique, si latens
est dolor in corpore famulae dei, dicenti sibi quid
doleat, sine dubitatione credatur ; sed tamen, utrum

---

a Eph. iii. 19 ; 1 Cor. xiii. 8.

b Compare the Rule of St. Benedict, 54 " quod si etiam a
parentibus suis ei quidquam directum fuerit, non praesumat
suscipere illud, nisi prius indicatum fuerit abbati. Quod si
iusserit suscipi, in abbatis sit potestate cui illud iubeat dari."

c With this compare Jerome, *Ep.* 125. 7 " sordes vestium
candidae mentis indicio sint ; vilis tunica contemptum
saeculi probet. . . . Balnearum fomenta non quaeras, qui
calorem corporis ieiuniorum cupis frigore extinguere " ; *id.*

give to the common good in preference to your own, the more progress you will know you have made, so that the love which endureth *a* may be conspicuous in everything needed for the wants that pass away. It follows, then, that even what a man or woman bestows upon the inmates of the monastery, be they daughters or relatives, whether the gift be clothing or any other things that may be regarded as necessaries, must not be received in secret, but it must lie in the power of the superior to put it to the common stock and to hand it over to any inmate that needs it.*b* If anyone conceal a gift bestowed on her, let her be sentenced and condemned for theft.

Let your garments be washed, either by yourselves 13 or by washer-women, at the discretion of the superior, so that excessive solicitude for clean raiment may not infect the soul with inward vileness.*c* Let the bathing of the body and the use of baths not be incessant, but be granted at the usual interval of time, that is, once a month. If, however, the need arising from any illness demands the washing of the body, let it not be too long postponed, and let it be done without murmuring for medical reasons ; if anyone refuse, let her do at the command of the superior what needs to be done for health's sake. But if she wishes it and it does not happen to be for her good, she must not give in to her desire, for there are times when what is pleasant is thought to be beneficial, even though it really do harm. Finally, if a handmaid of God has some hidden pain in the body, and tells what ails her, she should be believed without hesitation ; but still, if there be uncertainty

Ep. 107. 11 " mihi omnino in adulta virgine lavacra displicent."

sanando illi dolori quod delectat expediat, si non
est certum, medicus consulatur. Nec eant ad
balneas sive quocumque ire necesse fuerit minus
quam tres. Nec illa quae habet aliquo eundi necessitatem, cum quibus ipsa voluerit, sed cum quibus
praeposita iusserit, ire debebit. Aegrotantium cura,
sive post aegritudinem reficiendarum sive aliqua im-
becillitate etiam sine febribus laborantium, alicui
debet iniungi, ut ipsa de cellario petat quod cuique
opus esse perspexerit; sive autem quae cellario sive
quae vestibus sive quae codicibus praeponuntur, sine
murmure serviant sororibus suis. Codices certa hora
singulis diebus petantur; extra horam quae petierint,
non accipiant. Vestimenta vero et calciamenta
quando fuerint indigentibus necessaria, dare non dif-
ferant, sub quarum custodia sunt, quae poscuntur.

14 Lites aut nullas habeatis aut quam celerrime
finiatis, ne ira crescat in odium et trabem faciat de
festuca et animam faciat homicidam. Neque enim
ad solos viros pertinet, quod scriptum est : *Qui odit
fratrem suum, homicida est,* sed sexu masculino, quem
primum deus fecit, etiam femineus sexus praeceptum
accepit. Quaecumque convicio vel maledicto vel
etiam criminis obiectu alteram laeserit, meminerit

---

a Churches possessed libraries from an early date. They
are frequently referred to during the seizure of Christian
books in the Diocletian persecution. The Acts of Purgation
of Caecilian and Felix, for example, mention one in the
church at Cirta early in the fourth century, and Augustine
speaks of the library of his church at Hippo in *Ep.* ccxxxi.
7 " bibliothecam nostram, ut sint unde libri vel parentur
vel reparentur, adiuvare dignatus es," and also in *De
Haeres.* 80 " ipsum eius opusculum in nostra bibliotheca
invenire non potuimus." There is frequent mention of
church libraries in Jerome : *e.g. Ep.* 49. 3 " ecclesiarum

whether that which pleases her is suitable for curing her pain, let the doctor be consulted. When they go to the baths, or wherever they have to go, let there not be less than three ; and the sister who requires to go somewhere is not to go along with those she chooses herself, but with those the superior orders. The care of the sick, whether they be convalescing or be afflicted with some weakness, yet without fever, ought to be devolved upon someone, so that she herself may procure from the store-room what she sees to be needful for each. Further, the sister who has charge either of the store-room or the wardrobe or the library,[a] must serve her sisters without murmuring. Let the manuscripts be applied for at a fixed hour each day ; outside that hour those who apply for them are not to receive them. As for clothes and shoes, whenever they are required for those in need, let those who have charge of them not delay to supply what is asked for.

You should either have no quarrels or put an end 14 to them as speedily as possible, lest anger develop into hatred and make a beam out of a mote [b] and turn the soul to murder. For it is not only to men that the saying applies, " He that hateth his brother is a murderer," [c] but the female sex too has received this commandment along with the male sex, which God created first. Whoever has injured a sister by taunt or abuse, or even by casting up faults, must

bibliothecis fruere," 112. 9 " omnes ecclesiarum bibliothecas damnare cogeris," etc. Ambrose gives further testimony to the reading of books by nuns : *De Virginibus*, 3. 4. 15 " siquando rogaris ut cibum sumas, paulisper deponas codicem."

[b] Matt. vii. 3-5 ; Luke vi. 41-42. *Cf.* p. 107 above.
[c] 1 John iii. 15.

satisfactione quantocius curare quod fecit, et illa
quae laesa est, sine disceptatione dimittere. Si
autem invicem se laeserint, invicem sibi debita
relaxare debebunt propter orationes vestras, quas
utique quanto crebriores tanto sanctiores habere
debetis. Melior est autem, quae quamvis ira saepe
temptatur, tamen impetrare festinat ut sibi di-
mittat, cui se fecisse agnoscit iniuriam, quam quae
tardius irascitur et ad veniam petendam difficilius
inclinatur. Quae autem numquam vult petere
veniam aut non ex animo petit, sine causa est in
monasterio, etiamsi non inde proiciatur. Proinde
vobis a verbis durioribus parcite; quae si emissa
fuerint ex ore vestro, non pigeat ex ipso ore
proferre medicamenta, ex quo facta sunt vulnera.
Quando autem necessitas disciplinae minoribus co-
hercendis dicere vos verba dura compellit, si etiam
in ipsis modum vos excessisse sentitis, non a vobis
exigitur ut ab eis veniam postuletis, ne apud
eas, quas oportet esse subiectas, dum nimia servatur
humilitas, regendi frangatur auctoritas. Sed tamen
petenda est venia ab omnium domino, qui novit,
etiam eas, quas plus iusto forte corripitis, quanta
benivolentia diligatis. Non autem carnalis sed
spiritalis inter vos debet esse dilectio; nam quae
faciunt pudoris inmemores etiam feminis feminae
iocando turpiter et ludendo, non solum a viduis et
intactis ancillis Christi in sancto proposito constitutis
sed omnino Christianis nec a mulieribus nuptis nec a
virginibus sunt facienda nupturis.

remember to make amends at the first opportunity and heal the wound she has caused; and the injured sister must forgive her without further argument. But if they have caused mutual injury, they will require to grant mutual pardon because of your prayers, which from their frequency ought to be the holier. She who is often tempted by anger and yet hastens to beg for forgiveness from the sister whom she acknowledges she has hurt, is better than she who is slower to anger and is more stubborn in turning to seek for pardon. As for her who always refuses to seek for pardon or who seeks it without sincerity, she has no reason to be in the monastery, even if she is not expelled from it. Wherefore, refrain from harsh words; if they fall from your lips, do not think shame with the same lips that caused the hurt to utter words of healing. When, however, the needs of discipline compel the speaking of harsh words for the controlling of the younger inmates, you are not required to ask their pardon even if you feel that you have gone somewhat too far; otherwise, in observing too much humility towards those whose duty it is to be subject to you, you will undermine your authority in controlling them. But still you must seek pardon from the Lord of all, Who knows how great is the goodwill and love you have even for those whom you rebuke, perhaps, with undue severity. The love you bear each other ought, however, not to be carnal, but spiritual, for the things that immodest women do even to other women in low jests and pranks ought not to be done, not only by widows and chaste handmaidens of Christ following your holy way of life, but by Christians at all, be they married women or maidens destined for marriage.

15 Praepositae tamquam matri oboediatur honore servato, ne in illa offendatur deus, multo magis presbytero, qui omnium vestrum curam gerit. Ut ergo cuncta ista serventur et, si quid servatum non fuerit, non neglegenter praetereatur, sed emendandum corrigendumque curetur, ad praepositam praecipue pertinebit, ita ut ad presbyterum, qui vobis intendit, referat quod modum vel vires eius excedit. Ipsa vero non se existimet potestate dominante sed caritate serviente felicem. Honore coram hominibus praelata sit vobis, coram deo substrata sit pedibus vestris. Circa omnes se ipsam bonorum operum praebeat exemplum. Corripiat inquietas, consoletur pusillanimes, suscipiat infirmas, patiens sit ad omnes ; disciplinam libens habeat, metuens inponat. Et quamvis utrumque sit necessarium, tamen plus a vobis amari appetat quam timeri, semper cogitans deo se pro vobis reddituram esse rationem. Unde magis oboediendo, non solum vestri verum etiam ipsius miseremini, quia inter vos quanto in loco superiore, tanto in periculo maiore versatur.

16 Donet dominus ut observetis haec omnia cum dilectione tamquam spiritalis pulchritudinis amatrices et bono odore Christi de bona conversatione fraglantes, non sicut ancillae sub lege, sed sicut liberae sub gratia constitutae. Ut autem vos in hoc libello tamquam in speculo possitis inspicere, ne per oblivionem aliquid neglegatis, semel in septimana

---

^a Dan. xi. 4 ; Gal. v. 13.   ^b Titus ii. 7.   ^c 1 Thess. v. 14.

^d Similarly the Benedictine Rule describes the duties of the abbot : (64) " sciat sibi oportere prodesse quam praeesse . . . studeat plus amari quam timeri ; . . . (2) agnoscat pro certo quia in die iudicii ipsarum animarum est redditurus Domino rationem."

^e 2 Cor. ii. 15.   ^f Rom. vi. 14, 15.

Let the superior be obeyed like a mother, with all 15
due honour, so that you offend not God through
offending her; much more should you obey the
priest who has charge of you all. Upon the superior
particularly will fall the responsibility of seeing that
all these regulations are carried out and, if anything
is not carried out, of not carelessly passing over the
offence, but of applying the remedy to heal and
correct it; she may, further, refer to the priest-in-
charge any matter that goes beyond her province or
power. But let her think herself fortunate, not in
having authority to rule, but in having the love to
serve.^{a} In honour in the sight of men let her be
preferred to you; in the sight of God let her be
beneath your feet. Towards everyone let her show
herself " a pattern of good works." ^{b} Let her " warn
the unruly, comfort the feeble-minded, support the
weak, be patient to all." ^{c} Let her be cheerful in
maintaining discipline and fearful to impose it; and
although both are necessary, yet let her endeavour
to be more loved by you than feared, always bearing
in mind that she has to render an account of you to
God.^{d} Wherefore, by yielding her greater obedience,
have compassion on her as well as on yourselves,
because the higher her position is among you, the
greater is the risk she runs.

May the Lord grant you to observe all these rules 16
with love, as those whose affection is set upon spiritual
beauty and who are fragrant with the sweet savour
of Christ in your good conduct,^{e} not as bondswomen
under the law, but as free women under grace.^{f} In
order, however, that you may examine yourselves
in this treatise as in a mirror and may not neglect
any point through forgetfulness, let it be read to

vobis legatur, et ubi vos inveneritis ea quae scripta
sunt facientes, agite gratias domino bonorum omnium
largitori ; ubi sibi autem quaecumque vestrum videt
aliquid deesse, doleat de praeterito, caveat de futuro,
orans ut sibi debitum dimittatur et in temptationem
non inducatur.

No. 50 (Ep. CCXIV)

DOMINO DILECTISSIMO ET IN CHRISTI MEM-
BRIS HONORANDO FRATRI VALENTINO ET
FRATRIBUS QUI TECUM SUNT, AUGUSTI-
NUS IN DOMINO SALUTEM

1   Venerunt ad nos duo iuvenes, Cresconius et Felix,
de vestra congregatione se esse dicentes, qui nobis
rettulerunt monasterium vestrum nonnulla dissensione turbatum eo, quod quidam in vobis sic gratiam
praedicent, ut negent hominis esse liberum arbitrium
et, quod est gravius, dicant quod in die iudicii non
sit redditurus deus unicuique secundum opera eius.

---

^a Matt. vi. 12-13 ; Luke xi. 4.
^b Valentinus was abbot of the monastery at Hadrumetum,
the capital of Byzacenum (now Sousse, 100 miles south of
Tunis). Two of his monks, Florus and Felix, when visiting
the monastery at Uzala, read and copied Augustine's letter
to the presbyter Sixtus (Ep. cxciv.) on grace and free-will,
and on their return to Adrumetum read it to the monks
there, some of whom considered Augustine's teaching fatal
to the doctrine of free-will. The monastery was bitterly
divided on the question, so Valentinus sent Felix and
Cresconius, another of the disputants, to ascertain Augustine's
real opinions. The present letter is his reply. The two
monks were unwilling to wait at Hippo until some of his
anti-Pelagian treatises were copied for them, but he kept
them until Easter, writing another letter to Valentinus
(Ep. ccxv.) and composing for him the treatise *De Gratia*

you once each week, and when you find yourselves
practising the things written in it, render thanks to
the Lord, the giver of every good gift. But when
any one of you perceives herself deficient in some
point, let her lament the past and take precautions
for the future, praying both that her trespass may
be forgiven and that she may not be led into
temptation.[a]

No. 50 (Ep. CCXIV)

(A.D. 426 or 427)

TO VALENTINUS,[b] MY WELL-BELOVED LORD
AND BROTHER, HONOURED IN THE MEMBERS
OF CHRIST, AND TO THE BRETHREN WHO
ARE WITH YOU, AUGUSTINE SENDS GREET-
ING IN THE LORD

There have come to me two young men, Cresconius 1
and Felix, declaring themselves members of your
community, who have reported to me that there is some
disturbance and dissension in your monastery because
certain brethren are extolling grace to such an extent
that they deny the freedom of the human will and,
what is more serious, assert that on the day of judgement God will not render to every man according to

et Libero Arbitrio. Later, Valentinus replied in Ep. ccxvi.,
and Florus too visited Hippo, giving Augustine the chance
to mention the disputation at Hadrumetum in his Retracta-
tiones, ii. 66. In the Revue Bénédictine, xviii (1901), pp.
241-256, Dom Germain Morin has published a hitherto unknown, short letter from Augustine to Valentinus, with other
letters addressed by a priest Januarianus and Evodius to the
monks of Hadrumetum on this same occasion.

Etiam hoc tamen indicaverunt, quod plures vestrum non ita sentiant, sed liberum arbitrium adiuvari fateantur per dei gratiam, ut recta sapiamus atque faciamus et, cum venerit dominus reddere unicuique secundum opera eius, inveniat opera nostra bona, *quae praeparavit deus, ut in illis ambulemus.* Hoc qui sentiunt, bene sentiunt.

2   *Obsecro* itaque *vos, fratres,* sicut Corinthios obsecravit apostolus, *per nomen domini nostri Iesu Christi, ut id ipsum dicatis omnes et non sint in vobis schismata.* Primo enim dominus Iesus, sicut scriptum est in evangelio Iohannis apostoli, non venit, *ut iudicaret mundum, sed ut salvaretur mundus per ipsum*; postea vero, sicut scribit apostolus Paulus, *iudicabit deus mundum,* quando " venturus est," sicut tota ecclesia in symbolo confitetur, " iudicare vivos et mortuos." Si ergo non est dei gratia, quo modo salvat mundum ? Et si non est liberum arbitrium, quo modo iudicat mundum ? Proinde librum vel epistulam meam, quam secum ad nos supra dicti adtulerunt, secundum hanc fidem intellegite, ut neque negetis dei gratiam neque liberum arbitrium sic defendatis, ut a dei gratia separetis, tamquam sine illa vel cogitare aliquid vel agere secundum deum ulla ratione possimus, quod omnino non possumus. Propter hoc enim dominus, cum de fructu iustitiae loqueretur, ait discipulis suis : *Sine me nihil potestis facere.*

3   Unde supra dictam epistulam ad Sixtum, presbyterum ecclesiae Romanae, contra novos haereticos

---

    a Matt. xvi. 27.   *b* Eph. ii. 10.   *c* 1 Cor. i. 10.
        d John iii. 17.   *e* Rom. iii. 6.
      f 2 Tim. iv. 1 ; 1 Pet. iv. 5.   *g* John xv. 5.

his deeds.[a] But yet they have pointed out too that there are many of you who do not share these opinions, but confess that our free-will is aided by the grace of God so that we may think and do what is right, and that, when the Lord comes to render to every man according to his deeds, he will find our deeds good—deeds " which God hath before ordained that we should walk in them." [b] Those who hold these opinions, hold right opinions.

" I beseech you," therefore, " brethren," as the apostle besought the Corinthians, " by the name of our Lord Jesus Christ, that ye all speak the same thing and that there be no divisions among you." [c] For in the first place, the Lord Jesus, as is written in the Gospel of John the apostle, did not come " to condemn the world, but that the world through him might be saved " [d]; secondly, as the apostle Paul writes, " God shall judge the world," [e] when He has come, as the whole Church confesses in the Creed, " to judge the quick and the dead." [f] If then there is no grace of God, how does He save the world? And if there is no free-will, how does He judge the world? Wherefore, the treatise or letter of mine, which the afore-mentioned brethren brought with them to us, you are to understand in the light of that confession of faith, so that you neither deny the grace of God nor defend free-will in such a way as to sunder it from God's grace, as if without it we could by any means think or do anything well-pleasing to God— a thing which is utterly impossible. That is why the Lord, speaking about the fruits of righteousness, says to His disciples, " Without me ye can do nothing." [g]

So you must know that the letter I have mentioned was written to Sixtus, a priest of the Roman Church,

Pelagianos noveritis esse conscriptam, qui dicunt gratiam dei secundum merita nostra dari, ut qui gloriatur, non in domino sed in se ipso glorietur, hoc est in homine, non in domino. Quod prohibet apostolus dicens: *Nemo glorietur in homine*, et alio loco: *Qui gloriatur*, inquit, *in domino glorietur*. Illi vero haeretici se ipsos a se ipsis iustos fieri putantes, quasi hoc eis non deus dederit sed ipsi sibi, non utique in domino sed in semet ipsis gloriantur. Talibus dicit apostolus: *Quis enim te discernit?* Quod ideo dicit, quia de massa illius perditionis quae facta est ex Adam, non discernit hominem, ut eum faciat vas in honorem non in contumeliam, nisi deus. Sed quoniam homo carnalis et inaniter inflatus, cum audisset: *Quis enim te discernit?*, posset respondere vel voce vel cogitatione et dicere: " Discernit me fides mea, discernit me oratio mea, discernit me iustitia mea," mox apostolus occurrit cogitationibus eius et dixit: *Quid enim habes, quod non accepisti? Si autem et accepisti, quid gloriaris, quasi non acceperis?* Sic enim gloriantur quasi non acceperint, qui se a se ipsis iustificari putant ac per hoc in se ipsis non in domino gloriantur.

4 Propter quod ego in hac epistula, quae ad vos pervenit, probavi per testimonia scripturarum sanctarum, quae ibi potestis inspicere, et bona opera nostra et pias orationes et rectam fidem nullo modo

---

[a] 1 Cor. iii. 21; 1 Cor. i. 31; 2 Cor. x. 17.
[b] 1 Cor. iv. 7.
[c] Rom. ix. 21; 2 Tim. ii. 20.   [d] 1 Cor. iv. 7.

[e] The *ego* is probably designed to discredit once for all the suggestion made by some of the monks of Hadrumetum that the monk Florus had written it himself.

against the new heretics, the Pelagians, who declare
that the grace of God is bestowed according to our
merits ; so that he who glories has to glory, not in
the Lord, but in himself, that is, in man, not in the
Lord. Now this is forbidden by the apostle, in the
words, " Let no man glory in man," and in another
place he says, " He that glorieth let him glory in the
Lord." [a]   But these heretics, imagining that they
become righteous of themselves, as if it was they
themselves and not God who granted this to them,
consistently enough glory in themselves and not in
the Lord. To such the apostle says, " Who maketh
thee to differ from another ? ",[b] saying this on the
ground that what makes a man to differ from that mass
of perdition which had its origin in Adam and makes
him a vessel unto honour and not unto dishonour,[c] is
God alone. But since carnal man, swollen with empty
pride, might, on hearing the question " Who maketh
thee to differ from another ? ", make answer either in
thought or in word and say, " It is my faith that makes
me to differ ; my prayers that make me to differ ;
my righteousness that makes me to differ," the
apostle at once met these thoughts half-way and
said, " For what hast thou that thou didst not
receive ? Now, if thou didst receive it, why dost
thou glory, as if thou didst not receive it ? "[d]   For
they glory just as if they did not receive it, those
who imagine they are justified of themselves ; they
glory therefore in themselves and not in the Lord.

That is the reason why, in that letter that has come 4
into your hands, I, the author of it,[e] have proved from
passages of Holy Scripture, which you can examine in
it, that our good works and our holy prayers and our
right faith could certainly not have come into being

in nobis esse potuisse, nisi haec acciperemus ab illo
de quo dicit apostolus Iacobus : *Omne datum optimum
et omne donum perfectum desursum est descendens a
patre luminum*, ne quisquam dicat meritis operum
suorum vel meritis orationum suarum vel meritis
fidei suae sibi traditam dei gratiam, et putetur verum
esse quod illi haeretici dicunt, gratiam dei secundum
merita nostra dari, quod omnino falsissimum est ; non
quia nullum est meritum vel bonum piorum vel
malum impiorum—alioquin quo modo iudicabit deus
mundum ?—sed misericordia et gratia dei convertit
hominem, de qua psalmus dicit : *Deus meus, misericordia eius praeveniet me*, ut iustificetur impius, hoc
est ex impio fiat iustus, et incipiat habere meritum
bonum, quod dominus coronabit quando iudicabitur
mundus.

5   Multa erant quae vobis mittere cupiebam, quibus
lectis totam ipsam causam quae conciliis episcopali-
bus acta est adversus eosdem Pelagianos haereticos,
diligentius et plenius nosse possetis, sed festinaverunt
fratres qui ex numero vestro ad nos venerant, per
quos vobis non rescripsimus ista, sed scripsimus.
Nullas enim ad nos vestrae caritatis litteras ad-
tulerant ; tamen suscepimus eos, quoniam simplicitas
eorum satis indicabat nihil illos nobis potuisse con-
fingere. Ideo autem festinaverunt, ut apud vos
agerent pascha, quo possit adiuvante domino tam
sanctus dies vestram pacem quam dissensionem
potius invenire.

6   Melius autem facietis, quod multum rogo, si ipsum

---

within us, unless we had received them from Him of Whom the apostle James says, " Every good gift and every perfect gift is from above and cometh down from the Father of lights."[a] This makes it impossible for anyone to say that it is for the merit of his own works or the merit of his own prayers or the merit of his own faith that the grace of God was bestowed upon him, and to imagine that what these heretics say is true, that the grace of God is bestowed according to our merits. This is utterly untrue ; not because there are no merits—either good merits in the righteous, or evil merits in the unrighteous—otherwise how will God judge the world ?—but because a man is converted by the mercy and grace of God, of which the Psalm says, " As for my God, His mercy shall prevent me,"[b] so that the unrighteous may be justified, that is, be made just instead of unrighteous, and begin to possess that good merit which the Lord will crown when He comes to judge the world.

There are many communications I wished to send 5 you for your perusal ; you would then have had more exact and detailed knowledge of the whole action that was brought against these same Pelagians by the councils of bishops. But the brethren who came to us from your company had to hurry away. By them I am sending you this letter, which is not a reply to any of yours, for they brought none to us from your Charity. Yet we received them, as their straightforwardness was sufficient evidence that they were incapable of fabricating anything. Their purpose in hurrying away is to spend Easter with you, so that so holy a day may, with the Lord's help, find you in peace, rather than in strife.

It will, however, be better for you to do what I 6

a quo dicunt se fuisse turbatos, ad me mittere non gravemini. Aut enim non intellegit librum meum aut forte ipse non intellegitur, quando difficillimam quaestionem et paucis intellegibilem solvere atque enodare conatur. Ipsa est enim quaestio de gratia dei, quae fecit ut homines non intellegentes putarent apostolum Paulum dicere : *Faciamus mala, ut veniant bona.* Unde apostolus Petrus in secunda epistula sua : *Quapropter, inquit, carissimi, haec expectantes, satis agite inviolati et inmaculati apud eum reperiri in pace, et domini nostri patientiam salutem existimate, sicut et dilectissimus frater noster Paulus secundum eam quae data est ei sapientiam scripsit vobis ut et in omnibus epistulis loquens in eis de his, in quibus sunt quaedam difficilia intellectu, quae indocti et instabiles homines pervertunt sicut et ceteras scripturas ad proprium suum interitum.*

7   Cavete ergo quod tantus apostolus tam terribiliter dicit, et, ubi sentitis non vos intellegere, interim credite divinis eloquiis quia et liberum hominis est arbitrium et gratia dei, sine cuius adiutorio liberum arbitrium nec converti potest ad deum nec proficere in deum, et, quod pie creditis, ut etiam sapienter intellegatis, orate. Et ad hoc ipsum enim, id est ut sapienter intellegamus, est utique liberum arbitrium. Nisi enim libero arbitrio intellegeremus atque saperemus, non nobis praeciperetur dicente

---

a Rom. iii. 8.   *b* 2 Pet. iii. 14-16.

earnestly beg you will do ; send to me, if it will not trouble you, the brother who is said to have caused this dissension, for either he has misunderstood my book, or perhaps he has made himself misunderstood, in his attempt to elucidate and unravel a question which is very difficult and intelligible to few. It is no other than the question about God's grace, which has caused men of small intelligence to imagine that the apostle Paul says, " Let us do evil that good may come." [a] With reference to this the apostle Peter says in his second Epistle, "Wherefore, beloved, seeing that ye look for such things, be diligent, that ye may be found of Him in peace, without spot and blameless ; and account that the long-suffering of our Lord is salvation ; even as our beloved brother Paul also, according to the wisdom given unto him, hath written unto you ; as also in all his epistles, speaking in them in these things ; in which are some things hard to be understood, which they that are unlearned and unstable wrest, as they do also the other Scriptures, unto their own destruction." [b]

Take heed, then, to avoid what the great apostle 7 describes so fearsomely, and when you realize that you do not understand, put your faith for the present in the inspired statements that in man there is both free-will and divine grace, without the aid of which free-will can neither be turned to God nor make any advance towards God ; and pray that what you submissively put your faith in, you may come wisely to understand. And indeed it is for this very purpose that we have free-will, namely, that we may wisely understand, for unless we had freedom of will in understanding and practising wisdom, we should not be commanded in the words of Scripture, " Under-

scriptura: *Intellegite ergo, qui insipientes estis in populo ;
et stulti, aliquando sapite.* Eo ipso quippe, quo praeceptum atque imperatum est ut intellegamus atque
sapiamus, oboedientiam nostram requirit, quae nulla
potest esse sine libero arbitrio. Sed si posset hoc
ipsum sine adiutorio gratiae fieri per liberum arbitrium, ut intellegeremus atque saperemus, non
diceretur deo : *Da mihi intellectum, ut discam mandata
tua,* neque in evangelio scriptum esset : *Tunc
aperuit illis sensum, ut intellegerent scripturas,* nec
Iacobus apostolus diceret : *Si quis autem vestrum
indiget sapientia, postulet a deo, qui dat omnibus affluenter
et non inproperat, et dabitur ei.* Potens est autem
dominus, qui et vobis donet et nobis, ut de vestra
pace et pia consensione nuntiis celerrimis gaudeamus.
Saluto vos non solum meo nomine, sed etiam fratrum
qui mecum sunt, et rogo ut pro nobis concorditer
atque instanter oretis. Sit vobiscum dominus.
Amen.

No. 51 (Ep. CCXX)

DOMINO FILIO IN PRAESENTEM ET IN AETER-
NAM SALUTEM DEI MISERICORDIA PROTE-
GENDO ET REGENDO BONIFATIO AUGUS-
TINUS

1   Fideliorem hominem et qui faciliores haberet

---

a Ps. xciii. 8.   *b* Ps. cxviii. 125.   *c* Luke xxiv. 45.   *d* James i. 5.
  e See note on p. 322. Boniface had been recalled in
disgrace from Africa, but refused to go. War was declared
on him in 427, but he divided his opponents and defeated
them. After a period of hesitation, Boniface called the
Vandals to his aid, in May 429. The present letter was
written after Boniface had fallen into disgrace, but before
429 ; a translation of it is given by Hodgkin, *Italy and her
Invaders,* 376-476, vol. i. pp. 495-503. His account of
Aetius and Boniface, *ib.* pp. 456-462, should be read along

stand now, ye simple among the people ; and ye fools, at length be wise." [a] From the very fact, then, that we have been commanded and instructed to understand and be wise, it follows that our obedience is demanded, and it cannot exist unless through free-will. Yet if it were in our power of our own free-will to obey this precept to understand and be wise, without the assistance of grace, it would be useless to say to God, " Give me understanding, that I may learn Thy commandments," [b] nor would it be written in the Gospel, " Then opened He their understanding, that they might understand the Scriptures " [c] ; nor would the apostle James say, " If any of you lack wisdom, let him ask of God, Who giveth to all men liberally and upbraideth not, and it shall be given him." [d] But the Lord is able to grant both to you and to us, to rejoice in the speedy tidings of your peace and holy concord. I greet you, not only in my own name, but also in the name of the brethren who are with me, and I beseech you to pray for us with one heart and with all instancy. The Lord be with you ! Amen.

No. 51 (Ep. CCXX)

(A.D. 427)

TO MY LORD BONIFACE,[e] MY SON WHOM I COMMEND TO THE PROTECTION AND GUIDANCE OF GOD'S MERCY FOR PRESENT AND ETERNAL SALVATION, AUGUSTINE SENDS GREETING

I could never find a more trustworthy man or one 1

with that of Freeman, *Western Europe in the Fifth Century*, Appendix I: "Aetius and Boniface" (pp. 305-370), who tries to clear Boniface of the charge made by Procopius of inviting the Vandals to Africa.

accessus ad aures tuas ferens litteras meas, numquam potui reperire, quam nunc dominus obtulit
servum et ministrum Christi diaconum Paulum
ambobus nobis carissimum, ut aliquid tibi loquerer
non pro potentia tua et honore quem geris in isto
saeculo maligno, nec pro incolumitate carnis tuae
corruptibilis atque mortalis, quia et ipsa transitoria
est, et quam diu sit, semper incertum est, sed
pro illa salute quam nobis promisit Christus, qui
propterea hic exhonoratus atque crucifixus est, ut
doceret nos bona saeculi huius magis contemnere
quam diligere, et hoc amare et sperare ab illo, quod
in sua resurrectione monstravit ; *resurrexit* enim *a
mortuis nec iam moritur, et mors ei ultra non dominabitur.*

2　　Scio non deesse homines qui te secundum vitam
mundi huius diligunt et secundum ipsam tibi dant
consilia, aliquando utilia aliquando inutilia, quia
homines sunt et, sicut possunt, ad praesens sapiunt,
nescientes quid contingat sequenti diei.　Secundum
autem deum, ne pereat anima tua, non facile tibi
quisquam consulit, non quia desunt qui hoc faciant,
sed quia difficile est invenire quando tecum ista
possint loqui.　Nam et ego semper desideravi, et
numquam inveni locum vel tempus, ut agerem tecum
quod me agere oportebat cum homine quem multum
diligo in Christo.　Scis autem qualem me apud
Hipponem videris, quando ad me venire dignatus es,

---

^a Probably the Paul spoken of in the following letter.
　　^b 1 Cor. xv. 53.　　　　^c Rom. vi. 9.

who could have easier access to your presence **as**
bearer of my letter than the servant and minister of
Christ, the deacon Paul,[a] a dear friend of us both,
who has just now been provided for me by the Lord.
I must say something to you, not with regard to the
power and the honour you bear in this evil world,
nor with regard to the preservation of your corruptible
mortal body [b] (for it too is destined to pass away,
and how long it may endure is always uncertain),
but with regard to the salvation promised us by
Christ. Because of it He was degraded and crucified
here below, so that He might teach us rather to
despise than to desire the good things of this world,
and to set our affection and our hope upon that
which He revealed in His resurrection ; for He
" is risen from the dead and dieth no more ; death
hath no more dominion over Him." [c]

I know that you have no lack of friends who love **2**
you as far as your life in this world is concerned, and,
so far as it is concerned, give you advice, sometimes
useful, sometimes not ; for they are only human and
the highest wisdom they as such can have looketh
only to the present hour, and they do not know
what may happen on the morrow. But as far as God
is concerned, it is not easy for anyone to give you
advice that will prevent the destruction of your
soul ; it is not that you lack friends who would do
this, but because it is difficult for them to find an
opportunity of speaking of those subjects with you.
I myself, indeed, have always wanted to do so, but
I have never found the place or the time to deal with
you as I ought to deal with one for whom I have **a**
great affection in Christ. Yet you know what I was
like when you saw me at Hippo, on the occasion of

quia vix loquebar inbecillitate corporis fatigatus.
Nunc ergo, fili, audi me saltem per litteras tibi
sermocinantem, quas in periculis tuis numquam tibi
mittere potui, periculum cogitans perlatoris et cavens
ne ad eos, ad quos nollem, mea epistula perveniret.
Unde peto ut ignoscas, si putas me plus timuisse
quam debui ; tamen dixi, quod timui.

3 Audi ergo me, immo dominum deum nostrum per
ministerium infirmitatis meae ; recole qualis fueris
adhuc in corpore constituta religiosae memoriae
priore coniuge tua et recenti eius obitu quo modo
tibi vanitas saeculi huius horruerit et quo modo
concupieris servitutem dei. Nos novimus, nos testes
sumus, quid nobiscum apud Tubunas de animo et
voluntate tua fueris conlocutus. Soli tecum eramus
ego et frater Alypius. Non enim existimo tantum
valuisse terrenas curas quibus impletus es, ut hoc de
memoria tua penitus delere potuerint. Nempe omnes
actus publicos quibus occupatus eras, relinquere
cupiebas et te in otium sanctum conferre atque
in ea vita vivere, in qua servi dei monachi vivunt.
Ut autem non faceres, quid te revocavit, nisi quia

---

a It was probably on this occasion that Augustine preached
before him Sermon cxiv., the title of which states it was
delivered " praesente comite Bonifacio."

b Servitus Dei, in the narrower sense, is used of the
monastic life, just as *servus Dei*, in the narrower sense, is
used of a monk (*e.g. Serm.* 214. 8 " de servis Dei . . .
saepissime dicitur, ' Tot annos ille in illo vel in illo monasterio
sedit,' hoc est, requievit, commoratus est, habitavit " ; *Ep.*
clix. 1, etc.), but it is also used of the clergy (in No. 34, § 3,
it is used of priests) and of the Christian laity (*In Ioan. Ev.*
x. 7 " servus Dei, populus Dei, ecclesia Dei," and § 5 below).

c The modern Tobna, near El Kantara, which lies about
fifty miles north of Biskra. Tubunae became a *municipium*
418

your gracious visit to me [a] : I was so worn out and weak in body that I could scarcely speak. But now, my son, hearken to me when I converse with you by letter at least ; while you were in danger, I never had a chance of sending one to you, from apprehension of danger to the bearer and fear that my letter might come into the hands of people whom I should not have wished it to reach. I beg you, therefore, for forgiveness, if you have the impression that I was more apprehensive than I should have been ; yet I have stated that I was apprehensive.

Hear me, therefore ; nay, hear the Lord our God [3] through me, His feeble servant. Recall to mind what manner of man you were while your first wife, of hallowed memory, was still in the flesh, and how just after her death you took a horror of the vanity of this life, and how you longed to enter the service of God.[b] We know, we can testify, what you said in conversation with us at Tubunae [c] about your state of mind and your intentions, when brother Alypius and I were alone with you. Indeed, I do not think that the earthly cares which now engross you have so prevailed as to be able to wipe that conversation from your memory. You wanted, in fact, to abandon all the public business that engaged you and to retire to a holy retreat and to live the life lived by God's servants the monks. What was it that restrained you ? Only the reflection, which we urged on you, of

not later than the reign of Septimius Severus. Bishops of Tubunae are mentioned in 256, 411, and 484. Under the Byzantines a large fortress was built there, and the town retained its importance long after their dominion had passed away. There are now few remains from the period of the Roman Empire.

considerasti ostendentibus nobis quantum prodesset
Christi ecclesiis quod agebas, si ea sola intentione
ageres, ut defensae ab infestationibus barbarorum
quietam et tranquillam vitam agerent, sicut dicit
apostolus, *in omni pietate et castitate*, tu autem nihil
ex hoc mundo quaereres nisi ea quae necessaria
essent huic vitae sustentandae tuae ac tuorum,
accinctus balteo castissimae continentiae et inter
arma corporalia spiritalibus armis tutius fortiusque
munitus.

4 Cum ergo te esse in hoc proposito gauderemus,
navigasti uxoremque duxisti. Sed navigasse oboe-
dientiae fuit, quam secundum apostolum debebas
sublimioribus potestatibus ; uxorem autem non
duxisses, nisi susceptam deserens continentiam
concupiscentia victus esses. Quod ego cum com-
perissem, fateor, miratus obstipui ; dolorem autem
meum ex aliqua parte consolabatur, quod audivi te
illam ducere noluisse, nisi prius catholica fuisset facta.
Et tamen haeresis eorum qui verum filium dei
negant, tantum praevaluit in domo tua, ut ab ipsis
filia tua baptizaretur. Iam vero, si ad nos non falsa
perlata sunt, quae utinam falsa sint, quod ab ipsis
haereticis etiam ancillae deo dicatae rebaptizatae
sint, quantis tantum malum plangendum est fontibus

---

a These barbarians were not the Huns or Vandals from
the north, but, as §§ 6-7 show, the Moors from the inner
recesses of Africa.

b 1 Tim. ii. 2.

c Recalled to Italy after Valentinian's victory in 425,
Boniface was rewarded for his fidelity to Placidia and his
resistance to the usurper John by the grant of the administration of Africa and (probably) the title *Comes
domesticorum*. While in Italy he married the wealthy

the great advantage the work you were doing would
be to the churches of Christ, if you pursued it with
the sole purpose of protecting them from the hostile
attacks of barbarians,[a] so that they might live, as
the apostle says, " a quiet and peaceable life in all
godliness and honesty," [b] while you yourself would
seek from this world nothing but what was necessary
for the maintenance of your own life and that of your
household, girding yourself with the chastest continence, and wearing along with the armour of the
body the surer and stronger defence of the armour
of the spirit.

When, in consequence, we were rejoicing in this 4
design of yours, you sailed for Italy and you married
a wife [c]; your sailing was an act of obedience,
which you owed, according to the apostle, to " the
higher powers " [d]; but you would not have married
a wife if you had not been overcome by desire and
abandoned the continence you took upon yourself.
When I learned of this, I confess I was thunder-
struck with amazement, yet in some measure I
found consolation for my grief in the fact that I
heard you had refused to marry her until she turned
Catholic. But in spite of that, the heresy of those
who deny the true Son of God has acquired such
influence in your home that it was by them that
your daughter was baptized. If the report that
reached us was not untrue (and would to Heaven
that it were !), that those same heretics have even
re-baptized maidens consecrated to God, what
fountains of tears we should need now to bewail

Pelagia, an Arian, but she abandoned this heresy before her
marriage, only to return to it afterwards.
    [d] Rom. xiii. 1.

lacrimarum ! Ipsam quoque uxorem non tibi suf-
fecisse, sed concubinarum nescio quarum commixtione
pollutum loquuntur homines et forsitan mentiuntur.

5   Ista, quae omnibus patent, tot et tanta mala, quae
a te, posteaquam coniugatus es, consecuta sunt, quid
ego dicam ? Christianus es, cor habes,[a] deum times.
Tu ipse considera quae nolo dicere, et invenies de
quantis malis debeas agere paenitentiam, propter
quam tibi credo dominum parcere et a periculis
omnibus liberare, ut agas eam sicut agenda est,
sed si illud audias quod scriptum est : *Ne tardes
converti ad dominum neque differas de die in diem.*[b]
Iustam quidem dicis habere te causam, cuius ego
iudex non sum, quoniam partes ambas audire non
possum ; sed qualiscumque sit tua causa, de qua
modo quaerere vel disputare non opus est, numquid
coram deo potes negare quod in istam necessitatem
non pervenisses, nisi bona huius saeculi dilexisses,
quae tamquam servus dei, quem te ante noveramus,
contemnere omnino et pro nihilo habere debuisti et
oblata quidem sumere, ut eis utereris ad pietatem,
non autem negata vel delegata sic quaerere, ut
propter illa in istam necessitatem perducereris, ubi
cum amantur vana, perpetrantur mala,[c] pauca quidem

---

    [a] *Cor habere* is not a common phrase, but it is more
frequently used by Augustine than by any other, though the
Thesaurus Linguae Latinae fails to note the fact. It occurs
in Epp. lxxxv. 2, cxli. 3 ; *Util. Ieiun.* 7. 9 " habent cor,
sciunt lapidem sentire non posse " ; *In Ps.* lxxv. 16 " cor
habeant, non sint fatui " ; *cf. In Ps.* xxxiv. ; *Serm.* 2. 8 " ubicumque invenerint Christianum, solent . . . vocare hebetem,
insulsum, nullius cordis."

    [b] Ecclus. v. 8.

    [c] This refers to Placidia's recall of Boniface from Africa
at the treacherous instigation of Boniface's rival, and the con-

such a calamity! Further, people say that you have not been content with your own wife, but have degraded yourself by having intercourse with some concubines or other. But perhaps this is lying gossip.

These evils, numerous and grave and known to 5 everybody, have been perpetrated by you since your marriage, and so what am I to say? You are a Christian, you possess intelligence,[a] you cherish the fear of God. Consider for yourself the things I am unwilling to utter, and you will find how great are the evils for which you ought to do penance. I believe it is for that that the Lord is sparing you and delivering you from all dangers, so that you may do it as it should be done, but on condition that you hearken to the words, " Tarry not to be converted to the Lord and put not off from day to day." [b] You maintain that your cause is just,[c] but I cannot judge of that, for I am unable to hear both sides; but whatever your cause be, and of that at present there is no need of inquiry or discussion, can you deny before God that you would not have fallen into these straits if you had not loved the good things of this world, which like a servant of God, as we knew you to be formerly, you ought entirely to have despised and counted as nothing? Accepting what was bestowed on you, you should have employed it to advance your godliness; that which was denied you or was entrusted to you to administer, you should not have sought after in such a way as to reduce yourself because of it to the present straits, in which, because of the love felt for vain things, evil things are done—few, indeed, by you, but many because of

sequent disgrace into which Boniface fell. It was unjust, for Aetius betrayed both the Empress and his rival.

a te sed multa propter te et, cum timentur quae
ad exiguum tempus nocent, si tamen nocent, com-
mittuntur ea quae vere noceant in aeternum?

6 De quibus ut unum aliquid dicam, quis non videat
quod multi homines tibi cohaereant ad tuendam
tuam potentiam vel salutem, qui, etiam si tibi omnes
fideles sint nec ab aliquo eorum ullae timeantur
insidiae, nempe tamen ad ea bona quae ipsi quoque
non secundum deum sed secundum saeculum diligunt,
per te cupiunt pervenire, ac per hoc, qui refrenare et
compescere debuisti cupiditates tuas, explere cogeris
alienas? Quod ut fiat, necesse est multa quae deo
displicent, fiant. Nec sic tamen explentur tales
cupiditates; nam facilius resecantur in eis qui deum
diligunt, quam in eis, qui mundum diligunt, aliquando satiantur. Propter quod dicit scriptura
divina: *Nolite diligere mundum nec ea quae in mundo
sunt. Si quis dilexerit mundum, dilectio patris non est
in eo, quia omne quod in mundo est, concupiscentia
carnis est et concupiscentia oculorum et ambitio saeculi,
quae non est a patre, sed ex mundo est. Et mundus
transit et concupiscentia eius; qui autem facit voluntatem
dei manet in aeternum, sicut et deus manet in aeternum.*
Quando ergo poteris tot hominum armatorum,
quorum fovenda est cupiditas, timetur atrocitas,
quando, inquam, poteris eorum concupiscentiam qui
diligunt mundum, non dico satiare, quod fieri nullo

---

a 1 John ii. 15-17. Augustine quotes this text with an
additional clause (" sicut . . . aeternum ") which is not in
the Greek original, but is found in the Sahidic version, in
Cyprian, and in Lucifer of Calaris. The same reading is
given in Augustine's *Tract. in Ioan.* 2. 10, but *ib.* 2. 4 he
reads "quomodo ipse . . ." Like the Vulgate, Augustine's

you, and since fear is felt for things which hurt for only a short time (if indeed they hurt at all), things are done which really hurt for all eternity.

To mention only one of these things : who can fail 6 to see that many men cleave to you for the preservation of your power or your personal safety, who (assuming that they are all loyal to you and that you need not apprehend treachery from any one of them) yet desire through you to attain to those good things which they too love, not in order to please God, but from worldly motives ? As a result, you, whose duty it was to bridle and check your desires, are compelled to satisfy those of others ; and before that can be done, many things have to be done that are displeasing to God. Even so, such desires as theirs are not quite satisfied, for it is easier altogether to cut them off in those who love God, than ever to give them appeasement in those who love the world. That is why Holy Scripture says, " Love not the world nor the things that are in the world. If any man love the world, the love of the Father is not in him. For all that is in the world, the lust of the flesh, the lust of the eyes, and the pride of life, is not of the Father, but is of the world. And the world passeth away, and the lust thereof ; but he that doeth the will of God abideth for ever, as God abideth for ever." [a] When, then, will you succeed with so many armed men whose desires have to be humoured and whose vindictiveness is to be feared—when, I repeat, will you succeed in bringing the desires of these men who love the world, not to actual repletion (for that is simply impossible),

version interpolates into the second part of verse 16 an *est* which is not in the Greek original.

modo potest, sed aliqua ex parte pascere, ne universa plus pereant, nisi tu facias quae deus prohibet et facientibus comminatur ? Propter quod vides tam multa contrita, ut iam vile aliquid quod rapiatur, vix inveniatur.

7 Quid autem dicam de vastatione Africae, quam faciunt Afri barbari resistente nullo, dum tu talis tuis necessitatibus occuparis nec aliquid ordinas unde ista calamitas avertatur ? Quis autem crederet, quis autem timeret, Bonifatio domesticorum et Africae comite in Africa constituto cum tam magno exercitu et potestate, qui tribunus cum paucis foederatis omnes ipsas gentes expugnando et terrendo pacaverat, nunc tantum fuisse barbaros ausuros, tantum progressuros, tanta vastaturos, tanta rapturos, tanta loca quae plena populis fuerant, deserta facturos ? Qui non dicebant, quandocumque tu comitivam sumeres potestatem, Afros barbaros non solum domitos sed etiam tributarios futuros Romanae rei publicae ? Et nunc quam in contrarium versa sit spes hominum, vides. Nec diutius hinc tecum loquendum est, quia plus ea tu potes cogitare quam nos dicere.

8 Sed forte ad ista respondes illis hoc esse potius inputandum, qui te laeserunt, qui tuis officiosis

---

ᵃ Boniface had apparently not followed the advice given him by Augustine in No. 42 § 7 "divitiae saeculares, si desunt, non per mala opera quaerantur in mundo." The historian Olympiodorus is much more favourable to Boniface: ἦν δὲ καὶ δικαιοσύνης ἐραστὴς καὶ χρημάτων κρείττων.

ᵇ There is as yet no question of the Vandals, whose coming to Africa was at least a year later. Of this campaign in Africa against the Moors no details are known. Freeman,

but to a moderate gratification, in order to avoid a universal destruction, if you do not do the things that God forbids and for which His vengeance will fall on the doers ? And to afford them gratification, you see the havoc has been so widespread that now hardly anything, however small its value, can be found for them to plunder.[a]

And what shall I say about the devastation of **7** Africa that is being wrought by African barbarians ? They meet with no opposition, so long as you are taken up with the difficulties of your own situation and take no measures to avert this calamity. After the appointment of Boniface as Count of the Household and of Africa with so great an army and such extensive authority—Boniface, who, while tribune, aided by a few confederates, quelled all those tribes by force of arms and the menace of his name,[b]— who would ever believe, who would ever be afraid, that those barbarians would be so daring, would encroach so far, would spread such devastation, seize so much plunder, make desolate so many places that were once crowded with people ? Did not everyone declare that, as soon as you took over the authority of Count, the African barbarians would not only be subdued, but would actually be made tributary to the Roman Empire ? And now you see how men's hopes have been dashed to the ground. On this subject I need not linger, for your own mind can suggest more to you than I can say.

But perhaps you reply to this with the defence **8** that the blame must rather be laid upon those who have injured you, who instead of a fair reward for

Western Europe, pp. 327-328, discusses this sentence as it bears on the point of Boniface's appointment as Count.

virtutibus non paria sed contraria reddiderunt.
Quas causas ego audire et iudicare non possum;
tuam causam potius aspice et inspice, quam non cum
hominibus quibuslibet, sed cum deo habere te cognoscis; quia in Christo fideliter vivis, ipsum debes
timere ne offendas. Nam causas ego superiores
potius adtendo, quia, ut Africa tanta mala patiatur,
suis debent inputare homines peccatis. Verum tamen
nolo te ad eorum numerum pertinere, per quos malos
et iniquos deus flagellat poenis temporalibus quos
voluerit. Ipsis namque iniquis, si correcti non fuerint,
servat aeterna supplicia, quorum malitia iuste utitur
ut aliis mala ingerat temporalia. Tu deum adtende,
tu Christum considera, qui tanta bona praestitit et
tanta mala pertulit. Quicumque ad eius regnum
cupiunt pertinere et cum illo ac sub illo semper beate
vivere, diligunt etiam inimicos suos, bene faciunt
illis qui eos oderunt, et orant pro eis a quibus per-
secutionem patiuntur, et, si quando adhibent pro
disciplina molestam severitatem, non tamen amittunt
sincerissimam caritatem. Si ergo bona tibi sunt praestita quamvis terrena transitoria ab imperio Romano,
quia et ipsum terrenum est, non caeleste, nec potest
praestare nisi quod habet in potestate; si ergo bona
in te conlata sunt, noli reddere mala pro bonis; si
autem mala tibi inrogata sunt, noli reddere mala

---

a Matt. v. 44; Luke vi. 27-28.
b No writer is so fond of the word *transitorius* as Augustine,
and not infrequently he uses it in conjunction with *terrenus*,
as here (*e.g. Serm.* 113. 6). From him comes probably the use
of the phrase in the Rule of St. Benedict, §2, and in Gregory
the Great, *In Ezech.* ii. 10. 21.

the virtues you displayed in office, rendered you the very opposite. The rights or wrongs of that I personally am unable to examine and decide ; rather look at and look into your own case, not as it lies between you and any men, but as it lies, to your own personal knowledge, between you and God ; for as you live in Christ as a believer, you ought to cherish fear of giving offence to Him. The cases that engage my attention are rather those of the world above, for it is to their own sins that men ought to attribute the fact that Africa is undergoing such calamities. Nevertheless, I do not want you to be of the number of those evil and unrighteous men whom God uses to scourge with temporal punishments those whom He chooses ; since for the unrighteous themselves, whose evil nature He justly employs to inflict temporal evils on others, He reserves everlasting punishment, if they do not reform. But as for yourself, fix your mind upon God, turn your thoughts to Christ, Who has bestowed such great blessings and endured such great sufferings. Those who desire to attain to His kingdom and to live with Him and under Him in everlasting blessedness, love even their enemies, do good to those who hate them and pray for those who persecute them[a]; and if at any time in the interests of discipline they employ irksome severity, they do not, however, lay aside their sincere affection. If, then, benefits have been conferred upon you by the Roman Empire, though they be earthly and transitory [b] (for that Empire itself is earthly, and not heavenly, and it can bestow only what lies within its own power); if, then, benefits have been bestowed upon you, render not evil for good ; but if evil has been inflicted upon

Q 429

pro malis. Quid istorum duorum sit, nec discutere
volo nec valeo iudicare ; ego Christiano loquor : noli
reddere vel mala pro bonis vel mala pro malis.

9   Dicis mihi fortasse : " In tanta necessitate quid
vis ut faciam ? " Si consilium a me secundum hoc
saeculum quaeris, quo modo ista salus tua transitoria
tuta sit, et potentia atque opulentia vel ista servetur
quam nunc habes, vel etiam maior addatur, quid tibi
respondeam, nescio ; incerta quippe ista certum
consilium habere non possunt. Si autem secundum
deum me consulis ne anima tua pereat, et times
verba veritatis dicentis : *Quid prodest homini, si
totum mundum lucretur, animae autem suae damnum
patiatur?* habeo plane, quod dicam ; est apud me
consilium quod a me audias. Quid autem opus est
ut aliud dicam quam illud quod supra dixi : *Noli
diligere mundum nec ea quae in mundo sunt. Si quis
enim dilexerit mundum, non est caritas patris in illo,
quoniam omnia quae in mundo sunt, concupiscentia
carnis est et concupiscentia oculorum et ambitio saeculi,
quae non est a patre, sed ex mundo est. Et mundus
transit et concupiscentia eius ; qui autem fecerit voluntatem dei, manet in aeternum, sicut et deus manet in
aeternum?* Ecce consilium ; arripe et age. Hic
appareat, si vir fortis es ; vince cupiditates, quibus
iste diligitur mundus, age paenitentiam de praeteritis
malis, quando ab eis cupiditatibus victus per desi-

ᵃ Rom. xii. 17 ; 1 Thess. v. 15 ; 1 Pet. iii. 9.

ᵇ *Cf.* Ter. *Eun.* 57-63 "quae res in se neque consilium
neque modum Habet ullum, eam consilio regere non potes."

ᶜ Matt. xvi. 26 ; Mark viii. 36 ; Luke ix. 25. This seems
to be the only place where Augustine quotes the form
damnum patiatur; elsewhere (*De Serm. Dom.* 2. 50, *C.
Adim.* 18, *Serm.* 330. 3) he has either *detrimentum faciat,* or
detrimentum patiatur.

you, render not evil for evil.[a] Which of these two
has been your lot, I do not wish to discuss nor am I
able to decide ; for my part I am speaking to a
Christian : render not evil for good nor yet evil for
evil.

You perhaps say to me, " What do you want me [9]
to do in these straits ? " If you ask advice from me
as after the spirit of this world, how your safety,
transitory as it is, may be secured, and your power
and wealth either preserved in their present condition or increased to greater dimensions, I am at a
loss what to answer you ; things as uncertain as
these do not admit of any certain counsel.[b] But if,
as in the sight of God, you consult me about saving
your soul from destruction and fear the word of
Truth Who says, " What is a man profited, if he shall
gain the whole world and lose his own soul ? ",[c] I
certainly have an answer to give ; I am ready with
advice which you must hear from me. Yet what need
is there for me to say anything different from what
I have already said : " Love not the world, neither
the things that are in the world. If any man love
the world, the love of the Father is not in him. For
all that is in the world, the lust of the flesh and the
lust of the eyes and the pride of life, is not of the
Father, but is of the world. And the world passeth
away, and the lust thereof ; but he that doeth the
will of God, abideth for ever, even as God abideth
for ever." [d] Here is advice for you ; lay hold of it
and act upon it. Let it now be seen if you are a
strong man ; vanquish the desires with which you
love the world. Do penance for the misdeeds of
the past, when these desires had you vanquished

[d] 1 John ii. 15-17.

deria vana trahebaris. Hoc consilium si acceperis, si tenueris atque servaveris, et ad bona illa certa pervenies et cum salute animae tuae inter ista incerta versaberis.

10 Sed forte iterum quaeris a me, quo modo ista facias tantis mundi huius necessitatibus implicatus. Ora fortiter et dic deo, quod habes in psalmo : *De necessitatibus meis erue me.* Tunc enim finiuntur istae necessitates, quando vincuntur illae cupiditates. Qui exaudivit te et nos pro te, ut libereris de tot tantisque periculis visibilium corporaliumque bellorum, ubi sola ista vita quandoque finienda periclitatur, anima vero non perit, si non malignis cupiditatibus captiva teneatur, ipse te exaudiet, ut interiores et invisibiles hostes, id est ipsas cupiditates, invisibiliter et spiritaliter vincas et sic utaris hoc mundo tamquam non utens, ut ex bonis eius bona facias, non malus fias, quia et ipsa bona sunt nec dantur hominibus nisi ab illo, qui habet omnium caelestium et terrestrium potestatem. Sed ne putentur mala, dantur et bonis ; ne putentur magna vel summa bona, dantur et malis itemque auferuntur ista et bonis, ut probentur, et malis, ut crucientur.

11 Quis enim nesciat, quis ita sit stultus, ut non videat quod salus huius mortalis corporis et mem-

---

and empty passions dragged you in their train. If you will receive this advice and hold fast to it and keep it, you will both attain to those blessings which are certain and pass through the midst of these uncertain things without harm to your own soul.

But perhaps you ask me again how you are to accomplish this, involved as you are in the great distresses of this world. Be earnest in prayer and say to God the words you find in the Psalm, " Bring thou me out of my distresses," [a] for then are these distresses ended when those desires are overcome. He who has answered your prayers and our prayers for you and has delivered you from the many great dangers of the warfare in which men visibly risk their bodies, in which the stake is but this life that must sooner or later come to an end, while the soul escapes destruction unless it be held in captivity by evil desires—He will Himself also answer your prayer for an invisible and spiritual victory over your inward and invisible foes, that is these same desires, and help you to " use this world as not abusing it," [b] so that with its good things you may do good, instead of becoming evil. For these things are good in themselves and are not given to men save by Him Who has power over all things in heaven and in earth; and on the one hand they are bestowed upon the good, so that they may not be thought to be evil ; on the other, they are bestowed upon the evil, so that they may not be thought to be the great or supreme good ; and likewise they are taken away from the good, in order to try them, and from the evil, in order to punish them.

Who is so ignorant, who so foolish, as not to see that the health of this mortal body and the strength

brorum corruptibilium virtus et victoria de hominibus
inimicis et honor atque potentia temporalis et cetera
ista bona terrena et bonis dentur et malis et bonis
auferantur et malis ? Salus vero animae cum inmortalitate corporis virtusque iustitiae et victoria de
cupiditatibus inimicis et gloria et honor et pax in
aeternum non dantur nisi bonis. Ista ergo dilige,
ista concupisce, ista modis omnibus quaere. Propter
haec adquirenda et obtinenda fac elemosynas, funde
orationes, exerce ieiunia, quantum sine laesione tui
corporis potes. Bona vero illa terrena noli diligere
quanta libet tibi abundent. Sic eis utere, ut bona
multa ex illis, nullum autem malum facias propter
illa. Omnia quippe talia peribunt, sed bona opera
non pereunt, etiam quae de bonis pereuntibus fiunt.

12   Si enim coniugem non haberes, dicerem tibi quod
et Tubunis diximus, ut in castitate continentiae
viveres ; adderem quod tunc fieri prohibuimus, ut
iam te, quantum rerum humanarum salva pace
potuisses, ab istis bellicis rebus abstraheres et e
vitae vacares in societate sanctorum, cui tunc vacare
cupiebas, ubi in silentio pugnant milites Christi, no

---

a *Miles Christi,* like *servus Christi,* does not exclusively
mean " monks," but refers generally to Christian service
whether on the part of the laity (Ambr. *Ep.* 27. 15 " omne
qui sunt in ecclesia, Deo militant " ; Leo Magn. *Serm.* 89.
has the phrase *ecclesiasticus miles* of a layman), or of the
regular clergy (Aug. *Ep.* lx. 1 " ad militiam clericatu
eligantur," *Ep.* xxi. 1 " quo modo militetur "), or of monk
(Aug. *Ep.* cli. 8 " ne susciperet cingulum militiae Chris
tianae vinculum praepediebat uxorium "). This use was
natural extension of the idea of service connoted by *militare*
and it was encouraged by the Pauline phrase in 1 Tim. i. 1
" milites in illis bonam militiam," and 2 Tim. iv. 2 " nem
militans Deo . . ." In especial, *militare* was used b
Christian writers of the centuries of persecution to denot

of its corruptible members, and victory over men who are our foes, and honour and temporal power and all other earthly blessings, are bestowed upon both the good and the evil and are taken away from both the good and the evil ? But the health of the soul, along with the immortality of the body, and the strength of righteousness and victory over the desires that are our foes, and glory and honour and peace for evermore, are bestowed upon the good alone. These things, then, love and desire and seek by every possible means. To secure them and hold them fast, give alms, pour forth prayers, practise fasting as much as you can without harming your body ; but love not those earthly blessings, however much you may abound in them. Make such use of them that you do many good deeds by them and no single evil deed because of them. For all such things will pass away, but good deeds do not pass away, even those which are done with the aid of the good things that pass away.

If you had not a wife, I should tell you what we 12 said to you already at Tubunae, that you should live in the holy state of continence ; to that I should add what we then forbade you to do, namely, that you should withdraw from your military labours as far as is possible without endangering the peace of mankind, and obtain the leisure to follow that quiet life you then expressed your desire to follow, in the community of the holy, where the soldiers of Christ [a] contend in silence, not with the purpose of taking

the " service " of martyrs (Cypr. *Ep.* 60. 2 " milites Christi . . . prompte et animas et sanguinem tradere "). On the other hand, it was used too by Christian writers of the service of the world, sin, or the devil (Aug. *Conf.* ix. 8. 17 " relicta militia saeculari accinctus in Tua ").

ut occidant homines, sed ut expugnent *principes et potestates et spiritalia nequitiae*, id est diabolum et angelos eius. Hos enim hostes sancti vincunt, quos videre non possunt; et tamen, quos non vident vincunt, ista vincendo quae sentiunt. Sed ut te ad istam vitam non exhorter, coniunx impedimento est, sine cuius consensione continenter tibi non liceat vivere, quia, etsi tu eam post illa tua verba Tubunensia ducere non debebas, illa tibi tamen nihil eorum sciens innocenter et simpliciter nupsit. Atque utinam posses ei persuadere continentiam, ut sine impedimento redderes deo quod te debere cognoscis! Sed si cum illa agere non potes, serva saltem pudicitiam coniugalem et roga deum, qui te de necessitatibus eruat, ut, quod non potes modo, possis aliquando. Verum tamen, ut deum diligas, non diligas mundum; ut in ipsis bellis, si adhuc in eis te versari opus est, fidem teneas, pacem quaeras; ut ex mundi bonis facias opera bona et propter mundi bona non facias opera mala, aut non impedit coniunx aut impedire non debet. Haec ad te, fili dilectissime, ut scriberem, caritas iussit, qua te secundum deum, non secundum hoc saeculum diligo, quia et cogitans quod scriptum est: *Corripe sapientem et amabit te, corripe stultum et adiciet odisse te*, non te utique stultum sed sapientem debui cogitare.

---

^a Eph. vi. 12.   ^b Matt. xxv. 41.   ^c Prov. ix. 8.

men's lives, but of conquering "principalities and powers and spiritual wickedness,"[a] that is, the devil and his angels.[b] For these are the enemies whom the holy vanquish, enemies they cannot see ; and yet they vanquish the enemies they cannot see by vanquishing the objects of their senses. But to that kind of life I am prevented from urging you, for your wife stands in the way, and without her consent you cannot adopt a life of continence ; because, although you had no right to marry her after what you said at Tubunae, yet she became your wife in all innocence and single-mindedness, knowing nothing of your declaration. Yet would that you could persuade her to continence, so that with nothing in your way you could render unto God what you know you owe Him ! But if you cannot arrange that with her, preserve at least your conjugal chastity and ask God, Who can "bring you out of your distresses," to grant that you may be able to do sooner or later what you find impossible now. But yet, in order to love God, you must give up loving the world ; in your warfare (if you have still to be engaged in it) keep the faith and ensue peace ; use this world's goods to do good deeds, and to obtain this world's goods do not do evil deeds — in these duties a wife is not a hindrance, or ought not to be.

I have written thus to you, my beloved son, at the bidding of the love wherewith I love you, not in the way of this world, but in God's way. And when I recall to mind the words of Scripture, "Reprove a wise man and he will love thee ; reprove a fool and he will hate thee more,"[c] I had to think of you as surely not a fool, but a wise man.

No. 52 (Ep. CCXXVII)

[BEATI AUGUSTINI AD SENEM ALYPIUM DE CONVERSIONE DIOSCURI]

Frater Paulus hic est incolumis ; adportat negotiorum suorum secundas curas ; praestabit dominus,
ut etiam ipsa ultima sint. Multum vos salutat et
narrat gaudia de Gaviniano, quod ab illa sua causa
misericordia dei liberatus non solum Christianus sed
etiam fidelis sit valde bonus per pascha proxime
baptizatus, in corde atque in ore habens gratiam
quam percepit. Quantum eum desiderem, quando
explicabo ? Sed nosti ut eum diligam. Archiater
etiam Dioscorus Christianus fidelis est, simul gratiam
consecutus. Audi etiam quem ad modum ; neque
enim cervicula illa vel lingua nisi aliquo prodigio
domarentur. Filia eius, in qua unica adquiescebat,
aegrotabat et usque ad totam desperationem salutis
temporalis eodem ipso patre renuntiante pervenit.

ᵃ Dioscurus is unknown except from this letter. Brother
Paul is probably the Paul mentioned in the last letter. Nothing
is known of the business here spoken of, or of Gavinianus.

ᵇ *Fidelis* in this sense is contrasted with *catechumenus*, a
distinction which is as early as Tertullian (*Praescr. Haer.* 41
" quis catechumenus, quis fidelis, incertum est ; pariter
adeunt, pariter audiunt, pariter orant "). Jerome speaks
(*In Isaiam* xix. 19) of five orders in the Church : *episcopos,
presbyteros, diaconos, fideles, catechumenos,* and Augustine
(*Serm.* 21. 5) mentions a higher kind of faith, " qua fidelis
vocaris, accedens ad mensam Domini tui," and (*Serm.* 93. 2)
defines *fidelis* : " Fidelibus dico, eis quibus Christi corpus
erogamus." ᶜ Rom. x. 8.

ᵈ The *archiater* (ἀρχιατρός) was a municipal doctor,
appointed by the decurions and receiving a salary from the
town. They enjoyed, with their wives and families, special
privileges (*Cod. Theod.* xiii. iii. 1, 2, 3 " archiatri omnes

No. 52 (Ep. CCXXVII)

(A.D. 428 or 429)

[TO THE SENIOR ALYPIUS FROM AUGUSTINE, ABOUT THE CONVERSION OF DIOSCURUS [a]]

Brother Paul has arrived back safely; he reports that his affairs have been considered favourably; the Lord will grant that this may be the last of them. He sends you hearty greetings and gives us the joyful news about Gavinianus, that having secured deliverance, by God's mercy, from that case of his, he is now not only a Christian but has become a very admirable member of the Church,[b] having received baptism last Easter, and professing in his heart and with his mouth [c] the grace that was bestowed on him. I could never express the greatness of my longing for him, but you know how dear he is to me. The town physician,[d] Dioscurus, has also become a Christian and joined the Church, having received grace at the same time. I must tell you how it came about, for one so stiff-necked and sharp-tongued could have been subjugated only by a miracle.

His daughter, an only child, the pride of his life, was ill, and she reached a point when the recovery of her bodily health was quite despaired of, and her own father gave her up. The story goes (and its truth

... a praestationibus quoque publicis liberi immunesque permaneant "). Rome and Constantinople had these municipal doctors appointed in 368, and at Rome there were fourteen in all, one for each region. In Ep. xli. 2 Augustine speaks of one Hilarinus, whom he calls *Hipponiensem archiatrum et principalem*, and another is mentioned by one of his correspondents in Ep. ccxxx. 6.

Dicitur ergo—et constat, cum mihi hoc et ante
fratris Pauli reditum comes Peregrinus, vir laudabilis
et bene Christianus, qui cum eis eodem tempore baptizatus est, indicaret,—dicitur ergo ille senex tandem
conversus ad inplorandam Christi misericordiam voto
se obligasse Christianum fore, si illam salvam videret.
Factum est. At ille, quod voverat, dissimulabat
exsolvere. Sed adhuc manus excelsa. Nam repentina caecitate suffunditur statimque venit in mentem
unde illud esset. Exclamavit confitens atque iterum
vovit se, recepto lumine, impleturum esse quod
voverat. Recepit, implevit. Et adhuc manus excelsa. Symbolum non tenuerat aut fortasse tenere
recusaverat et se non potuisse excusaverat. Deus
viderit. Iam tamen post festa omnia receptionis
suae in paralysin solvitur multis ac paene omnibus
membris, tunc somnio admonitus confitens per
scripturam ob hoc sibi dictum esse accidisse, quod
symbolum non reddiderit. Post illam confessionem
redduntur officia membrorum omnium nisi linguae
solius. Se tamen didicisse symbolum ideoque me-

---

[a] Apparently mentioned only here.

[b] This is a Biblical phrase, occurring in Exod. xiv. 8,
Num. xxxiii. 3, and Deut. xxxii. 27, where it seems to imply
" with unbroken pride," or the like. Similar is Job xxxviii.
15 " auferetur ab impiis lux sua, et brachium excelsum
confringetur."

[c] *Teneo*, thus used, is found in Plautus, Virgil (*Ecl.* ix. 45
" numeros memini, si verba tenerem "), Martial (iv. 37
" teneo melius ista, quam meum nomen "), and others,
though Cicero always uses *memoria tenere.* Augustine uses
it both with *memoria,* and without (*In Ioan. Ev.* 69. 4 " si
tenueritis quod audistis " ; *Quant. An.* 7. 12 " nosse hoc
plane ac tenere volumus "). Candidates for baptism were expected to memorize the Creed, which it was forbidden to write
down (*Retr.* i. 17 speaking of his book *De Fide et Symbolo,*

is vouched for by the fact that even before the return
of brother Paul it was told me by Count Peregrinus,[a]
an admirable man and a thorough Christian, who
received baptism at the same time as they did)—the
story goes then that the old man finally turned to
implore the pity of Christ and bound himself by a
vow to become a Christian, if he saw her out of
danger. That prayer was granted, but in spite of
that he neglected to fulfil his vow. But his hand
was still high.[b] For suddenly he is smitten with
blindness and it immediately occurred to him why
that had happened. He cried out, confessing his
fault, and made another vow that, if he received back
his sight, he would fulfil his earlier vow. He received
it back, he fulfilled his vow. And still his hand was
high.[b] He had not memorized[c] the Creed, or perhaps
had refused to memorize it, and had offered the excuse
that he could not. Let God be judge. But just after
the completion of the ceremony of his admission, he
fell into a paralytic seizure affecting many, if not all,
of his members. Then, being warned in a dream, he
confessed in writing that he had been told this had
befallen him for the reason that he had failed to
repeat the Creed. After that confession the use of all
his limbs was restored to him, saving only his tongue.
Yet he confessed on paper that in spite of that

which he wrote without putting the Creed in writing, " ut
tamen non fiat verborum illa contextio quae tenenda memoriter competentibus traditur " ; *Serm.* 212. 2 " nec ut
eadem verba Symboli teneatis, ullo modo debetis scribere,
sed audiendo perdiscere; nec . . . scribere, sed memoriter
semper tenere " ; *Serm.* 58. 1 " quicumque vestrum non
bene reddiderunt, habent spatium, teneant ; quia die sabbati
audientibus omnibus qui aderunt reddituri estis, die sabbati
novissimo, quo die baptizandi estis ").

moria iam tenere nihilo minus in eadem temptatione
litteris fassus est, et omnis est ab eo deleta nugaci-
tas, quae, ut scis, multum dedecorabat naturalem
quandam eius benignitatem eumque insultantem
Christianis faciebat valde sacrilegum. Quid dicam
domino, nisi *hymnum canamus et superexaltemus eum
in saecula*? Amen.

No. 53 (Ep. CCXXIX)

DOMINO MERITO INLUSTRI ET MAGNIFICEN-
TISSIMO ATQUE IN CHRISTO CARISSIMO
FILIO DARIO AUGUSTINUS

1   A sanctis fratribus et coepiscopis meis Urbano et
Novato, qualis sis vir et quantus, accepi, quorum
alteri apud Carthaginem in Hilarensi oppido et modo
in Siccensi, alteri autem apud Sitifim te nosse pro-
venit. Per hos ergo factum est ut nec ego te habere

---

[a] Judith xvi. 15; Dan. iii. 57.

[b] Darius, a high official at the court of Valentinian III.,
was sent in 429 to Africa to negotiate a peace between
Count Boniface and the Emperor. He was accompanied by
his son Verimodus, alluded to at the end of the letter.
Augustine here writes congratulating him on making peace
with the Vandals.

[c] This Urbanus is most probably the bishop of Sicca, who
was originally a member of Augustine's monastery at Hippo
(Ep. cxlix. 34); he became bishop there before 418. He is
best remembered as the central figure in that Council of 418
which decreed that no African cleric should prosecute an
appeal overseas (*cf.* p. 364 above)—a decree of great importance in the controversy about the supremacy of the see
of Rome. Sicca (or Sicca Veneria, so-called from its famous
temple to Astarte, whom the Romans identified with Venus)

seizure he had learned the Creed and still retained it
in his memory. And thus was destroyed in him all the
scurrility which, as you know, was a great blemish
on his natural kindness and made him, when he
mocked Christians, a very sacrilegious man. What
shall I say save " Let us sing a hymn to the Lord
and highly exalt Him for ever " [a]? Amen.

No. 53 (Ep. CCXXIX)

(A.D. 429)

AUGUSTINE TO DARIUS,[b] MY DESERVEDLY
    ILLUSTRIOUS AND MOST DISTINGUISHED
    LORD AND SON WARMLY CHERISHED IN
    CHRIST

From my holy brethren and fellow-bishops Urbanus [1]
and Novatus [c] I have learned of your character and
high position ; one of them had the good fortune to
make your acquaintance in the town of Hilari near
Carthage and recently at Sicca, the other at Sitifis.
Through them it has been brought about that I too

is the modern Le Kef, lying about 125 miles south-west of
Tunis ; its strategical position on the great roads between
Numidia and Proconsular Africa gave it great importance.
    Novatus was bishop of Sitifis (Sétif) in Mauretania ; he
was addressed by Augustine in No. 22 above. The *Hilarense
oppidum* I have not succeeded in locating. One of the four
manuscripts of this letter reads *larensi*, whis is probably the
adjectival form of the name *Lares*, an important town
10 miles south-east of Sicca Veneria and prominent during
the war with Jugurtha (Sallust, *Iug.* 90). Though at a
considerable distance from Carthage, it was within Carthaginian territory, and was easy for Darius to reach from
Sicca, so I am inclined to adopt the reading *Larensi* here in
place of the unidentifiable *Hilarensi*.

incognitum possem. Neque enim quia me infirmitas corporis et geminum frigus, id est hiemis et aetatis, non sinit coram tecum conloqui, ideo non te vidi ; nam iste mihi etiam praesens, quando ad me venire dignatus est, ille autem litteris, non faciem tuae carnis sed cordis ostendit, ut tanto suavius quanto interius te viderem. Hanc faciem tuam etiam in sancto evangelio et nos et tu ipse propitio deo tamquam in speculo laetissimus inspicis, ubi scriptum est a veritate dicente : *Beati pacifici, quoniam filii dei vocabuntur.*

2 Magni quidem sunt et habent gloriam suam non solum fortissimi sed etiam, quod verioris origo laudis, fidelissimi bellatores et quorum laboribus atque periculis dei protegentis atque opitulantis auxilio hostis indomitus vincitur, quies rei publicae pacatisque provinciis comparatur ; sed maioris est gloriae ipsa bella verbo occidere quam homines ferro, et adquirere vel obtinere pacem pace non bello. Nam et hi qui pugnant, si boni sunt, procul dubio pacem sed tamen per sanguinem quaerunt ; tu autem, ne cuiusquam sanguis quaereretur, es missus. Est itaque aliis illa necessitas, tibi ista felicitas. Proinde, domine merito inlustris et magnificentissime atque in Christo carissime fili, gaude isto tuo tam magno et vero bono et fruere in deo, unde sumpsisti ut talis

---

[a] Matt. v. 9.

cannot regard you as unknown to me. For the fact that my bodily weakness and the twofold cold, of winter and of old age, does not permit me to have converse with you face to face, has not prevented me from seeing you, for one of these friends, when present with me on a visit he was good enough to make, revealed to me the countenance of your heart, if not of your body, and the other did so by letter, so that I have all the greater pleasure in seeing the more inward man. This countenance of yours both you and I, by God's favour, behold with joy in the Holy Gospel, as in a mirror, where the words are written that were uttered by Him who is truth: "Blessed are the peacemakers, for they shall be called the children of God."[a]

Those men are indeed great and they have their own honour who as warriors display not only great courage but also (what is the source of more genuine praise) great fidelity, and by their toils and perils, with the assistance of God's protection and aid, subdue foes before invincible, and procure peace for the state and for the tranquillized provinces. But it is a greater glory to slay war with a word than men with the sword and to gain and maintain peace by means of peace, not by means of war. For even those who fight are certainly seeking peace, if they are good men, but seeking it by the shedding of blood, while you have been sent to prevent the seeking of anyone's blood. Others are therefore under the necessity of taking life, while you have the felicity of sparing it. Wherefore rejoice, my deservedly illustrious and most distinguished lord and son warmly cherished in Christ, in the great and genuine blessing that is yours and enjoy it in the Lord to Whom you owe it that you

esses et talia gerenda susciperes. Confirmet deus
quod per te operatus est nobis. Accipe hanc
salutationem nostram et tuam dignare rependere.
Sicut mihi scripsit frater Novatus, egit ut me excellentia et eruditio tua etiam in meis opusculis
nosset. Si ergo legisti quae dedit, ego quoque in-
notui interioribus tuis sensibus, non multum dis-
plicens, quantum existimo, si propensiore caritate
quam severitate legisti. Non est multum sed multum
gratum, si pro litteris nostris et his et illis unam nobis
epistulam reddas. Saluto etiam pignus pacis, quod
domino deo nostro adiuvante feliciter accepisti, ea
dilectione qua debeo.

No. 54 (Ep. CCXXXI)

AUGUSTINUS SERVUS CHRISTI MEMBRORUM-
QUE CHRISTI DARIO FILIO MEMBRO
CHRISTI IN IPSO SALUTEM

1   Quod acceperim libenter litteras tuas, mea rescripta indicio esse voluisti. Ecce rescribo et tamen
rescriptis hoc indicare non possum vel istis vel
quibuslibet aliis, sive breviter sive prolixissime
scribam ; neque enim aut paucis aut multis verbis

---

are what you are and that you have undertaken the task it is yours to accomplish. May God " strengthen that which He hath wrought for us through you "[a]! Accept this my greeting and be good enough to repay it with one from you. As I am informed by the letter of my brother Novatus, he has taken steps to make your learned Excellency acquainted with me also in my writings. If, then, you have read the works he gave you, I too have become known to your more inward perceptions, nor would you, I imagine, find me very unsatisfactory, if your reading has been done with greater inclination to love than to harshness. It is not asking very much, but it will be very much appreciated, if in return for my writings, both this one and those others, you send me a single letter. I greet too with all due affection the pledge of peace,[b] whom you have been happy enough to receive by the favour of the Lord our God.

No. 54 (Ep. CCXXXI)

(A.D. 429)

AUGUSTINE, SERVANT OF CHRIST AND OF THE
MEMBERS OF CHRIST, TO DARIUS,[c] MY SON,
A MEMBER OF CHRIST, GREETING IN HIM

You wanted a reply from me as evidence that I 1
have received your letter with joy, so, see, I send
you one. And yet in a reply, be it this one or
any other, it is impossible for me, whether writing
briefly or at great length, to make that evident, for
neither a few words nor many can be evidence of

447

indicari potest quod indicari verbis non potest. Et
ego quidem parum eloquor, etsi multum loquor ;
sed nulli eloquenti omnino concesserim ut qualicumque et quantacumque epistula sua affectum explicet, quem fecit in me tua, quod non possum ego,
etiam si eum possit ita in animo meo videre sicut ego.
Restat ergo sic tibi indicare quod scire voluisti, ut
in verbis meis, et quod non indicant, sentias. Quid
igitur dicam nisi delectatum me esse litteris tuis
valde valde ? Repetitio verbi huius non est repetitio
sed quasi perpetua dictio ; quia enim fieri non posset
ut semper diceretur, ideo factum est ut saltem
repeteretur ; sic enim fortasse dici potest quod dici
non potest.

2   Hic si quaerat aliquis quid me tandem in tuis tam
valde litteris delectaverit, utrum eloquium, respondebo : " Non " ; et ille forsitan respondebit : " Ergo
laudes tuae " ; sed de his quoque respondebo :
" Non," nec ideo, quia non sunt ista in illa epistula ;
nam et eloquium ibi tantum est, ut et optimo te
natum ingenio et talibus disciplinis satis eruditum
praeclarissime luceat, et prorsus plena est meis
laudibus. " Ergone," ait quispiam, " non te ista
delectant ? " Immo vero ; " neque enim mihi,"
ut ait quidam, " cornea fibra est," ut haec non sentiam
vel sine delectatione sentiam. Delectant et ista ;

---

^a Pers. i. 47.

what words cannot make evident at all. And for
my part, though I have the gift of copious expression,
I have only a limited power of self-expression ; yet
I would certainly not admit that any man, however
gifted with the power of expression, could describe
in a letter, no matter how good or how long, the
feelings awakened in me by your letter ; it is quite
beyond my power, and he cannot observe them
within me as I do myself. It only remains for me,
then, to give you the evidence you wanted to have in
such a way that in my words you may feel evidence
of what they cannot express. So what shall I say
but this, that I was very, very pleased with your
letter ? The repetition of that word is not so much
a repetition as a constant utterance, but since the
perpetual utterance of it is quite impossible, I have
done the only thing possible by at least repeating
it. In this way, perhaps, things may be uttered that
completely defy utterance.

At this point, if anyone were to ask what after all 2
it was in your letter that pleased me so very much,
if it was its eloquence, I shall say "No"; he will
perhaps reply, "Then it was the praise of yourself,"
and to that too I shall say "No"; not for the
reason that your letter was without these, for it was
eloquent enough very notably to reveal the fact that
your natural endowments are of the finest quality
and that your training in the literary disciplines has
been good ; and, further, your letter was full of
praises of myself. "And so," someone may say,
"things of that kind give you no pleasure ?" It is
the other way round, for, as someone has remarked,
"my heart is not made of horn,"[a] that I either do not
feel such things or feel them without pleasure. I do

449

sed ad illud, quo me valde dixi esse delectatum,
quid sunt ista? nam eloquium tuum me delectat,
quoniam graviter suave est vel suaviter grave;
meis autem laudibus cum profecto nec omnibus
delecter nec ab omnibus, sed eis qualibus me dignum
esse arbitratus es, et ab eis qualis es, id est qui
propter Christum diligunt servos eius, etiam laudibus
meis me delectatum in litteris tuis negare non
possum.

3   Viderint graves et periti viri quid de illo The-
mistocle sentiant, si tamen hominis nomen verum
recolo, qui cum in epulis, quod clari et eruditi
Graeciae facere solebant, canere fidibus recusasset
et ob hoc indoctior haberetur totumque illud iucun-
ditatis genus aspernatus esset, dictum illi est:
"Quid ergo audire te delectat?" Ad quod ille
respondisse fertur: "Laudes meas." Viderint ergo
quo fine qua intentione illud dixisse crediderint vel
ipse qua dixerit. Erat enim secundum hoc saeculum
vir magnificus. Nam etiam cum ei dictum fuisset:
"Quid igitur nosti?" "Rem publicam," inquit,
"ex parva magnam facere." Ego autem, quod ait
Ennius: "Omnes mortales sese laudari exoptant,"
partim puto adprobandum, partim cavendum. Ut
enim appetenda est veritas, quae procul dubio
est, etiam si non laudetur, sola laudabilis, sic ea
quae facile subrepit, vanitas in hominum laude
fugienda est; haec est autem, cum vel ipsa bona

  [a] Cic. *Pro Arch.* 9. 20; Plut. *Them.* 2; Cic. *Tusc. Disp.*
1. 2. 4.
  [b] Enn. *Ann.* 560 (ed. Vahlen).

take pleasure in even such things as these, but, alongside that which made me, as I said, very pleased, what are such things after all ? Your eloquence does give me pleasure, so gravely sweet and so sweetly grave it is ; with the praise of myself, however, though certainly I neither find pleasure in every kind nor from every man, but only in such as you consider me worthy to receive and from men such as you are, who for Christ's sake love His servants—even with the praise of myself contained in your letter I cannot deny that I was very well pleased.

Let serious-minded and experienced men consider **3** what opinion they should form of the well-known Themistocles[a] (if I remember his name aright), who at a banquet, on refusing to play on the lyre, a usual practice among the distinguished and learned men of Greece, and being on that account deemed a less cultured person, and scorning all that kind of amusement, is said, when asked what he did take pleasure in hearing, to have made answer, " My own praises." Let such men consider what they think the aim and intention of this remark was or what was the intention of the speaker. He was, indeed, a very high-minded man, in the eyes of this world, for when the further question was asked him, " What then do you know ? " he replied, " How to make a small state great." For myself, however, I hold that the saying of Ennius that " All mortal men are eager to be praised,"[b] is partly to be approved of, partly to be taken as a warning. For just as truth is to be sought after, as being without a doubt the only thing deserving of praise, even if praise be withheld, so is the easily and furtively developing pride in the praise of men to be shunned. And that is the case when, on the one hand, those good

quae laudatione digna sunt, non putantur habenda,
nisi laudetur ab hominibus homo, vel ea quoque
vult in se multum quisque laudari, quae aut exigua
laude aut etiam vituperatione digniora sunt. Unde
Horatius Ennio vigilantior ait :

> laudis amore tumes? sunt certa piacula, quae te
> ter pure lecto poterunt recreare libello.

4 Ita tumorem de amore laudis humanae velut
serpentis morsum medicinalibus verbis quasi ex-
cantandum putavit. Docuit itaque nos per apostolum suum magister bonus neque propterea nos recte
vivere et recte facere, ut laudemur ab hominibus,
id est finem recti nostri non in hominum laudibus
ponere et tamen propter ipsos homines quaerere
laudes hominum. Etenim cum laudantur boni, non
laudatis sed laudantibus prodest. Nam illis, quantum ad ipsos adtinet, quod boni sunt sufficit ; sed
eis, quibus expedit imitari bonos, gratulandum est,
cum ab eis laudantur boni, quoniam sic indicant eos
sibi placere, quos veraciter laudant. Dicit ergo
apostolus quodam loco: *Si hominibus placerem, Christi
servus non essem*, et idem dicit alio loco : *Placete
omnibus per omnia, sicut et ego omnibus per omnia
placeo*, sed adiungens causam : *Non quaerens quod
mihi utile est, sed quod multis, ut salvi fiant*. Ecce
quod quaerebat in laude hominum, ubi etiam dicebat :
*De cetero, fratres, quaecumque sunt vera, quaecumque
pudica, quaecumque casta, quaecumque sancta, quaecum-*

  ᵃ Hor. *Ep.* i. 1. 36-37.

  ᵇ 1 Thess. ii. 4; Matt. v. 16; for the phrase *cf.* Pers. i. 48
  " sed recti finemque extremumque esse recuso ' Euge ' tuum
  et ' belle.' "   ᶜ Gal. i. 10.

  ᵈ 1 Cor. x. 33. The words *Placete omnibus per omnia* is
  only his paraphrase of the preceding verse: *Sine offensione
  estote Iudaeis et gentibus et ecclesiae Dei.*

qualities that are worthy of being praised are thought
not worth possessing unless a man is praised by his
fellows, or, on the other hand, when a man desires
great praise for things which are worthier of either
slight praise or even censure. Hence Horace was
much more cautious than Ennius in saying [a]:

> Swell you with lust for praise? Then read thrice o'er
> Some book whose charms are potent to restore.

You see he thought that the swelling arising from
the lust for human praise was to be, as it were, charmed
away, like some serpent's bite, by healing words.
The Good Master has accordingly taught us by His
apostle not to live right and do right with the object
of being praised by men, that is, not to make the
praise of men the motive of our doing right, and yet
He has taught us for men's sake to seek men's praise.[b]
For when good men are praised, the praise confers a
benefit on those who bestow it, not on those who
receive it. For as far as concerns the good, the fact
that they are good is sufficient, but the others, whose
interest it is to imitate the good, are to be congratu-
lated when they bestow praise on the good, since by
doing so they show that they are pleased by those
whom they praise in sincerity. So the apostle says
in a certain passage, " If I yet pleased men, I should
not be the servant of Christ," [c] and he says in another
passage, Please all men in all things, " even as I
please all men in all things [d] "; but he adds the
reason, " Not seeking mine own profit, but the profit
of many that they may be saved." See what he
sought in men's praise, of which he says further,
" Finally, brethren, whatsoever things are true,
whatsoever things are honest, whatsoever things are

que carissima, quaecumque bonae famae, si qua virtus, si qua laus, haec cogitate ; quae didicistis et accepistis et audistis et vidistis in me, haec agite et deus pacis erit vobiscum. Cetera igitur quae supra commemoravit, virtutis nomine amplexus est, dicens *" si qua virtus "* ; illud autem quod subiecit *" quaecumque bonae famae,"* alio uno verbo congruo prosecutus est dicendo *" si qua laus."* Quod itaque ait : *Si hominibus placerem, Christi servus non essem*, sic utique accipiendum est tamquam dixerit : " Si bona quae facio, fine laudis humanae facerem, laudis amore tumescerem." Volebat ergo apostolus placere omnibus et eis placere gaudebat, non quorum laudibus tumescebat in se ipso, sed quos laudatus aedificabat in Christo. Cur ergo me non delectet laudari abs te, cum et vir bonus sis, ne me fallas, et ea laudes quae amas et quae amare utile ac salubre est, etiam si non sint in me ? Neque hoc tibi tantum sed etiam mihi prodest. Si enim non sunt in me, salubriter erubesco, atque ut sint, inardesco. Ac per hoc, quae agnosco mea in laude tua, gaudeo me habere et abs te illa ac me ipsum diligi propter illa ; quae autem non agnosco, non solum ut ipse habeam, desidero consequi, verum etiam ne semper in mea laude fallantur qui me sinceriter diligunt.

---

[a] Phil. iv. 8-9.

just, whatsoever things are pure, whatsoever things are lovely, whatsoever things are of good report ; if there be any virtue, and if there be any praise, think on these things. Those things, which ye have both learned and received and heard and seen in me, do ; and the God of peace shall be with you." [a] So the other things he mentioned above he included under the word "virtue," saying, "If there be any virtue"; what he meant by the words, "Whatsoever things are of good report," he followed up by the single, appropriate phrase, "If there be any praise." So his words, "If I yet pleased men, I should not be the servant of Christ," are to be understood in this way, as if he had said, "If I were doing the good I do with the motive of receiving human praise, I should be 'swelling with the lust for praise.'" The apostle wanted therefore to please all men, and found joy in pleasing those whom he edified in Christ by receiving their praise, not those whose praise made him swell within himself. Why should I not therefore find pleasure in being praised by you, when you are (unless I am mistaken in you) a good man and bestow your praise upon the things which you admire and which it is profitable and wholesome for you to admire, even if they be lacking in me ? This benefits not only you, but me too, for if they are lacking in me, it is wholesome for me to be shamed and inflamed with desire to acquire them. And so the qualities I recognize in your praises as my own I rejoice in possessing and in having you love them and me for their sake ; those on the other hand that I fail to recognize as mine I yearn to acquire, not only in order to possess them for myself, but also to keep those who have a genuine love for me from being deluded when they praise me.

5 Ecce quam multa dixi et quid sit illud quod me longe amplius eloquio tuo, longe amplius laudibus meis in tuis litteris delectavit, non adhuc dixi. Quid autem putas esse, o bone homo, nisi quod te talem virum etiam non visum feci amicum, si tamen non visum dicere debeo, cuius non corpus sed animum in ipsis tuis litteris vidi, ubi de te non sicut antea fratribus meis, sed mihi credidi? Quis enim esses iam quidem acceperam, sed qualis erga me esses nondum tenebam. Ex hac amicitia tua etiam laudes meas, quae me quo fine delectent, satis dixi, multo uberius ecclesiae Christi non dubito profuturas, quando quidem etiam labores meos in defensione evangelii adversus reliquias impiorum daemonicolarum sic habes, sic legis, sic amas, sic praedicas, ut in eis tanto fiam notior, quanto es ipse nobilior; eos enim latentes inlustris inlustras clarusque declaras, et ubi prodesse posse perspicies, ignorari omnino non sines. Si unde id sciam quaeris, talis mihi apparuisti in litteris tuis. Hinc iam vide quantum me illae litterae delectare potuerint, si bene de me existimans, cogitas quantum me Christi lucra delectent. Iam vero quod te ipsum, qui, ut scribis, a parentibus, ab avis et postrema usque gentis prole Christi iura percipere potuisti, tamen adversus gentiles ritus ut numquam alias eisdem laboribus

See how much I have said, and I have not yet 5
said what it is in your letter that delighted me far
more than your eloquence, far more than your praise
of myself. What else do you think it is, honoured Sir,
than this, that I have gained the friendship of a man
of your character, even without seeing you—if I ought
to use the words " without seeing you," when I have
seen your mind, if not your body, in your letter ; in it
I gained an impression of you not, as before, from the
testimony of my brethren, but for myself. Already,
indeed, I had been told what manner of man you were,
but I had not experienced what kind of man you were
towards me. But I am sure that from this friendship
of yours even my praises (which delight me in a way I
have already sufficiently spoken of) will redound all
the more richly to the profit of the Church, since you
possess and study and admire and commend even my
labours in defence of the Gospel against the remnant of
ungodly demon-worshippers to such an extent that, in
proportion to your high station, I gain all the greater
reputation ; illustrious yourself, you add lustre to
their lowliness, and celebrated yourself, you celebrate
them, and wherever you see that they can do good,
you will certainly not allow them to remain unknown.
If you ask me how I know that, it is as such that you
have shown yourself to me in your letter. See now
from this how great delight your letter was able to
give me, if, with your good opinion of me, you think
how delighted I am by gains for Christ. And when
you inform me that you yourself, who have had the
good fortune, as you say in your letter, to acquire
Christian rights from your parents, your grand-
parents, and even your remotest ancestry, were yet
helped by my efforts in the contest with pagan rites

meis adiutum esse significas, parumne cogito quantum boni aliis et quam multis, quam claris et quam
facile quamque salubriter per illos ceteris quibus
talia conveniunt, possint scripta nostra te commen-
dante ac disseminante conferre ? Aut hoc cogitans
possumne parvorum vel mediocrium gaudiorum
iucunditate perfundi ?

6   Quia igitur non potui verbis explicare quantam
delectationem de tuis litteris ceperim, unde me delectaverint, dixi. Iam quod nequivi satis dicere, id
est quantum delectaverint, tibi coniciendum relinquo.
Sume itaque, mi fili, sume, vir bone et non in superficie sed Christiana caritate Christiane, sume, inquam,
etiam libros quos desiderasti, confessionum mearum ;
ibi me inspice, ne me laudes ultra quam sum, ibi
non aliis de me crede sed mihi, ibi me adtende et
vide quid fuerim in me ipso per me ipsum. Et si
quid in me tibi placuerit, lauda ibi mecum quem
laudari volui de me, neque enim me, quoniam *ipse
fecit nos et non ipsi nos* ; nos autem perdideramus
nos, sed qui fecit, refecit. Cum autem ibi me inveneris, ora pro me, ne deficiam, sed perficiar ; ora,
fili, ora. Sentio quid dicam, scio quid petam ; non
tibi videatur indignum et quasi ultra merita tua ;
fraudabis me magno adiutorio, si non feceris. Non
solum tu, sed etiam omnes qui me ex ore tuo di-

---

a Ps. xcix. 3.
b Here Augustine has an untranslatable four-fold jingle
with *facio, reficio, deficio, perficio* ; several times elsewhere
he has the triple paronomasia, as *In Ioan. Ev.* 1. 12 " si per
te deficis, Ille te reficiat qui te fecit," *In Ps.* 94. 10 "a te
deficere potes, tu teipsum reficere non potes; Ille reficit qui
te fecit." The play upon *deficere* and *reficere* is a favourite
with him (*In Ioan. Ev.* 11. 5, 52. 3; *In Ep. Ioan.* 3. 1, 4. 5;
458

as by nothing else, can I think it a small matter, the amount of good that through your commendation and circulation my writings can bestow on others, and they numerous and famous, and through them easily and profitably on other people in need of some such message ? Or with that thought in mind can I be imbued with the satisfaction of joys that are only slight or commonplace ?

Since then I could not express in words the extent of 6 the delight your letter gave me, I have spoken of that in it which was the source of my delight, and now I leave you to conjecture for yourself what I have been unable sufficiently to tell, that is, the delight it gave me. Take then, my son, take, excellent Sir, Christian that you are not on the surface only, but with Christian love—take, I repeat, those books of my Confessions that you asked for ; in them behold me, so that you praise me not beyond what I am ; in them give your belief to me, not to others who speak of me ; in them observe me and see what I was of myself, by myself, and if anything in me gives you pleasure, join me in praising for it Him Whom I desired to have praise from me, and not myself ; for " He hath made us and not we ourselves "[a]—indeed we had destroyed ourselves, but He Who made us, re-made us. And when in them you find me, pray for me that I may not suffer defeat,[b] but may be made complete ; pray, my son, pray. I realize what I am saying ; I know what I am asking ; let it not seem to you un-fitting and beyond your merits ; you will deprive me of great assistance, if you do it not. Pray for me, not only you, but all others who have learned to love me

In Ps. 36 ; *Serm.* 1. 11, 38. 16, 94. 10, 109. 6, 145. 4, 159. 8, 9, 190. 2 ; *Discip. Chr.* 13. 14 ; *C. Sec.* 17 ; *Ep.* 144. 2, etc.).

lexerint, orate pro me. Hoc eis me petivisse indica,
aut, si multum nobis tribuitis, iussisse nos existimate quod petimus; et tamen date petentibus vel
obtemperate iubentibus: orate pro nobis. Lege
litteras dei et invenies ipsos arietes nostros apostolos
petisse hoc a filiis suis sive praecepisse auditoribus
suis. Ego certe, quoniam hoc a me petisti pro te,
quantum faciam, videt qui exaudiat, qui videbat
quia et ante faciebam; sed redde etiam in hac re
dilectionis vicem. Praepositi vestri sumus, grex
dei estis; considerate et videte pericula nostra
maiora esse quam vestra, et orate pro nobis—hoc
enim et nobis conducit et vobis—ut bonam rationem
de vobis reddamus pastorum principi et omnium
nostrum capiti pariterque evadamus huius mundi
periculosiores blanditias quam molestias, nisi cum
pax eius ad hoc proficit quod apostolus orare nos
monuit, id est *ut quietam vitam et tranquillam agamus
in omni pietate et caritate.* Si enim desit pietas et
caritas, quid est ab illis et a ceteris mundi malis
tranquillitas et quies, nisi luxuriae perditionisque
materies sive invitamentum sive adiumentum?
Ut ergo habeamus *quietam et tranquillam vitam in
omni pietate et caritate,* quod oro pro vobis, orate pro
nobis, ubicumque estis, ubicumque sumus; nusquam
enim non est, cuius sumus.

---

[a] 1 Pet. v. 2; Hier. xiii. 17. The ram is used of the
apostles because they are leaders of the flock (Cassiod. *In
Ps.* 28. 1 " arietes apostoli accipiendi sunt, qui tanquam
duces gregum in caulas Domini perduxerunt populum
Christianum "), and so occasionally in Augustine (*Serm.*
135. 7, 311. 2; *In Ps.* 64. 18, etc.), but, as suggested
by the sacrifice offered by Abraham, the ram is frequently
employed as a figure of Christ (*Civ. Dei*, xvi. 32 " quis erat

from your lips ; inform them of this my request, or rather, if you esteem me highly, consider that my request is a command ; in any case, grant my request or carry out my command : pray for me. Read God's letters and you will find that the apostles themselves, the leaders [a] of the flock, requested this from their children or enjoined it on their hearers. For myself, since you make the same request from me for yourself, He Who answers prayer sees to what extent I am doing it, and saw to what extent I was doing it even before ; but in this matter do you show me an equal return of love. We are your overseers, and you are God's flock. Reflect and see that our dangers are greater than yours, and pray for us (for this profits both us and you) that we may render a good account of you to the Chief Shepherd [b] and Head of us all and that we may likewise escape this world's allurements, more dangerous than its afflictions, unless when its peace makes for that for which the apostle warned us to pray, that is, "that we may lead a quiet and peaceable life in all godliness and honesty." [c] For if godliness and honesty be wanting, what is quietness and peace-ableness from those and the other evils of the world but an opportunity for self-indulgence and destruction, either by inviting to it or by assisting towards it ? So, then, that we may obtain this " quiet and peaceful life in all godliness and honesty " which my prayers ask for you, let your prayers ask it for me, wherever you are, wherever we are ; for He is everywhere, " Whose we are." [d]

ille aries [at the sacrifice of Isaac] . . . nisi Iesus?"), and as such it is frequently found in Christian epigraphy.

[b] 1 Pet. v. 4.   [c] 1 Tim. ii. 2.
[d] Act. xxvii. 23.

7   Misi et alios libros, quos non petisti, ne hoc tantum
modo facerem quod petisti : de fide rerum quae
non videntur, de patientia, de continentia, de providentia, et unum grandem de fide et spe et caritate.
Hos omnes si dum es intra Africam, legeris, iudicium
tuum mitte de illis, aut mitte nobis aut quod nobis
a domino sene Aurelio mittatur, ibi dimitte. Quamquam et ubicumque fueris, speramus inde litteras
tuas et hinc tu, dum possumus, nostras. Suscepi
gratissime quae misisti, ubi et salutem meam
quamvis corporalem, quoniam vis me utique sine
impedimento malae valitudinis deo vacare, et bibliothecam nostram, ut sit unde libri vel parentur vel
reparentur, adiuvare dignatus es. Rependat tibi
dominus et hic et in futuro saeculo bona quae talibus,
qualem te esse voluit, praeparavit. Pignus pacis
apud te depositum nostrumque utrique dulcissimum,
sicut ante a me salutari, ita nunc resalutari peto.

No. 55 (Ep. CCXXXII)

DOMINIS   PRAEDICABILIBUS   ET   DILECTIS-
    SIMIS   FRATRIBUS   MADAURENSIBUS,
    QUORUM   PER   FRATREM   FLORENTIUM
    EPISTULAM ACCEPI, AUGUSTINUS

1   Si forte illi qui inter vos catholici Christiani sunt,
talia mihi scripta miserunt, hoc tantum miror, quod

---

^a For Aurelius see p. 40, note.
^b For the library at Hippo see note on p. 398.
^c 1 Cor. ii. 9.   ^d Verimodus, his son, as on p. 446.
^e To this point the letters have been arranged in chrono-
logical order, but the remaining letters cannot be dated and
are grouped in two divisions, controversial letters, and
letters to private individuals. Florentius is not further
known; Madaura was mentioned on p. 16, note *b*. The

I am sending other books as well, though you did 7
not ask for them ; I did not want to do only what you
asked and nothing more. They are *On Faith in Things
Unseen*, *On Patience*, *On Continence*, *On Providence*, and
a bulky book *On Faith, Hope and Charity*. If you read
all these while in Africa, send me your opinion of
them ; either send it to me or send it to a place from
which it can be sent to me by my lord, the Senior
Aurelius.[a] Yet wherever you are, I hope to receive
letters from you and to send some to you while I am
able. I have been very glad to receive the materials
you were kind enough to send to the assistance both
of my health, though it is only of the body, since you
want me to suffer no impediment in the devotion of
my time to God, and also of our library,[b] so that we
may have the means of either preparing books or
repairing them. May the Lord recompense you,
both in this life and in the life to come, with those
blessings He has prepared [c] for such as He has willed
that you should be! I beg you to convey my greetings
once again, as you did before, to the pledge of peace [d]
entrusted to you and very dear to us both.

No. 55 (Ep. CCXXXII)

AUGUSTINE TO MY PRAISEWORTHY LORDS
AND WELL-BELOVED BRETHREN OF MA-
DAURA, WHOSE LETTER I RECEIVED BY THE
HANDS OF BROTHER FLORENTIUS [e]

If perchance those who are Catholic Christians 1
among you have sent me a letter of this kind, my

letter is interesting for its indication of the survival and
the strength of paganism, for which see also Nos. 5-6, 16
and 24 above.

non suo potius quam ordinis nomine. Si autem **re**
vera omnes aut prope omnes ordinis viri ad me
dignati estis litteras dare, miror quod " patri " et
" in domino salutem " scripsistis, quorum mihi super-
stitiosus cultus idolorum, contra quae idola facilius
templa vestra quam corda clauduntur, vel potius quae
idola non magis in templis quam in vestris cordibus
includuntur, cum magno est dolore notissimus, nisi
forte iam de salute ipsa quae in domino est, per
quam me salutare voluistis, tandem prudenti consideratione cogitatis. Nam si non ita est, quaeso
vos, quid laesi, quid offendi benivolentiam vestram,
ut me titulo epistulae vestrae inridendum potius
quam honorandum esse putaretis, domini praedicabiles et dilectissimi fratres ?

2   Quod enim scripsistis: " Patri Augustino in
domino aeternam salutem," cum legerem, tanta spe
subito erectus sum, ut crederem vos ad ipsum
dominum et ad ipsam aeternam salutem aut iam
esse conversos aut per nostrum ministerium desiderare converti. Sed ubi legi cetera, refriguit
animus meus ; quaesivi tamen ab epistulae perlatore
utrum iam vel essetis Christiani vel esse cuperetis.
Cuius responsione posteaquam comperi nequaquam
vos esse mutatos, gravius dolui, quod Christi nomen,
cui iam totum orbem subiectum esse conspicitis, non
solum a vobis repellendum. sed etiam in nobis inridendum esse credidistis. Non enim potui cogitare

---

ᵃ The *Ordo* was the Senate of the *municipium*, or
municipal town of the Provinces ; sometimes it is called *curia*.
Its members are *decuriones* or *curiales*. See too No. 24 § 8
"cum leges . . . episcopus ordini replicasset." The word
Senatus was at this time reserved for the Senate at Rome.
    ᵇ As was ordered by the laws of 399 (*Cod. Theod.* **xvi. x.**
464

only surprise is that it was in the name of the municipal senate ^{a} instead of their own. But if, in very truth, you all or almost all of the municipal senate have deigned to write to me, I am surprised that you have written the words " To Father Augustine " and " Salutation in the Lord "; for to my great grief I am well aware of your superstitious devotion to idols, against which idols it is easier to close your temples ^{b} than your hearts, or rather those idols are more enclosed in your hearts than they are in your temples. But perhaps you have at last given wise consideration and thought to that salutary life which is in the Lord and in which you wanted to give me salutation. For if it be not so, I ask you, praiseworthy lords and well-beloved brethren, what harm have I done to your Benevolences, what offence have I given, that you should think fit to mock at me by the superscription of your letter instead of honouring me ?

For when I read the words you wrote, " To Father Augustine, eternal salutation in the Lord," I was suddenly uplifted with such hope as to believe that you had already turned to this Lord and this eternal salvation, or were through my ministry desirous of turning. But when I read the rest, my spirit was chilled ; I inquired, however, from the bearer of the letter whether you were already Christians or were anxious to become so. After learning from his answer that you were in no way changed, I was the more deeply grieved that you thought fit not only to spurn from you the name of Christ to which you see the whole world already in subjection, but even to make mock of it in my person. For I was

15-18) and 408 (*ib.* XVI. x. 19), when the pagan temples were confiscated or turned to public uses.

alterum dominum, secundum quem posset episcopus
"pater" a vobis vocari, praeter dominum Christum,
et si esset hinc aliqua de interpretatione vestrae
sententiae dubitatio, subscriptione epistulae tolle-
retur, ubi aperte posuistis : "Optamus te, domine,
in deo et Christo eius per multos annos semper in
clero tuo gaudere." Quibus omnibus perlectis atque
discussis, quid aliud mihi occurrere potuit aut cuilibet
homini potest, nisi aut veridico aut fallaci scribentium
animo haec esse conscripta ? Sed si veridico animo
ista scribitis, quis vobis ad hanc veritatem inter-
clusit viam ? Quis aspera dumeta substravit ? Quis
rupium praerupta inimicus opposuit ? Postremo
quis basilicae ianuam ingredi cupientibus clausit, ut
in eodem domino per quem nos salutatis, eandem
salutem nobiscum habere nolitis ? Si autem fallaciter
atque inridenter haec scribitis, itane tandem mihi
negotia vestra curanda inponitis, ut nomen eius per
quem aliquid possum, audeatis non veneratione
debita adtollere, sed insultatione adulatoria ventilare ?

3   Sciatis me, carissimi, cum ineffabili pro vobis
tremore cordis haec dicere ; novi enim quanto
graviorem et perniciosiorem causam sitis habituri
apud deum, si frustra vobis haec dixero. Omnia
quae praeteritis temporibus erga humanum genus
maiores nostri gesta esse meminerunt nobisque

unable to think of any other Lord in whom a bishop could be addressed by you as " Father," except the Lord Christ ; and if there were any doubt on this point about the meaning of the words you used, it would be removed by the closing sentence of your letter, in which you plainly put the words, " We pray, my lord, that always in company with your clergy you may rejoice in God and His Christ for many years." After reading it all and pondering it, what else could I, what else can any man, think than that it was written either as a genuine expression of the writers' mind or with an intention to deceive ? But if what you wrote is a genuine expression of your mind, who has barred your way to this truth ? Who has strewn it with sharp thorns ? Who has out of enmity set up steep rocks against you ? Who, finally, has shut the church door in your face when you sought to enter, that you refuse to be partakers with us of that same salvation in that same Lord by whom you gave us salutation ? But if it was with the intention to deceive and to mock that you wrote what you did, is that indeed the way in which to lay upon me the conduct of your affairs, not exalting with due honour the name of Him through Whom it is possible for me to do anything, but having the effrontery to bandy it about with insulting flattery ?

You must understand, my dear friends, that it is 3 with unspeakable quaking of the heart on your account that I say this to you, for I realize how much greater will be the seriousness and the doom of your case before God, if what I say to you has no effect. There is nothing that has happened to the human race in past times and has been recorded and handed down to us by our ancestors, nothing either that we

tradiderunt, omnia etiam quae nos videmus et
posteris tradimus, quae tamen pertinent ad veram
religionem quaerendam et tenendam, divina scriptura
non tacuit, sed ita omnino cuncta transeunt, ut tran-
situra esse praedicta sunt. Videtis certe populum
Iudaeorum avulsum a sedibus suis per omnes fere
terras disseminatum atque diffusum ; et origo eiusdem populi et incrementa et regni amissio et per
cuncta dispersio sicut praedicta, ita facta sunt.
Videtis certe ex ipso populo verbum dei legemque
prodeuntem per Christum, qui ex illis mirabiliter
natus est, omnium gentium fidem occupasse atque
tenuisse ; ita haec omnia praenuntiata legimus, ut
videmus. Videtis certe multos praecisos a radice
Christianae societatis, quae per sedes apostolorum
et successiones episcoporum certa per orbem pro-
pagatione diffunditur, de sola figura originis sub
Christiano nomine quasi arescentia sarmenta gloriari,
quas haereses et schismata nominamus ; praevisa,
praedicta, scripta sunt omnia. Videtis certe simulacrorum templa partim sine reparatione conlapsa,
partim diruta, partim clausa, partim in usus alios
commutata, ipsaque simulacra vel confringi vel in-
cendi vel includi vel destrui, atque ipsas huius saeculi
potestates, quae aliquando pro simulacris populum
Christianum persequebantur, victas et domitas non
a repugnantibus sed a morientibus Christianis et

---

* Like the temple of Caelestis at Carthage, which was
closed for pagan worship in 391, but consecrated by bishop
Aurelius in 399 as a Christian church. In *C. Gaud.* i. 38. 51
Augustine speaks of pagan temples overthrown by the
Donatists ; " pagani quorum certe templa evertistis et ba-
silicas construxistis." The passage in *Serm.* 163. 2 bears a
resemblance to the text : " loca ipsa terrena [*i.e.* pagan

experience and hand down to our posterity, that Holy Scripture has not spoken of, as far as it pertains to the seeking and the holding of true religion; everything comes to pass exactly as it was foretold it would come to pass. You plainly see the Jewish people torn from their abode and dispersed and scattered throughout almost the whole world; the origin of that people and its development and the loss of its realm and its dispersion everywhere— everything has happened just as it was foretold. You plainly see that the word of God and the law that came forth from that same people through Christ (Who was miraculously born of them) has laid fast hold upon the faith of all the nations; all these things, as we may read, were predicted just as we see them. You plainly see many cut off from the root of the Christian society, which through the sees of the apostles and the succession of bishops is spread abroad in unmistakable diffusion throughout the world, who yet boast, under cover of the Christian name, of the mere outward likeness they bear to their origin, like withered branches, which we term heresies and schisms; it was all foreseen, foretold and put down in writing. You plainly see some of the temples of idols fallen into ruin and not restored, some cast down, some closed, some converted to other uses,[a] and the idols themselves either smashed to pieces or burned or destroyed; and you see how the powers of this world, who at one time for the sake of their idols persecuted the Christian people, are vanquished and subdued by Christians who did not take up arms but laid down their lives, and have now turned

temples] in melius convertuntur, alia diruuntur atque franguntur, alia in meliores usus commutantur."

contra eadem simulacra, pro quibus Christianos
occidebant, impetus suos legesque vertisse et imperii
nobilissimi eminentissimum culmen ad sepulcrum
piscatoris Petri submisso diademate supplicare.

4 Haec omnia divinae scripturae, quae in manus
omnium iam venerunt, ante longissima tempora
futura esse testatae sunt ; haec omnia tanto robus-
tiore fide laetamur fieri, quanto maiore auctoritate
praedicta esse in sanctis litteris invenimus. Numquidnam, obsecro vos, numquidnam solum iudicium
dei, quod inter fideles atque infideles futurum esse
in eisdem litteris legimus, cum illa omnia, sicut praedicta sunt, venerint, numquidnam solum iudicium
dei venturum non esse putabimus ? Immo vero
veniet, sicut omnia illa venerunt. Nec quisquam
erit homo nostrorum temporum, qui se in illo iudicio
de sua possit infidelitate defendere, cum Christum
cantet et iustus ad aequitatem et periurus ad fraudem
et rex ad imperium et miles ad pugnam et maritus
propter regimen et uxor propter obsequium et pater
propter praeceptum et filius propter oboedientiam et
dominus propter dominationem et servus propter
famulatum et humilis ad pietatem et superbus ad
aemulationem et dives, ut porrigat, et pauper, ut
sumat, et ebriosus ad phialam et mendicus ad ianuam

---

^a Augustine is probably not thinking of any specific
incident, but he might well have had in mind the subjection of
the Emperor Theodosius to the Church under St. Ambrose.
And yet, in spite of his eloquence here, he acknowledges
elsewhere that Rome itself was still given over to idolatry
(*Conf.* viii. 2-3) ; in Ep. xxxvi. 4, he speaks of the Church
as "toto terrarum orbe diffusam, exceptis Romanis." This
fact accounts for the scant sympathy he shows at the fall
of Rome (*Excid. Urbis*, ii.). His language here is paralleled
by the words of St. John Chrysostom (*C. Iud. et Gent.* § 9):
ἐν τῇ βασιλικωτάτῃ πόλει Ῥώμῃ, πάντα ἀφιέντες, ἐπὶ τοὺς τάφους

their attacks and their laws against the very idols for whose sake they were in the habit of slaying Christians; and you see the most eminent dignitary of this noble Empire lay aside his crown and bow in supplication before the tomb of the fisherman Peter.[a]

All these things were long, long ago foretold to 4 be coming to pass by the testimony of Holy Scripture, which has now come into the hands of everyone : all of them have happened, to our joy and to the greater strengthening of our faith as we find the Holy Scripture foretold them with a more imposing authority. Are we then, I ask you, to imagine that it is God's judgement alone, which those same Books foretell to their readers as deciding between the believing and the unbelieving—are we then to imagine that this judgement of God's alone will not come about, when all those other things came about just as they were foretold ? Yea, verily, just as they all came about, so it too will come. Nor will there be any man of our times who at that judgement will be able to put forward any defence for being an unbeliever, when the name of Christ is on every man's lips : the righteous invokes it for justice, and the perjurer for deceit and the king for rule and the soldier for battle and the husband for establishing his authority and the wife as a sign of her submission and the father for his commands and the son for his obedience, the master for his lordship and the servant for his service, the humble man for piety and the proud man for ambition, the rich man when he gives away and the poor man when he receives, the drunkard in his cups and the beggar at the gate, and

τοῦ ἁλιέως καὶ τοῦ σκηνοποιοῦ τρέχουσι καὶ βασιλεῖς καὶ ὕπατοι καὶ στρατηγοί.

et bonus, ut praestet, et malus, ut fallat, et Christianus venerator et paganus adulator; omnes Christum
cantant et, qua voluntate atque ore cantent, eidem
ipsi, quem cantant, rationem sine dubio reddituri
sunt.

5 Est quiddam invisibile, ex quo creatore principio
sunt omnia quae videmus, summum, aeternum, in-
commutabile et nulli effabile nisi tantum sibi. Est
quiddam, quo se ipsa summitas maiestatis narrat et
praedicat, non inpar gignenti atque narranti, verbum
quo ille qui verbum gignit, ostenditur. Est quaedam
sanctitas, omnium quae sancte fiunt, sanctificatrix,
ipsius incommutabilis verbi, per quod narratur illud
principium, et ipsius principii, quod pari se verbo
narrat, inseparabilis et indivisa communio. Quis
autem hoc totum, quod non dicendo dicere conatus
sum et dicendo non dicere, quis hoc possit serenis-
sima et sincerissima mente contueri eoque contuitu
beatitudinem ducere, atque in id quod intuetur,
deficiens quodam modo se oblivisci et pergere in
illud, cuius visione sibi vilis est, quod est inmortalitate
indui et obtinere aeternam salutem, per quam me
salutare dignamini—quis hoc possit, nisi qui omnes

---

a Salvian, *Gub. Dei*, iv. 15. 71, gives similar testimony
to the common use of the name of Christ: " Quis est
omnino hominum saecularium praeter paucos, qui non ad
hoc semper Christi nomen in ore habeat ut peieret? Unde
etiam pervulgatum hoc fere et apud nobiles et apud ignobiles
sacramentum est: ' per Christum quia hoc facio,' ' per
Christum quia hoc ago,' . . . Et quid plura? In id penitus
deducta res est, ut . . . Christi nomen non videatur iam
sacramentum esse, sed sermo." Augustine seems nowhere
else to refer to this practice, but he frequently does speak
of the profane invocation of God's name, which he confesses
having been addicted to himself (*Serm.* 180. 10, " iuravimus

the good man that he may do good and the bad man that he may deceive, both the Christian worshipper and the pagan time-server—all repeat the name of Christ, and with what purpose and what lips they repeat it, to that same Christ, whose name they repeat, they shall most assuredly render an account.[a]

There is an invisible something from which, as a [5] creator and first cause, all that we see derives its being, supreme, eternal, unchangeable and inexpressible save only to itself. There is a something by which that supreme majesty utters and declares itself, the Word, not inferior to its begetter and utterer, by which He Who begets the Word reveals Himself. There is a certain holy thing, the sanctifier of everything that is begotten in sanctity, which inseparably and undividedly unites that unchangeable Word, through which the First Principle utters itself, with the First Principle, which utters itself in the Word which is its equal. Who could contemplate with perfectly tranquil and pure mind this whole, which I have attempted to express without expressing it and by expressing it not to express, and from that contemplation draw blessedness, and lose and forget self in that object of contemplation, and press forward to that which, once seen, makes man hold himself as nothing—which means to be clothed with immortality and to lay hold upon that eternal salvation, in which you think fit to give me salutation —who could do this, save he who, confessing his sins,

et nos passim, habuimus istam teterrimam consuetudinem et mortiferam "; *cf. Serm.* 307, 4-5, and for the common habit, *Serm.* 12. 3, 180). He also mentions, in *Serm.* 4. 6, the familiar habit of swearing " per lumina mea."

superbiae suae toros inanes peccata sua confitens complanaverit seque substraverit mitem atque humilem ad excipiendum doctorem deum ?

6   Quoniam ergo a vanitate superbiae prius ad humilitatem deponendi sumus, ut inde surgentes solidam celsitudinem teneamus, non potuit nobis hoc tanto magnificentius quanto blandius inspirari, ut nostra ferocitas non vi sed persuasione sedaretur, nisi verbum illud, per quod se angelis indicat deus pater, quod virtus et sapientia eius est, quod corde humano visibilium rerum cupiditate caecato videri non poterat, personam suam in homine agere atque ostendere dignaretur, ut magis homo timeret extolli fastu hominis quam humiliari exemplo dei. Itaque non Christus regno terreno decoratus, nec Christus terrenis opibus dives, nec Christus ulla terrena felicitate praefulgens, sed Christus crucifixus per totum terrarum orbem praedicatur, quod riserunt prius populi superborum et adhuc rident reliquiae, crediderunt autem prius pauci, nunc populi, quia tunc ad fidem paucorum et contra inrisionem populorum, cum Christus crucifixus praedicaretur, claudi ambulabant, muti loquebantur, surdi audiebant, caeci videbant, mortui resurgebant. Sic tandem animadvertit terrena superbia nihil in ipsis terris esse potentius humilitate divina, ut etiam saluberrima humilitas humana contra insultantem sibi superbiam divinae imitationis patrocinio tueretur.

---

[a] 1 Cor. i. 24.   [b] 1 Cor. i. 23.
[c] Matt. xi. 5 ; Luke vii. 22.

has laid low all the empty swellings of his pride and prostrated himself in meekness and humility to receive God as his teacher?

Since then we have first to be reduced from the vanity of pride to humility, so that rising thence we may acquire real exaltation, it was impossible for us to have communicated to us this spirit (the more glorious for its very gentleness) whereby our ungovernableness is subdued by persuasion instead of by force, had not this Word—through Whom God the Father reveals Himself to the angels,[a] Who is His strength and wisdom, Whom the human heart, blinded by the desire for things visible, was unable to perceive—condescended to act out His part in human form and exhibit His being in such a way as to make mankind more afraid of being uplifted by the pride of man than of being brought low by the example of God. So the Christ Who is preached throughout the world is not a Christ Who is adorned with an earthly kingdom, nor a Christ rich in earthly possessions, nor a Christ shining with any earthly splendour, but Christ crucified.[b] This was a matter for ridicule at first by proud nations and still is to a remnant, but it was a matter for faith first to a few, now to nations, for then according to the faith of the few and in spite of the ridicule of the nations, when Christ crucified was preached, the lame walked, the dumb spoke, the deaf heard, the blind saw, and the dead rose again.[c] Thus at last conviction was brought to the pride of the world that nothing in the world itself was more potent than divine humility, so that under the protection of that divine example the most wholesome human humility may find shelter against the scornful assaults of pride.

7 Expergiscimini aliquando, fratres mei et parentes mei Madaurenses ; hanc occasionem scribendi vobis deus mihi obtulit. Quantum potui quidem in negotio fratris Florenti, per quem litteras misistis, sicut deus voluit, adfui et adiuvi ; sed tale negotium erat, quod etiam sine opera mea facile peragi posset; prope omnes enim domus ipsius homines qui apud Hipponem sunt, noverunt Florentium et multum eius orbitatem dolent. Sed epistula mihi a vobis missa est, ut non inpudens esset epistula mea, cum occasione a vobis accepta idolorum cultoribus de Christo aliquid loqueretur. Sed obsecro vos, si eum non inaniter in mea epistula nominastis, ut non inaniter vobis haec scripserim. Si autem me inridere voluistis, timete illum, quem prius iudicatum inrisit superbus orbis terrarum et nunc iudicem subiectus expectat ; erit enim testis affectus in vos cordis mei per hanc, quantum potui, paginam expressus, erit testis vobis in iudicio eius, qui credentes sibi confirmaturus est et incredulos confusurus. Deus unus et verus vos ab omni huius saeculi vanitate liberatos convertat ad se, domini praedicabiles et dilectissimi fratres.

---

^a The editors say that Augustine uses the term " fathers " here because he was born at Tagaste, which is not far from Madaura, and studied in Madaura as a boy.

NO. 55 (Ep. CCXXXII)

Awake at last from your slumbers, ye men of [7] Madaura, my brethren and my fathers! [a] This opportunity of writing to you has been furnished me by God. As far as was possible, I stood by and gave my assistance, as God willed, in this affair of brother Florentius, who brought your letter to me ; but the affair was such that even without my aid it could very easily have been carried through, for almost all the men of that family who are at Hippo know Florentius and deeply lament his bereavement. But your having sent a letter to me made it not presumptuous in me to write to you and, availing myself of the opportunity you provided, to say something to idol-worshippers about Christ. But I beseech you, if your naming of Him in your letter was not a vain gesture, that what I have written to you may not be in vain. If you wanted to make mock of me, fear Him Who on being at first condemned was made mock of by the proud world, which now awaits Him in subjection as Judge. For my heart's desire for you, expressed as well as I could in these pages, will be a witness against you at His judgement, when He will confirm those who believe in Him and confound those who do not. May the one true God free you from all the vanity of this world, my praiseworthy lords and well-beloved brethren, and turn you to Himself.

477

No. 56 (Ep. CCXLV)

DOMINO DILECTISSIMO ET VENERABILI FRA-
TRI ET CONSACERDOTI POSSIDIO ET QUI
TECUM SUNT FRATRIBUS AUGUSTINUS ET
QUI MECUM SUNT FRATRES IN DOMINO
SALUTEM

1 Magis quid agas cum eis qui obtemperare nolunt,
cogitandum est, quam quem ad modum eis ostendas
non licere quod faciunt. Sed nunc epistula sanctitatis tuae et occupatissimum me repperit et celerri-
mus baiuli reditus neque non rescribere tibi neque
ad ea quae consuluisti, ita ut oportet, respondere
permisit. Nolo tamen de ornamentis auri vel vestis
praeproperam habeas in prohibendo sententiam, nisi
eos qui, neque coniugati neque coniugari cupientes,
cogitare debent quo modo placeant deo. Illi autem
cogitant quae sunt mundi, quo modo placeant vel viri
uxoribus vel mulieres maritis, nisi quod capillos nudare
feminas, quas etiam caput velare apostolus iubet,
nec maritatas decet ; fucari autem pigmentis, quo
vel rubicundior vel candidior appareat, adulterina

---

^a For Possidius see pp. 128, 190 above.
^b 1 Cor. vii. 32-34.   ^c 1 Cor. xi. 5-6.
^d The habit of painting the face was denounced by all
the Christian writers : Tertullian, *De Cult. Fem.* ii. 7
" videbo an eum cerussa et purpurisso et croco et in illo
ambitu capitis resurgatis " ; Cyprian, *De Hab. Virg.* 14,
blames the fallen angels for teaching " oculos nigrore
fucare et genas mendacio ruboris inficere et mutare adul-
terinis coloribus crinem " ; Ambr. *De Virginibus*, i. 6. 28
" quaesitis coloribus ora depingant, dum viris displicere
formidant " ; and frequently by Jerome : *Ep.* 54. 7 " quid
facit in facie Christianae purpurissus et cerussa ? " ; *Ep.*
107. 5 " cave ne aures perfores, ne cerussa et purpurisso

No. 56 (Ep. CCXLV)

TO MY WELL-BELOVED LORD AND VENERABLE
BROTHER AND FELLOW-PRIEST, POSSIDIUS,[a]
AND THE BRETHREN WHO ARE WITH YOU,
AUGUSTINE AND THE BRETHREN WHO ARE
WITH ME SEND GREETING IN THE LORD

What you are to do with those who refuse to 1
comply requires more consideration than how you
can show them that what they are doing is unlawful.
But at present the letter of your Holiness has found
me extremely busy and at the same time the bearer's
great haste to return has not allowed me either to
make no reply to you or to give an adequate answer
to the problems on which you asked my advice.
Still, I should not like you to make any over-hasty
decision about the forbidding of ornaments of gold
or finery, except that those who are neither married
nor desirous of being married ought to be thinking
how they may please God. For that class of people
think of worldly things, how they may, if they are
husbands, please their wives, or if wives, please their
husbands[b]; the one exception is that it is not becoming
in women, even in those who are married, to uncover
their hair, since the apostle bids them cover the
whole head.[c] But as for painting the face[d] so that it
may appear ruddier or fairer, this is immoral deceit.

. . . ora depingas." In *Doct. Chr.* iv. 21. 49 Augustine
quotes passages from Cyprian and Ambrose on women who
paint the face, and in *De Bono Viduitatis*, 19. 24, he advises
a virgin and a widow "simulatum candorem ac ruborem et
pigmentis illitum non adhiberetis, etiamsi viros haberetis;
non putantes dignos quos falleretis, nec vos quae fallere
deberetis."

fallacia est, qua non dubito etiam ipsos maritos se nolle decipi, quibus solis permittendae sunt feminae ornari secundum veniam, non secundum imperium. Nam verus ornatus maxime Christianorum et Christianarum non tantum nullus fucus mendax verum ne auri quidem vestisque pompa, sed mores boni sunt.

2   Execranda autem superstitio ligaturarum, in quibus etiam inaures virorum in summis ex una parte auriculis suspensae deputantur : non ad placendum hominibus sed ad serviendum daemonibus adhibentur. Quis autem possit speciales nefariarum superstitionum prohibitiones in scripturis invenire, cum generaliter apostolus dicat : *Nolo vos socios fieri daemoniorum,* et iterum : *Quae enim consonantia Christi ad Belial?* nisi forte, quia Belial nominavit et generalem societatem daemoniorum prohibuit, licet Christianis sacrificare Neptuno, quia nihil proprie de

---

^a These amulets were used especially to cure diseases, and their use seems to have been common at this time. Augustine repeatedly refers to it (*In Ps.* 33, *Serm.* 2, 18 ; 93. 20 ; *In Ioan. Ev.* 3. 14 ; *Serm.* 286. 7, 318. 3, etc.) and in *De Doctr. Chr.* ii. 20. 30 mentions it among other charms, especially the earrings spoken of in the text: ' ad hoc genus [superstitionis] pertinent omnes etiam ligaturae atque remedia . . . sive in praecantationibus, sive in quibusdam notis quos ' characteres ' vocant, sive in quibusque rebus suspendendis atque illigandis vel etiam aptandis quodammodo . . . ad quasdam significationes aut occultas aut etiam manifestas ; . . . sicut sunt inaures in summo aurium singularum aut de struthionum ossibus ansulae in digitis, aut cum tibi dicitur singultienti, ut dextera manu sinistrum pollicem teneas." He complains too that the *ligaturae* had the name of Christ written on them, so as to avert the suspicion of the Christians (*In Io. Ev.* 7. 6), and that it was a common practice to fasten a copy of the Gospels to the head, if it ached, as a doubly sure *ligatura* (*ib.* 7. 12).

I am quite sure that even their own husbands do not want to be so taken in, and they are the only people for whom women should be allowed to adorn themselves, and that as a concession, not as a command. For not only is lying paint no real adornment of Christian men and women, nor yet is the ostentation of gold and finery ; but a good character is.

It is an accursed superstition to wear amulets,[a] 2 among which must be reckoned also the earrings[b] that men wear on the top part of the ear on one side ; they are employed not to please men, but to do homage to devils. Who could expect to find in the Scriptures individual prohibitions of every kind of ungodly superstition, when the apostle says in general terms, " I would not that ye should have fellowship with devils,"[c] and again, " For what concord hath Christ with Belial ? ",[d] unless in naming Belial and forbidding in general terms fellowship with devils, he perchance allowed Christians to sacrifice to Neptune, because we do not read that any prohibition was made of Neptune specifically.[e]

[b] The habit of wearing earrings is denounced by Cyprian, *De Hab. Virg.* 14 " an vulnera inferre auribus Deus voluit, quibus innocens adhuc infantia et mali saecularis ignara crucietur, ut postea de aurium cicatricibus et cavernis pretiosa grana dependeant, gravia etsi non suo pondere, mercium tamen quantitate ? " and Jerome, *Ep.* 127. 3 " illae solent purpurisso et cerussa ora depingere . . . et auribus perforatis Rubri Maris pretiosissima grana suspendere." These passages refer to the wearing of earrings by women : there is scanty evidence for their use by men.

[c] 1 Cor. x. 20.   [d] 2 Cor. vi. 15.

[e] The cult of Neptune is mentioned several times by Augustine and seems to have been fairly common in North Africa (*C. Cresc.* iii. 78. 89 ; *Doctr. Chr.* iii. 7. 11 ; *In Ps.* 183 ; *Serm.* 2, 5 ; *In Ps.* 145, 6. 12, etc.).

Neptuno vetitum legimus. Moneantur interim miseri, ut, si obtemperare nolunt praeceptis salubrioribus, saltem sacrilegia sua non defendant, ne maiore se scelere implicent. Quid autem cum eis agendum sit, si solvere inaures timent et corpus Christi cum signo diaboli accipere non timent ?

De ordinando autem, qui in parte Donati baptizatus est, auctor tibi esse non possum ; aliud est enim facere, si cogaris, aliud consulere ut facias.

No. 57 (Ep. CCXLVI)

LAMPADIO AUGUSTINUS

1 De quaestione fati ac fortunae, qua tuum animum non leviter moveri et, cum praesens essem, adverti et nunc tuis litteris gratius certiusque cognovi, rescriptum tibi non parvi voluminis debeo, quod dominus praestabit ut ita explicem, quem ad modum novit tibi congruere ac saluti fidei tuae. Non enim parvum malum est perversis opinionibus non solum ad committendum blandimento voluptatis adduci, sed etiam ad defendendum peccatum a medicamento confessionis averti.

2 Illud sane quanto citius ac breviter noveris, omnes leges atque instituta omnia, disciplinae, laudes, vituperationes, exhortationes, terrores, praemia, sup-

---

[a] Lampadius appears to be mentioned only here.

482

Meanwhile, let those unhappy people be warned that if they refuse to comply with these more wholesome counsels, they must at least refrain from defending their acts of irreverence, from fear of involving themselves in greater guilt. Yet what are we to do with them, if they are afraid to put off their earrings and are not afraid to receive the body of Christ while wearing the devil's badge?

I cannot accept responsibility for the ordaining of one who was baptized in the Donatist party; it is one thing to do it if you are compelled, and another thing to advise you to do it.

No. 57 (Ep. CCXLVI)

AUGUSTINE TO LAMPADIUS *

On the problem of Fate and Chance, which is seri- 1 ously perturbing your mind, as I noticed when I was with you and am now assured in a more gratifying and definite manner by your letter, I ought to reply to you at considerable length; the Lord will enable me to furnish you with such an explanation as He knows will be best suited for you and for your spiritual welfare. For it is no slight evil that perverted opinions not only induce men by the allurement of pleasure to commit sin, but lead them away from the remedy of confession to a defence of their sin.

Let me, however, at once and in a word assure 2 you of this, that all legislation and all rules, all repressions, all commendations, censures, exhortations, menaces, rewards, punishments, and all other things

483

plicia, ceteraque omnia quibus humanum genus administratur et regitur, penitus labefactari atque subverti nihilque in eis omnino iustitiae remanere, nisi voluntas sit causa peccandi. Quanto ergo licentius et aequius mathematicorum inprobamus errores, quam divinas leges vel etiam domorum nostrarum curam damnare atque abicere cogimur, quod nec ipsi mathematici faciunt! Nam cum aliquis eorum hominibus nummatis fatua fata vendiderit, mox ut oculum a tabellis eburneis ad domus suae moderamen ac sollicitudinem revocaverit, non solum vocibus sed etiam plagis emendat uxorem, non dico si petulantius iocantem, sed si inmoderatius per fenestram aspicientem animadverterit. Quae tamen si ei dicat: "Quid me caedis? Venerem caede, si potes, a qua cogor hoc facere," tunc vero ille non curat, quam vana verba componat fallendis extraneis, sed quam iusta verbera inponat corrigendis suis.

3 Quando ergo quisque, cum reprehendi coeperit, causam convertit in fatum et ideo se culpari non vult, quia fato se dicit coactum fecisse id quod arguitur,

---

ᵃ *Mathematicus* was the popular term for "astrologer" from the time of Tacitus and Juvenal, and Augustine follows other writers in explaining that the proper term is *genethliaci* (*Doct. Chr.* ii. 21. 32 ; *Div. Quaest.* xlv. 2). In *Conf.* iv. 3, he tells how he once consulted astrologers himself. He often has occasion to point out the absurdity of their pretensions (*Gen. ad Litt.* 2. 35 ; *In Ioan. Ev.* 8. 11 ; *In Ps.* 40. 3, 61. 23, 140. 9 where he repeats very nearly the words of this letter : "mathematicus si uxorem suam paulo petulantius viderit conversari . . . aut fenestram crebro repetere, nonne arripit, verberat, et dat disciplinam? Respondeat illi uxor : ' Si potes, Venerem caede, non me ' " ; *Ep.* lv. 12-13, where he repeats his argument that to believe them is to deny the

by which the human race is controlled and governed,
are utterly overthrown and subverted and left devoid
of any particle of justice, if the cause of sinning is
not the will. How much more legitimate and right,
therefore, is it for us to reject the errors of the
astrologers,[a] than to be forced to condemn and
repudiate the divine laws or even the supervision
of our own households. The astrologers themselves
do not do so, for when one of them has sold his silly
horoscopes to wealthy persons and turns his eyes
away from the ivory tablets to the management and
supervision of his own household, he immediately
reproves his wife, not with objurgations only but even
with blows, if he finds her not to say engaged in
froward dalliance, but even looking too much out of
the window. Yet if she were to say to him : " Why
do you beat *me* ? Beat Venus, if you can, for it is
the influence of her planet that makes me do this,"
his concern then is not what empty jargon he can
concoct for the deception of strangers, but what just
lashes he can inflict for the correction of his own
household.[b]

When a man, then, upon receiving censure, throws **3**
the responsibility on Fate and therefore declines to
accept the blame on the ground that it was under
the compulsion of Fate that he did the action which

freedom of the will). Astrologers were condemned both by
civil laws (in 357, 358, 370, 409), and by ecclesiastical
councils, but they continued to flourish.

[b] The careful and prolonged jingle in *verba componat
fallendis extraneis* and *verbera inponat corrigendis suis* is
almost beyond reproduction in English. The play on *verba*
and *verbera*, or *verbero*, is not infrequent in Augustine
(*Ep.* clxxxv. 15 ; *Fid. et Symb.* 3. 3 ; *In Ioan. Ev.* 37. 4).
So in No. 59. 1, *abripui* and *subripui*.

redeat ad se ipsum, servet hoc in suis, non castiget
servum furem, non de contumelioso filio conqueratur,
vicino inprobo non minetur. Quid enim horum
faciens iuste facit, si omnes a quibus iniurias patitur,
non culpa sua sed fato inpelluntur ut faciant? Si
autem iure proprio et patris familias diligentia, quos-
cumque homines pro tempore in potestate habet,
hortatur ad bonum, deterret a malo, imperat suae
voluntati ut obtemperent, honorat eos qui sibi ad
nutum oboediunt, vindicat in eos qui se contemnunt,
rependit gratiam beneficis, odit ingratos, egone ex-
pectabo ut contra fatum disputet, cum tanta eum
non verbis sed factis eloqui deprehendam, ut prope
manibus suis omnes mathematicorum lapillos supra
capita eorum frangere videatur? His itaque paucis
si aviditas tua contenta non est et librum aliquem
de hac re, quem diutius legas, desideras, patienter
tibi sunt expectandae vacationes nostrae et rogandus
deus, qui et otium et facultatem satiando de hac re
animo tuo tribuere dignetur. Ero tamen alacrior,
si et saepe commemorare me litteris tuam non
piguerit caritatem, et quid de hac epistula sentias,
rescribendo edocueris.

is condemned, let him come to himself again and observe this same principle in dealing with those attached to him ; let him refrain from chastising a servant who steals ; let him utter no complaint of an abusive son and no threats to an offensive neighbour. Would he be acting justly in doing any of these things, if all those who do him some injury are driven to perform such actions, not by any fault of their own, but by Fate ? If, however, from his personal rights and his responsibility as the head of a household, he exhorts to good those persons who for the time being are under his authority, deters them from doing evil and commands them to carry out his will, honours those who obey his nod, punishes those who set him at naught, renders thanks to the obliging, and hates those who are ill-disposed—shall I expect him to argue against Fate, when I find him proclaiming, not in words but in deeds, such convictions as to make him almost appear to be breaking with his own hands all the tables of the astrologers over their own heads ?

So then, if these few remarks do not appease your thirst for information and you desire on this subject a book that will take a longer time to read, you must await with patience until I have a free interval, and ask God to be pleased to grant me both the leisure and the ability to satisfy your mind on this question. Yet my eagerness will be increased, if your charity does not grudge to write often and remind me, and also to reply informing me what you think about this letter.

No. 58 (Ep. CCLIV)

DOMINO BEATISSIMO ET VENERABILI AC DE-
SIDERABILI FRATRI ET CONSACERDOTI
BENENATO ET QUI TECUM SUNT FRA-
TRIBUS AUGUSTINUS ET QUI MECUM SUNT
FRATRES IN DOMINO SALUTEM

Puella de qua mihi scripsit sanctitas tua, in ea
voluntate est, ut, si aetas ei iam matura esset, nulli
in nuptiis conveniret. In ea vero aetate est, ut, si
voluntatem nubendi haberet, nulli adhuc dari vel
promitti deberet. Huc accedit quia eam deus in
ecclesia sic tuetur, ut contra inprobos tueatur, non
ut cui voluero tradi possit, sed ut a quo non oportet
rapi non possit, domine Benenate dilectissime et
venerabilis frater. Condicio itaque quam insinuare
dignatus es, non mihi displicet, si nuptura est;
utrum autem nuptura sit, etsi illud quod in ore
habet magis optamus, nunc tamen ignoramus, quia
in his annis est ut et quod se dicit velle esse sancti-
monialem, iocus sit potius garrientis quam sponsio
profitentis. Deinde habet materteram, cuius vir
honorabilis frater noster Felix, cum de hac re
contulissem cum illo—neque enim possem aliter

---

^a Benenatus was bishop of Tugutiana, the site of which
is not known. The girl referred to was an orphan whom her
father, a *vir spectabilis* (probably a magistrate), had entrusted to the guardianship of the Church. Four letters were
written by Augustine about her : cclii. to one Felix, declining
to take any action concerning her without consulting another
guardian, ccliii. to Benenatus, expressing surprise at receiving
through him the proposal for a marriage with a pagan, ccliv.
here translated, and clv. to Rusticus, the pagan who had sought
her hand, bluntly refusing his request. The practice of caring
for orphans dates from the early years of the Church, and it

No. 58 (Ep. CCLIV)

TO BENENATUS,[a] MY SAINTLY AND REVERED LORD AND LONGED FOR BROTHER AND FELLOW-PRIEST, AND THE BRETHREN WHO ARE WITH YOU, AUGUSTINE AND THE BRETHREN WHO ARE WITH ME SEND GREETING IN THE LORD

The girl about whom your Holiness wrote to me is so minded, that if she were once of full age, she would not be joined in marriage to anyone ; but her present age is such that, even if she had a mind to marry, she ought not at this stage to be given or betrothed to any man. In addition to this, my lord Benenatus, brother revered and well-beloved, the protection God is giving her in the church is a protection against wicked men, not an opportunity to give her over to anyone I choose, but an opportunity to defend her from seizure by any unsuitable person. The condition, therefore, that you are good enough to suggest seems to me satisfactory, if she gets married ; at present, however, while I have greater hopes she will carry out the intention she now expresses, I do not know if she will get married, because at her age the declaration that she wants to be a nun is rather the whim of an irresponsible babbler than the vow of one solemnly pledging herself. Further, she has an aunt married to our esteemed brother Felix ; when I consulted him about this (for I could not do other-

was regarded as fitting that the duties of guardianship should be undertaken by the clergy. Augustine refers to this in *Serm.* 176. 2 : " Pro magno commendantur episcopis patrimonia pupillorum . . . Pupillum tuetur episcopus, ne mortuis parentibus ab extraneis opprimatur."

vel deberem,—non quidem invitus accepit, immo
etiam gratulatus est ; sed iure amicitiae non im-
portune doluit, quod eis nihil inde sit scriptum.
Fortassis enim, quae nunc non apparet, apparebit et
mater, cuius voluntatem in tradenda filia omnibus,
ut arbitror, natura praeponit, nisi eadem puella in
ea iam aetate fuerit ut iure licentiore sibi eligat ipsa
quod velit.   Illud quoque cogitet sinceritas tua, quia
si mihi de nuptiis eius potestas summa ac tota tribuatur atque ipsa quoque iam matura et nubere
volens, cui voluero, se tradendam sub deo iudice
mihi committat, sic dico et verum dico mihi placere
istam condicionem, ut propter deum iudicem non
possim respuere meliorem.   Quae utrum adventura
sit, utique incertum est.   Quapropter videt caritas
tua quanta consideranda concurrant, ut nunc a me
cuiquam promitti omnino non possit.

No. 59 (Ep. CCLVIII)

DOMINO MERITO SUSCIPIENDO ET IN CHRISTO
DILECTISSIMO AC DESIDERANTISSIMO FRA-
TRI MARCIANO AUGUSTINUS IN DOMINO
SALUTEM

1   Abripui vel potius subripui et quodam modo

---

^a This is the only place where Marcianus is mentioned.

wise nor ought I to do otherwise), so far was he from being reluctant to agree to it that he actually expressed his delight, but he regretted that they had no written instructions on the matter, as their friendly relations not unreasonably entitled him to expect. For perhaps the girl's mother will come forward, though she has not come forward as yet, and her wishes about the handing over of her daughter naturally have, in my opinion, precedence over all others, unless the girl is by that time of an age to have a more legitimate claim to choose for herself what she wants. Take this point too into consideration, my true friend, that if supreme and undivided power over her marriage were entrusted to me and she herself, if of age and desirous of marrying, left me free, with God as my Judge, to give her hand to the one I desired, then I declare, and declare with sincerity, my satisfaction with the condition you suggest, provided that, because of God my Judge, I should not be repudiating a better one ; but whether a better one will turn up, is naturally uncertain. So your Charity will see how many considerations conspire to make it quite impossible for me at present to promise her to anyone.

No. 59 (Ep. CCLVIII)

TO MARCIANUS,[a] MY LORD DESERVEDLY HON-
OURED AND BROTHER CHERISHED IN CHRIST
AND LONGED FOR, AUGUSTINE SENDS
GREETING IN THE LORD

I have torn myself away from my many pre- 1
occupations (or rather have slipped away and, so to

furatus sum memet ipsum multis occupationibus
meis, ut tibi scriberem antiquissimo amico, quem
tamen non habebam, quam diu in Christo non
tenebam. Nosti quippe ut definierit amicitiam
" Romani," ut ait quidam, " maximus auctor Tullius
eloquii." Dixit enim et verissime dixit : " Amicitia est rerum humanarum et divinarum cum
benivolentia et caritate consensio." Tu autem, mi
carissime, aliquando mihi consentiebas in rebus
humanis, cum eis more vulgi frui cuperem, et mihi
ad ea capessenda, quorum me paenitet, favendo
velificabas, immo vero vela cupiditatum mearum
cum ceteris tunc dilectoribus meis inter praecipuos
aura laudis inflabas. Porro in rebus divinis, quarum
mihi illo tempore nulla eluxerat veritas, utique in
maiore illius definitionis parte, nostra amicitia claudi-
cabat ; erat enim rerum tantum modo " humanarum " non etiam " divinarum," quamvis " cum
benivolentia et caritate consensio."

2   Et posteaquam illa cupere destiti, tu quidem
perseverante benivolentia salvum me esse cupiebas
salute mortali et ea rerum prosperitate felicem,
quam mundus optare consuevit. Et iam sic itaque
aliquantum tibi erat mecum rerum humanarum
benivola et cara consensio. Nunc ergo quantum de
te gaudeo, quibus explicem verbis, quando eum
quem quoquo modo habui diu amicum, habeo iam
verum amicum ? Accessit enim rerum etiam consensio divinarum, quoniam, qui mecum temporalem

---

a Lucan, *B.C.* vii. 62-63, quoted again by Augustine in
Ep. cxliii. 3 and *Civ. Dei*, xiv. 18.
b Cicero, *Lael.* vi. 20.

speak, stolen myself away from them) in order to write
to you, my oldest friend ; and yet I did not really
have you as a friend until I clove to you in Christ.
You know, to be sure, the definition of friendship
given by " Tully, the greatest master of the Roman
tongue," as he has been called[a] ; he said, and said
very truly, " Friendship is agreement, with kindliness
and affection, on things human and divine." [b] At one
time, my dear friend, you were in agreement with me
about things human, when it was my wish to
enjoy them as the common people do, and by your
encouragement you stretched my sails to the eager
pursuit of things whereof I am now ashamed—or
rather, along with the rest of my admirers of that
time (and you were among the chief of them) you
filled the sails of my ambitions with the breeze of
praise. On the other hand, our friendship was de-
fective on the side of things divine, of which at that
period no gleam of truth had come to me, though
they form the more important half of that definition ;
it included only the human things, not those as well
that are divine, although it was " agreement with
kindliness and affection."

And after I abandoned those desires, you with 2
persistent kindliness desired that in earthly welfare
I should do well and be successful with that material
prosperity which the world is wont to wish for one,
and so, because of this, you still to some extent shared
with me this kindly and affectionate agreement on
things human. So, now, how can I explain in words the
joy I have of you, when he who was so long my friend in
some kind of way, is at last my friend in a genuine way ?
For there has been added the agreement in things
divine as well, since you, who formerly spent this

vitam quondam iucundissima benignitate duxisti,
nunc in spe vitae aeternae mecum esse coepisti.
Modo vero etiam de rebus humanis inter nos nulla
dissensio est, qui eas rerum divinarum cognitione
pensamus, ne plus eis tribuamus quam modus earum
iustissime postulat, nec eas iniquo contemptu ab-
iciendo creatori earum domino rerum caelestium
atque terrestrium faciamus iniuriam. Ita fit, ut
inter quos amicos non est rerum consensio divinarum,
nec humanarum esse plena possit ac vera. Necesse
est enim, ut aliter quam oportet humana aestimet,
qui divina contemnit, nec hominem recte diligere
noverit, quisquis eum non diligit qui hominem fecit.
Proinde non dico : "Nunc mihi plenius amicus es,
qui eras ex parte," sed, quantum ratio indicat,
nec ex parte eras, quando nec in rebus humanis
mecum amicitiam veram tenebas. Rerum quippe
divinarum, ex quibus recte humana pensantur,
socius mihi nondum eras, sive quando nec ipse in
eis eram sive posteaquam ego eas utcumque sapere
coepi, a quibus tu longe abhorrebas.

3   Nolo autem suscenseas, nec tibi videatur absurdum
quod illo tempore, cum in vana mundi huius aestuarem,
quamvis me multum amare videreris, nondum eras
amicus meus, quando nec ipse mihi amicus eram sed
potius inimicus. Diligebam quippe iniquitatem, et

temporal life with me in the most charming kindness, have now begun to be with me in the hope of life eternal. Now, indeed, even on things human there is no disagreement between us, for we weigh them in the knowledge of things divine, so as not to concede to them more than their measure most justly demands, nor yet to slight their Creator, the Lord of things heavenly and earthly, by throwing them away with undeserved contempt. It is on these grounds that those friends who are not in agreement about things divine cannot be in complete and genuine agreement about things human either ; for of necessity one who has a contempt for things divine must hold a different opinion from what he should hold about things human, and anyone who does not love Him Who made man has not learned to love man aright. Hence I do not say that now you are more completely my friend, instead of being, as you were before, only partially so ; but, as far as reason can show, you were not even partially so before, since the friendship you cherished with me then was not even genuine in things human : for, assuredly, you were not yet my comrade in those things divine by which the human things are rightly weighed. Partly it was that at that time I had no interest in them myself, partly that after I began to have a taste (however slight) for them, you still entertained for them a strong aversion.

I do not want you to feel annoyed or to think it 3 absurd that at that time, when I was aflame with desire for this world's empty show, you were not yet my friend, although you seemed to have a great affection for me ; for then I was not even a friend to myself, but an enemy instead. For I loved iniquity,

vera, quia divina, sententia est, qua scriptum est in
sanctis libris : *Qui autem diligit iniquitatem, odit
animam suam.* Cum ergo odissem animam meam,
verum amicum quo modo habere poteram ea mihi
optantem, in quibus ipse me ipsum patiebar inimicum ? *Cum vero benignitas et gratia salvatoris nostri
inluxit mihi non secundum merita mea sed secundum
ipsius misericordiam,* tu ab hac alienus quo modo esse
poteras amicus meus, qui, unde beatus esse possem,
penitus ignorabas et non in hoc me amabas, in quo
mihi ipse iam fueram utcumque amicus effectus ?

4 Gratias itaque domino, quod te mihi amicum
facere tandem aliquando dignatur. Nunc enim
nobis est " rerum humanarum et divinarum cum
benivolentia et caritate consensio " in Christo Iesu
domino nostro, verissima pace nostra. Qui duobus
praeceptis cuncta praeconia divina conclusit dicens :
*Diliges dominum deum tuum ex toto corde tuo et ex tota
anima tua et ex tota mente tua,* et : *Diliges proximum
tuum tamquam te ipsum ; in his duobus praeceptis tota
lex pendet et prophetae.* In illo primo rerum divinarum,
in hoc secundo rerum humanarum est cum benivolentia et caritate consensio. Haec duo si mecum
firmissime teneas, amicitia nostra vera ac sempiterna
erit et non solum invicem nos sed etiam ipsi domino
sociabit.

5 Quod ut fiat, exhortor gravitatem et prudentiam
tuam, ut iam etiam fidelium sacramenta percipias ;

---

a Ps. x. 5, the Vulgate version, after the Septuagint ὁ δὲ
ἀγαπῶν ἀδικίαν μισεῖ τὴν ἑαυτοῦ ψυχήν ; the English reads,
" But the wicked and him that loveth violence, his own soul
hateth."

b Titus iii. 4-5.   *c* Cicero, *Lael.* vi. 20.

and that saying that is written in the Holy Books is true, because divine : " He that loveth iniquity hateth his own soul." [a] Hating then my own soul as I did, how could I have a true friend in one who wished me those things in which I was suffering myself to be my own enemy ? " But after that the kindness and love of God our Saviour " [b] dawned upon me, not according to my merits, " but according to His mercy," how could you, when you were a stranger to it, be my friend ? That which could give me happiness was quite unknown to you, nor did you love me in that wherein I had already been made a friend (however poor) unto myself.

Thanks be therefore to the Lord, that He is good 4 enough to make you a friend of mine now at last ; for now we have that " agreement, with kindliness and affection, about things human and divine " [c] in Christ Jesus our Lord, Who is our real peace. In two commandments He has summed up all God's injunctions, saying : " Thou shalt love the Lord thy God with all thy heart and with all thy soul and with all thy mind " and " thou shalt love thy neighbour as thyself ; on these two commandments hang all the law and the prophets." [d] In the first of these is " agreement, with kindliness and affection " about things divine, in the second, about things human. If you are with me in holding these two commandments with tenacity, our friendship will be genuine and everlasting and it will join us not merely to each other but also to the Lord Himself.

That this may be so, I exhort you, my wise and 5 honoured friend, now also to partake of the Sacraments available for those in full communion, for

[d] Matt. xxii. 37, 39, 40, etc.

decet enim aetatem et congruit, quantum credo, moribus tuis. Memento quid mihi dixeris profecturo, comicum quidem de Terentio recolens versum sed tamen aptissimum et utilissimum :

nunc hic dies aliam vitam adfert, alios mores postulat.

Quod si veraciter dixisti, sicut de te dubitare non debeo, iam profecto sic vivis ut sis dignus baptismo salutari remissionem praeteritorum accipere peccatorum. Nam omnino non est, cui alteri praeter dominum Christum dicat genus humanum :

te duce, si qua manent sceleris vestigia nostri,
irrita perpetua solvent formidine terras.

Quod ex Cymaeo, id est ex Sibyllino carmine se fassus est transtulisse Vergilius, quoniam fortassis etiam illa vates aliquid de unico salvatore in spiritu audierat, quod necesse habuit confiteri. Haec tibi, domine merito suscipiende et in Christo dilectissime ac desiderantissime frater, sive pauca sive forsitan multa sint, utcumque occupatissimus scripsi. Tua sumere rescripta desidero et te nomen vel dedisse inter competentes vel daturum esse iam iamque cognoscere. Dominus deus, in quem credidisti, et hic et in futuro saeculo te conservet, domine merito suscipiende et in Christo dilectissime ac desiderantissime frater.

---

^a From what follows it is clear that Augustine wanted his friend to be baptized. The habit of postponing baptism as long as possible was still very common ; Basil, Gregory of Nazianzus and Chrysostom, though the sons of Christian mothers, received baptism only when of mature years, and Augustine himself was baptized only at the age of 33. Infant baptism was not the general rule until the following century. For *fidelis* in the sense of " a communicant" see p. 438. ^b Terence, *Andr.* 189.

^c Virgil, *Buc.* iv. 13-14, Rhoades's translation.

this would become one of your age *a* and be appropriate, in my opinion, to your character. Remember your remark to me when I was on the point of leaving you ; you recalled that verse from one of Terence's comedies, but still, though from a comedy, very apposite and proper :

> To-day now introduces a different life
> and demands a different character.*b*

If you were sincere in quoting it, as I have no right to doubt you were, you certainly are living now in such a way as to be worthy of receiving through the saving rite of baptism the remission of your past sins. There is none other at all, save the Lord Christ, to whom the human race can say :

> Under Thy guidance, whatso tracks remain
> Of our old wickedness, once done away,
> Shall free the earth from never-ceasing fear.*c*

Virgil confessed to adopting this thought from the Cumaean, that is, the Sibylline, prophecy, and perhaps that seer too had had some message to her spirit about the only Saviour, which she had of necessity to confess.

This, my lord deservedly honoured and brother cherished in Christ and longed for, be it little or be it perchance much, I have at any rate written you, though in one way and another extremely engrossed in business. I long to receive a reply from you and to learn at any moment that you have entered your name among the candidates for baptism or are on the point of doing so. May the Lord God, in Whom you have put your trust, keep you, my lord deservedly honoured and brother cherished in Christ and longed for, both here and in the world to come !

No. 60 (Ep. CCLXII)

DOMINAE RELIGIOSISSIMAE FILIAE ECDICIAE[a] AUGUSTINUS IN DOMINO SALUTEM

1 Lectis litteris reverentiae tuae et earum perlatore
interrogato, quae interroganda restabant, vehementer
dolui sic te voluisse agere cum marito, ut aedificium
continentiae, quod in eo iam construi coeperat, amissa
perseverantia in adulterii ruinam miserabiliter laberetur. Cum enim lugendus esset, si post continentiam votam deo iamque actu ipso moribusque
susceptam reverteretur ad coniugis carnem, quanto
magis nunc demersus in interitum profundiorem
lugendus est, qui tam abrupta dissolutione moechatur
iratus tibi perniciosus sibi, tamquam in te acerbius
saeviat, si ipse pereat! Hoc autem tantum mali
accidit, dum tu eius animum non qua debuisti
moderatione tractasti, quia, etsi carnali consortio iam
ex consensu vobis non miscebamini, in ceteris tamen
rebus coniugali obsequio viro tuo mulier servire
debuisti, praesertim cum ambo essetis membra
corporis Christi.[b] Et utique, si maritum infidelem
fidelis habuisses, agere te conversatione subdita
oportuit, ut eum domino lucrareris, sicut apostoli
monuerunt.

2 Omitto enim, quod ipsam continentiam, illo non-

---

[a] Ecdicia is not otherwise known.
[b] Eph. v. 30, etc.

No. 60 (Ep. CCLXII)

TO THE MOST DEVOUT LADY, MY DAUGHTER ECDICIA,[a] AUGUSTINE SENDS GREETING IN THE LORD

After reading your Reverence's letter and asking 1
its bearer the questions that remained to be asked,
I have been very greatly grieved that you chose so to
act towards your husband that the edifice of chastity
which had already begun to be built up in him has,
through his failure to persevere, toppled to the pitiful
downfall of adultery. If after making to God a vow
of chastity and already undertaking its observance in
deed and in disposition, he had returned to his wife's
body, his case would have been deplorable enough ;
but how much more deplorable is it now that he has
plunged to deeper destruction, with such precipitate
collapse into adultery, furious towards you, in-
jurious to himself, as if his rage at you would be
the more violent if he accomplished his own ruin !
This great mischief has come about because you
failed to treat him with the moderation you ought,
for although by agreement you were no longer
coming together in carnal intercourse, yet in all other
things you ought to have shown the subjection of a
wife to your husband in compliance with the marriage-
bond, especially as you were both members of the
body of Christ.[b] Indeed, if you, a believer, had had
a husband who was an unbeliever, it would have
been your duty to conduct yourself with submissive-
ness, as the Apostles enjoined, so as to win him to
the Lord.

I leave out of account the fact that I know you 2

501

dum volente, non secundum sanam doctrinam te
suscepisse cognovi. Neque enim corporis tui debito
fraudandus fuit, priusquam ad illud bonum quod
superat pudicitiam coniugalem, tuae voluntati voluntas quoque eius accederet, nisi forte non legeras
nec audieras vel non adtenderas apostolum dicentem:
Bonum est homini mulierem non tangere; propter fornica-
tiones autem unusquisque suam uxorem habeat et una-
quaeque suum virum habeat. Uxori vir debitum reddat,
similiter autem et uxor viro. Uxor non habet potestatem
corporis sui sed vir; similiter autem et vir non habet
potestatem corporis sui sed mulier. Nolite fraudare
invicem nisi ex consensu ad tempus, ut vacetis orationi,
et iterum ad id ipsum estote, ne vos temptet Satanas
propter incontinentiam vestram. Secundum haec verba
apostolica, etiam si se ipse continere voluisset et tu
noluisses, debitum tibi reddere cogeretur et illi deus
inputaret continentiam, si non suae sed tuae cedens
infirmitati, ne in adulterii damnabile flagitium
caderes, maritalem tibi concubitum non negaret;
quanto magis te, quam magis subiectam esse de-
cuerat, ne ipse quoque in adulterium diabolica
temptatione traheretur, in reddendo huius modi
debito voluntati eius obtemperare convenerat, cum
tibi voluntatem continendi acceptaret deus, quia
propterea non faceres, ne periret maritus!

3   Sed hoc, ut dixi, omitto, quoniam postea tibi

ᵃ 1 Cor. vii. 1-5.

took this chastity upon yourself before he consented, which was not according to sound doctrine, for he should not have been defrauded of the debt you owed him of your body, before his will too joined with yours in seeking that good which is above conjugal chastity. But perhaps you had not read or heard or meditated upon the apostle's words : " It is good for a man not to touch a woman ; nevertheless, to avoid fornication, let every man have his own wife and let every woman have her own husband. Let the husband render unto the wife due benevolence ; and likewise also the wife unto the husband. The wife hath not power of her own body, but the husband ; and likewise also the husband hath not power of his own body, but the wife. Defraud ye not one the other, except it be with consent for a time, that ye may give yourselves to prayer ; and come together again that Satan tempt you not because of your incontinency."[a] According to these words of the apostle's, even if he had desired to practise chastity and you had not, he would be bound to " render you due benevolence," and God would give him credit for chastity, since he would have been granting you marital inter-course through regard not for his own weakness but for yours, so as to prevent you from falling into the damnable sin of adultery. How much more fitting was it that you, who ought to have been in greater subjection, should give way to his desire in the rendering of this benevolence, so that he might not be led by the devil's tempting into adultery, since your desire for chastity would have been acceptable to God, as you were unable to carry it out for fear of driving your husband to destruction!

I leave this fact, as I said, out of account, because **3**

nolenti sibi ad reddenda coniugalia debita consentire ad eadem continentiae pacta ipse consensit et tecum continentissime diu vixit suoque consensu a peccato illo, quo ei debitum carnis negabas, ipse te absolvit. Non ergo iam in tua causa ista vertitur quaestio, utrum redire debeas ad concubitum viri. Quod enim deo pari consensu ambo voveratis, perseveranter usque in finem reddere ambo debuistis, a quo proposito si lapsus est ille, tu saltem constantissime persevera. Quod te non exhortarer nisi quia tibi ad hoc ipse consenserat. Nam si numquam tenuisses eius adsensum, numerus te nullus defendisset annorum, sed post quantum libet tempus me consuluisses, nihil tibi aliud responderem nisi quod ait apostolus : *Uxor non habet potestatem corporis sui sed vir.* De qua potestate sic tibi iam permiserat continentiam, ut eam tecum et ipse susciperet.

4 Sed illud est quod minus te observasse contristor, quia tanto humilius et oboedientius ei obsequi in domestica conversatione debuisti, quanto ille religiosius tibi rem tam magnam etiam imitando concesserat. Non enim quia pariter temperabatis a commixtione carnali, ideo tuus maritus esse destiterat ; immo vero tanto sanctius inter vos coniuges manebatis, quanto sanctiora concorditer placita servabatis. Nihil ergo de tua veste, nihil de auro

---

* 1 Cor. vii. 4.

after you had refused to consent to render him this conjugal benevolence he consented to the same bond of continence and lived for a long time in the greatest continence with you ; and by consenting he absolved you from your sin in denying him carnal benevolence. So now in this problem of yours the question is not involved whether you ought to return to intercourse with your husband ; for what you both with one consent vowed unto God, you both ought to have persevered unto the end in paying ; even if he has fallen away from your resolution, do you at least persevere in it with the utmost fidelity. I should not be urging you to this course unless for the fact that he gave you his consent to that plan ; for if you had never obtained his assent, no lapse of years would excuse you, but had you consulted me, however long afterwards, I should have made you no other answer than the saying of the apostle : " The wife hath not power of her own body, but the husband." [a] By this power of his he had already allowed you to practise continence and undertook to practise it with you himself.

But this is the point which I am grieved you did 4 not observe more carefully : you were bound to give way to him in your private conduct with all the greater humility and submission, since he had so devotedly followed your example and conceded you so much. For he had not ceased to be your husband because you had both agreed to abstain from carnal intercourse ; instead of that, the tie that bound you to each other as husband and wife remained all the more holy because of the greater holiness of the resolutions you were with one accord carrying out. You had no right, therefore, to do anything with

vel argento vel quacumque pecunia, rebus ullis
terrenis tuis, sine arbitrio eius facere debuisti,
ne scandalizares hominem qui deo tecum maiora
voverat et ab eo quod de tua carne licita potestate
posset exigere, se continenter abstinuerat.

5   Denique factum est ut vinculum continentiae,
quo se dilectus innexuerat, contemptus abrumperet
et iratus tibi non parceret sibi. Sicut enim mihi
rettulit perlator epistulae tuae, cum cognovisset
quod omnia vel paene omnia quae habebas, nescio
quibus duobus transeuntibus monachis tamquam
pauperibus eroganda donaveris, tunc ille detestans
eos tecum et non dei servos sed domus alienae
penetratores et tuos captivatores et depraedatores
putans, tam sanctam sarcinam quam tecum subierat,
indignatus abiecit. Infirmus enim erat et ideo tibi,
quae in communi proposito fortior videbaris, non erat
praesumptione turbandus sed dilectione portandus,
quia, etiamsi ad ipsas elemosynas largius faciendas
forte pigrius movebatur, posset et ista condiscere,
si tuis inopinatis non feriretur expensis, sed ex-
pectatis invitaretur obsequiis, ut etiam hoc quod

---

^a These were probably wandering monks, who were
numerous in Africa; Augustine describes them in *De
Opere Monachorum* 28. 36: "tam multos hypocritas sub
habitu monachorum usquequaque dispersit [diabolus],
circumeuntes provincias, nusquam missos, nusquam fixos,
nusquam stantes, nusquam sedentes. Alii membra martyrum, si tamen martyrum, venditant; alii fimbrias et phy-
lacteria sua magnificant; alii parentes vel consanguineos
suos in illa vel in illa regione se audisse vivere et ad eos
pergere mentiuntur; et omnes petunt, omnes exigunt,
aut sumptus egestosae egestatis, aut simulatae pretium

your garments, anything with your gold or silver or money or with any of your earthly property, without his approval, for fear of scandalizing a man who had joined you in vowing more important things to God and had continently refrained from what he had lawful authority to demand from your body.

Finally, it came about that when scorned he burst 5 the bond of continence with which he had girt himself when loved, and from anger with you, did not hesitate to harm himself. For, as the bearer of your letter informed me, when he learned that you had given away everything, or nearly everything, that you possessed to two passing monks,[a] of some kind or other, as if it were alms you were giving to the poor, then he cursed them and you together, and thinking that they were the kind of men who " creep into other people's houses," and not servants of God, and that they had " led you captive "[b] and plundered you, he was provoked to throw off the holy obligation he had undertaken along with you. For he was weak, and therefore, since you seemed the stronger in your common resolution, he required to be supported by your love and not disquieted by your obstinacy ; even if he happened to be slower in being moved to greater generosity in giving those alms, he could have learned even that from you, had he not been exasperated by your unlooked-for extravagance, but won over to it by the compliance he expected from you ; so even this

sanctitatis." They are the monks referred to in the Benedictine Rule as *gyrovagi*, the worst class of monks, " qui tota vita sua per diversas provincias ternis aut quaternis diebus per diversorum cellas hospitantur, semper vagi et numquam stabiles et propriis voluptatibus et gulae illecebris servientes."

[b] 2 Tim. iii. 6.

temere sola fecisti, multo consultius dilectione concordi multoque ordinatius et honestius ambo faceretis,
nec blasphemarentur servi dei, si tamen hoc fuerunt
qui marito absente atque nesciente ab ignota muliere
et aliena uxore tanta sumpserunt, et laudaretur deus
in operibus vestris, quorum esset tam fida societas,
ut a vobis communiter teneretur non solum summa
castitas verum etiam gloriosa paupertas.

6 Nunc autem inconsiderata festinatione adtende
quid feceris. Ut enim de illis monachis, a quibus te
ipse non aedificatam sed spoliatam esse conqueritur,
ego bene sentiam nec homini prae ira turbatum
oculum habenti contra dei fortasse famulos facile
consentiam, numquid tantum bonum est quod
pauperum carnem largioribus elemosynis refecisti,
quantum malum est quod viri tui mentem a tam bono
proposito subruisti ? An cuiusquam tibi temporalis
salus carior esse debuerat quam huius aeterna ?
Nonne si ampliorem misericordiam cogitans ideo
pauperibus res tuas erogare differres, ne scandalizatus
maritus tuus deo periret, uberiores tibi deus elemosynas inputaret ? Proinde, si recolis quid ad-
quisiveras, quando lucrata fueras virum tuum ut
tecum Christo sanctiore castitate serviret, intellege,
per illas elemosynas tuas quibus cor eius eversum

---

a Ps. vi. 8, "turbatus est prae ira oculus meus " (Vulgate :
" turbatus est a furore . . .")

that you did of yourself so indiscreetly, you would in harmonious affection have done together with much more deliberation, much more orderliness and more decency, and no blasphemy would have been directed at servants of God (if that is what those men really were, who accepted such large sums from a woman they did not know, another man's wife, in the absence of her husband and without his knowledge) and praise would have arisen to God from your works. In them your companionship would have been so trustful that you would jointly have embraced not only the strictest chastity, but also glorious poverty.

Now, however, by your ill-advised haste see what **6** you have done. For although I were to think the best about those monks by whom he complains you were not edified but robbed, and were not readily to take the part of a man whose eye was confused by anger *a* against those who were perhaps God's servants, is the good you have done in refreshing the bodies of the poor by your over-generous alms as great as the evil you have done in subverting your husband's mind from his virtuous resolution ? Or ought anyone's temporal welfare to have been more precious to you than his eternal welfare ? Would not God have credited you with still richer alms, if, meditating a wider sphere of mercy, you had postponed the distribution of your wealth to the poor in order to avoid putting a stumbling-block in your husband's way and making him die to God ? So, if you recall what you gained when you won your husband to the service of Christ with you in holier chastity, you can understand how much weightier is the loss with which you have been smitten

est, quanto graviore damno percussa fueris, quam sunt illa lucra quae caelestia cogitabas. Si enim habet ibi magnum locum panis fractus esurienti, quantum locum ibi credenda est habere misericordia qua homo eripitur diabolo, tamquam leoni rugienti et quem devoret inquirenti !

7   Neque hoc ita dicimus, ut, si quisquam scandalizatus fuerit de bonis operibus nostris, ab eis desistendum putemus ; sed alia causa est alienarum alia necessariarum in societate aliqua personarum, alia fidelis alia infidelis, alia parentum erga filios alia filiorum erga parentes, alia postremo ea quae in his rebus vel maxime intuenda est, viri et uxoris, ubi mulierem coniugatam non licet dicere : " Facio quod volo de meo," cum et ipsa non sit sua sed capitis sui, hoc est viri sui. *Nam sic quaedam,* ut commemorat apostolus Petrus, *mulieres sanctae, quae in deum sperabant, ornabant se subiectae suis viris, sicut Sarra obsequebatur Abrahae dominum eum vocans, cuius,* inquit, *factae estis filiae,* cum ad Christianas, non ad Iudaeas feminas loqueretur.

8   Quid autem mirum, si pater communem filium nolebat huius vitae sustentaculis a matre nudari, ignorans quid sectaturus esset, cum in aetate grandiuscula esse coepisset, utrum monachi professionem an ecclesiasticum ministerium an coniugalis necessitudinis vinculum ? Quamvis enim ad meliora excitandi et erudiendi sint filii sanctorum,

---

a Isai. lviii. 7.   *b* 1 Pet. v. 8.
c Eph. v. 23.   *d* 1 Pet. iii. 5-6.

510

through your almsgiving, which overturned his heart,
than is the gain which you thought you were laying
up in heaven. For if the breaking of bread for the
hungry [a] has a great place there, how great must we
believe to be there the place of the compassion by
which a man is snatched from the devil, " as a roar-
ing lion seeking whom he may devour " [b] !

Now, by this I do not mean that if our good **7**
works put a stumbling-block in anyone's way, we
should imagine that we must cease from them ; but
the case of strangers differs from that of those bound
to us by any tie : that of the believer differs from
that of the unbeliever, that of parents towards their
children from that of children towards their parents,
and finally the case (which in the present circumstances must be particularly considered) of a husband
and a wife, where the married woman has no right
to say, " I shall do what I like with what is my own."
She is not her own, but belongs to her head, that is,
her husband, [c] " for after this manner," as the apostle
Peter reminds us, [d] " the holy women also, who trusted
in God, adorned themselves, being in subjection unto
their own husbands, even as Sara obeyed Abraham,
calling him lord ; whose daughters," he says, though
he was speaking to Christian not to Jewish women,
" ye have become."

And was it surprising that a father refused to **8**
have the son of both of you stripped by his mother
of the means of supporting this life, when he did not
know what career he would pursue when he came to
be a little older, whether he would undertake the
vows of a monk or service in the Church or the tie
of marriage relations ? For although the children
of holy parents should be prompted and trained for

unusquisque tamen *proprium donum habet a deo alius
sic, alius autem sic,* nisi forte talia prospiciens et
praecavens reprehendendus est pater, cum beatus
apostolus dicat : *Quisquis autem suis et maxime
domesticis non providet, fidem denegat et est infideli
deterior.* Cum vero de faciendis ipsis elemosynis
loqueretur, ait : *Non ut aliis refectio, vobis autem
angustia.* Pariter ergo consilium de omnibus haberetis, pariter moderaremini quid thesaurizandum esset
in caelo, quid ad vitae huius sufficientiam vobis et
vestris vestroque filio relinquendum, ne aliis esset
refectio, vobis autem angustia. Et in his disponendis
atque faciendis si quid tibi forte melius videretur,
suggereres viro reverenter eiusdemque auctoritatem
tamquam tui capitis sequereris oboedienter, ut
omnes qui sanum sapiunt, ad quos posset hoc bonum
vestrum fama perferre, de domus vestrae fructu ac
pace gauderent, et adversarius revereretur, nihil
habens de vobis dicere pravi.

9 Porro si de faciendis elemosynis et in pauperes
inpendendis rebus tuis, de quo bono opere et magno
tam evidentia praecepta sunt domini, cum viro tuo
fideli et tecum sancta continentiae pacta servante
consilium communicare deberes eiusdemque non
spernere voluntatem, quanto magis de habitu atque
vestitu nihil tibi praeter eius arbitrium mutandum
vel usurpandum fuit, unde nihil divinitus legimus

---

a 1 Cor. vii. 7.   *b* 1 Tim. v. 8.
c 2 Cor. viii. 13, where the Vulgate reads " non ut aliis **sit**
remissio, vobis autem tribulatio."

better things, still " every man hath his proper gift of God, one after this manner, and another after that "[a]; unless indeed a father is to be blamed who exercises foresight and caution about such things, though the apostle says, " But if any provide not for his own, and specially for those of his own house, he hath denied the faith and is worse than an infidel."[b] But when he speaks of almsgiving, he says, " I mean not that other men be eased, and ye burdened."[c] Together, you should deliberate on all matters, together you should apportion what treasure you should lay up in heaven and what you should leave as a sufficiency in this life for yourselves and your household and your son, so that " other men " should not " be eased and ye burdened." And in the ordering and doing of this, if any better plan happened to occur to you, you should have suggested it to your husband with deference and with obedience submitted to his authority as that of your head. In this way all sensible people to whom the report could come of this good thing in you would rejoice at the fruitfulness and peace of your household, and your adversary would be put to shame, having nothing to say about you that was amiss.

Further, if in the matter of alms-giving and be- 9 stowing your property upon the poor—a good work and important, about which the Lord has given such unmistakable commandments—it was your duty to take common counsel with your husband, a Christian and observing with you the holy vow of continence, and not to scorn his wishes, how much more necessary was it for you, not to change or to adopt against his will anything in the way of attire or dress—a thing about which there are

513

imperatum! Scriptum est quidem mulieres esse debere
in habitu ordinato, aurique circumpositio et intortio
crinium et cetera huius modi, quae vel ad inanem
pompam vel ad inlecebram formae adhiberi solent,
merito reprehensa sunt. Sed est quidam pro modulo
personae habitus matronalis a viduali veste dis-
tinctus, qui potest fidelibus coniugatis salva religionis
observantia convenire. Hunc te maritus si deponere
noluit, ne te velut viduam illo vivente iactares, puto
quia non fuerat in hac re usque ad dissensionis
scandalum perducendus magis inoboedientiae malo
quam ullius abstinentiae bono. Quid est enim ab-
surdius quam mulierem de humili veste viro superbire,
cui te potius expediret obtemperare candidis moribus
quam nigellis vestibus repugnare, quia etsi te in-
dumentum monachae delectabat, etiam hoc gratius
posset marito observato exoratoque sumi quam illo
inconsulto contemptoque praesumi ? Quod si omnino non sineret, quid tuo proposito deperiret ?
Absit ut hinc displiceres deo, quod coniuge tuo

---

* 1 Tim. ii. 9 ; 1 Pet. iii. 3.

ᵇ Two orders of widows are to be discriminated : (1) those
who were maintained by the Church and who gave a return
of either prayer or good works (*cf. Stat. Eccl. Antiq.* 103
"viduae quae stipendiis ecclesiae sustentantur tam assiduae
in Dei opere esse debent ut et meritis et orationibus suis
ecclesiam adjuvent"); (2) a more honourable order, not
confined to those over 60 or in need of support, who gained
merit from abstaining from a second marriage. The widows
who had taken this vow were distinguished by a special
dress (" vestis fuscior," Jerome, *Ep.* 38. 5), and the distinction
seems to have been much coveted. This class of widows

no divine orders for us to read. It is, indeed,
written that women should have " modest apparel,"
and " the wearing of gold " and " the broidering
of the hair "[a] and other suchlike things, usually
employed either for empty show or to give allurement
to the body, are deservedly condemned. But there
is a kind of matronly dress, befitting a person's
station, distinct from the garments of a widow, which
may become Christian wives without affronting
Christian decorum. If your husband did not wish you
to put that aside, so that you should not vaunt yourself
as a widow while he was still alive,[b] I am of opinion
that on this point he should not have been driven to
the scandal of quarrelling with you, for the harm done
by your disobedience was greater than the good
you did by any of your self-repression. For what is
more preposterous than a wife's domineering over
her husband about a humble garment, when it would
be more becoming in you to yield him compliance in
shining deeds than to contend with him about
gloomy clothes ? Even if a nun's dress pleased you,
you would have been happier in assuming even it
when you had shown due regard for your husband
and received his permission, than in presuming to
don that other, without asking his advice or paying
him any respect. And if he altogether refused to
allow it, wherein would your resolution have been the
loser ? Far be it from us to imagine you would dis-

performed duties much like deaconesses, and by the eighth
century they were compelled to leave their private houses
and live in communities. Eventually, too, the order of
widows was confused with that of deaconesses, and the
ceremony of assuming widow's dress was performed before
the bishop, instead of remaining simply a private act of the
widow herself.

nondum defuncto non induereris sicut Anna, sed
sicut Susanna.

10 Neque enim et ille qui tecum iam coeperat
custodire tam magnum continentiae bonum, etiamsi
coniugale, non viduale, voluisset ut acciperes indu-
mentum, ad indecentem quoque te compulisset
ornatum, quo etsi aliqua dura condicione cogereris,
posses habere in superbo cultu cor humile. Nempe
apud patres Esther illa regina deum timens, deum
colens, deo subdita, marito regi alienigenae non
eundem secum colenti deum tamen subiecta
serviebat. Quae cum extremo periculo non suo
tantum sed etiam gentis suae, qui tunc erat
populus dei, domino prosterneretur orando, in ipsa
oratione sua dixit ita sibi esse ornatum regium sicut
pannum menstrualem ; et ita orantem confestim
exaudivit, qui *cordis inspector* eam verum dicere
scivit. Et utique maritum habebat multarum
mulierum virum et deorum alienorum falsorumque
cultorem. Tu autem, si et ille in proposito quod
tecum susceperat, perduraret nec a te offensus in
flagitium corruisset, maritum habebas non solum
fidelem et verum deum tecum colentem sed etiam
continentem, qui procul dubio propositi vestri non

---

a i.e. By wearing a matron's dress instead of a widow's
dress. "Anna" is the prophetess of S. Luke ii. 36-38, one
of the godly remnant of Israel that was looking for the
coming of the Messiah; she is taken by the Fathers as a proto-
type of true and holy widowhood. The story of Susanna is
told in the apocryphal part of Daniel, ch. xiii ; she is the

please God by wearing, while your husband was still alive, not the dress of Anna, but of Susanna.[a]

Nor even if he had wished you to put on the dress of a matron and not of a widow, would he who had already begun with you to observe the great virtue of continence, have been driving you also to adopt adornment that was unbecoming ; even had he compelled you to it by some galling condition, you could have had a humble heart beneath your haughty finery. Surely, in the time of the patriarchs, Queen Esther feared God, worshipped God and obeyed God, and yet in submission served the foreign king, her husband, who did not worship the same God as she did. At a time of the utmost danger, not to herself alone but to her race as well, who were then God's chosen people, she prostrated herself before God in prayer, and said in her prayer that she regarded her royal adornment " as a menstruous rag "[b]; and so her prayer was immediately heard and answered by Him "that pondereth the heart,"[c] Who knew that she was speaking the truth. And yet her husband was a man with many wives and worshipped strange, false gods. But you, if your husband had persevered in the resolution he had undertaken with you and had not fallen into sin on provocation from you, you had a husband who was not only a believer and a worshipper with you of the true God, but was also practising continence, and who undoubtedly, recollecting your common

type of the chaste matron. See, for example, St. Ambrose's praises of Susanna, Anna and the Virgin Mother, as types of chastity in the wife, the widow and the virgin (*De Vid.* 4. 21-25).

[b] Esther xiv. 16.　　　　　　[c] Prov. xxiv. 12.

inmemor, etsi te ad coniugalia cogeret indumenta,
ad superba tamen ornamenta non cogeret.

11   Haec tibi scripsi, quoniam me consulendum putasti, non ut tuum rectum institutum sermone meo
frangerem, sed quod te inordinate et incaute agente
viri tui factum dolerem. De cuius reparatione debes
vehementissime cogitare, si vere ad Christum vis
pertinere. Indue itaque humilitatem mentis, et
ut te deus conservet perseverantem, noli maritum
contemnere pereuntem. Funde pro illo pias et
assiduas orationes, sacrifica lacrimas tamquam vulne-
rati sanguinem cordis et scribe ad eum satisfactionem,
petens veniam, quia in eum peccasti, quod praeter
eius consilium et voluntatem de rebus tuis fecisti
quod faciendum putasti, non ut te paeniteat tribuisse
pauperibus sed eum boni tui operis participem et
moderatorem habere noluisse. Promitte de cetero
in adiutorio domini, si et illum suae turpitudinis
paenituerit et continentiam quam deseruit, re-
petiverit, te illi, sicut decet, in omnibus servituram
ne forte, ut ait apostolus, *det* illi *deus paenitentiam et*
resipiscat *de diaboli laqueis, a quo* captivus tenetur
secundum ipsius voluntatem. Filium autem vestrum,
quoniam de legitimis eum et honestis nuptiis sus-
cepisti, magis in patris quam in tua esse potestate
quis nesciat ? Et ideo ei negari non potest, ubicumque illum esse cognoverit et iure poposcerit ; ac per
hoc, ut secundum tuam voluntatem in dei possit

---

^a 2 Tim. ii. 25-26.

resolution, even if he did compel you to wear matronly
dress, would nevertheless not have compelled you to
wear proud ornaments.

I have written this to you, since you thought fit to
ask my advice, not in order to undermine your
righteous design by any words from me, but because
I am grieved at what your husband has done as
a result of your irregular and imprudent conduct.
It is your duty most earnestly to think how he may
be restored, if your wish to belong to Christ is sincere.
Put on therefore humility of mind, and in order that
God may keep you while you persevere, do not you
scorn your husband while he perishes. Pour forth
for him devoted and constant prayers; offer the
sacrifice of tears as though they were the blood of a
stricken heart, and write him an apology, begging his
forgiveness for that you sinned against him in doing
with your property what you thought should be
done, without asking his advice and consent; not
that you should repent of having given to the poor,
but of having refused to let your husband share and
direct your good deeds. Promise for the future, with
the help of the Lord, that, if he repents of his evil conduct and returns to the continence he had abandoned,
you will be subject to him, as it is fitting you should
be, in all things, "if peradventure God will give him
repentance and that he may recover himself out of
the snare of the devil, by whom he is taken captive
at his will."[a] And as for your son, who does not know
that, since you got him in lawful and honourable wedlock, his father has greater authority over him than
you have? So he cannot be denied him, when he
learns his whereabouts and claims him by law.
Hence, in order that he may be nurtured and

nutriri et erudiri sapientia, necessaria illi est etiam
vestra concordia.

No. 61 (Ep. CCLXVIII)

DOMINIS DILECTISSIMIS ET DESIDERANTISSIMIS
SANCTAE PLEBIS CUI MINISTRO MEMBRIS
CHRISTI AUGUSTINUS IN DOMINO SALUTEM

1 Notissima mihi et probatissima devotio sanctitatis
vestrae in domino nostro Iesu Christo fiduciam dedit,
ut etiam absens praesumerem unde praesens gaudere
consuevi, qui semper spiritu vobiscum sum, non
solum quia gratia domini nostri Iesu Christi tantae
suavitatis flagrare non cessat, sed etiam quia me
ipsum, qui vobis in evangelio servio, angustiam pati
non permittitis. Cum enim frater noster Fascius debito
decem et septem solidorum ab opinatoribus urgeretur
ut redderet, quod ad praesens unde explicaret
se, non inveniebat, ne corporalem pateretur iniuriam
ad auxilium sanctae ecclesiae convolavit. Illi etiam
exactores, cum proficisci cogerentur et ideo dilationem
dare non possent, gravissimis me querelis onera-
verunt, ita ut eis illum traderem aut, quod sibi deberi
ostendebant, unde acciperent, providerem. Cumque
obtulissem Fascio ut vestram sanctitatem de necessi-

---

a In this letter to his congregation at Hippo, Augustine
appeals for a collection to enable him to repay to Macedonius a debt he had incurred to relieve their townsman
and fellow-Christian, Fascius, who being pressed by creditors,
took sanctuary in the church. By a law of Theodosius
(*Cod. Theod.* ix. 45. 1-3) Fascius was liable to seizure and
removal, unless the bishop discharged the debt. This
Augustine did by borrowing, but as Fascius has not repaid
him, he appeals for their help.

trained, as you would have him, in the wisdom of
God, it is essential for him too that you both should
be in harmony.

No. 61 (Ep. CCLXVIII)

TO THE MEMBERS OF CHRIST, MY WELL
BELOVED AND MUCH LONGED FOR LORDS
OF THE HOLY CONGREGATION TO WHICH
I MINISTER, AUGUSTINE SENDS GREETINGS
IN THE LORD [a]

Your devotion, my holy brethren, to our Lord Jesus 1
Christ, well known to me and often tested, has given
me, though absent, reason to place reliance in that
wherein I have been wont to rejoice when present:
in spirit I am always with you, not only because the
great sweetness of the grace of our Lord Jesus
Christ ever continueth its fragrance, but also because you do not suffer me, who am your servant
in the Gospel, to endure any hardship. Now, our
brother Fascius was being pressed for payment of
a debt of seventeen solidi [b] by the tribute-gatherers
and found for the moment no way of escape from
his entanglement; wherefore, so as not to suffer
bodily injury, he fled to the protection of Holy
Church.[c] And as those tax-collectors were compelled to take their departure and so were unable to
grant him a respite, they heaped on me the most
grievous abuse, declaring that I ought to hand him
over to them or to furnish the means wherefrom
they could receive the debt which they proved was
owing them. I made the offer to Fascius to speak to

[b] This amounted to about £16.
[c] For sanctuary see p. 209.

521

tatibus eius adloquerer, pudore deterritus, ne facerem
deprecatus est. Ita ego maiore necessitate coartatus
a fratre nostro Macedonio decem et septem solidos
accepi, quos in causam eius continuo dedi, promittente
illo quod ad certum diem cum eis reddendis posset
occurrere, et consentiente, ut si non posset occurrere,
sermo de illo fieret ad vestram misericordiam, quam
fraternam fratribus exhibere consuestis.

2 Nunc ergo, quoniam absens est, restat ut sub-
veniatis non illi, quem nemo compellat absentem,
sed pollicitationi meae, cuius existimatio vobis
semper est praesens. Iam enim dies ad quem se
promiserat occursurum, transactus est, et ego ei qui
solidos suos fidei meae commisit, quid respondeam,
non invenio, nisi ut faciam quod me facturum esse
promisi. Sed quoniam non sum de hac re com-
monitus, ut die pentecostes, quando aderat maior
vestra frequentia, sermonem inde facerem, peto ut
has litteras pro lingua mea praesente habere digne-
mini admonente vos et exhortante in cordibus vestris
deo et domino nostro, cui credidistis, qui numquam
discedit a nobis timentibus et honorantibus nomen
suum, in quo vobis et nos semper coniuncti sumus,
quamvis corpore a vobis profecti esse videamur, qui
vobis de isto bonorum operum semine messem vitae
aeternae promittit, dicente apostolo : *Bonum autem
facientes non deficiamus; tempore enim suo metemus
infatigabiles. Itaque, dum tempus habemus, operemur
bonum ad omnes, maxime autem ad domesticos fidei.*

---

a This is probably a citizen of Hippo and a member of
Augustine's church, and not the Macedonius who was
vicar of Africa in 414, when he was entrusted with the
duty of enforcing the imperial decrees against the recusant
Donatists. Several of the letters exchanged between him
and Augustine are extant (*Epp.* cliii.-clv.).

you, holy brethren, about his needs, but, deterred by shame, he implored me not to do it. So I myself, under pressure of greater needs, accepted seventeen solidi from our brother Macedonius,[a] and these I immediately handed over on his behoof, while he promised that on a certain day he could meet the repayment, and agreed that if he was not able to meet it, an appeal should be made for him to that compassion of yours, which it is your habit to display as a brotherly feeling for our brethren.

Wherefore, now that he is absent, it remains for 2 you to give your backing, not to him, for no one can apply compulsion to him in his absence, but to my promise, for with you my good name and fame are always present. For already the day on which he promised he would meet the debt, is past and gone, and I find no reply to make to him who gave me the amount on trust, save to do what I promised I would do. But since I had no information about this matter on the day of Pentecost, so that I might have made an appeal when the crowd at Church was greater than usual, I ask you to be good enough to take this letter as my voice, while in your hearts Our Lord and God speaks warning and exhortation ; in Him you have put your trust, and He never leaves us so long as we fear and honour His name ; in Him I too am united with you, although in body I seem to have departed from you ; from Him comes the promise of the harvest of eternal life from this seed of good works, for the apostle says : " And let us not be weary in well-doing, for in due season we shall reap if we faint not. As we therefore have opportunity, let us do good unto all men, especially unto them who are of the household of

Quoniam ergo domesticus fidei est, Christianus fidelis, catholicus frater noster, pro cuius supplenda necessitate vos peto ut faciatis quod dominus imperat, sine tristitia, sine murmuratione et cum laetitia et hilaritate facite; deo enim creditis non homini, quia ille promittit vos nihil eorum quae misericorditer facitis, perdituros, sed in illo die cum usuris inmortalibus recepturos. Et quoniam ipse apostolus dicit: *Hoc autem dico: Qui parce seminat, parce et metet*, intellegere debetis tempus esse, ut donum vitae aeternae, cum adhuc in ista vita sumus, festinanter et alacriter comparemus, quia, cum finis saeculi venerit, non dabitur nisi eis qui per fidem sibi hoc emerunt, antequam videre potuissent.

3 Scripsi etiam presbyteris, ut, si quid minus fuerit post conlationem sanctitatis vestrae, compleant ex eo quod habet ecclesia, dum tamen vos, secundum quod placet, hilariter offeratis, quia sive de vestro sive de ecclesia detur, omnia dei sunt, et devotio magis vestra dulcior erit thesauris ecclesiae, sicut apostolus dicit: *Non quia quaero datum, sed requiro fructum.* Laetificate ergo cor meum, quia de fructibus vestris gaudere cupio; vos enim estis arbores dei, quas assiduis imbribus etiam per nostrum ministerium rigare dignatur. Tueatur vos dominus ab

---

ᵃ Gal. vi. 9-10. ᵇ Matt. xxv. 34-40.
ᶜ 2 Cor. ix. 6. ᵈ Phil. iv. 17.
ᵉ The mention of fruits suggests to him the trees that bring forth good fruits (Matt. iii. 10, etc.), and he immediately applies the Scriptural idea to those he is addressing —a frequent device with him. *Cf.* Ep. xxi. 5 " arbores vivae " (p. 38 above); Ep. lxxiv. 2 " fingite vos ante tempus messis fugere permixta zizania, quia vos estis Sola zizania "; *Serm.* 11. 1 " Deus . . . excolens ecclesiam suam velut agrum suum, quaerens fructum de arboribus suis"; 72. 1

faith."[a] Since then he is of the household of faith,
a member of the Christian Church, a Catholic brother
of our own, for the satisfaction of whose needs I ask
you to do what the Lord bids you do, do it without
grudging, without complaint, and with gladness and
cheerfulness ; for your trust is in God, not in man,
and He has promised that you will lose nothing of
the things you do in mercy, but will receive
them on that day with eternal usury.[b] And since the
apostle himself says, "But this I say, He which
soweth sparingly shall reap also sparingly,"[c] you
should understand that now is the time for us, while
we are still in this life, to purchase with haste and
cheerfulness the gift of eternal life ; for when the
end of the world comes, it will be given only to those
who through faith have bought it for themselves
before it was possible for them to see it.

I have written to the priests as well that, if there 3
be any deficiency after the offering made by you,
my holy friends, they should make it up from the
Church's store, provided that you have all made
cheerful offering, each man as he will ; for whether
the gift come from you or from the Church, it is all
God's, yet your devotedness will be far more acceptable than the treasures of the Church, as the apostle
says, "Not because I desire a gift, but I desire that
fruit may abound."[d] Gladden my heart, then, for I
wish to have joy of your fruits ; for you are God's
trees which even through my ministry He deigns to
water with unceasing showers.[e] May the Lord keep

"admonuit nos Dominus ut bonae arbores simus"; 36. 4.
"arboribus bonis et fidelibus hanc adlocutionem praebet
apostolus"; 72. 2 "quisquis igitur homo hodie bonus est,
id est, arbor bona . . ."

T

omni malo et hic et in futuro saeculo, domini
dilectissimi et desiderantissimi fratres.

No. 62 (Ep. CCLXIX)

BEATISSIMO AC VENERABILI FRATRI ET CON-
SACERDOTI NOBILIO AUGUSTINUS

Tanta est sollemnitas ad quam me affectus tuae
fraternitatis invitat, ut corpusculum meum ad vos
traheret voluntas, nisi teneret infirmitas. Possem
venire, si hiems non esset; possem hiemem contemnere, si iuvenis essem; aut enim ferret rigorem
temporis fervor aetatis aut temperaret frigus aetatis
fervor aestatis. Nunc hieme iter tam prolixum non
suffero cum annositate algida, quam mecum fero,
domine beatissime, sancte ac venerabilis frater et
consacerdos. Salutationem debitam reddo meritis
tuis; salutem vero meam commendo precibus tuis,
poscens et ipse a domino, ut dedicationem tantae
fabricae pacis prosperitas prosequatur.

---

[a] Augustine writes excusing himself on grounds of his
age and feebleness and of the winter season, from attending
the dedication of a church. Nobilius is not known and his
name does not elsewhere appear. From internal evidence
this appears to be among the last letters Augustine wrote:
the remaining letter in the complete collection is from the

you from all evil, both in this world and in the world
to come, my well-beloved lords and much longed
for brethren.

No. 62 (Ep. CCLXIX)

AUGUSTINE TO MY SAINTLY AND REVERED BROTHER AND FELLOW-PRIEST, NOBILIUS •

So important is the ceremony to which your
brotherly affection invites me, that I should drag
my poor body to you with willingness, were it not
detained by weakness. I might have come, had it
not been winter ; I might have scorned the winter,
had I been young ; for either the glow of youth
would have endured the rigour of the season, or
else the glow of summer would have allayed the chill
of age. As it is, my saintly lord, my holy and revered
brother and fellow-priest, in winter I cannot bear
so lengthy a journey since I must bear with me the
frigidity of great age. I return the greeting that
I owe to your merits ; my own welfare I commend
to your supplications, while beseeching the Lord
myself that peace and prosperity may follow upon
the dedication of so great a building.

hand of an unknown correspondent. The date of the present
piece is probably the winter of 429–430.

INDEX

The references are to letters, as numbered in this selection, and to paragraphs.

528

INDEX

appoint the clergy, **17.** 1; declares he did not write a book against Jerome, **20.** 2; on legacies left to monasteries, **21.** 1-6; urges the Calamans to adopt Christianity, **24** n.; a reader of Virgil, 2 n.; on the immorality of the pagan gods, 4; on the disturbances of June the 1st, 8; his contempt for pagan writings, **28.** 2; his books *De Musica*, 3; on the Psalms, 4; on being praised by his friend, **29.** 3-5; his weak health, **31.** 1; on the sanctity of oaths, **33.** 11; his friendship with Marcellinus, **34** n.; on the punishment of criminals, 1, 2; his controversy with Pelagius, **36** n.; on the connexion of soul and body, **38.** 1; on visions, 2; his argument against toleration, **39.** 2; on free-will, 3-5; on baptism, 4 n.; on charity, 6; his *De Trinitate*, **40**; his *De natura et gratia*, **41** n.; on the Pelagian heresy, 3-10; death of, **42.** 1 n.; on military service, 4-6; on love, **44.** 1, 2; his approval of conjugal continence, **45.** 1 n., 3; **51.** 12; development of monasticism among women due to, **48.** 1 n.; his monastic Rule, **49.** 5-16; his letter on grace and free-will, **50** n., 2-7; on bodily adornment, **51.** 1, 2; on praise, **54.** 2-4; his advice to Ecdicia on conjugal chastity, **60**

Augustine, St., of Canterbury, **10.** 1 n.

Augustinian Rule, the, **49.** 5-16

Aurelius, Bishop, 8; **17**; **39.** 8 n.; **40** n.; **43.** 1; **54.** 7

Baal Addir, **6.** 2 n.

Bacchus, deprives men of reason, **6.** 4

Bagai, **39.** 8 n.

Balearic Islands, **15** n.

Baptism, adult, Augustine on, **39.** 4 n.; **59.** 4 n.

Barbarus, **38.** 1

Barnabas, **33.** 6

Baths, once a month, **49.** 13

Bede, **47.** 2 n.

Bee, the, if it sticks in the honey dies, **4.** 2

Benedict, St., Rule of, **49.** 12 n., 15 n.; **51.** 8 n.; **60.** 5 n.

Benenatus, Bishop of Tugutiana, **58**

Bethlehem, Jerome in, **9** n.; **20** n.; **43.** 1 n.

Bishop, the difficulty of worthily discharging the duties of, **7.** 1; legal duties of, **24.** 7; translation of, forbidden, **47.** 7 n.

Biskra, **51.** 8

Boniface, Bishop of Cataquas, **25.** 3

Boniface, Count, Governor of Africa, note on his life, **42.** 1 n.; his disgrace, **51.** 1 n.; his marriage, 4 n.; barbarian invasions under, 7; **54** n.

Boniface, Pope, **47.** 1 n., 6, 9

Bonum, donum, **45.** 3 n.

Britain, **44.** 1 n.

Britons, the, **44.** 1 n.

Bulla, **18.** 1

Byzacena, **39.** 8 n.; **50** n.

Cabrera, **15** n.

Caecilian, Bishop of Carthage, **39.** 7-9; his Act of Purgation, **49.** 13 n.

Caecilianus, Roman legate, note on his life, **23** n.

Caelestis, temple of, consecrated as a church, **45.** 3 n.

Caesarea, note on its history, **47.** 8 n.

Cain, **41.** 8

Calama, **13.** 2 n., 3; **19** n.; pagan festivals held at, **24** n., 10

Caligula, **47.** 8 n.

Campania, **14** n.

Capitulum, portion of Scripture, **10.** 2 n.

Capraria, **15** n.

Caprera, famous for manufacture of goat's-hair garments, **15.** 4 n.

Capua, **23** n.

Carthage, Church of, **8.** 4; Augustine's lectures in, **9** n.; Council of, **17.** 2 n.; **36** n.; **41** n.; **48.** 1 n.; Caecilianus in, **22** n.; **38.** 3; conference of, **39.** 7 n.; Synod of, **47.** 8 n.; **53.** 1; **55.** 3 n.

Cassiciacum, **1.** 1 n.; **2.** 1 n.; **24.** 2 n.; **38** n.

529

INDEX

Castellum, Augustine's definition of, **47**. 2 n.

Cataquas, **25**. 3

Catechumens, not present at prayers, **33**. 5 n.

Cathedra, defined, **47**. 7 n.

Catholica, the Church Catholic, **47**. 9 n.

Catholics, disputes between, and Donatists, **34** n.

Cato, a model of pagan virtue, **24**. 4

Celer, proconsul of Africa, a Donatist, **47**. 5

Celestine, Bishop of Rome, note on his life, **44**. 1 n., 4, 7 ; **47**. 9 n.

Cemeteries, drunkenness in, **8**. 3, 6

Chalcedon, Council of, **47**. 2 n.

Chambering and wantonness, a great sin, **8**. 3

Character Domini, **39**. 3 n.

Characteres, **56**. 2 n.

Charity, **39**. 6

Charus, a deacon, **41**. 7 n.

Chastity, conjugal, **51**, 60

Cherchel, **47**. 8 n.

Choir, in the early Church, **10**. 8 n.

Christ, swearing by, **55**. 4 n.

Christian names, **29** n.

Christians, their secret worship of God, **5**. 3 ; worship God only, **6**. 5 ; concessions made to induce people to become, **10**. 9 ; massacre of, at Sufes, **16** ; their attitude towards their enemies, **27**. 1, 2

Chrysostom, his correspondence with Italica, **26** n.

Churches, as sanctuaries, **30**. 1 n. ; **66**. 1

Cicero (Tully), his *Dialogues*, **6**. 3 ; his *De Republica*, **3** n. ; on friendship, **59**

Circumcellions, break into the church at Asna, **10**. 12 ; their violence, **34**. 1 n.

Cirta, made Bishop of, **9**. 1 ; **30** n. ; **49**. 13 n. See also Constantine

Claudian, patronized by Stilicho, **25**. 3 n.

Cinacina, the goddess of purification, **6**. 2

Coelestius, **41** n.

Columella, **6**. 2 n.

Comes per Africam, **30**. 1 n.

Constantine, or Cirta, named after the Emperor, **11**. 5 n. ; **13**. 3 ; a stronghold of Donatists, **35** n.

Constantine, Emperor, presents the Lateran to the Church, **10**. 10 n. ; allows appeals to Bishops in civil suits, **24**. 7 n. ; allows churches to be used as sanctuaries, **30**. 1 n.

Constantinople, municipal doctors in, **52** n.

Cor habere, **51**. 5 n.

Cordis aures, **46** n.

Cornelius, **42**. 4

Corrigere, intransitive, **49**. 3 n.

Corsica, **15** n.

Cosmetics, **56**. 1 n.

Creed, candidates for baptism expected to memorize the, **52** n.

Cresconius, monk, **50**. 1

Crispinus, Donatist Bishop of Calama, **19** n.

Cyprian, **48**. 1 n. ; **51**. 9 n.

Darius, note on his life, **53**. 1 n.

David, his clemency, **34**. 2 ; **42**. 4

Death, the journey to, alone to be planned, **3**. 2 ; not feared by those who die to bodily affections, **3**

Deficere, reficere, **54**. 6 n.

Demetrias, the virgin, **37** n.

Devil-worshippers, **14**

Diocletian, **30**. 1 n. ; **47**. 8 n. ; persecution under, **49**. 13 n.

Dioscurus, the physician, **52**

Diospolis, Synod of, **36** n. ; **41**. 1 n., 7 n.

Dominica in albis, **11**. 3 n.

Donatist heresy, **47**. 2 n.

Donatist party, the, terrorize Numidia, **10**. 12 n. ; incident of the violent young man who joined, **11**. 2, 3

Donatists, disputes between, and Catholics, **34** n. ; edicts against, **25** n. ; **27**. 2 ; **28**. 1 n. ; **35** n. ; **36**. 2 n. ; **39**. 7 n., 8 n., 9 ; **49**. 4 n. ; **61**. 1 n.

Donatus, priest of Mutugenna, **39**. 7

Donatus, priest of the Donatist party, **17**. 1, 2 ; **39** n.

Donatus, Proconsul of Africa, **17** n.

Drunkenness, condemned by St. Paul, **8**. 3 ; in cemeteries, **3**, 6 ;

INDEX

INDEX

INDEX

534

INDEX

Printed in Great Britain by R. & R. CLARK, LIMITED, *Edinburgh*

THE LOEB CLASSICAL LIBRARY

VOLUMES ALREADY PUBLISHED

LATIN AUTHORS

1

THE LOEB CLASSICAL LIBRARY

Cicero : De Officiis. Walter Miller.
Cicero : De Oratore, etc. 2 Vols. Vol. I : De Oratore,
 Books I and II. E. W. Sutton and H. Rackham. Vol. II :
 De Oratore, Book III ; De Fato ; Paradoxa Stoi-
 corum ; De Partitione Oratoria. H. Rackham.
Cicero : De Republica, De Legibus, Somnium Scipionis.
 Clinton W. Keyes.
Cicero : De Senectute, De Amicitia, De Divinatione.
 W. A. Falconer.
Cicero : In Catilinam, Pro Murena, Pro Sulla, Pro
 Flacco. Louis E. Lord.
Cicero : Letters to Atticus. E. O. Winstedt. 3 Vols.
Cicero : Letters to his Friends. W. Glynn Williams.
 3 Vols.
Cicero : Philippics. W. C. A. Ker.
Cicero : Pro Archia, Post Reditum, De Domo, De Ha-
 ruspicum Responsis, Pro Plancio. N. H. Watts.
Cicero : Pro Caecina, Pro Lege Manilia, Pro Cluentio,
 Pro Rabirio. H. Grose Hodge.
Cicero : Pro Caelio, De Provinciis Consularibus, Pro
 Balbo. R. Gardner.
Cicero : Pro Milone, In Pisonem, Pro Scauro, Pro
 Fonteio, Pro Rabirio Postumo, Pro Marcello, Pro
 Ligario, Pro Rege Deiotaro. N. H. Watts.
Cicero : Pro Quinctio, Pro Roscio Amerino, Pro Roscio
 Comoedo, Contra Rullum. J. H. Freese.
Cicero : Pro Sestio, In Vatinium. R. Gardner.
[Cicero] : Rhetorica ad Herennium. H. Caplan.
Cicero : Tusculan Disputations. J. E. King.
Cicero : Verrine Orations. L. H. G. Greenwood. 2 Vols.
Claudian. M. Platnauer. 2 Vols.
Columella : De Re Rustica ; De Arboribus. H. B. Ash,
 E. S. Forster, E. Heffner. 3 Vols.
Curtius, Q. : History of Alexander. J. C. Rolfe. 2 Vols.
Florus. E. S. Forster : and Cornelius Nepos. J. C. Rolfe.
Frontinus : Stratagems and Aqueducts. C. E. Bennett
 and M. B. McElwain.
Fronto : Correspondence. C. R. Haines. 2 Vols.
Gellius. J. C. Rolfe. 3 Vols.
Horace : Odes and Epodes. C. E. Bennett.
Horace : Satires, Epistles, Ars Poetica. H. R. Fairclough.
Jerome : Select Letters. F. A. Wright.
Juvenal and Persius. G. G. Ramsay.

THE LOEB CLASSICAL LIBRARY

Livy. B. O. Foster, F. G. Moore, Evan T. Sage, A. C. Schlesinger and R. M. Geer (General Index). 14 Vols.

Lucan. J. D. Duff.

Lucretius. W. H. D. Rouse.

Martial. W. C. A. Ker. 2 Vols.

Minor Latin Poets: from Publilius Syrus to Rutilius Namatianus, including Grattius, Calpurnius Siculus, Nemesianus, Avianus, with "Aetna," "Phoenix" and other poems. J. Wight Duff and Arnold M. Duff.

Ovid: The Art of Love and other Poems. J. H. Mozley.

Ovid: Fasti. Sir James G. Frazer.

Ovid: Heroides and Amores. Grant Showerman.

Ovid: Metamorphoses. F. J. Miller. 2 Vols.

Ovid: Tristia and Ex Ponto. A. L. Wheeler.

Petronius. M. Heseltine: Seneca: Apocolocyntosis. W. H. D. Rouse.

Plautus. Paul Nixon. 5 Vols.

Pliny: Letters. Melmoth's translation revised by W. M. L. Hutchinson. 2 Vols.

Pliny: Natural History. 10 Vols. Vols. I-V and IX. H. Rackham. Vols. VI-VIII. W. H. S. Jones. Vol. X. D. E. Eichholz.

Propertius. H. E. Butler.

Prudentius. H. J. Thomson. 2 Vols.

Quintilian. H. E. Butler. 4 Vols.

Remains of Old Latin. E. H. Warmington. 4 Vols. Vol. I (Ennius and Caecilius). Vol. II (Livius, Naevius, Pacuvius, Accius). Vol. III (Lucilius, Laws of the XII Tables). Vol. IV (Archaic Inscriptions).

Sallust. J. C. Rolfe.

Scriptores Historiae Augustae. D. Magie. 3 Vols.

Seneca: Apocolocyntosis. Cf. Petronius.

Seneca: Epistulae Morales. R. M. Gummere. 3 Vols.

Seneca: Moral Essays. J. W. Basore. 3 Vols.

Seneca: Tragedies. F. J. Miller. 2 Vols.

Sidonius: Poems and Letters. W. B. Anderson. 2 Vols.

Silius Italicus. J. D. Duff. 2 Vols.

Statius. J. H. Mozley. 2 Vols.

Suetonius. J. C. Rolfe. 2 Vols.

Tacitus: Dialogus. Sir Wm. Peterson: and Agricola and Germania. Maurice Hutton.

Tacitus: Histories and Annals. C. H. Moore and J. Jackson. 4 Vols.

THE LOEB CLASSICAL LIBRARY

TERENCE. John Sargeaunt. 2 Vols.
TERTULLIAN: APOLOGIA AND DE SPECTACULIS. T. R. Glover:
  MINUCIUS FELIX. G. H. Rendall.
VALERIUS FLACCUS. J. H. Mozley.
VARRO: DE LINGUA LATINA. R. G. Kent. 2 Vols.
VELLEIUS PATERCULUS AND RES GESTAE DIVI AUGUSTI. F. W.
  Shipley.
VIRGIL. H. R. Fairclough. 2 Vols.
VITRUVIUS: DE ARCHITECTURA. F. Granger. 2 Vols.

GREEK AUTHORS

ACHILLES TATIUS. S. Gaselee.
AELIAN: ON THE NATURE OF ANIMALS. A. F. Scholfield.
  3 Vols.
AENEAS TACTICUS, ASCLEPIODOTUS AND ONASANDER. The
  Illinois Greek Club.
AESCHINES. C. D. Adams.
AESCHYLUS. H. Weir Smyth. 2 Vols.
ALCIPHRON, AELIAN AND PHILOSTRATUS: LETTERS. A. R.
  Benner and F. H. Fobes.
APOLLODORUS. Sir James G. Frazer. 2 Vols.
APOLLONIUS RHODIUS. R. C. Seaton.
THE APOSTOLIC FATHERS. Kirsopp Lake. 2 Vols.
APPIAN'S ROMAN HISTORY. Horace White. 4 Vols.
ARATUS. *Cf.* CALLIMACHUS.
ARISTOPHANES. Benjamin Bickley Rogers. 3 Vols. Verse
  trans.
ARISTOTLE: ART OF RHETORIC. J. H. Freese.
ARISTOTLE: ATHENIAN CONSTITUTION, EUDEMIAN ETHICS,
  VIRTUES AND VICES. H. Rackham.
ARISTOTLE: GENERATION OF ANIMALS. A. L. Peck.
ARISTOTLE: METAPHYSICS. H. Tredennick. 2 Vols.
ARISTOTLE: METEOROLOGICA. H. D. P. Lee.
ARISTOTLE: MINOR WORKS. W. S. Hett. "On Colours,"
  "On Things Heard," "Physiognomics," "On Plants,"
  "On Marvellous Things Heard," "Mechanical Problems,"
  "On Indivisible Lines," "Situations and Names of
  Winds," "On Melissus, Xenophanes, and Gorgias."
ARISTOTLE: NICOMACHEAN ETHICS. H. Rackham

THE LOEB CLASSICAL LIBRARY

ARISTOTLE: OECONOMICA AND MAGNA MORALIA. G. C. Armstrong. (With Metaphysics, Vol. II.)

ARISTOTLE: ON THE HEAVENS. W. K. C. Guthrie.

ARISTOTLE: ON THE SOUL, PARVA NATURALIA, ON BREATH. W. S. Hett.

ARISTOTLE: THE CATEGORIES. ON INTERPRETATION. H. P. Cooke; PRIOR ANALYTICS. H. Tredennick.

ARISTOTLE: POSTERIOR ANALYTICS. H. Tredennick; TOPICS. E. S. Forster.

ARISTOTLE: SOPHISTICAL REFUTATIONS. COMING-TO-BE AND PASSING-AWAY. E. S. Forster. ON THE COSMOS. D. J. Furley.

ARISTOTLE: PARTS OF ANIMALS. A. L. Peck; MOTION AND PROGRESSION OF ANIMALS. E. S. Forster.

ARISTOTLE: PHYSICS. Rev. P. Wicksteed and F. M. Cornford. 2 Vols.

ARISTOTLE: POETICS; LONGINUS ON THE SUBLIME. W. Hamilton Fyfe; DEMETRIUS ON STYLE. W. Rhys Roberts.

ARISTOTLE: POLITICS. H. Rackham.

ARISTOTLE: PROBLEMS. W. S. Hett. 2 Vols.

ARISTOTLE: RHETORICA AD ALEXANDRUM. H. Rackham. (With Problems, Vol. II.)

ARRIAN: HISTORY OF ALEXANDER AND INDICA. Rev. E. Iliffe Robson. 2 Vols.

ATHENAEUS: DEIPNOSOPHISTAE. C. B. Gulick. 7 Vols.

ST. BASIL: LETTERS. R. J. Deferrari. 4 Vols.

CALLIMACHUS: FRAGMENTS. C. A. Trypanis.

CALLIMACHUS: HYMNS AND EPIGRAMS, AND LYCOPHRON. A. W. Mair; ARATUS. G. R. Mair.

CLEMENT OF ALEXANDRIA. Rev. G. W. Butterworth.

COLLUTHUS. *Cf.* OPPIAN.

DAPHNIS AND CHLOE. *Cf.* LONGUS.

DEMOSTHENES I: OLYNTHIACS, PHILIPPICS AND MINOR ORATIONS: I-XVII AND XX. J. H. Vince.

DEMOSTHENES II: DE CORONA AND DE FALSA LEGATIONE. C. A. Vince and J. H. Vince.

DEMOSTHENES III: MEIDIAS, ANDROTION, ARISTOCRATES, TIMOCRATES, ARISTOGEITON. J. H. Vince.

DEMOSTHENES IV-VI: PRIVATE ORATIONS AND IN NEAERAM. A. T. Murray.

DEMOSTHENES VII: FUNERAL SPEECH, EROTIC ESSAY, EXORDIA AND LETTERS. N. W. and N. J. DeWitt.

DIO CASSIUS: ROMAN HISTORY. E. Cary. 9 Vols.

5

THE LOEB CLASSICAL LIBRARY

DIO CHRYSOSTOM. 5 Vols. Vols. I and II. J. W. Cohoon. Vol III. J. W. Cohoon and H. Lamar Crosby. Vols. IV and V. H. Lamar Crosby.

DIODORUS SICULUS. 12 Vols. Vols. I-VI. C. H. Oldfather. Vol. VII. C. L. Sherman. Vol. VIII. C. B. Welles. Vols. IX and X. Russel M. Geer. Vol. XI. F. R. Walton.

DIOGENES LAERTIUS. R. D. Hicks. 2 Vols.

DIONYSIUS OF HALICARNASSUS : ROMAN ANTIQUITIES. Spelman's translation revised by E. Cary. 7 Vols.

EPICTETUS. W. A. Oldfather. 2 Vols.

EURIPIDES. A. S. Way. 4 Vols. Verse trans.

EUSEBIUS : ECCLESIASTICAL HISTORY. Kirsopp Lake and J. E. L. Oulton. 2 Vols.

GALEN : ON THE NATURAL FACULTIES. A. J. Brock.

THE GREEK ANTHOLOGY. W. R. Paton. 5 Vols.

THE GREEK BUCOLIC POETS (THEOCRITUS, BION, MOSCHUS). J. M. Edmonds.

GREEK ELEGY AND IAMBUS WITH THE ANACREONTEA. J. M. Edmonds. 2 Vols.

GREEK MATHEMATICAL WORKS. Ivor Thomas. 2 Vols.

HERODES. *Cf.* THEOPHRASTUS : CHARACTERS.

HERODOTUS. A. D. Godley. 4 Vols.

HESIOD AND THE HOMERIC HYMNS. H. G. Evelyn White.

HIPPOCRATES AND THE FRAGMENTS OF HERACLEITUS. W. H. S. Jones and E. T. Withington. 4 Vols.

HOMER : ILIAD. A. T. Murray. 2 Vols.

HOMER : ODYSSEY. A. T. Murray. 2 Vols.

ISAEUS. E. S. Forster.

ISOCRATES. George Norlin and LaRue Van Hook. 3 Vols.

ST. JOHN DAMASCENE : BARLAAM AND IOASAPH. Rev. G. R. Woodward and Harold Mattingly.

JOSEPHUS. 9 Vols. Vols. I-IV. H. St. J. Thackeray. Vol. V. H. St. J. Thackeray and Ralph Marcus. Vols. VI and VII. Ralph Marcus. Vol. VIII. Ralph Marcus and Allen Wikgren. Vol. IX. L. H. Feldman.

JULIAN. Wilmer Cave Wright. 3 Vols.

LONGUS : DAPHNIS AND CHLOE. Thornley's translation revised by J. M. Edmonds ; and PARTHENIUS. S. Gaselee.

LUCIAN. 8 Vols. Vols. I-V. A. M. Harmon ; Vol. VI. K. Kilburn ; Vol. VII. M. D. Macleod.

LYCOPHRON. *Cf.* CALLIMACHUS.

LYRA GRAECA. J. M. Edmonds. 3 Vols.

LYSIAS. W. R. M. Lamb.

THE LOEB CLASSICAL LIBRARY

MANETHO. W. G. Waddell. PTOLEMY: TETRABIBLOS. F. E. Robbins.

MARCUS AURELIUS. C. R. Haines.

MENANDER. F. G. Allinson.

MINOR ATTIC ORATORS. 2 Vols. K. J. Maidment and J. O. Burtt.

NONNOS: DIONYSIACA. W. H. D. Rouse. 3 Vols.

OPPIAN, COLLUTHUS, TRYPHIODORUS. A. W. Mair.

PAPYRI. NON-LITERARY SELECTIONS. A. S. Hunt and C. C. Edgar. 2 Vols. LITERARY SELECTIONS (Poetry). D. L. Page.

PARTHENIUS. *Cf.* LONGUS.

PAUSANIAS: DESCRIPTION OF GREECE. W. H. S. Jones. 5 Vols. and Companion Vol. arranged by R. E. Wycherley.

PHILO. 10 Vols. Vols. I-V. F. H. Colson and Rev. G. H. Whitaker; Vols. VI-X. F. H. Colson; General Index. Rev. J. W. Earp.
   Two Supplementary Vols. Translation only from an Armenian Text. Ralph Marcus.

PHILOSTRATUS: IMAGINES: CALLISTRATUS: DESCRIPTIONS. A. Fairbanks.

PHILOSTRATUS: THE LIFE OF APOLLONIUS OF TYANA. F. C. Conybeare. 2 Vols.

PHILOSTRATUS AND EUNAPIUS; LIVES OF THE SOPHISTS. Wilmer Cave Wright.

PINDAR. Sir J. E. Sandys.

PLATO: CHARMIDES, ALCIBIADES, HIPPARCHUS, THE LOVERS, THEAGES, MINOS AND EPINOMIS. W. R. M. Lamb.

PLATO: CRATYLUS, PARMENIDES, GREATER HIPPIAS, LESSER HIPPIAS. H. N. Fowler.

PLATO: EUTHYPHRO, APOLOGY, CRITO, PHAEDO, PHAEDRUS. H. N. Fowler.

PLATO: LACHES, PROTAGORAS, MENO, EUTHYDEMUS. W. R. M. Lamb.

PLATO: LAWS. Rev. R. G. Bury. 2 Vols.

PLATO: LYSIS, SYMPOSIUM, GORGIAS. W. R. M. Lamb.

PLATO: REPUBLIC. Paul Shorey. 2 Vols.

PLATO: STATESMAN. PHILEBUS. H. N. Fowler: ION. W. R. M. Lamb.

PLATO: THEAETETUS AND SOPHIST. H. N. Fowler.

PLATO: TIMAEUS, CRITIAS, CLITOPHO, MENEXENUS, EPISTULAE. Rev. R. G. Bury.

PLUTARCH: MORALIA. 15 Vols. Vols. I-V. F. C. Babbitt;

7

THE LOEB CLASSICAL LIBRARY

Vol. VI. W. C. Helmbold; Vol. VII. P. H. De Lacy and B. Einarson; Vol. IX. E. L. Minar, Jr., F. H. Sandbach, W. C. Helmbold; Vol. X. H. N. Fowler; Vol. XI. L. Pearson and F. H. Sandbach; Vol. XII. H. Cherniss and W. C. Helmbold.

PLUTARCH: THE PARALLEL LIVES. B. Perrin. 11 Vols.

POLYBIUS. W. R. Paton. 6 Vols.

PROCOPIUS: HISTORY OF THE WARS. H. B. Dewing. 7 Vols.

PTOLEMY: TETRABIBLOS. *Cf.* MANETHO.

QUINTUS SMYRNAEUS. A. S. Way. Verse trans.

SEXTUS EMPIRICUS. Rev. R. G. Bury. 4 Vols.

SOPHOCLES. F. Storr. 2 Vols. Verse trans.

STRABO: GEOGRAPHY. Horace L. Jones. 8 Vols.

THEOPHRASTUS: CHARACTERS. J. M. Edmonds; HERODES, etc. A. D. Knox.

THEOPHRASTUS: ENQUIRY INTO PLANTS. Sir Arthur Hort. 2 Vols.

THUCYDIDES. C. F. Smith. 4 Vols.

TRYPHIODORUS. *Cf.* OPPIAN.

XENOPHON: CYROPAEDIA. Walter Miller. 2 Vols.

XENOPHON: HELLENICA, ANABASIS, APOLOGY, AND SYMPOSIUM. C. L. Brownson and O. J. Todd. 3 Vols.

XENOPHON: MEMORABILIA AND OECONOMICUS. E. C. Marchant.

XENOPHON: SCRIPTA MINORA. E. C. Marchant.

VOLUMES IN PREPARATION

ARISTOTLE: HISTORIA ANIMALIUM (Greek). A. L. Peck.
BABRIUS (Greek) AND PHAEDRUS (Latin). B. E. Perry.
PLOTINUS (Greek). A. H. Armstrong.

DESCRIPTIVE PROSPECTUS ON APPLICATION

LONDON   CAMBRIDGE, MASS.
WILLIAM HEINEMANN LTD   HARVARD UNIV. PRESS